A Child of Christian Blood

A Child of Christian Blood

MURDER AND CONSPIRACY
IN TSARIST RUSSIA:
THE BEILIS BLOOD LIBEL

Edmund Levin

SCHOCKEN BOOKS
NEW YORK

Grateful acknowledgment is made to M. E. Sharpe, Inc., for permission to reprint
material from "The Iushchinskii Murder and the Expert Psychiatric-Psychological
Opinion," by V. M. Bekhterev, translated by Lydia Razran Stone, from *Journal of
Russian & East European Psychology,* vol. 41, no. 2 (March–April 2003).
English translation copyright © 2003 by M. E. Sharpe, Inc.
Reprinted with permission. All rights reserved.

The excerpt from "The Prioress's Tale" has been adapted from *The Canterbury Tales
and Faerie Queen: With Other Poems of Chaucer and Spenser,* by D. Lang Purves
(Edinburgh: William P. Nimmo, 1870).

Library of Congress Cataloging-in-Publication Data
Levin, Edmund.
A child of Christian blood : murder and conspiracy in Tsarist Russia : the Beilis
blood libel / Edmund Levin.
pages   cm.
Includes bibliographical references and index.
ISBN 978-0-8052-4299-7
1. Blood accusation—Russia. 2. Christianity and antisemitism—Russia.
3. Antisemitism—Russia—Case studies. 4. Russia—Trials, litigation, etc. I. Title.
BM585.2.L48 2013   305.892'4047—dc23   2013019938

www.schocken.com

Jacket photograph © Juliet Ferguson/Alamy
Jacket design by Ben Denzer
Book design by M. Kristen Bearse

Printed in the United States of America
First Edition
2   4   6   8   9   7   5   3   1

To the Memory of Selene and Martin Levin

There was in Asia, in a great city,
Among Christian folk, a street of Jewry,
Sustained by a lord of that country
For foul usury and lucre of villainy,
Hateful to Christ and to his company;
And through the street men might ride and wend
For it was free and open at either end.

A little school of Christian folk there stood
Down at the farther end, in which there were
Many children, born of Christian blood.

—from "The Prioress's Tale,"
The Canterbury Tales, Geoffrey Chaucer

Contents

Preface

In the spring of 1911, a young boy was found stabbed to death in a cave on the desolate outskirts of the city of Kiev, then part of the Russian Empire, his body riddled with some fifty puncture wounds. Four months later, a troop of police and gendarmes raided the home of a Jewish brick factory clerk named Mendel Beilis and dragged him off to prison in the middle of the night. Beilis's trial for the murder of thirteen-year-old Andrei Yushchinsky, which took place in the fall of 1913, was the most sensational court case of its time and surely one of the most bizarre ever tried in an ostensibly civilized society. The case was front-page news around the world. The reason for the intense international attention: the Russian state had charged Beilis not simply with the boy's murder but with the ritual Jewish killing of this Christian child.

Beilis was an improbable candidate on whom to pin a crime supposedly associated with his "race." As a Jew, he was barely observant and of modest religious learning. But soon after the discovery of the body, the Russian anti-Semites known as the Black Hundreds were leveling the centuries-old slander known as the blood libel or blood accusation. A leaflet passed out at the boy's funeral proclaimed, "The Yids have tortured Andrusha Yushchinsky to death!" If a Jew was to be accused, Beilis turned out to be, for reasons that will become clear, the most convenient choice. Only slowly comprehending the tremendous significance of his case, Beilis found himself at the center of an anti-Semitic maelstrom.

The notion that, for their demonic purposes, Jews commit ritual murder to obtain Christian blood, generally the blood of children, had its origins in Western Europe in the twelfth and thirteenth centuries. The blood libel was a hardy and persistent bacillus, sometimes lying dormant for decades, then erupting virulently. At the turn of the previous century a spate of alleged "ritual murder" cases arose across Central and Eastern Europe. But there had never been a court case like the Beilis trial in Kiev, a prosecution that was pursued with the full backing of the state.

The corrupt and decadent Russia of Tsar Nicholas II was pervaded by a violently paranoid fear of "Jewish power," as evidenced by the some fourteen hundred different government statutes and regulations limiting where Jews could live, what schools they could attend, and which professions they could pursue. In the century's first few years the Black Hundreds killed and maimed hundreds of Jews in horrifying pogroms, with imperial officials often willfully ignoring the violence. It was around this time that Russian anti-Semites are believed to have fabricated the notorious *Protocols of the Elders of Zion,* the Jews' supposed secret plan for world domination.

In its judicial procedures, if not in its genuine respect for human rights, Russia emulated the West, with the full apparatus of courts, judges, and juries. To prove the charge of ritual murder, the prosecution would duly produce expert witnesses: pathologists, clergymen, even a psychological profiler. That the methods of Western justice could be so perverted in the service of this case is part of what gives Mendel Beilis's story so much of its eerie resonance. The toxic mixture of the medieval and the modern was a formula whose destructive power would be fully realized in the heart of Europe a generation later.

I first heard of the Beilis case as a boy from my Russian Jewish grandmother, who would recount tales of the old country, and of the Jews' persecution under the tsars, around the dinner table. (How I wish now I had written those tales down.) I recall her once telling a story or two and then saying with a half shake of her head and a pained and bitter smile, "And Mendel Beilis!" as if those three words contained a world.

Many years later, moved by that memory to learn more about the case, I was surprised to find that the last book about it had been written nearly a half century earlier and that the only account based on primary sources had been published in the Soviet Union in the early 1930s. I also learned that, after the fall of the Soviet state, the archival materials—including the original case files—had become accessible to foreign scholars. But no one had mined them to tell the full story of the Beilis affair from its strange beginnings to its dramatic and ambiguous conclusion.

Within weeks I was scrolling through thousands of documents on microfilm, later supplemented by hundreds more obtained directly from the archives, many of which were labeled "top secret." My effort to reconstruct the two-and-a-half-year drama took me to Kiev, now the capital of Ukraine. A hundred years to the day after the crime, I was walking the city's streets, retracing the route young Andrei Yushchinsky had taken for a secret rendezvous with his best friend on the last day of his life. As I sat in the main Kiev library, reading remarkably well-preserved daily newspapers, I felt as if I was reliving the events as they happened.

The secret documents and other materials, especially the transcript of the thirty-four-day trial, do indeed contain a world—a complex and a fascinating one. The story encompasses the vast and varied panorama of East European Jewish life in the era: one of fantastically wealthy Jews, such as Kiev's beet sugar magnates, of poor Jews, and of working-class Jews like Beilis who saved their kopeks to send their children to Russian schools, hoping to give them a better life. But the story takes in much more: not only the network of the Jews' persecutors and their intrigues, but the many good Christian Russians who tried to stop the case, and a parade of both colorful and malevolent lowlifes who figured into Beilis's fate. The story also offers a surprising window into the revolutionary underground, which was to produce the men who would rule Russia in just half a decade's time.

I found the characters to be exceptionally vivid and diverse. Among them: the murdered boy, Andrei Yushchinsky, an illegitimate child, poor and abused, often hungry, perennially hoping for the return of his real father who he believed would spirit him away from his squalor; Nikolai Krasovsky, "Russia's Sherlock Holmes," who attempted to find Andrei's real killers in defiance of the regime and would pay for it dearly; the demonic criminal gang leader Vera Cheberyak, a figure worthy of one of the great Russian novelists; and Mendel Beilis himself, the proverbial ordinary man trapped in extraordinary circumstances.

Beyond Russia's borders, the frame-up of an innocent man provoked widespread indignation and drew in some of the era's greatest personages. In Western Europe, the case struck an unpleasantly familiar chord; when Beilis was arrested, only five years had passed since the final exoneration in 1906 of the French officer Alfred Dreyfus, a Jew who had been falsely convicted of treason and imprisoned on

Devil's Island. Leading cultural, political, and religious figures such as Thomas Mann, H. G. Wells, Anatole France, Arthur Conan Doyle, and the archbishop of Canterbury rallied to Beilis's defense.

The story reaches across the ocean, to America, where the Beilis case made for an inspiring if often tardy and ineffectual collaboration between Jews and non-Jews. Rallies headlined by the likes of social reformer Jane Addams drew thousands. But in a cross-cultural convergence of hatred, America also had its own notorious, and uncannily similar, anti-Semitic court case unfolding at almost exactly the same time. In August 1913, Leo Frank, a Georgia pencil-factory manager, was convicted on a wrongful charge of killing a young female employee. Both cases presented themselves as surprisingly problematic and contentious matters for America's Jewish leadership.

Within Russia, the Beilis case reached to the heights of a decrepit regime on the verge of collapse. The story's trail leads up the chain of command, from local functionaries to ministers and all the way to Tsar Nicholas II, whose role—though its specifics are elusive—I believe was crucial. In all of its deceit, corruption, and sheer absurdity, the Beilis case powerfully illuminates the final chapter of the Romanov dynasty. Russians were haunted by a sense that their world was disintegrating: they shared an intuition of disaster, though they did not know what form it would take. The Beilis case fed into that anxiety, with Russians across the political spectrum pointing to it as a warning sign of a regime in a terminal state of decay.

I have been careful to present the characters in this book only in light of what they knew at the time. But the reader would do well to bear in mind what the characters do not know: that nearly all of them will be exterminated or swept away—doomed to execution or exile, to the firing squad or the émigré café. While some of the players may have merited their fates, many others did not; they were the best that Russia had to offer, exemplars of the liberal intelligentsia. Russia arguably has never recovered from their loss.

Despite its remarkable resonance in its own time and beyond, the Beilis case has been strangely neglected. Bernard Malamud, inspired by its power, used it as the basis for his Pulitzer Prize– and National Book Award–winning 1967 novel, *The Fixer.* But not only has there been no full-length nonfiction treatment of the case in nearly fifty years, there is not a single book recounting the complete story of the investigation and the trial, based on the original sources, from beginning to end. This book tells the full story of the case for the first time, exposing its genesis in the minds of a few fanatics and its path to worldwide cause célèbre.

The blood libel has been called the "master libel" against the Jews. It directly inspired the rampant metaphor of the Jews as economic "bloodsuckers." And more subtly, it's been argued, it underlies the slander of the Jews as a disloyal, conspiratorial, and parasitical force that exploits its hosts, sucking society's energy. The Beilis affair, as the outstanding example of the blood libel in the modern era, merits the closest study.

A hundred years after Mendel Beilis was first led into a Kiev courtroom, the killing of Andrei Yushchinsky remains a rallying point for the extreme right fringe in Russia and Ukraine. The Blood Libel today has its greatest mainstream acceptance in the Middle East, where it has been featured in major newspapers such as Saudi Arabia's *Al Riyadh,* propounded by a Cairo University professor, and been the subject of a book by a Syrian government minister. And in the Middle East, the Jew as vampire or bloodsucker is an all-too-common trope. Still, if the twentieth century has taught us anything, it is that societies that consider themselves "enlightened" need especially to be on their guard against infection by irrational hatred. The ordeal of Mendel Beilis stands as a cautionary reminder of the power and persistence of a murderous lie. In the twenty-first century, the blood libel is still with us.

This is a work of nonfiction based chiefly on primary sources—principally the trial transcript and the voluminous case files in the State Archives of the Kiev Region—and contemporary Russian newspaper accounts, as well as selected articles from the Yiddish press. What I refer to as Mendel Beilis's "Lost Memoir"—a lengthy, multipart interview the defendant gave to the Yiddish newspaper *Haynt* (Today) in 1913 that had likely lain unread for a century—has been especially useful in completing a portrait of the man in the dock.

All words in quotation marks come from a transcript, document, newspaper report, or the recollection of a direct participant. No details—no matter how strange they may seem—have been invented.

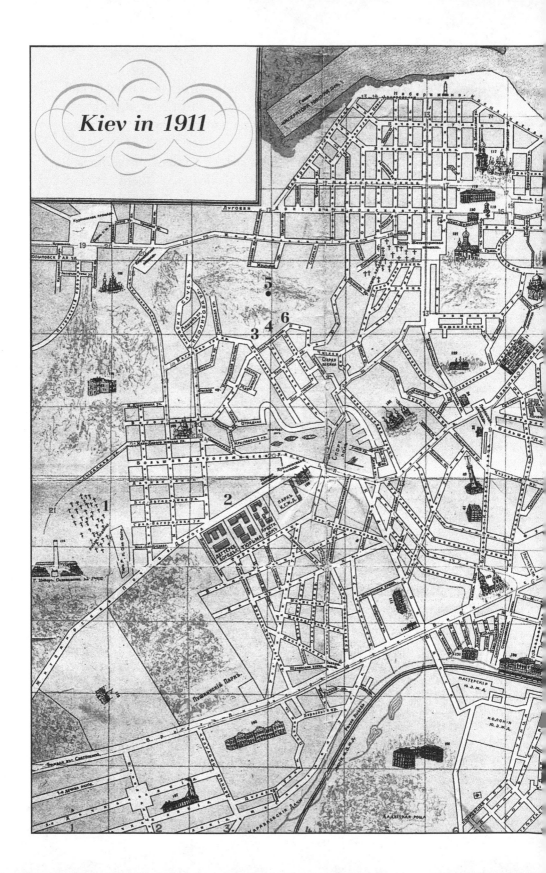

Kiev in 1911

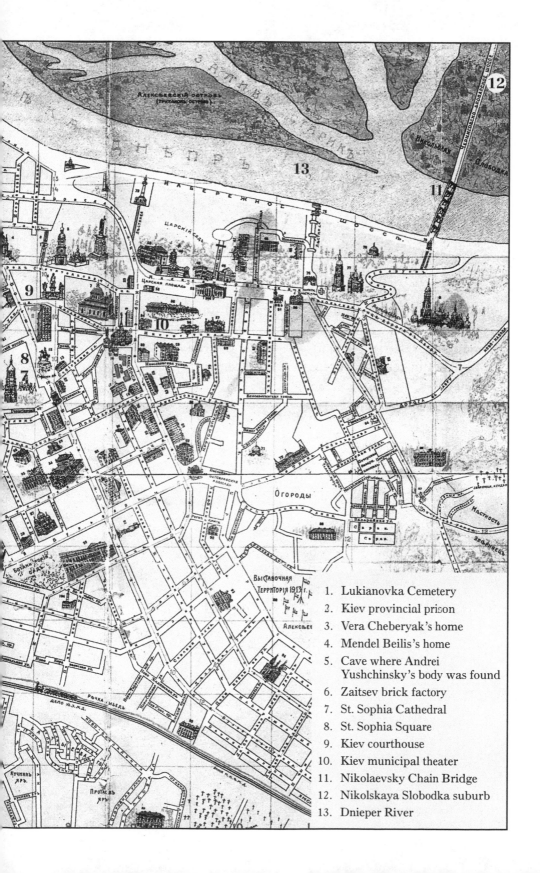

1. Lukianovka Cemetery
2. Kiev provincial prison
3. Vera Cheberyak's home
4. Mendel Beilis's home
5. Cave where Andrei Yushchinsky's body was found
6. Zaitsev brick factory
7. St. Sophia Cathedral
8. St. Sophia Square
9. Kiev courthouse
10. Kiev municipal theater
11. Nikolaevsky Chain Bridge
12. Nikolskaya Slobodka suburb
13. Dnieper River

A Note on Dates and Terminology

All dates in the text are given according to the Julian (Old Style) Calendar, in use in Russia until 1918, which lagged thirteen days behind the Gregorian Calendar used in the West.

In the following narrative, I have generally preferred the term "blood accusation" to the more common "blood libel," judging it more appropriate to the story of a court case where the validity of the charge is at issue. But the blood accusation has been, always and everywhere, a libel.

Cast of Characters

BEILIS'S DEFENDERS: OFFICIALS, POLICE, AND JOURNALISTS

Detective Nikolai Krasovsky, a provincial police official and former Kiev police detective brought in to investigate the Yushchinsky murder

Detective Evgeny Mishchuk (mish-CHOOK), chief of Kiev's investigative police, or chief detective

Vasily Fenenko, Kiev's Investigating Magistrate for Especially Important Cases

Nikolai Brandorf, a prosecutor in the Kiev regional court, comparable to a district attorney (referred to as "the local prosecutor"), who tries to stop the Beilis prosecution

Stepan Brazul-Brushkovsky (brah-ZOOL broosh-KAWF-skee), an ambitious Kiev journalist

Arnold Margolin, a scion of one of Russia's wealthiest families and Beilis's first attorney

Vladimir D. Nabokov, a leading liberal jurist and journalist (and father of the novelist Vladimir V. Nabokov)

Vasily Shulgin, an anti-Semitic newspaper editor and politician

BEILIS'S ATTORNEYS

Oskar Gruzenberg, Russia's most prominent Jewish attorney and head of the legal team

Nikolai Karabchevsky, one Russia's most famous attorneys

Vasily Maklakov, brother of interior minister Nikolai Maklakov

Alexander Zarudny, well-known defender of revolutionaries

Dimitry Grigorovich-Barsky, a Kiev attorney

THE PROSECUTION

Oskar Vipper, the lead prosecutor

Alexei Shmakov, technically an attorney for Andrei's mother (referred to as a "civil prosecutor")

Georgy Zamyslovsky, a right-wing member of the State Duma, technically an attorney for Andrei's mother (referred to as a "civil prosecutor")

WITNESSES FOR THE DEFENSE

Amzor Karaev, a young revolutionary

Sergei Makhalin, a young revolutionary who teamed up with Amzor Karaev to help Beilis

Mikhail Nakonechny, a shoemaker and neighbor of Beilis's

Evdokia [Dunya] Nakonechnaya, his daughter

Ekaterina Diakonova, an acquaintance of Vera Cheberyak's
Zinaida Malitskaya, Vera Cheberyak's downstairs neighbor
Professor P. K. Kokovtsov, one of Russia's most distinguished
    Hebraists
Professor I. G. Troitsky, an expert on the Jewish religion at the
    St. Petersburg Theological Seminary
Rabbi Jacob Mazeh, the chief rabbi of Moscow

WITNESSES FOR THE PROSECUTION

Vera Cheberyak (see Lead Players, above)
Vasily Cheberyak, her husband
Ludmila Cheberyak, her daughter
Father Justin Pranaitis, a Catholic priest who testifies as an expert
    on Judaism
Dr. Ivan Sikorsky, a professor of psychiatry at a Kiev university
Dr. Dimitry Kosorotov, a forensic pathologist
Kazimir Shakhovsky and *Ulyana Shakhovskaya* (known as "the
    Lamplighters"), witnesses who saw Andrei on the morning he
    disappeared
Anna "the Wolf" Zakharova, an alcoholic derelict

ASSORTED RIFFRAFF

Pavel Mifle, Vera Cheberyak's former lover
Ivan Kozachenko, a cellmate of Beilis's
Anna Darofeyeva, a woman who murdered her husband

ASSORTED POLITICIANS AND OFFICIALS

Peter Stolypin, Russian prime minister and minister of the interior.
    Assassinated in September 1911.
Vladimir Kokovtsov, successor to Peter Stolypin as prime minister
General Pavel Kurlov (koor-LAWF), deputy minister of the interior
    and head of the Corps of Gendarmes
Colonel Alexander Shredel, head of the Kiev division of the Corps of
    Gendarmes

ANDREI YUSHCHINSKY'S FAMILY

Alexandra Prikhodko, Andrei's mother
Luka Prikhodko, Andrei's stepfather, Alexandra's husband
Natalia Nezhinskaya, Andrei's aunt, Alexandra Prikhodko's sister
Fyodor Nezhinsky, Andrei's uncle, Alexandra Prikhodko's brother

A Child of Christian Blood

"Why Should I Be Afraid?"

Two boys were looking for buried treasure.

Early in the afternoon of March 20, 1911, a pair of gymnasium students of twelve or thirteen set off to explore the Berner Estate, a scruffy piece of wilderness adjoining the Lukianovka neighborhood on the northern outskirts of Kiev. A dozen or so acres in size, strewn with mysterious mounds, ruts, and ravines and dotted with brush, the Berner Estate had an outstanding feature irresistible to adventurous boys: its numerous caves. The caves had been uncovered accidentally by road workers some six decades earlier, causing considerable excitement among archaeologists and would-be treasure hunters. According to legend, treasure grounds were distinguished by unusual rock formations such as the ones found on the estate. A local landowner, convinced that the caves harbored the lost trove of an early eighteenth-century Cossack leader, ordered an intensive search back in the 1850s.

Treasure was said to be watched over by vengeful guardian spirits, but if the men obeying the landowner's command were at all fearful of supernatural forces, they were also thorough; by the time archaeologists arrived, every cave but one had been scraped clean of every human artifact. In that sole untouched cave, however, they found the earliest known traces of Kiev's first Neolithic inhabitants. These were remarkable discoveries—a flint blade, pottery shards, and a burned-out granite hearth so brittle from repeated firings that a trespasser could pulverize the stone to powder just by gripping a piece of it with his fingers. Further excavation of the area unearthed some two thousand human skeletons. The Berner Estate had been a burial ground.

By that spring day in 1911, the archaeologists were long gone, and the area had become a no-man's-land, a local newspaper branding it "a place for the Lukianovka children's games, where local hooligans and derelicts have convenient refuge." But the lore persisted of lost

Cossack treasure, hidden by a leader or "hetman," or by the rebellious eighteenth-century plunderers known as the Haidamaks. In the imaginations of the two young boys that March afternoon, somewhere within this broad, bleak slope, only a thousand feet from their neighborhood's crooked streets, vast riches lay hidden. Standing at the crest of the slope, which was rather steep, the boys could see the brownish ribbon of the Dnieper River, which marked Kiev's upper boundary. To the right, about halfway down, they could see the awnings and chimneys of the brick factory owned by the Jew Zaitsev. The neighborhood children liked to sneak onto the factory grounds and play there until the watchman chased them off.

The boy in charge of the expedition, Peter Elansky, led his friend Boris Beloshchitsky downhill to a cave dug into the side of a small mound. At either end of the mound were two trees, standing like sentries, their roots intertwined above its black mouth. On the ground near the cave lay something that caught Peter's eye—a torn-up school composition book. He read the name inscribed on the cover, but it meant nothing to him.

Boris was afraid of entering the cave. Treasure, everyone knew, could be guarded by the Haidamaks' angry ghosts. But Peter did not hesitate. This cave was a perfect place for a Cossack to have stashed his gains, with an entrance about three and a half feet high and two and a half feet wide—small enough to discourage adults, but big enough for a boy to scuttle through in a crouch.

The entrance to the cave was partially blocked with melting snow. With the temperature now barely above freezing, Kiev was three days into the spring thaw that each year turned the city's dirt streets into muddy rivers and aroused fears that the great Dnieper would brim over in another disastrous flood. A small stream of water trickled into the cave, but inside it was dry. After creeping six feet in, Peter could see that the cave forked at right angles into two niches. He could stand up easily now—inside, in places, the cave was more than five feet high. He looked first into the left-hand niche. He saw a figure, slumped against the wall. At first he thought it was a doll. Then he thought it was a woman. He had surely seen innumerable drunks passed out on the streets of Lukianovka, which had drinking establishments on nearly every corner. But this was motionlessness of a more peculiar and scary sort.

Peter ducked out of the cave and ran to get his stepfather, Leonty Sinitsky, who happened to be a police department paramedic. He was skeptical—surely, he thought, the boy was imagining things. But at about two p.m., he went with his stepson to the cave to check. He wriggled halfway in. There was not much light, but he could see there was a human figure, which looked to him like a man with a beard. He was seized by a fear that someone might be waiting within the cave to stab him. He squirmed out and ran with Peter to a nearby church, where he knew a policeman ought to be on duty.

A few moments later a policeman's whistle rang out, rousing a beat cop who, informed of the situation, went with Sinitsky and his stepson to the cave. The officer squeezed in and lit a match. The body belonged to a boy, he said, not a man or a woman, and he was dead. Clad only in a shirt and knee-length underwear and a single threadbare sock, it was lying in a semi-upright position, its hands tied behind with twine. Directly above the body, five school composition books were wedged into a crevice in the cave wall. A belt lay on top of the half-bare legs, which were bent and crossed. When the belt was turned over, it revealed an inscription: Andrei Yushchinsky Kiev-St. Sophia Religious School.

Sinitsky and the police officer stood over the body, its image flashing out of the gloom with each new match the officer struck. The policeman wanted to take the belt out of the cave, but Sinitsky stopped him—he knew that nothing should be removed from the scene until investigators arrived. Sinitsky, present by happenstance, would turn out to be the only person who tried to prevent the disastrous mishandling of the crime scene. When reinforcements arrived, a certain Officer Rapota, a stout fellow, found he could not squeeze himself into the cave. A shovel appeared. The snow was cleared away, and with it any clues it might have contained.

Just three hundred yards away from the cave, a Jewish clerk, Mendel Beilis, was sitting at his desk in his office on the edge of the Zaitsev brick factory, where he had been working since before dawn. "As I looked through the window," he later recalled, "I saw people hurrying somewhere, all in one direction. It was a usual thing to see individual workers coming to the factory, or passers-by. But now there were people in large groups, walking rapidly from various streets." When he stepped outside to find out what was going on, he was told that the body of a boy had been found nearby. He considered this disturbing news for a moment, and then went back to filling out receipts for the endless convoy of horse-drawn carts leaving the factory laden with bricks.

Soon it seemed all of Lukianovka was streaming into the Berner Estate, with a local newspaper reporting that "crowds of the curious surrounded the cave in a thick circle." Many of the onlookers wanted to get into the cave; reinforcements arrived but the officers had a hard time holding back the crowd. Everything should have been left undisturbed until the arrival of the lead detective; instead, the belt, the five notebooks (on which were also inscribed the same name, Andrei Yushchinsky), and some pieces of newspaper smeared with blood were sent back to the precinct house. The boy's jacket and cap, found lying in the right-hand niche, were placed outside the cave, free for people in the gathering crowd to pick up and examine.

Among the first onlookers that the police invited into the cave to try to identify the body was Vera Cheberyak, the mother of Andrei Yushchinsky's best friend, Zhenya. Cheberyak was a notorious figure in Lukianovka. Some years earlier she had blinded her lover, a French accordion player, with sulfuric acid, yet somehow escaped punishment. She was also reputed to be the keeper of a den of thieves, a fence for stolen goods, and a sometime procuress. For years, somewhat incongruously, she had been married to a respectable civil servant, with whom she had three children. When she saw the body, Vera Cheberyak told the police that the child did resemble a friend of her son's but the name on the belt was not familiar to her. She knew the boy only by a nickname, "Domovoi" or "Goblin." Later that day, she returned to the cave with Zhenya, who had told her his friend's real name was Yushchinsky. Mother and son were led through the cave's well-cleared entrance and into the left-hand niche. When the boy saw the body, he said, "Yes mama, that's definitely him. It's Goblin."

Nearly everyone in Andrei Yushchinsky's world seemed to have a nickname. "Honeybunch," "Frog," "Wolfie," "Snub-Nose," "Crooked Arm," "Crosseyed," "Sailor." The provenance could be obvious or obscure. But once a Russian child was given a nickname, there was no outgrowing it. It followed you to the brink of the grave, where it was finally left behind, and a proper Christian name and surname etched on the nameplate affixed to the simple cross. Andrei, though, would be denied even that small dignity. His grave marker would always tell a half truth. Andrei was legally barred from bearing the name of the father who had sired him and then abandoned him and his mother, when he was less than two years old, to serve in the tsar's army, it was said, somewhere in the Far East.

Friends noticed Andrei avoided saying his last name, Yushchinsky, his mother's maiden name, which was a mark of his illegitimate birth. (Some only learned of it for the first time after his death.) But he certainly liked to talk about his father. He mentioned him often, insisting to his friends that he would eventually be reunited with this mythical man, Feodosy Chirkov, who could not even give him his name. He would declare dreamily to his friends that his father would soon reappear and summon his son to go live with him, and how he would take only his grandmother along with him, not his mother or even his beloved aunt Natalia, because if he took them with him, people would think his father wanted only to beget another child with one woman or another, and he was not going to let people think that. At other times, he envisioned the reunion as happening in the more distant future. As soon as he came of age, he told his friends, he would track his father down in the Far East, where he was surely still alive and waiting for him.

As for his Christian name, all his life the family called Andrei by the usual Russian diminutive, "Andrusha." But he was known to nearly everyone else in Lukianovka by his nickname, "Domovoi." The word is usually translated as "goblin," but "house spirit" gives a more accurate idea of its meaning. A *domovoi* is a kind of dwarfish, impish poltergeist. In Slavic folklore, the *domovoi* (from the root *dom,* meaning "home") is the true master and protector of your household. If you are a good tenant of your residence, he will treat you well, tend the hearth and livestock, and safeguard your domicile. If you anger him, he will play tricks on you, make terrifying noises, throw crockery around in the dead of night.

Vera Cheberyak claimed it was her own Zhenya who had bestowed the nickname on the boy when Andrei was little because he wore a red hat, just as *domovois* were said to, but she made the claim only after both boys were dead. Perhaps the moniker's origin had something to do with Andrei's stature; as he entered adolescence, he seemed to grow hardly at all. But a neighbor who had known Andrei from his earliest years believed the nickname came about because of the boy's restlessness after dark. Andrei would roam the streets at night alone. "I would ask him: 'Why are you walking around so late? Aren't you afraid?'" the neighbor recounted. "And he would say: 'Why should I be afraid of anything?'"

On the morning of Saturday, March 12, 1911, Andrei awoke around six a.m. He got up carefully enough not to rouse his two brothers who slept in the same room. His mother and stepfather were both at work, so he didn't have to worry about anyone asking him any questions. He could focus on his plans for this special day without having to waste his boyish ingenuity on lies. Andrei had a secret on this day. Maybe he thought of it as a reward for all the dogged schoolwork he had done. He was going to play hooky—the only time he was known to have done so—and visit his old neighborhood of Lukianovka.

In the kitchen he washed his hands with cold water—there was no soap and no mirror to help him groom his blond hair. He was lucky that morning there was some leftover borscht to eat for breakfast; more often than not there was nothing at all, and he would go hungry until the afternoon or later. The deprivation had likely stunted his growth. At thirteen, Andrei was barely four feet four inches tall. (The autopsy report would find his body to be "of weak build and not well nourished.")

The borscht itself evinced the family's desperation. The day before, Andrei's mother, Alexandra, had gone to her own mother, complaining that she didn't have a single kopek. Alexandra's tiny income from taking in laundry and selling vegetables door-to-door, and her husband Luka's wages as a bookbinder, were barely enough to fend off starvation. Alexandra's mother had given her sixteen kopeks, enough to make the pot of soup with potatoes, beets, cabbage, and sunflower-seed oil.

Alexandra's sister, Andrei's aunt Natalia, had come by that night and taken the potato peels for her cow (outside its urban center, much of Kiev in those days was more village than city, and many people kept livestock). She tried the borscht and found it sour. But for Andrei the next morning a little of the borscht with a crust of bread made for a good start to his day.

The house had no clock. But Andrei somehow always woke up on time. His teachers said his attendance record was good and he always arrived punctually at eight thirty a.m. As Andrei left the house that Saturday morning, he appeared to be on his way to the Kiev-St. Sophia Religious School (a six-day school week was the norm in Russia) where he was studying with the eventual goal of becoming a Russian Orthodox priest. Prodded by his aunt Natalia, he had worked with a tutor (who had found him to be "very receptive," though "a little moody") for nine months to prepare for the school entrance exam. He had attended school regularly since the fall of the previous year and had received average grades, no mean accomplishment considering his circumstances.

He wore a blouse, embroidered by his mother, dark trousers, a cap with the school badge, a uniform jacket, and a padded felt coat. He bound his schoolbooks with the two leather straps his aunt Natalia, who paid for his schooling, had given him for Christmas. His schoolwork required only three books or so each day, but he always carried all seven or eight, plus a half-dozen notebooks with him because he was afraid one of his younger half brothers would tear them up if he left them at home.

Andrei went down a few steps to the street—the building stood on pillars, insurance against a modest flood. A boy who lived next door, Pavel Pushka, saw Andrei leave the house, slinging over his shoulder the heavy load of books, which were mere props that day. Pavel walked along with him a bit, but Andrei didn't say a word.

The previous fall, Andrei's family had moved from Lukianovka to Nikolskaya Slobodka, just outside the city on the Dnieper's left bank. Andrei still did not feel at home there. He would play in the street with the shopkeepers' sons, and some of the Jewish children (his new neighborhood was an area where Jews could live freely), but he had no real friends. He must have missed Lukianovka, where he ran with his best friends Zhenya, Ivan the cabdriver's son, and Andrei Maistrenko, whose mother was a state liquor store cashier. But they rarely all played together; when Andrei was with Zhenya they liked it to just be the two of them.

As Andrei walked westward past the mostly commercial storefronts of Slobodka's dreary streets, he may have looked forward to strolling across the magnificent entrance to the city of Kiev, the famous Nikolaevsky Chain Bridge over the Dnieper. Half a mile long, with four stone towers, each one hundred feet tall, it was the longest suspension bridge in the world when it was completed in 1856.

Little more is known about what Andrei did after he crossed that bridge. He was spotted at a market that morning about a half hour from home; he may have been looking to buy gunpowder for his homemade gun, which was his passion. He had fashioned it out of a piece of pipe he'd bought for thirty kopeks. (A handy boy—later, at the trial, his grandmother Olympiada said, "Whatever he saw, he made.") Maybe he was planning all the while to obtain the gunpowder from Zhenya, who made his own. Whatever the exact nature of his plans, walking at a good pace, it took him over an hour to get to the Cheberyak house in Lukianovka. He knocked on the door and Zhenya came out to play.

A little before seven a.m. on that Saturday, a lamplighter named Kazimir Shakhovsky was walking home, ladder on his shoulder, having filled the streetlamps on his route with kerosene. He lived on Polovetskaya Street, about fifty steps away from Zhenya Cheberyak's home on Upper Yurkovskaya Street. He remembered the day well because he was on his way back from his boss's house, where he had just got a ruble advance on his salary and a fresh batch of kerosene. At home, his wife, Ulyana, took the ruble and headed to the grocery store. On the way, she saw Andrei and his friend Zhenya standing on the corner of Polovetskaya and Upper Yurkovskaya talking and eating candy. She noticed Andrei was not wearing a coat and was carrying his belt of books. She spent ten kopeks on some bread and sausage that her husband ate for breakfast.

Kazimir left the house, passing the state liquor store on the ground floor of the Cheberyaks' building, which was already open, meaning it was a little past eight a.m. (the Russian Empire, brutal in so many ways, indulged its drinkers), and came upon Andrei and Zhenya, who were still standing on the sidewalk and talking, a little farther down the street from where Ulyana saw them. Kazimir noticed that Andrei had a jar about two inches tall with something black inside that he was sure was gunpowder. The boy was excited to see "Lamplighter," according to Kazimir, though it is not clear why. "He ran up to me and hit me on my shoulder with his hand and asked me where I was going," the man recalled. "He hit me pretty hard—it hurt, so I got angry . . . I told him he had no business knowing where I was going." Turning around, he spat out, "Bastard!"

If Andrei was hurt by this word, which he must have heard many, many times in his brief life, he did not show it. "Gramps, where are you going? Take me with you," he pleaded. Kazimir was going out to catch goldfinches to sell live at the market; Andrei, who had a net and liked to catch birds, would have enjoyed that. But Lamplighter pushed ahead to his destination, leaving Andrei behind, the taunt of "bastard" ringing in his ears. He was the last person known to have seen Andrei alive.

A short time after the body was discovered, Mendel Beilis answered a knock at the door of his home on Upper Yurkovskaya Street, which was located in the same two-story building at the entrance to the factory that housed his office. The Beilis household constituted a tiny Jewish outpost in a part of Kiev otherwise off-limits even to those Jews fortunate enough to receive government permits to live in the city. Russia's Jews were subject to a vast, oppressive, and ever-growing burden of more than a thousand discriminatory statutes and regulations restricting where they could live, where they could worship, which schools they could attend, and what kind of work they could perform. In principle, Jews could only live in the fifteen western provinces known as the "Pale of Settlement," which did not include Kiev. The Beilis family was only granted permission to live in Kiev, and the special privilege of living in this neighborhood, thanks to the intervention of the brick factory owner, Jonah Zaitsev, with the authorities.

Beilis found a Russian neighbor was paying him a call. He knew the man was a proud member of the "Black Hundreds," Russia's anti-Semitic movement of right-wing nationalists, but that was not a barrier to social interaction between them. Beilis got along well with his Christian neighbors and had a friendly relationship with at least one other Black Hundred member. A man could hate Jews as a group and get on perfectly well with them individually.

The neighbor delivered an odd piece of news, telling Beilis that "my paper"—the organ of his local Black Hundred group—was declaring that the boy Andrei Yushchinsky had been murdered by Jews for "ritual" purposes. Beilis would not recall perceiving this report as a threat to him or even to other Jews, and in fact the man may well have just been sharing the local news or even trying to convey to Beilis a friendly warning of possible anti-Jewish reprisals for the boy's killing. As the days passed, the brick factory clerk gave it little thought.

During his fifteen years in Kiev, Mendel Beilis had only once felt mortal fear as a Jew, during the terrible pogrom of 1905, when the mobs had killed scores of Jews and vandalized nearly every Jewish residence and place of business down to the lowliest stall. But when the violence began, a local priest had a guard put on Beilis's house. Beilis had done the priest a number of favors, including arranging to sell him bricks at a discount to build a school for orphans, and allowing his funeral processions to take a shortcut across the factory grounds to the cemetery. (A nearby Christian factory owner refused the request—the priest would often tell people that the Jew had helped him out, while the Christian had not.) After the pogrom ended, the great Yiddish writer and Kiev native Sholem Aleichem wrote his daughter that no one was spared: "They have beaten our millionaires—the Brodskys, the Zaitsevs . . ." Indeed, the mansions of the Zaitsevs and the even wealthier Brodskys, in a fine part of town, were ransacked, while Beilis's house was one of the few Jewish homes in the city to go untouched.

After the revolutionary and anti-Semitic turmoil of 1905 subsided, the brick factory resumed operation. Jonah Zaitsev, a sugar magnate, used the profits from the factory to help maintain the Jewish Surgical Hospital, a state-of-the-art facility open free of charge to indigent patients of all faiths, which he had founded with a thirty-thousand-ruble donation, in honor of the wedding of Tsar Nicholas II and Alexandra in 1894. He and other Jewish notables hoped that such beneficent institutions would testify to the community-mindedness of Kiev's Jews and their loyalty to the regime. The 1905 pogrom had been an unfortunate step backward, but the hospital's good works continued. In working at the factory, Mendel Beilis, it could be said, was doing his part to win the goodwill of the Russian people and state.

A week after the ghastly discovery in the cave, Andrei's burial in the cemetery of his old Lukianovka neighborhood was a kind of homecoming, with the funeral drawing scores of mourners. His former tutor presided, and as he intoned the Russian Orthodox service he noticed pieces of paper fluttering into the open grave. At first, he assumed they were farewell notes written by friends and schoolmates. But the mimeographed sheets, caught by the breeze as bewildered mourners perhaps let them slip from their hands, spoke not of grief but of hatred and revenge:

> Orthodox Christians! The Yids have tortured Andrusha Yushchinsky to death! Every year, before their Passover,* they torture to death several dozens of Christian children in order to get their blood to mix with their matzo. They do this to commemorate the suffering of our Savior, whom they tortured to death on the cross. The official doctors found that before the Yids tortured Yushchinsky, they stripped him naked, tied him up, stabbing him in the principal veins so as to get as much blood as possible. They pierced him in fifty places. Russians! If your children are dear to you, beat the Yids. Beat them up until there is not a single Yid left in Russia. Have pity on your children! Avenge the unfortunate martyr. It is time! It is time!

Police soon arrested a young man named Nikolai Pavlovich on suspicion of incitement to violence for handing out the inflammatory leaflets. They were unsigned, but there was little doubt about who lay behind their creation. The Okhrana, Russia's secret police, confirmed the twenty-two-year-old Pavlovich was "known to the division" as a member of the foremost Black Hundred organization, the Union of Russian People, and of the local right-wing youth group, the Society of the Double Headed Eagle. The tsarist security forces kept close watch on any significant political organization, even if it was ostensibly friendly to the imperial regime. Pavlovich, a sometime metalworker and petty criminal, was a typical specimen of one slice of the Black Hundreds, which included a substantial criminal element—men who did not shrink from assault, robbery, or murder. But the Black Hundreds were also the first genuine right-wing movement that united all Russia's social classes—peasants, workers, priests, shopkeepers, nobles—in defense of the tsar, against every enemy. Above all, against the Jews. The Black Hundreds would play a central and sinister role in the Yushchinsky case. Their success in elevating a local murder into a national rallying cry epitomizes this historical moment in Imperial Russia. The venom released by the murder of Andrei Yushchinsky would signal the progressive

---

* Passover that year fell on March 31.

moral and societal rot that had taken hold in Russia, and which within a half-dozen years would fatally undermine the tsarist regime.

Russia in these years was, as the noted historian W. Bruce Lincoln described it, a society "consumed by a sense of doom." One of the era's greatest poets, Alexander Blok, would date his intense anxiety for the future of Russia to the very season of Andrei's killing, the spring of 1911, when he wrote, "one could already begin to sense the smell of burning, blood and iron in the air." When Russia's most gifted artists and writers fixed their gaze on the future, they saw impending desolation, the fulfillment of the dread prophecies of the New Testament's book of Revelation, including the coming of the Antichrist. The politically minded on both the right and the left also expressed their anxiety in metaphors. They often talked of living "on a volcano." Within a few years, the liberal politician Vasily Maklakov (who would be one of Mendel Beilis's defense attorneys) would famously compare Russia to an automobile being driven down a steep and hazardous road at breakneck speed by "a mad chauffeur," heedless of all danger, resistant to the advice of competent drivers, steering Russia to inevitable destruction. All understood that the man at the wheel in this allegory was Tsar Nicholas II.

Nicholas himself, ruler of the largest country on earth—sprawling on either side of the Urals, to cover a third of the European continent and a third of Asia—shared the sense of foreboding. Many observers commented on his strong fatalism, which deepened with the years. "The emperor's salient characteristic," one of his ministers remarked, "is mystic resignation." Nicholas made much of the coincidence of his birthday with the Russian Orthodox feast day of Job, the "righteous and blameless" man in the Old Testament who maintained his faith in God despite a plague of undeserved misfortune. "I have a presentiment— more than a presentiment, a secret conviction," he once confided to his prime minister, Peter Stolypin, "that I am destined for terrible trials." He added with resignation, though, that unlike Job, to whom the Lord had restored everything he had lost and more, "I shall not receive my reward on this earth."

Even if he saw himself as a figure destined to be beset by tribulation, Nicholas dismissed apocalyptic fears for the country's future, even though Russia had experienced a revolution—the first in its history—just a few years earlier, in 1905. Nicholas's complacency stemmed from the pride he took in his supposed personal bond with his subjects. To a degree, the connection he felt was based on reality. The tsar, in fact, had much in common with men like the Jew-hating, petty criminal and Black Hundred rabble-rouser Nikolai Pavlovich. Both belonged to the Union of Russian People; Nicholas was an honorary member. The tsar was deeply grateful to malefactors like Pavlovich because they had helped him keep his throne. In December 1905, after a chaotic year for Russia, he had warmly accepted the organization's official badges for himself and his son, the tsarevich Alexis, telling a delegation, "I believe with your help I and the Russian people will succeed in defeating the enemies of Russia."

The Black Hundreds had emerged as malevolent and potent antagonists to the tsar's enemies amid the chaos of the 1905 Russian Revolution, which had threatened the very existence of the three-hundred-year-old Romanov dynasty. Russia had long had revolutionaries, but until 1905 it had never endured an actual revolution. Which is not to say that the country had previously enjoyed domestic tranquillity: a generation earlier, Russians had virtually invented modern political terrorism. In 1881, a radical group called the People's Will assassinated Nicholas's grandfather, Tsar Alexander II, in what is regarded as history's first suicide bombing. (Ironically, this "Tsar-Liberator" who had freed the serfs was the most liberal sovereign Russia would ever have.) In the first years of the new century, successor groups of radicals—preeminently the party of Socialist Revolutionaries, which was inspired by native populist thinkers as well as Karl Marx—were killing tsarist officials by the thousands. (In the most murderous year, from the fall of 1905 to the fall of 1906, the dead numbered 3,611.) The radicals' taste for imperial blood enthralled rather than appalled much of the educated liberal public, who initially viewed the bombings, murders, and robberies (or "expropriations") as acts of romantic and heroic despair. Expressing support for the revolutionaries was considered, in the words of one contemporary observer, "a sign of good manners," showing you were on the right side of history. In 1905 the revolutionaries suddenly became a mortal threat to the decrepit autocracy, weakened as it was by a disastrous war with Japan. The revolution began with "Bloody Sunday" on January 22 when the police fired on a large demonstration of workers marching to the Winter Palace in St. Petersburg. There followed strikes, peasant uprisings, and even rebellions in the armed forces, the most famous of which was the mutiny on the battleship *Potemkin* in the Black Sea. The year culminated in the world's first general strike and the tsar's grudging issuance of the October Manifesto, in which the "unlimited" sovereign found himself forced to make odious concessions, including the creation of the first elected parliament in Russia's history.

During that traumatic year, Black Hundred groups functioned as vigilante or paramilitary organizations in support of the tsarist regime, fighting in the streets against its opponents, attacking bystanders whom they suspected of antigovernment sympathies, and assassinating liberal politicians. Black Hundred thugs were known to waylay people—especially Jews and university students—whom they suspected of disloyalty and force them to kneel in front of an image of the tsar. They were most notorious, in Russia and abroad, for perpetrating murderous pogroms across the empire in 1905 and 1906, including in Kiev. Contrary to suspicions at the time and subsequently, historians have found little in the way of premeditation or planning. Still, some three thousand Jews were killed, and thousands more injured, as the marauders attacked people in the street and went from house to house, searching cellars where any Jews may have tried to hide. Countless Jewish homes and businesses were damaged and destroyed.

Nicholas never actively incited violence against the Jews, but he took palpable satisfaction from seeing the mobs heed the vigilantes' infamous call: "Beat the Yids. Save Russia." Manifesting a shared vocabulary with men such as Pavlovich, he wrote to his mother, the dowager empress Maria, in October 1905:

> In the first days after the Manifesto, the bad elements boldly raised their heads, but then a strong reaction set in and the whole mass of loyal people took heart. The result, as is natural and usual with us, was that the people became enraged by the insolence and audacity of the revolutionaries and socialists; and because nine tenths of them are Yids, the people's whole wrath turned against them. That is how the pogroms happened.

Nicholas acted as the protector of the most infamous Black Hundred rabble-rouser of the time, the "Mad Monk" Iliodor. At the very moment Andrei was being buried, Iliodor was reaching the height of his renown. Iliodor propagandized, in its purest form, the ideology of the Russian right, which, in the words of historian Jacob Langer, "revolved around a view of the Jews as a race of superhuman power spreading evil on a biblical scale." Based in the southern Russian city of Tsaritsyn (now Volgograd, formerly Stalingrad), Iliodor proselytized his creed to crowds in the thousands. "The Jew drinks human blood," he declaimed. "The Jew regards it as a pious deed to kill a Christian, the Antichrist will spring from Jewish stock, the Jew is accused by God, the Jew is the source of all evil in the world." The Mad Monk was so charismatic that he could reduce his female followers to a "tearful hysteria." A contemporary observer was struck by the curious combination of his "delicate, beautiful, feminine face" and "powerful will" that held his enthusiasts spellbound as he preached sermons vowing to drown every last Jew in the Black Sea.

Iliodor's moniker was no exaggeration. The Mad Monk was a genuinely unbalanced demagogue. He once slandered the wife of a wealthy timber merchant for supposedly wearing a low-cut dress and singing "filthy" songs at a charitable event (a fund-raiser for a temperance society, no less). The affair was taken up by the prime minister himself—an unavoidable intervention, given that Iliodor was a revered leader of a movement esteemed by the tsar. Such absurdities were routine in the end-time of the Romanovs, when a culture of intrigue mixed with operetta-style lunacy had deeply infected the Russian imperial court and government. Prime Minister Peter Stolypin, in fact, dared to side with the offended lady, ordering "rapid and decisive measures to protect the citizens of Tsaritsyn from public insults" of the kind inflicted by the Mad Monk. But the government was hesitant to the point of paralysis when it came to dealing with Iliodor's more serious and even murderous threats to public order. Stolypin privately called Iliodor a "fanatic" and spreader of "Black Hundred propaganda" who weakened the government's authority. But Iliodor had insinuated himself into the court's inner circle. He had secured the patronage of the powerful, and no less mad, "holy man" Grigory Rasputin, who was then at the height of his legendary and hypnotic influence over the royal family. The Church had tried to exile Iliodor to a remote parish, but Tsar Nicholas intervened to save him—"out of pity," he said, for the holy man's followers. The Mad Monk was untouchable.

Iliodor's story lays bare the strange and paradoxical rules of the game in end-stage tsarist Russia. Iliodor targeted not just what he called the Jewish-led "Satan's band," but rich capitalists and landowners as well; he even called for the prime minister to be put to death. He was truly a subversive force. Tsar Nicholas, however, saw in him not an enemy bent on undermining the state but a kindred spirit, one of the "mass of loyal people" who defended him from the "insolence" of his enemies, "nine tenths" of whom he believed were Jews. And for Nicholas, the supposed archaic purity of Iliodor's Russianness—his closeness to the *narod,* the people—trumped any concerns about his effect on the polity. The tsar's obsession with a pure Russia foretold a monarchy that was losing all sense of reality and becoming susceptible to fantasies of the darkest kind.

As it turned out, a few months after the death of Andrei Yushchin-sky, Iliodor would self-destruct before he could put his talents to work in a case that might well have given him the ultimate pulpit for his anti-Semitic screeds. He betrayed his protector Rasputin, threatening to reveal the holy man's debauchery, but was outmaneuvered, and ended up exiled and defrocked. It would fall to others to exploit the boy's murder for their own ends.

At Andrei's grave site, the mourners and provocateurs must have noticed a strange circumstance. While the deaths of children were tragically common in Russia, one aspect of the service surely distinguished it from any other child's funeral the mourners may have attended: the parents were not present. Andrei's schoolmates and teachers were there. His aunt Natalia, in the final stages of tuberculosis, stood there in the cold. Vera Cheberyak was there with Zhenya and her two daughters. But as Andrei lay in his open coffin—his wounds covered by makeup, a cypress cross tied around his neck with a ribbon, wearing his one spare pair of school uniform trousers, with ten one-kopeck coins in the right pocket—his mother and stepfather were at the local police precinct, under arrest.

The story of the family's three-month ordeal at the hands of the authorities, omitted or glossed over in the standard accounts of the case, is essential to understanding how the murder of a poor, troubled boy burgeoned from a family tragedy to a matter of state on the imperial agenda to a bizarre trial that would be followed the world over.

The trajectory of the case is conventionally portrayed as a line leading from an investigation infused with official anti-Semitism straight to the Jew in the dock. But the path that led from "the Yushchinsky murder" to "the Beilis affair" is as twisted as one of Kiev's winding streets.

Andrei's family did seem to harbor the essential elements required of a routine domestic tragedy: an illegitimate child, a resentful step-father, rumors of violent quarrels and abuse. As investigators talked to friends, neighbors, and relatives, their suspicions could only have grown. A teacher of Andrei's had been sure something at home was wrong: "Thin, troubled . . . silent. He walked the halls alone." Class-mates knew that Andrei often came to school hungry. Many witnesses told the authorities that Andrei's mother beat him. Zhenya Cheberyak said, "There were times when Andrusha's mother would punish him, she would beat him sometimes with her hand, sometimes with a belt, for example when she'd send him somewhere and he didn't go, and then she would thrash him for that. His mother never beat him badly, but a little, and never beat him so that he'd bleed."

But there were indications the beatings went beyond the routine. "I know that Alexandra . . . disliked Andrei very much," an elderly neigh-bor testified, and claimed he saw her beat him several times. "What she beat him for, I don't know, but through the fence I could see how awfully she treated him." He reported that "as soon as his mother started beating him [Andrei] would run to his Aunt Natalia." A class-mate confirmed that "his mother punished him often, and . . . when his mother beat him he'd always run to his aunt."

Andrei's maiden aunt Natalia was the boy's savior and protector. "Since I had no children of my own, I very much loved my sister's illegitimate son . . . Andrusha . . . and I decided to raise him and make something of him," she said in a deposition after Andrei's death, just months before she died of tuberculosis. A woman with a rare entrepre-neurial streak, she ran a workshop out of her apartment, which made decorative boxes for a store on Kiev's main street, Kreshchatik. Her income was modest, but it enabled her to pay for Andrei's education.

Natalia claimed to investigators that she had no idea who killed Andrei and did not suspect anyone. She insisted that Luka Prikhodko, Andrei's stepfather, was by nature "quiet, sober, modest and hardwork-ing." But Natalia did not completely conceal from the authorities the family's tensions, admitting that her sister sometimes resented the way she displaced her as the dominant figure in Andrei's life. Natalia was loving, but she could be harsh as she tried to keep the boy on the right path. Sometimes, Natalia said, "I would scream at [Andrusha] and he'd burst out crying. Then Alexandra would say she didn't want me to pay for Andrusha's education and I shouldn't dare insult him. There were frequent scenes like that."

Whatever suspicions Natalia had would have carried great weight with investigators because she was more a mother to Andrei than anyone else in the boy's life. From his earliest years he called his mother "Sashka" (a diminutive of Alexandra)—never "mama." Zhenya said, "When I asked Andrusha if he loved his stepfather and his mother, he always answered that he loved his aunt more than anyone." Natalia did not share her most disturbing suspicions with the police, but she did voice them in the presence of the local pub owner, Dobzhansky, who knew Andrei well—the boy would drop by the pub to have an egg for breakfast when he had a few extra kopeks—and was one of those who identified his body. In a sworn deposition Dobzhansky recounted how, after Andrei's body was found, a "very despondent" Natalia "walked up to the cave and said 'Andrusha was killed by no one other than his own people.'"

The man in charge of following up these leads, at this point, was Detective Evgeny Mishchuk, head of the Criminal Investigation Department of the Kiev police. Though he had some two decades of experience in law enforcement, he was of dubious competence and his investigative methods were reprehensible. He was gullible, reckless, and politically maladroit—qualities that would make him vulnerable to his enemies. Soon he would be the first victim of what would become a conspiracy to ensure that a Jew stood accused. But Mishchuk was honestly convinced that the family was involved in the crime—he utterly dismissed the "ritual murder" hypothesis—and he attempted to prove his theory with ruthless zeal.

On March 24, just four days after Andrei's body was found, Mishchuk personally arrested Luka and Alexandra Prikhodko, who was then four months pregnant, as well as Alexandra's brother Fyodor Nezhinsky, accusing them of the boy's killing. According to Alexandra, she implored, "Arrest me, but just allow me to bury my son, and I'll come back." Mishchuk answered: "It's not allowed to let a murderer like you go."

Only after the arrest was there a hunt for actual evidence to justify the charges against the couple. Mishchuk was following the standard course of action for the police of the era: suspects were identified on whatever flimsy grounds presented themselves and then brought in for questioning. With the couple in custody, he then stepped up the quest for physical clues. The police searched the Prikhodkos' home on March 25 and 26, employing the same finesse they demonstrated at the cave. "They broke everything and destroyed everything," Andrei's grandmother later testified. "I screamed and cried, 'What are you doing?'" When she protested, she said, "They told me they'd pistol whip me." The police chiseled out seven pieces of plaster with dark brown spots from the walls and took some of Alexandra's and Luka's clothes, which also had blood-colored spots. Alexandra was interrogated for twelve of her thirteen days in custody from nine a.m. until one or two in the morning. Like many innocent people, under interrogation she began to look only more guilty. Mishchuk reported: "Questioned in that regard [about the spots] Alexandra Prikhodko at first declared that it wasn't blood, and then started saying that it could have gotten on the clothes because of a nosebleed." The couple were released on April 5. The spots on the clothes turned out to be vegetable juice. No blood was found anywhere in the apartment. The couple, having been deprived of a chance to grieve in dignity, returned after thirteen days to find a home that Luka said had been "rifled through, turned upside down, broken." Luka said, "It was a time when I didn't know whether to live or die."

As for Mendel Beilis, some time after his Black Hundred neighbor dropped by to tell him of the accusation that Andrei had been killed by the Jews, he became aware that the police were taking the investigation in quite a different direction, pursuing Andrei's family. If he had originally dismissed his neighbor's report, Beilis was likely now even more inclined to push it out of his mind, especially since Mishchuk and other investigators were disregarding the "ritual" version, and the focus on Andrei's family would continue for weeks after their initial arrest and release. Beilis, moreover, would soon hear there was a new suspect in the murder: his neighbor Vera Cheberyak. The name was a familiar one. She lived just a few dozen yards down the street from him, and he had long known of her villainous reputation. But it did not enter his mind that he had anything to fear from her or from the machinations of some of the most powerful men in Russia.

2

"The Vendetta of the Sons of Jacob"

In the days after Andrei Yushchinsky's funeral, the city entered its full spring thaw. In time for Easter, "the cold and cloudy weather," the *Kievan* effused, "gave way to wonderful, warm, spring days . . . as if Nature herself had acted in sympathy toward the holiday celebration." The Dnieper came alive with ferries. In another month, the city's celebrated chestnut trees would be flowering. Peddlers would take to the streets shoeless, leaving behind their precious felt boots until the next winter. But spring always brought an intimation of doom as well, of death by drowning or disease. As the temperature passed the freezing point, the river threatened to flood and the open sewers in the city's poorer districts ran free (the city fathers hesitated at the expense of covering the festering ditches, with one councilman arguing, "Why should we worry about cholera when all around us we have plague, diphtheria, scarlet fever and syphilis?") This year, thankfully, the city had been spared serious flooding. But the discovery of Andrei's body had unleashed another elemental, unpredictable, and destructive force that set the city on edge. The Black Hundreds were in a state of righteous rage. Jews prepared to hide in cellars or flee the city in fear of a coming pogrom.

For the Jews of the empire, Eastertide was always a menacing time. In the past, the holiday season had been marked by some of Russia's most notorious pogroms. This year, in the aftermath of Andrei's death, a pogrom seemed a near certainty. The day before Easter, on April 9, the newspaper *Zemshchina* (roughly, "The Realm") published an article headlined "A Ritual Murder." Based on allegedly leaked details of the autopsy report, the article affirmed that "the totality of the available information establishes that we are dealing here with a ritual murder, committed by a Jewish Hasidic sect."

The article caused a sensation and indicated a turning point in the case. This was not a leaflet handed out by an agitator at a funeral. This was an article in the newspaper controlled by one of the most prominent Black Hundred leaders, the State Duma (parliament) member N. E. Markov, soon to become president of the Union of Russian People. "A Ritual Murder" was widely reprinted, including in the almost equally far-right but much more widely read newspaper the *Moscow Gazette*. That paper noted in a companion piece the "alarming rumor" spreading in Kiev that the case might be quashed and the perpetrators left unpunished. The paper complained "our Judeophile press is trying . . . to place the blame on anyone at all except persons of the Jewish tribe and faith." The author appeals for action: "[The Jews'] complicity in the use of human blood in ritual meals cannot be hidden . . . The blood of the unfortunate Yushchinskys [of the world] cries out to the heavens!"

Further fueling the Black Hundreds' outrage was the stalled police investigation. Nearly a month after the discovery of Andrei's body, Vasily Fenenko, Kiev's Investigating Magistrate for Especially Important Cases, declared that the police had reached a dead end. No progress at all had been made toward apprehending Andrei's killer or killers. On April 14, 1911, Fenenko posted an appeal to the citizenry in the local Kiev papers:

> Neither the circumstances nor the motive of the crime have been established and the investigation . . . has been hindered by an insufficiency of material . . . The Investigating Magistrate requests all persons who have any information about this case to inform him of such verbally or in written form.

The day-to-day sleuthing was still in the hands of Evgeny Mishchuk, chief detective of Kiev's police force. But within days of the discovery at the cave, Fenenko had been assigned major responsibility for overseeing the investigation. The ostensible reason for the assignment had been the unusual nature of the murder. But there is some indication that Fenenko was chosen in part because it was believed he would unquestioningly carry out orders from above. If this was their expectation, his superiors in the Kiev Judicial Chamber were utterly mistaken. Fenenko was not a man meekly to carry out orders that conflicted with his common sense, let alone his conscience. A lifelong bachelor who lived with his childhood nanny, at the age of thirty-six Fenenko had settled into a premature and respectable middle age. He was, by all accounts, honest, competent, and incorruptible. If at times he sounded self-righteous, he was indeed a righteous man. Fenenko regarded his integrity to be his proudest possession. As the case unfolded, this quality would not necessarily prove an asset.

By mid-April Fenenko found himself in an extremely uncomfortable position. The Black Hundreds were decrying the incompetence of the investigation and the injustice to Andrei's memory. Their outrage at the authorities, at this point, was entirely justified. Detective Mishchuk's stewardship of the case had been a fiasco. The police had brutalized Andrei's family. In the eyes of the far-right wing in Kiev, the police were guilty of other offenses against the Russian people, as well. Nikolai Pavlovich, the young man they believed had only tried to warn of the Jewish menace at Andrei's funeral, was under arrest. Several of his fellow "Eaglets"—members of the local far-right group Society of the Double Headed Eagle—had also been detained, and police had searched the group's headquarters. Fenenko's appeal to the citizenry for assistance only proved that he was, at best, incompetent, at worst (and the worst was only too believable), complicit in the worldwide Jewish conspiracy. How could anyone accept his absurd contention that the physical evidence led nowhere? To the Far Right, the motive of the crime and the nature of the perpetrators were as obvious as Andrei's four dozen wounds.

The Far Right employed the publicly reported details of the crime to craft a tale of Jewish villainy that rabble-rousers could use to incite a murderous mob. In truth, however, Andrei's corpse told the story not of some methodically executed blood ritual but of a crime committed in a frenzy, with no rational purpose other than, possibly, revenge.

The coroner submitted his autopsy report on April 25. The pathologists determined the first wounds came as Andrei was surprised from behind. The time of death, based on the undigested beets and potatoes in his stomach, was judged to be three to four hours after his morning meal. There were no signs of resistance. The murder weapon was established to be an awl with a diamond-shaped shaft whose tip had once broken off and later been resharpened. A frugal workingman's tool.

The report laid out a barrage of injuries to Andrei's body:

A. *External examination.* The body is lying on its back on a table in the dissection hall of the office of forensic medicine, dressed in a white homespun linen shirt with embroidery on the chest, collar, cuffs, sleeves, and hem. The collar of the shirt is open. The button on the left side, two button loops on the right side, and almost every part of the shirt are covered with spots, smears, and spatters of dried blood . . .

B. *Injuries.* Shaving the hair on the head to the scalp, and cleaning the scalp of clay and clotted blood, reveals four linear 3–7-millimeter-long wounds in the middle part of the crown and a 4-millimeter wound of the same shape on the skin of the left temple. The right temple is covered with fourteen punctate stab wounds. These punctures are scattered on the outer edge of the temple, but are arranged in straight rows on the inner edge . . . There are four linear wounds on the right side of the neck, toward the nodding muscles, each about .5 centimeter long, and another similar wound under the left side of the lower jaw. There are two more in the area of the Adam's apple and two stab wounds on the left cheek.

   On the left side of the chest between the nipples and the hypochondrium [area below the ribs], there are seven stab wounds, of which the first is right below the nipple, the second 2 cm below the first, the third and fourth at the same height and 3 cm to the right, the fifth 1 cm below the third, the sixth 3 cm below the third, and the seventh 4.5 cm below the third . . .

   There are eight stab wounds in the central area of the xiphoid process [lower part of the sternum]. There are five stab wounds on the right side along the axillary line, of which the first is over the sixth rib, the second in the ninth intervertebral space, the third above the tenth rib, and the fourth midway between the hypochondrium and the pelvis, and the fifth at the edge of the iliac bone.

   There are four stab wounds on the right side of the back along the shoulder blade line between the hypochondrium and the pelvis.

In all, the city coroner, Dr. A. M. Karpinsky, noted fifty wounds. A second autopsy reckoned their number at forty-seven, which would become the official count, with thirteen wounds on the right temple rather than fourteen. The first wounds, which were to the head and neck, the experts agreed, would have been fatal on their own. By matching the holes in the fabric with the wounds on his head, it was later determined that Andrei was wearing his cap tilted slightly upward and boyishly cocked to the left when the powerful initial blows penetrated the top of his skull, driving bits of bone into the skull cavity, the awl's shaft spearing through the dura mater into the dural sinus, which carries blood from the brain. The wounds to the neck followed, causing profuse bleeding. While the head and neck wounds would have eventually caused death, they did not immediately kill the boy. Death came only twenty to thirty minutes later, due to the wounds he had suffered to the heart. In one place, the weapon was driven into the heart so deeply and with such force that the handle left an impression on the skin.

In Kiev and in the empire's capital of St. Petersburg, the threat of a pogrom alarmed government officials as much as it did Kiev's Jews. Even though the prosecution of the case over the next two and a half years would suggest little in the way of official sympathy for the Jews, the tsar's top officials first became involved out of concern with preventing anti-Jewish violence. They did not act out of compassion. The regime's top priority was the preservation of public order. Straight through to the end of the trial, the government was preoccupied with preventing the case from causing any disturbance in Russian society at an intensely volatile time.

Within days of the discovery of the body, St. Petersburg had taken notice of the murder. By March 27, the day of Andrei's funeral, the minister of justice was being copied on the prosecutors' reports. On April 1, the Ministry of the Interior adjured the Kiev region's governor to keep it informed about the case.

Pavel Alexandrovich Kurlov, the deputy minister of the interior, commander of the Corps of Gendarmes, and overall supervisor of the imperial security apparatus, was an ironic, even perverse choice to monitor the case. Perhaps no senior official in the ministry had as much Jewish blood on his hands. During the wave of pogroms in 1905, when he was governor of Minsk, he had given the marauders free rein. There was hardly anyone to whom Kiev's Jews would have been more unwilling to entrust their fate.

The situation appeared relatively quiet until the appearance of the "Ritual Murder" article on April 9, when public mutterings grew increasingly ominous. On April 13, Kiev's governor, A. F. Giers, dispatched his first telegraphic distress call to General Kurlov, warning that a pogrom might be imminent. Right-wing organizations, he reported, were growing convinced that the government was engaged in a cover-up of the murder. On April 17, far-right groups were planning a public requiem for Andrei. Signs were mounting that the Black Hundreds would follow it with a massacre.

The authorities did not want a pogrom to take place. But what would they do to stop one? What actions would they take to restrain the bands of thugs whom they considered useful allies and even secretly admired? Much would depend on how the infamous Kurlov decided to respond to Giers's warning. Would he order steps toward protecting the Jewish population? Or would he give the vigilantes carte blanche, as he had done six years earlier in Minsk, when more than a hundred Jews were killed and nearly five hundred wounded, and his men fired on a largely Jewish group of demonstrators, shooting most of them in the back?

Venal, unprincipled, and a master of the most convoluted intrigues, Kurlov was the extravagant embodiment of all the corruption and decay in a regime riddled with innumerable schemers, sycophants, and incompetents. A former governor of Kiev as well as Minsk, he was not unintelligent, but his main talent was for relentless bureaucratic advancement against all obstacles. He was said to owe his position to the empress Alexandra herself, who supposedly installed him as the protector of her beloved spiritual guide Rasputin. To the extent that Kurlov had principles, they were those of the Far Right. And having taken personal loans from the treasurer of the Union of Russian People, he was literally in the Black Hundreds' debt.

Kurlov never made a move that he did not perceive to be in his own interest, which makes his decision   untainted by any sense of honor or justice—especially notable. Kurlov replied to Governor Giers's agitated telegram on the same day he received it in the clearest and most direct fashion. "It is vital," he wrote, "to take the most decisive measures to maintain order; a pogrom must be avoided at all costs." Other officials quickly issued numerous orders in the same vein. Black Hundred vigilantes had helped save the regime during the 1905 revolution, and its gratitude for that service was immense. But that moment had passed. The priority now was the preservation of order, even if it meant protecting Jews.

The local authorities prohibited the public requiem set for April 17. Despite the ban, a crowd of 150 or so hard-core "Unionists" gathered at Andrei's grave. When the presiding priest hinted that the Jews were responsible for the murder, a police officer on the scene warned him that "such talk only inflames people's passions." The crowd dispersed without incident.

In dealing with the Far Right, though, the authorities mixed their warnings against violence with gestures of appeasement. Pavlovich, and several other Eaglets who had been detained, were released "for lack of evidence." Behind the scenes, local Black Hundred leaders were coddled and kowtowed to. Preeminent among them was nineteen-year-old Vladimir Golubev. A Kiev university student and secretary of the city's "patriotic" youth organization, Double Headed Eagle, Golubev could serve as a general refutation of the "great man" school of history. The head of a small, struggling group that was in fact losing members, Golubev, more than anyone, can be said to have created the case that would shock and dumbfound the world.

If Pavlovich represented the Black Hundreds' criminal element, Golubev, the son of a professor at a Kiev religious academy, characterized its more reputable contingent. Fanatically sincere in his anti-Semitic beliefs, he was, in his way, a man of principle. One historian has called him a kind of "Black Hundred idealist." Once, when he learned that a railroad was owned largely by Jews, he refused to buy a ticket and demonstratively walked several dozen miles along the tracks. After Andrei's body was found, Golubev became obsessed with the case and launched an independent investigation. He was certain that a Jew had committed the crime, and he would not rest until he found a Jew whom the authorities would agree to charge. He even slept overnight once in the cave, which had served as such a fine natural morgue for Andrei; his enemies said he did it on a bet, but perhaps he was hoping for some paranormal insight into the crime.

His efforts would be rewarded. "Student Golubev," as he was invariably called, was the freshest incarnation of an eight-hundred-year-old archetype: the dogged Christian detective who perceives in an unsolved murder a monstrous Jewish plot.

Golubev was taking on the role originated in the twelfth century by the Welsh monk Thomas of Monmouth. Around the year 1149, Thomas took it upon himself to investigate the unsolved murder of William of Norwich, a twelve-year-old apprentice skinner who had been found dead five years earlier, on the day before Easter in 1144. It was Thomas who laid the foundation for the medieval and modern myth of Jewish ritual murder. The origin of the myth can, rather astoundingly, be pinpointed to a specific time and place and an individual instigating mind. The foundational moment came in 1150, when Thomas published the first portion of his *The Life and Miracles of Saint William the Martyr of Norwich*. Thomas, as historian Gavin Langmuir has written, "did not alter the course of battles, politics or the economy. He solved no philosophical or theological problems." Yet he created a myth that burrowed deeply into the Western mind "and caused, directly or indirectly, far more deaths than William's murderer could ever have dreamt of committing."

According to Thomas's account, the week before Easter in 1144, a man claiming to be the archdeacon's cook came to young William's mother asking permission for the boy to work in his kitchen. Taking some money from the supposed cook, the mother allowed her son to be led away. Five days later the boy's body was found in the woods outside the city. The boy's uncle, who was a priest, rose before the local church synod to accuse the city's Jews of the crime, but this charge met with skepticism from local notables, including the bishop of Norwich, the church prior, and the sheriff. Still, the people of Norwich grew angry at the city's Jews, and the sheriff gathered them in the castle to assure their safety. The danger passed. No Jews, nor anyone else, were charged. Poor William, said like Andrei to be a "neglected" and "poor ragged little fellow" when alive, lay increasingly forgotten in his churchyard grave.

When Thomas arrived in Norwich he became obsessed with solving the mystery of William's murder, and he determined to prove that the boy was a martyr whose spirit could perform miracles. Like Golubev, his twentieth-century Russian avatar, Thomas was motivated by a dangerous mixture of true belief and personal ambition. As the propagator of the cult of a new martyr, and the caretaker of the boy's sacred relics (for Thomas parlayed his advocacy into a position as sacristan of William's shrine), he would acquire dramatically enhanced prestige.

In *The Life and Miracles of Saint William,* Thomas introduced the novel idea of ritual murder as a Jewish Passover rite. He also pioneered the sophistry, the twisting of evidence, and the calculated obtuseness that would mark all subsequent accusations of Jewish ritual murder. Thomas set an example for the ages by producing eyewitnesses who, long after the crime, came forward with vivid stories implicating the Jews (" . . . a certain poor maid-servant . . . through the chink in the door . . . managed to see the boy . . ."); in his caustic railing against the skeptics who refused to accept the victim as a true martyr (their "saucy cavils" irked him); and by accusing the Jews of bribing the authorities ("giving a hundred marks to the sheriff they were rid of their fear").

But the most notorious and fraught motif he introduced, after the accusation of ritual murder itself, is the character of the apostate Jew who publicly reveals his people's clandestine and insidious rite, one that is justified by their scripture. Thomas hears "from the lips" of a converted Jew, a monk named Theobald, how the Jews of Spain gather every year in the French city of Narbonne (which was, in fact, an important center of Jewish learning and leadership) to plot the annual sacrifice demanded by their ancient texts.

Theobald disclosed to Thomas that the Jews believe that without the shedding of Christian blood they cannot obtain their freedom or ever even have hope of returning to the land of their fathers from which they had been exiled. Therefore they have to sacrifice a Christian somewhere in the world "in scorn and contempt of Christ." The Jewish elders assembled in Narbonne cast lots for all the countries of the world where Jews lived, and in 1144, the lot fell on Norwich. All the synagogues in England then gave their consent that the deed be carried out there. According to Thomas, the truth of Theobald's words—"uttered by one who was a converted enemy, and had been privy to the secrets of our enemies"—were beyond doubt. Thomas did not succeed in having any Jews charged with the crime. But he did elevate William into a martyr murdered by the Jews. The ritual-murder myth spread throughout England and worked its way into the heart of the culture, as evidenced by "The Prioress's Tale," Geoffrey Chaucer's story of the martyrdom of a pious seven-year-old child "of Christian blood":

> *This cursed Jew hym hent [grabbed], and heeld hym faste,*
> *And kitte his throte, and in a pit hym caste . . .*
> *The blood out crieth on your cursed deed!*

The notion that the Jews actually required human blood for their rituals arose when the myth spread to the Continent. The blood accusation, in its full form, emerged in the German town of Fulda in 1235. On Christmas day of that year, while a miller and his wife were at church, their mill burned down with their five sons inside. The Jews of Fulda were accused of slaughtering the children before the blaze was set and draining off their blood into waxed bags, to utilize it in some sort of ritual or medicine. On December 28, 1235, thirty-four Jews in Fulda were killed—by the town's outraged citizens, according to one account, or by crusaders, in another version of the incident—and became the first known victims of the blood accusation. The authors of the calumny that Jews need human blood for ritual purposes remain unknown. But it is likely the blood accusation sprang from the creative imaginations of some Fulda inhabitants or passing crusaders in 1235, who were inspired to embroider the original slander of Thomas of Monmouth.

The governing powers of Europe quickly understood the danger that the emergent myth presented to the state. Frederick II, the Holy Roman emperor, sought to stamp out the inflammatory accusation and the public's wrath against the Jews; like Thomas of Monmouth, he turned for help to Jewish apostates, but with the opposite purpose. In 1236, just months after the Fulda massacre, he convened an assembly of Jewish converts to Christianity from across Europe. They found that none of the Jews' sacred texts indicated they were "greedy for human blood." Accepting their judgment, Frederick declared the Jews of Fulda to be exonerated and forbade anyone from ever again making such a charge. His imperial edict was followed in 1247 by a papal bull from Innocent IV, declaring the blood accusation to be false. But once the potent fiction had lodged in people's minds, not even the Vicar of Christ, in all his purported infallibility, had the power to stop its spread.

Golubev did not know of his debt to Thomas of Monmouth (who was by then an obscure figure even to scholars, not having earned the renown he surely craved). But Golubev was likely acquainted with the works of anti-Semitic pseudo-scholarship then circulating in Russia, and so would have been familiar with the five slaughtered brothers of Fulda; Andreas of Rinn, supposedly killed by the Jews on the "Judenstein" or Jew-Stone in 1462; and Simon of Trent, a murdered boy whose case codified the blood accusation's essentials in 1475, establishing the motif of Christian blood being used to bake Passover matzo. Golubev also undoubtedly knew of the most notorious cases of the past three decades, nearly all of which originated to the west of Russia.

The blood accusation in the case of Andrei Yushchinsky would soon cause the tsarist regime to be condemned in the West for its shocking retrogression to a medieval mentality of prejudice and vengeance. Yet nearly forgotten amid the outrage was that some of the most "civilized" parts of Europe had recently witnessed the largest outbreak of ritual murder charges in three centuries. According to the most reliable count, for the decade from 1891 to 1900, there were seventy-nine significant ritual murder cases in Europe where specific allegations were made to the authorities or at least gained wide popular currency. Only five cases took place in the Russian Empire. The majority were in Austria-Hungary (thirty-six) and Germany (fifteen). Men like Golubev knew the most notorious of them like a catechism. A handful had come to trial. Kutaisi (Georgia, part of the Russian Empire) 1879: nine Jews, tried in the murder of a six-year-old girl. Tisza-Eszlar (Hungary) 1882: a Jewish synagogue sexton, tried in the murder of a fourteen-year-old servant girl. Xanten (Prussia) 1891: a Jewish butcher, accused of killing a five-year-old-boy, whose throat had been slit ear-to-ear. Polna (Bohemia) 1899: a twenty-two-year-old cobbler's apprentice, tried in the murder of a nineteen-year-old seamstress. Konitz (Prussia) 1900: a Jewish butcher and an animal skinner, accused in the killing and dismembering of an eighteen-year-old gymnasium student.

As Golubev combed the area around the cave for clues and canvassed the Lukianovka neighborhood for witnesses, he must have been conscious of his potential place in history. With the ambiguous exception of Polna (where the defendant was convicted, but the state officially rejected the ritual motive), in every recent case the Jewish suspects had, frustratingly, been exonerated. Moreover, these cases had been treated primarily as local matters. In modern times, no ritual murder case had had the unmitigated support of a European central government. Golubev sought to change the legacy of the modern blood accusation: he would enlist the highest authorities in the empire behind his cause, including, he hoped, the sovereign himself.

Within months, Golubev's amateur sleuthing would have a decisive impact on the official investigation. At this point, however, the authorities were pressuring the young hothead to refrain from inciting violence. Careful not to offend him or his comrades, they cajoled him into promising, on his honor, that he would do nothing to instigate attacks on the Jews, at least through the end of the summer. The deputy head of the Kiev Okhrana, or secret police, reported in mid-April that "everything has turned out all right. Golubev has quieted down. They have decided to postpone their action until the Sovereign's departure from Kiev [that is, after the tsar's planned visit in August] . . . (B)eating the Yids . . . they've postponed until fall."

But even though Golubev had been "quieted down," the threat of a pogrom still felt real, both to Kiev's Jews and to the government. The pages of the right-wing press were filled with venomous screeds declaring that the four dozen wounds on the "boy martyr" were clearly the work of Jews who were part of a powerful cabal that had duped inept investigators or, more likely, bought them off.

The government and the extreme right both contended for control over the case. On April 18, the minister of justice, Ivan Shcheglovitov, asked Prime Minister Stolypin to pay it special attention; he also met with the tsar, possibly briefing him on it for the first time. On the same day, the justice minister also sent a telegram to Kiev, removing the case from the purview of the local police and prosecutor and putting it under the personal supervision of Grigory Chaplinsky, prosecutor of the Kiev Judicial Chamber (a post somewhat analogous to that of a U.S. state attorney general). The justice minister instructed Chaplinsky to deliver regular, detailed reports; the local murder case would now be followed in its minutest details at the highest levels of the government.

Also on April 18, the extreme right proceeded with a plan to shame and threaten the government in the most public forum: the State Duma. The right-wing deputies met secretly to discuss passing a resolution that would demand the government explain why it was not treating Andrei's killing as a ritual murder.

On the afternoon of Saturday, April 23, came the first serious acts of anti-Jewish violence connected with the Yushchinsky murder. Black Hundred thugs began attacking Jews on the street at random in the largely Jewish suburb of Nikolskaya Slobodka on the left bank of the Dnieper, where Andrei had lived. "The entire Sabbath day . . . the 'Unionists' [members of the Union of Russian People] took a 'stroll' . . . pulling 'pranks' on all the Jews that they encountered," reported the Kiev correspondent of the Yiddish newspaper *Haynt*. "These 'jokes' often ended sadly, many Jews ending up bandaged . . . Many Jews . . . hide in their attics or even escape over the Dnieper to Kiev." But the city of Kiev itself soon felt unsafe. "Various dark rumors have begun to spread," *Haynt* reported, "one worse than the other" about impending revenge being taken on the Jews for Andrei's murder. Kiev's Jews—at least "those who take an interest in other things besides sugar and the stock exchange," sniped the reporter—were seized by fear of a full-fledged pogrom.

The jibe was directed at the Jewish denizens of the city's famous stock exchange, who remained preoccupied with their furious buying and selling of sugar-backed notes and securities (Kiev, despite much poverty, was something of a beet boomtown) before heading off to relax at the card tables, the one place where Jews and Gentiles could mix easily. But even the stock traders must have paused to take notice when, on April 29, the far-right faction introduced its resolution on the Duma floor charging the Kiev administration with obstructing the Yushchinsky investigation. The authorities were wasting time going down false paths, persecuting the poor boy's mother, the resolution declared, "instead of addressing the question of the fanatical Jewish sect whose members committed the murder." By Black Hundred standards, the tone of the document was measured. N. E. Markov, the Black Hundred leader who commissioned the "Ritual Murder" article, mounted the Duma rostrum to make his group's demands, and threats, entirely clear. Markov was in every sense an outsize figure. Enormously tall, with dark, curly hair, he was said to bear a resemblance to the six-foot-eight-inch tsar Peter the Great, earning him the nickname "the Bronze Horseman," after the statue of Peter in St. Petersburg immortalized in Alexander Pushkin's poem. Even compared with his fellow rightists, his views were extreme: he was among a minority that seriously raised the question of expelling all of Russia's Jews.

"We must pursue the whole malignant sect, the Jewish sect, which sends its butchers to collect the blood of Christian children, which prepares these butchers who collect children's blood in cups and distributes this blood to the Jews—to feast on their Paschal lamb, to feast on their Passover, made of the blood of Christian infants," Markov declaimed in the thundering bass voice that packed the galleries. He and his brethren had been told by the government not to worry, he said, that a fine investigator was on the case, that behind him was the prosecutorial apparatus, and that "we can just fall asleep"—but the judicial authorities had betrayed his trust. He bluntly threatened a pogrom. "When the Russian people find that there is no possibility of exposing in court the Jew who cut up a child and drained the blood out of him, that neither the court, nor the police, nor the governors nor the ministers, nor the supreme legislative institutions would be of assistance—that day, gentlemen, there will be pogroms of Jews. But neither I . . . nor the Union of Russian People will create the pogrom. You yourself will create the pogrom. That pogrom will not be the kind we've seen so far, it will not be a pogrom of Yid feather beds, but all the Yids, down to the very last one, will be wiped out."

The resolution provoked a boisterous floor fight. A Social Democratic deputy, according to one account, "amid yells of defiance from the Right benches, denounced the [so-called] 'Real Russians' as 'a band of robbers and murderers.'" Liberals and mainstream conservatives deplored what they said was an incitement to violence and the promulgation of paranoid medieval fantasies that were bringing shame upon Russia. The resolution failed by a vote of 108 to 93. The narrow numerical loss was something of a moral victory for the Black Hundreds.

Markov's genocidal histrionics led Kiev's Jews to prepare for the worst. "The most fearful two days"—Saturday, April 30, and Sunday, May 1, the two days after the Duma debate—"passed in an unusually oppressive mood on the part of the entire population," *Haynt*'s Kiev correspondent wrote. In the Jewish neighborhoods "there was a kind of strange death-silence." Jews who had the financial means checked into hotels, where they would be relatively safe. Hundreds of Jewish families packed their suitcases and began to flee the city.

The Black Hundreds' triple-pronged attack on the regime—in the press, in the Duma, and on the streets of Kiev—deeply unnerved the upper echelons of the tsar's government. Thanks to the fecklessness of the local investigation into Andrei's murder, this case could no longer be managed haphazardly at a distance, with a minister prodding a vice minister, who prodded a governor, who prodded a police official. The central government would now impose direct oversight on the investigation.

On April 29, 1911, as the Duma debated the rightist resolution, the Justice Ministry official Alexander Liadov boarded a train in St. Petersburg bound for Kiev. Liadov—vice director of the ministry's First

Department, head of the Second Criminal Division—was the kind of bureaucrat often referred to as "colorless and faceless." The impact of such a figure is easily underappreciated, especially in a drama like the Yushchinsky affair, with so many vivid characters contending for attention. But complex plots often require at least one such transparently functional character, and in his limited stage time Liadov would set key plot mechanics into motion.

Exactly what Liadov's orders were from his boss, justice minister Ivan Shcheglovitov, is not known. If they were written down, they have been lost. Most likely they were given verbally, with things said or hinted at that no one wanted put to paper. But it can be deduced from subsequent events that, as he arrived in Kiev, Liadov had a threefold mission. Its first two aspects were straightforward, comprehensible, and expedient. Liadov was to defuse the explosive young Black Hundred leader, Golubev, who was conducting his own independent investigation of Andrei's murder and could ignite a pogrom whenever he chose to. Second, he was to make sure the investigation appeared to be in competent hands: the bumbling Mishchuk had to be replaced by someone with an unassailable reputation. Liadov's third imperative, however, was neither straightforward nor sensible. As he settled into his Kiev hotel suite, he mentally unpacked this part of his brief: to focus investigators on the "ritual version"—the notion that Andrei had been killed by Jews for his blood to make matzo for their Passover meals.

Why was Liadov pursuing the very scenario that the government feared as incendiary? The government was, after all, determined to prevent anti-Jewish violence "at all costs." If the abiding priority of the state was to preserve order, why would it pursue the most inflammatory possible course, one that would threaten its interests, both foreign and domestic?

Liadov's mission marks the start of this central mystery of the Yushchinsky affair. Russia, if measured by its skein of legal restrictions on Jews, was the most anti-Semitic country in the world, but this alone is not sufficient to explain how a medieval fantasy could engender a conspiracy at the highest levels of the tsar's government. Was Liadov's brief the result of some arcane political calculation? Possibly. But the answer may lie at a more atavistic level—within the warped mentality of a doomed regime and, ultimately, in the mind of the tsar himself. If there is one constant in the late period of imperial Russian decadence, it was the urge of all officials to please the tsar, or those whose positions depended on the tsar's favor. The tsar himself was notoriously inscrutable. In what remained an essentially absolute monarchy with profound rot at its core, much depended on what officials thought the tsar thought about a matter, or thought he would think about it if he took the time to think about it. Liadov and the rightists knew that the tsar planned an official visit to Kiev at the end of the summer, when the unsolved murder of a poor Christian boy promised to cast a shadow over his tour. Well aware that the proponents of the blood accusation would be hoping for a sign of imperial favor for their cause, Liadov had to recognize the signal importance of his mysterious but calculated mission.

The day after his arrival in Kiev Liadov initiated his first delicate maneuver by summoning Golubev to his hotel suite for a meeting with him and the chief prosecutor, Chaplinsky. The young extremist was in a hostile mood. He refused to talk to Chaplinsky, whom he was meeting for the first time, regarding him as an enemy. Liadov told the young man that if he had anything to say, the prosecutor would listen. When Golubev insisted that "we"—that is, his band of thugs—"have an interest in preventing that horror," meaning ritual murder, Liadov had his opening. He gave Golubev an uncompromising warning but presented the threat in the most empathetic manner possible. Liadov later recounted the conversation as accurately as he could remember it.

"I don't think it would be in your interest to organize a pogrom," he told Golubev.

"Why?" Golubev replied.

"Because," Liadov said, "the Sovereign is expected to visit [Kiev]. If any of your fellow members cause a pogrom and there are disturbances in Kiev, then you'll have as much chance of seeing the festivities as of seeing your own ears [as the Russian saying goes], and it probably would be more pleasant for you and your organization to see the Sovereign."

"That thought never occurred to me," Golubev replied obligingly. "I promise you that there will be not be a pogrom."

Perhaps out of politeness, Golubev apparently did not mention that he had heard exactly the same line of coaxing from the Kiev Gendarmes two weeks earlier. Liadov believed he had found the perfect psychological lever and reported to the justice minister, "The desire to avoid a pogrom [on Golubev's part], as I came to understand, was aroused *exclusively* by the fear that if there were disturbances in Kiev, then the visit of the sovereign would not take place." However, it would be a mistake to interpret this as implying official approval of a future pogrom to occur *after* the tsar's visit. Liadov was clearly only using the tsar's visit as an excuse for Golubev to back down without losing face. When the threat of pogroms emerged later, officials would act quickly to suppress them without recourse to excuses.

In any event, believing he had defused Golubev, Liadov now prepared to fulfill his aim of steering the investigation toward the motive of the "ritual version."

From the whisperings about the progress of the investigation, the prominent Jews of Kiev felt reassured. The Yiddish press was reporting (inaccurately) that, thanks to Liadov's intervention, the ritual-murder theory had been decisively rejected. Weeks earlier, after "the dark rumors" of violence had begun to spread, Jewish community leaders in Kiev conferred about what to do. They considered offering a reward for the apprehension of Andrei's killer or killers but rejected the proposal as likely only to draw more unwanted suspicion. Although some wanted to issue a proclamation declaring the Jewish people innocent of the crime, in late April, *Haynt* reported, Jewish leaders reached a consensus to employ a "tactic of remaining silent and waiting." They would "patiently refrain from anything that might anger the dark gangs." That is, they had decided to do nothing. The reaction of Kiev's Jewish leadership was typical of the inertia and cautiousness, as well as a pragmatism shading into wishful thinking, which often characterized its response to threats from outside.

The community's leaders represented their course of inaction as an opportunity for the Jews to show their inner strength. "In such a dangerous situation [Kiev's Jews] sit and grind their teeth and remain silent; this is truly a courageous act that only Jews who understand the term 'a time to be silent' are capable of," *Haynt* reported, referring to Ecclesiastes 3:7 ("A time to be silent, a time to speak"). When to stand up to the authorities and when to hold one's tongue in the face of danger and oppression was a fraught and divisive question for Russia's Jews. But in this case it seemed that the sage counsel of the rabbis and sugar barons had proven prudent.

These were not naive men. They claimed history, as well as common sense, on their side. For all its anti-Semitism—its segregation of the Jews in the Pale of Settlement, its funding of the Black Hundreds, its past toleration, if not outright encouragement, of pogroms—the tsarist state had propagated the blood accusation only inconsistently. To be sure, the record was disturbingly mixed. In 1817, Tsar Alexander I approved a decree that barred accusations of ritual murder against Jews based only on the prejudice of their supposed need for Christian blood. There had to be evidence. If "suspicion should fall upon the Jews [in a case of child-murder]," the decree said, "then an investigation should be carried out following the legal procedures that are followed when investigating people of any other religion, when they are accused of murder." Yet in 1823, Alexander ordered the investigation of a thoroughly baseless charge of ritual murder in the Belarusian town of Velizh that dragged on for more than a decade as the authorities arrested much of the Jewish communal leadership and shuttered the synagogue by imperial degree. Only in 1835 did Alexander's successor, Nicholas I, finally quash the Velizh case. But the notoriously reactionary Nicholas, known as the "Gendarme of Europe," rejected his advisers' counsel to reaffirm Alexander's 1817 declaration, averring "that there truly exist among the Jews fanatics or sectarians, who consider Christian blood necessary for their rites."

Still, over the previous century such cases had, in fact, been fairly rare in Russia, with only a half-dozen or so significant prosecutions. Russia's only conviction for ritual murder, of a group of Jewish soldiers in Saratov in the 1856 deaths of two young boys, had attracted little attention. Popular rumors of ritual murders did play a role in inciting pogroms in 1903 in Kishinev, but the state had not endorsed the accusations. The most recent actual court case, in 1900–1902, involved a Jewish barber in Vilna named David Blondes. He was convicted of assaulting, but not attempting to kill, a female servant who claimed he had wanted her blood. In convicting him, the court did not affirm the crime's supposed ritual nature (the woman's wounds amounted to a few scratches). The case was notable for exposing a definite timidity among Jewish leaders in defending their people against the ritual murder charge. When Blondes was convicted on the assault count, some in the Jewish community, and even one of his own attorneys, recommended that he accept his prison sentence of a few months. An appeal, it was feared, could only promote the ugly libel against the Jews and inflame the Christian populace. Blondes, urged by Oskar Gruzenberg, the empire's most prominent Jewish defense attorney, courageously decided to challenge the verdict. He wrote Gruzenberg from prison, "Am I really going to have to suffer from a false accusation, just because I was born a Jew?" He understood the case was not just about him but the entire Jewish people. On appeal, he was given a new trial and a jury cleared him of all charges.

Yet now the imperial government was preparing to abet a vengeful demand by political extremists for Jewish blood, even though investigators had discovered no indication of ritual murder. Liadov and his Kiev associates had only one possible shred of evidence on which to build a case. Andrei's mother, Alexandra, had received a strange and disturbing letter, the envelope addressed to "Yushchinskaya—Mother of the Murdered Boy." The anonymous author claimed that "on the day of the murder I saw your boy walking on Lukianovskaya [Street] with some sort of Jew. Near St. Fyodor's Church an old Jew joined them . . . That was probably your boy [I saw] . . . I was plagued with a thought that wouldn't leave me alone. The fact is that I had the thought, and what if . . . the Jews need blood for the Passover holiday and a thin boy will be their victim." The letter, postmarked March 24, was signed, "A Christian." A similar letter was sent to the coroner. But the "Christian Letters" would ultimately prove more useful to the defense than the prosecution. They would attract extraordinary attention when the defense put forward the theory that the missives were written at the behest of the real killers and held the key to solving the case.

In the initial investigation, before Liadov had come on the scene, mutterings swirled in the streets of Kiev that a Jewish cabal had killed the boy Andrei. The police had canvassed the Slobodka suburb and the boy's old neighborhood of Lukianovka, interviewing numerous residents and potential witnesses—and heard the same rumors repeated over and over again. Typical was the weary answer of a man named Tolkachev: "At the market they're saying all sorts of things—at first they said it looked like he was killed by his mother, then they said Andrusha was killed by the Yids, now I'm not sure I know what they're saying."

One of the last people to be questioned in this initial phase of the investigation, sometime in April, was Vera Cheberyak, who was happy to aggravate the rumors. Investigators were aware, of course, of her villainous reputation; she and her gang were currently under investigation in two major robberies, including the theft of two thousand rubles' worth of revolvers. But they viewed her mainly as the woman who, along with her son, had helped identify Andrei's body and had no reason to speculate that her criminal activity was related to Andrei's murder. They might have thought differently if they had known that Cheberyak had withheld a vital piece of information: her son Zhenya had gone out to play with Andrei the morning he disappeared. Revealing that fact would have made it clear that the murdered boy had last been seen alive just a few dozen yards from her doorstep. She told the police nothing of particular note, but she did volunteer that she was surer than most about who had killed Andrei. Having seen the Black Hundreds' leaflets at the funeral, she said, "Now it seems to me that Andrusha was probably killed by Jews since no one in general needed Andrusha dead." She admitted, though, "I cannot offer proof confirming my supposition."

Just a few days after Vera Cheberyak's testimony, Alexander Liadov set about searching for proof of the "supposition" that a Jew had committed the crime. The motives of Vera Cheberyak and those of the state would eventually intersect and produce one of the stranger collaborations in judicial history. But that lay many months in the future. Meanwhile, three obstacles stood in the way of any attempt to pin Andrei's murder on Jews: the lack of evidence, the absence of witnesses, and the opposition of the two respected local officials in charge of the case—the local prosecutor, Nikolai Brandorf, and Investigator Vasily Fenenko.

Liadov later claimed that he had no preconceived notions about what he sought to find. But according to Fenenko, in early May, when Liadov summoned him and a number of others for a meeting in his rooms at the European Hotel, he revealed a very definite view of the case—a view he made it clear was shared by the man who had sent him on this mission. The meeting would turn out to be one of the most pivotal events in the whole affair. Liadov, in Fenenko's telling, declared that "the Minister of Justice does not doubt the ritual character of the murder." Chaplinsky, Kiev's chief prosecutor, piped in that he was glad to hear that the minister was of the same opinion as he was. One participant in the meeting expressed the fear that propagating the blood accusation could provoke a pogrom. Chaplinsky, according to Fenenko, replied he would have no objection "if the Jews were beaten up a bit." Given the government's intense concern with preserving order, it is inconceivable that Chaplinsky meant this remark to be taken seriously. In fact, just days earlier, Chaplinsky himself had warned the justice minister about the danger of a pogrom. But the sardonic taunt exposed the government's official stance: in this matter, Jews were targets.

Investigator Fenenko and Prosecutor Brandorf believed the ritual-murder explanation of the crime was absurd. The autopsy reports told a story of homicidal rage and possibly revenge, not of a calm and deliberate ritual for collecting blood. In the days leading up to Liadov's arrival from St. Petersburg on May 1, the two men must have felt under increasing pressure to produce a definitive dismissal of the ritual-murder hypothesis. But how could they dispose of the ridiculous charge once and for all? One approach would be to profile the mind of the killer or killers based on the autopsy and what evidence there was at the crime scene. In late April, before Liadov's arrival, Brandorf recommended to Investigator Fenenko that he retain a renowned professor of psychiatry, Ivan Sikorsky, to analyze the full range of evidence. Students of the case have long assumed, quite reasonably, that Chaplinsky must have recommended Sikorsky, hoping that he would support the ritual accusation. But the documents suggest that getting Sikorsky involved in the case was very possibly Brandorf's idea. Brandorf may have sincerely hoped that seeking the distinguished professor's opinion would help lay the ritual accusation to rest. But it was a step that would help tip the case into madness.

Professor Emeritus Ivan Sikorsky of Kiev's St. Vladimir University was one of Russia's most eminent psychiatric researchers. While his achievements would soon be far outshone by those of his son, the aviation pioneer Igor Sikorsky—already gaining fame in 1911 as the inventor of the helicopter—Ivan was so esteemed that he had once been honored by the great Leo Tolstoy with an audience at his estate at Yasnaya Polyana. He was the author of works on general psychology, and numerous specialized studies on subjects ranging from child development to the effect of fatigue on intellectual function, which were widely published and cited abroad. He had started out his career as an anatomist-pathologist and was active in promoting the new science of criminalistics and the systematic use of psychiatric expertise in the courts. He was considered an expert on religious fanaticism and folk belief: his most popularly known work was a report on the horrific mass suicide in the town of Ternov, where twenty-five members of a Christian cult had themselves intentionally buried alive.

Sikorsky could by all rights have been considered the ideal man to evaluate the evidence in a case centering on questions of human anatomy and the fanatical mind. But his arrogant devotion to the pseudoscience of his day inspired and reinforced in him a virulent racism and anti-Semitism that would prove profoundly destructive to the cause of justice he professed to support. Sikorsky emerged as a full-fledged anti-Semite only very late in life, not long before Andrei's murder. An early indication of his noxious system of thinking can be found in his preoccupation with "sectology," the study of religious sectarianism, a discipline that had an inevitably political slant.

Russians at all levels of society were engaged in a scattershot spiritual awakening, with a proliferation of unconventional forms of belief, or "God-seeking," a quest for meaning amid the turbulence and trauma of the modern age. The most renowned God-seeker, Leo Tolstoy, had died only a few months earlier in the fall of 1910: his search had led him to a Christian-anarchist, pacifist philosophy that rejected basic tenets of the Orthodox Church, resulting in his excommunication. The search for the transcendent drew God-seeking intellectuals and members of the upper class to mysticism, spiritualism, and Eastern religions and healing. Tsar Nicholas and the empress Alexandra, in their devotion to a spiritual guide, were in many ways typical God-seekers of their era. (In fact, before Rasputin, in the years 1900–1902 the royal couple had formed a close bond with another mystic and faith healer, the Frenchman Philippe Nizier-Vachod, who was sent packing when his powers failed to help the empress conceive a male heir.) The lower classes were drawn to individual charismatic leaders in a popular religious revival that was rightly regarded by the Russian Orthodox Church as a threat to its authority. Some charismatic leaders were even imprisoned.

Sikorsky's worldview was largely constrained by the pseudosciences of his day, from social Darwinism to physiognomy. (In his analysis of a photograph of Fyodor Kovalev, the young man who buried alive the twenty-five Ternov cultists, Sikorsky wrote, "The left eyebrow is a little higher than the right, while the muscle around the eye on the right side is contracted more strongly than on the left, as a consequence of which the right eye seems smaller than the left one. This irregularity of his expression . . . constitutes a sign of degeneration and indicates Kovalev's belonging to a psychopathic family.") Sikorsky idolized Herbert Spencer, the renowned British social Darwinist and, like Spencer, simultaneously believed in Darwinism and the very theory it had discredited, Lamarckism, the inheritance of acquired characteristics, including ancestors' learned behavior. (Attributes could travel curious paths indeed: a widow, Sikorsky believed, could have children with a second husband bearing "the outer traits and character of the first husband.")

Sikorsky's pseudoscientific principles easily extended into ardent and avowed racism. Central to his beliefs was the notion that the races could be divided into two types, "higher" and "lower." During their meeting in 1890, Leo Tolstoy already sensed something not quite right about this professor, who apparently treated him to a disquisition on his obsession, the danger of national "hereditary degeneration." After Sikorsky took his leave, Tolstoy wrote in his diary of the man's "astonishing foolishness" and added one curious but pungent remark: "A nice fellow—but gone rotten."

When it came to the Yushchinsky case, however, the problem with Sikorsky was not his pseudoscientism or, exactly, his racism; racial pseudoscience was widespread in the era. Rather, it was that these intellectual foundations gave rise to a late-blooming, fanatical anti-Semitism that would poison his inquiry into the murder. Sikorsky had previously expressed alarm about the rising number of Jews in the empire and hinted that Jews were responsible for the plague of Russian alcoholism. ("Moneylenders"—their ethnicity was clear—supposedly lent the common folk the funds to buy liquor on what the professor called "ruinous terms.") He emerged as a full-fledged political anti-Semite in April 1910, when he delivered an address at the Club of Russian Nationalists. (The term "nationalists" generally referred to a political group that was somewhat more moderate than the Black Hundreds.) While wars used to be primarily over territory, Sikorsky argued, now one of the main aims of the enemies of the Russian people was "spiritual destruction." At the front lines of this conflict was an army of scribbling low-lifes in the liberal press, ideological warriors who attacked the nation's great men. Behind them, Sikorsky declared, stood a certain "opponent" of the Russian people. "This opponent consists of those pious people who hourly, from the depths of their offices, send up their prayers to the Almighty so that he would not lessen their profits on their international loans. These pious people . . . believe in the power of gold." Again, he did not need to specify the ethnicity of this "opponent."

When Sikorsky received the official request to consult on the notorious Yushchinsky case, he must have been gratified. His academic career had been in decline; he had found himself pushed aside by younger colleagues. He welcomed this unexpected opportunity to regain his prominence and determined to make the most of it. Sikorsky's academic writings could be long-winded, but for this case he would coin a memorably concise statement of the blood accusation: deftly epigrammatic, it would echo through the trial and beyond.

Liadov explored the cave where Andrei's body had been found. He met with Professor Sikorsky and they visited the anatomical theater, where they were shown the victim's preserved organs, and conferred with Dr. Nikolai Obolonsky, who had performed a second autopsy on the boy.

Given the case's notoriety, the authorities had retained Dr. Obolonsky and autopsy specialist N. N. Tufanov of St. Vladimir University's department of forensic medicine to perform an independent examination of the corpse. They did not endorse the ritual version but would not rule it out. Their autopsy report differed from the coroner's in only one significant respect: they concluded that in the course of the crime "there took place the body's almost complete exsanguination" and that the cause of death was "acute blood loss." As will later become clear, these conclusions were dubious. They were likely rendered under pressure from high officials.

Liadov then went to Kiev's Monastery of the Caves to meet a monk named Ambrosius. If Golubev was a Christian detective like Thomas of Monmouth, then Ambrosius was an avatar of the renegade Jew Theobald, the "converted enemy" who reveals his people's clandestine rituals.

Ambrosius was the first "expert" in the case to testify to the existence of ritual murder.

He claimed that during his residence at another monastery:

> I had numerous occasions to talk on the subject (of ritual murder)
> with various people, in particular with two Orthodox monks who
> had been converted from the Jewish religion to the Christian . . .
> All these discussions . . . gave me reason to believe that among
> the Jews, especially the Hasidim, it is the custom to obtain blood,
> particularly by the murder of Christian boys. This blood is
> required for the preparation of the Paschal matzos for the follow-
> ing reasons:
> According to the Talmud blood is the symbol of life; the Jews are
> the sole masters of the world and all other peoples are simply their
> slaves; and so the blood of Christian boys in the matzos symbolizes
> that to the Jews is given the right to take the lives of those slaves . . .
> The Jews want this to be known by non-Jews, too, and that is why
> the body of a Christian from which the blood is taken must not be
> completely destroyed . . . When such bodies are found, the Jews
> arranged it so that there is no clue to the place where the murder
> was committed, but the non-Jews who find the body are made to
> remember that the Jews have a right to their lives as masters of life
> and death.

Ambrosius also claimed that "there must be a specific number of
wounds in such cases in a specific part of the body: the number of wounds
is approximately forty-five." In his May 1911 deposition Ambrosius
acknowledged that he himself had not personally studied the alleged
Jewish texts concerning the ritual murder of Christians. Moreover, he
admitted that the two monks who were his main sources were "Can-
tonists," Jews who had been impressed as early as the age of twelve into
the tsar's army for twenty-five years and knew little of their religion.
Liadov nonetheless was highly impressed with Ambrosius's testimony.

On May 8, Professor Sikorsky rendered his psychological profile of
the perpetrators. It was based on an astounding interpretation of the
autopsy materials. "All the damage and wounds were inflicted by a
steady and confident hand, one that was neither trembling in fear, nor
moving with exaggerated scope and force out of rage," he pronounced.
While Fenenko and Brandorf believed the four dozen wounds, all over
Andrei's body, many with no clear purpose, testified to a crime committed in a frenzy, Sikorsky insisted, "This was precise, ruthless, cold-

blooded work, such as might have been performed by someone who was accustomed to slaughtering." Chaplinsky reported these revelatory findings to the justice minister:

> Professor Sikorsky, based on considerations of an historical and anthropological character, considers the murder of Yushchinsky, in its chief and consistent characteristics—the slow draining of blood, torture, and killing of the victim—typical of a series of similar murders which have happened repeatedly in Russia and other countries. The psychological basis of this type of murder, in the opinion of Professor Sikorsky, is the "racial revenge and vendetta of the sons of Jacob."

"The racial revenge and vendetta of the sons of Jacob." This was a powerful new formulation. Unlike Golubev and Ambrosius, Sikorsky was no one's avatar. In the drama of the blood accusation he had created a new role—the psychiatric explorer—and added modern elements to the myth. "The nationality which commits this horrible deed," Professor Sikorsky concluded, "as it is scattered among other nations, brings with it the traits of its racial psychology." Race, genetics, inherited behavior—Sikorsky renovated the myth with pseudoscientific rigor. It was a signal achievement. The Jews had committed such "horrible" deeds in the past that they had become conditioned to perform them in the future and for all time. Murder was in their blood.

Liadov now declared himself to be confident that the crime had the character of a secret ritual. Based on what he had heard from Professor Sikorsky, Ambrosius, and the pathologist, he later said, he had "formed the personal conviction that Yushchinsky was killed by Jews." But who was the culprit?

Liadov began to play detective, taking an unusual interest for a high official in the investigation's operational details. He called attention to the testimony of the boy Pavel Pushka who said Andrei would buy gunpowder from a Jew in Slobodka. According to Fenenko, Liadov instructed him "that as soon as the identity of this Jew was determined, he should be charged and placed under arrest."

The gunpowder-selling Jew was never found, but another Jew of interest was identified. In a deposition on May 5, 1911, Golubev told investigators:

Near [the area of the cave] there is located the enormous estate of the Yid Zaitsev. The manager of that estate and of the brick factory [there] is a certain Yid Mendel . . . who after the discovery of Yushchinsky's body behaved somewhat strangely, giving out candy to children and asking them not to say anything to the police.

This is the first mention in the official record of Mendel Beilis. (Beilis was not the "manager," but the clerk of the brick factory. All the rest of the report was unsubstantiated rumor.) Questioned the following day, Golubev again mentioned "the little Jew Mendel." He told the authorities, "My personal opinion is that the murder was probably committed either [at the Zaitsev estate] or at the Jewish hospital" adjoining the factory, though adding with unaccustomed humility, "Of course, I am not able to present proof of that."

Golubev would now dedicate himself to providing that proof.

3

"A Certain Jew Mendel"

On May 4, 1911, Nikolai Krasovsky, a provincial police official in western Ukraine, received an urgent telegram. The message was brief and clear: "By order of the governor, go to Kiev."

Until the previous fall, Krasovsky had been the acting head of the criminal investigation division of the Kiev police force—the city's chief detective. He had taken over the division three years earlier in the wake of a tremendous scandal. The then head of the division, Spiridon Aslanov, was exposed as being in the pay of Kiev's notorious "King of Thieves." The King, a flamboyant crook who also went by the nickname "Stovepipe Hat," boasted of an income of a hundred thousand rubles a year and prided himself on stealing only from the well-off, sharing his booty generously with his small army of pickpockets, burglars, and second-story men. The gifts that he bestowed on Detective Aslanov, including a ring studded with precious stones, were for him the cost of doing business.

After Aslanov's arrest, Krasovsky quickly gained respect by cracking a slew of cold cases. By the fall of 1908 he had become celebrated as the Sherlock Holmes who solved Kiev's most sensational crime, the Ostrovsky murder case. The stabbing deaths of a middle-aged couple in their home, along with a young acquaintance, their laundress, and a seamstress, had traumatized the city. As the killers remained at large day after day, the Kiev journalist and politician Vasily Shulgin wrote, "It seemed as if a dark cloud were hanging over the city . . . Crowds of people stood for hours in front of that house [where the murders were committed], gloomy and distraught, staring at those walls with superstitious horror."

In lifting that cloud, Krasovsky displayed stunning investigative virtuosity. He had a fair mastery of forensic science. (The field was surprisingly well advanced in Imperial Russia, whose chemists had devised tests still used today for detecting trace amounts of blood and certain poisons.) He had great powers of observation. He was a master of interrogation. Tallish and kindly looking, with blue eyes, a bushy mustache, and an unhurried air, he knew how to get people—ordinary folk and criminals—to tell him things. He was also cunning, fearless, and always willing to stand his ground. When detectives found jewelry purportedly belonging to the Ostrovskys in the home of a known thief, Krasovsky alone was unconvinced that he was the perpetrator. He proceeded to prove that engravings on the jewelry had been fabricated by a vengeful criminal (who himself had nothing to do with the murders) to incriminate his enemies. In a city with the highest crime rate in the empire, where two out of three cases went unsolved, Krasovsky was considered a hero for tracking down the four actual killers, one of them a psychopath who admitted to ten other murders and boasted of his ability to stab a person to death while shedding hardly any blood (the technique involved partial strangulation, then two stabs to the heart).

In an attempt to escape the hangman, the defendants appealed for help to the most famous Russian of his time, Count Leo Tolstoy, claiming they had only faithfully followed the famous writer's Christian anarchist precepts. (The era's spiritual ferment had seemingly penetrated even into the underworld.) "We acted according to your teachings because they had money and we didn't. Defend us," they wrote him in a postcard they sent from prison. Tolstoy, whose greatest wish at this stage of his life was to convey tenets of morality to common people, was greatly distressed by the notion that these men had operated under his influence. Tolstoy's estranged wife, Sophia, took the opportunity to torment her husband, arguing that the men could indeed rightfully consider themselves to be his followers. Tolstoy, who deeply and publicly opposed capital punishment, is not known to have lent these killers his support. (Tolstoy's morality, incidentally, extended to the acceptance of non-Christians as his equals. In November 1910, when the count died in a remote rural train station while fleeing his wife after a final quarrel, Russia's Jews lost their most prominent Christian defender. It is fascinating to imagine the role he might have played in the Yushchinsky affair had he lived a few months longer. In a late interview, Tolstoy told the *New York Times,* "How do I account for all this anti-Jewish feeling in Russia? We often dislike more those whom we harm than those who harm us.")

Krasovsky, given his record, surely deserved to have the "acting" removed from his title. But, as was so typical of the era, superior talent failed to be rewarded. Evgeny Mishchuk, who had served in St. Petersburg and no doubt had curried favor there, received the permanent chief detective post. But now Mishchuk had outrageously bungled the investigation into Andrei's murder, and Krasovsky had been summoned—from exile, one might say—to lead the police investigation into what would shortly become the most infamous murder case of the age.

At this sensitive moment, after the fiasco of the arrest of Andrei's family, and in the face of the Black Hundreds' incendiary anti-Semitic propaganda, the government needed a politically reliable professional of solid reputation to take charge. Renowned for his skill as a detective, Krasovsky was also, for reasons not entirely clear, well regarded by the right-wing Union of Russian People. Grigory Chaplinsky, the chief prosecutor and advocate for the blood accusation, thought he could find no better man for the job. But Chaplinsky had been in the Kiev post only about two months and did not really know Krasovsky, and ultimately he would want someone who would do as he was told. In that regard, Krasovsky—stubborn, crafty, incorruptible, but more than capable of dishonesty when necessary to his goals—would turn out to be a disastrous choice.

Krasovsky accepted the new mission reluctantly. The year before, after losing out to Mishchuk for the job of Kiev's chief detective, he had happily settled into a new post in the provincial city of Khodorkov. He was wary of getting involved in another highly publicized case, having learned from experience, as he later said, that "I never got anything from it but intrigues and trouble from co-workers and others involved." From the outset his apprehensions were disturbingly confirmed. Alexander Liadov, the St. Petersburg functionary sent to Kiev to oversee the case, insisted that Krasovsky's participation be kept secret. No one would inform Mishchuk that he was effectively being relieved from the case. Krasovsky knew Mishchuk would surely find out soon enough what his old rival was up to, and he could be expected to attempt his revenge. Complicating matters still further, the Corps of Gendarmes—a secret police force empowered to arrest people with no formal charges—was conducting its own secret investigation. Over the next few months the case would become a round-robin of intrigues and backstabbing that would exceed Krasovsky's greatest fears.

In early May, the far-right youth group leader, Vladimir Golubev, had identified as a person of interest a clerk at the Zaitsev brick factory, Mendel Beilis. But, within a few days, "the Yid Mendel," as Golubev called him, fell away as an object of the investigation. The day after receiving Golubev's supposed tip, Vasily Fenenko, the upstanding investigating magistrate, surveyed the Zaitsev factory and the area around it. Fenenko had been annoyed by Golubev's habit of arriving at his office unannounced, ranting about Jews and blood and murder. But Liadov, whose mission was to focus the investigation on finding a Jew, had already made sure Golubev would be treated with respect, his "leads" acted upon promptly. The results of Fenenko's survey were reported to the justice minister himself: "On the Zaitsev estate nothing suspicious was found and no cellars, which Golubev mentioned, turned out to be there." On May 11, in a report to the justice minister, Chaplinsky noted the suspicions about "the Jew Mendel" but stated that, "regarding the factual side of the investigation, the witnesses have not given any significant material for solving the case."

The right-wing press was appalled by what it believed to be the disastrous outcome of Liadov's visit to Kiev (a mirror image of the equally incorrect view in the Jewish press, as noted earlier, of Liadov as a hero). On May 14, 1911, as Liadov departed for St. Petersburg, the newspaper of the Union of Russian People, the *Russian Banner,* despairingly asked its readers, "Do you doubt that the Worldwide Yid will spare millions on suppressing this case? Do you doubt that this worldwide moneylender and swindler will threaten [Russia's] international loans . . . [and] international complications if the case . . . isn't suppressed?" The authorities, it was clear, "have yielded [to the Jews] in violation of the law, the truth, and the self-esteem of the Russian people." The paper was convinced that the killers would never be brought to justice. As for the Jews' adherence to the Ecclesiastical admonition about times to be silent—pointed to with such pride in the Jewish press—this, too, could only be seen as sinister. "The Yids found that the only means of saving themselves is silence. Therefore not one Yid has said anything about the murder."

The complaints of the Black Hundreds initially appear bewildering. Had not Liadov fawned over Kiev's young right-wing leader? Did he not put a distinguished new detective on the case? Had he not signaled the Justice Ministry's approval of "the ritual version"? The continued indignation of the right wing exposes a paradox: even as top officials placated the local vigilantes, no one had informed the Far Right's national leaders of this. The *Russian Banner* protested that St. Petersburg had not sent a single decent detective and that the case remained "under an impenetrable cover of secrecy." The disconnect might be the result of routine bureaucratic ineptitude (a safe assumption for a regime where often even the right hand did not know what the right hand was doing). Or it might have been the product of some never-revealed intrigue (two of the most popular words in tsarist officials' memoirs are "intrigue" and "camarilla"). But the authorities in Kiev and St. Petersburg had good reasons to keep the Far Right ignorant of the investigation.

At this point in the inquiry, the officials privately advocating for the blood accusation likely hesitated. Having sought to "find a Jew," they had to acknowledge that no suitable Jew—one against whom witnesses could be produced—had been found. So, for now, they kept secret from the public the judgment of the distinguished psychiatrist Ivan Sikorsky that Andrei's murder was an instance of the "revenge of the sons of Jacob." In the absence of a flesh-and-blood suspect, such a revelation could only highlight the failure of the authorities to find the actual perpetrators, inflame the populace, and increase the possibility of a pogrom, which, as officials often stated, would be "most undesirable." It would be some weeks before they could ready a case against a suitable Jew. Meanwhile, Krasovsky was taking the investigation in a very different direction.

Krasovsky "was not distinguished by especially firm moral qualities," the local prosecutor, Nikolai Brandorf, later recalled with disapproval, "and was capable, when needed, of conducting a double game." But a double game, or even a triple or quadruple game, it could be argued, was exactly what an investigator was required to play in this case. To maintain his freedom of action, Krasovsky had to indulge the Black Hundreds. He frequently met with Golubev and his chief investigator— a sometime police informer, moneylender, and former bordello proprietor named Rozmitalsky—and pronounced himself favorably disposed to the possibility that the crime was a ritual murder. Making his charade somewhat easier was the absence of any other persuasive theory of the case: at this point, he could honestly say, *anything* might be true.

Ironically, while Krasovsky had been unsettled by Liadov's conspiratorial machinations, the St. Petersburg official had done him a great service by creating a breathing space in which he could try to solve the case. Liadov's obeisance to Golubev and his crew, and the other actions he had taken, did not yet constitute a full-blown anti-Semitic conspiracy. The conciliatory gestures having been made to Kiev's Far Right, Krasovsky and the other investigators were allowed to pursue leads as they pleased.

Immediately after arriving in Kiev, Krasovsky made a detailed survey of the physical evidence. He was appalled by the destruction of the crime scene by the police and public, which had left only the paltriest scraps of evidence to work with. A trace amount of semen was detected on a blood-soaked piece of pillowcase found in Andrei's jacket pocket, pointing to a possible sexual motive for the crime. On the belt buckle, there were two clearly visible fingerprints—above and below the first letter of the word "School"—but, frustratingly, dusting with two types of powder failed to "develop" them. In the absence of a murder weapon, the four dozen wounds on the body pointed to no particular suspect. Imprinted in a muddy blotch on Andrei's jacket was the figure a small Christmas tree, which turned out to be the distinctive mark of the rare Columbus brand of galoshes; the footprint, however, could not be matched to a suspect. The clay encrusted on Andrei's clothes matched that in the cave and yielded no clues about the location of the murder, although Krasovsky did tease out one significant hypothesis. Based on meteorological reports that showed the only days when the temperature in Kiev was above freezing were March 16 and March 19, he believed the body had been dragged into the cave on one of those days, when wet clay and leaves could have stuck to the boy's clothes and then dried. (This contradicted the conclusion of the autopsy report that the body had been taken to the cave while still in rigor mortis, within about twelve to twenty-four hours after death.) Krasovsky surveyed the Zaitsev brick factory in late May and, like Fenenko, came away convinced that the crime could not have taken place there. He briefly talked to Mendel Beilis and asked to look at his shoes. He found no Columbus galoshes, only a worn-out pair of the more common Conductor brand.

In the absence of physical evidence or eyewitnesses, to solve the case

Krasovsky would have to induce people to say things they did not want to say. A way would have to be found to sway souls, until unspeakable memories made lips begin to move and unintended words were uttered. Some might think the investigator's methods amounted to coercion, but Krasovsky thought he was only after the truth. With the evidence at hand, he could not solve this crime. But perhaps he could find the killer by disinterring the secret history of Andrei's family in all its bitterness, resentment, and despair.

What Krasovsky had learned about the family—and, more important, what the family said about itself—had aroused his deepest suspicions. The arrest of the family had been a fiasco, with Andrei's relatives defended in the Duma itself, as the Far Right raged against the police for victimizing them. But that did not deter Krasovsky from focusing on them with renewed vigor. If the Black Hundreds had believed Krasovsky would be better than that contemptible tool of the Jews, Detective Mishchuk, they would soon be disappointed. Russia's Sherlock Holmes was coming to believe that Andrei had indeed been killed, as his aunt Natalia suspected, by "one of his own."

Andrei's stepfather, Luka Prikhodko, seemed to have a solid alibi. His boss, whose name was Kolbasov, swore that Luka had spent ten straight days and nights at the bookbinding workshop where he worked, sleeping and taking his meals there. But there was an emotional entanglement between them that surely gave pause to the psychologically minded Krasovsky. The two men were drinking companions and it was rumored that Luka was having an affair with Kolbasov's wife. It was hard to say whether this fraught relationship made Kolbasov more or less believable as an alibi witness, but clearly his motives could be complex.

There were still too many reasons to believe that Luka, and perhaps his wife, Alexandra, who was Andrei's mother, and her brother, Fyodor Nezhinsky, were involved in the crime. And a primal motive was now coming into clearer focus: money. It had been reported to the investigators that at the cave, after Andrei's body was found, witnesses had heard his uncle Fyodor declare that Andrei had been killed by his stepfather, and possibly other family members, "because of the promissory note." Questioned by the police, Fyodor confirmed that he had indeed accused his brother-in-law, Luka, and that he believed that money was the motive.

At this point, another mysterious character—talked about, obsessed about, but never seen—finally enters the story in a ghostly manner. Andrei's absent father, Feodosy Chirkov, whom his mother never married, lived with her for two years. While she was pregnant with their second child, a daughter who died shortly after birth, he left Kiev to fulfill his military service in the tsar's army. Around that time, his family's modest estate was sold and he received a share of the proceeds. By the time of Andrei's murder no one knew for sure if he was dead or alive, though rumor had it he had perished during the Russo-Japanese War.

Chirkov liked to play cards and was said by an acquaintance to "associate with a not especially reputable crowd." People who knew him had little doubt he would swiftly spend his inheritance. But after Chirkov's exit, the legend grew that he had bequeathed a "promissory note." Alexandra would often boast—particularly to her mother if the older woman reproached her for having an illegitimate son—that money existed in Andrei's name, perhaps a thousand rubles. Andrei, who longed for his father (he was said to ask passing soldiers if they knew of him), filled the emotional void by making his mother's story his own. He told one of his Jewish friends that his father had left him six hundred rubles and he lived on the interest. Until the day he died, he wanted to believe his father was providing for him.

The "promissory note" was a private myth, a weapon in a family battle, and a young boy's consolation. But after the murder, when tears might have washed old resentments away, it emerged like a malicious *domovoi* to haunt the family. Inexorably, the presumed motive called into being the requisite trappings of guilt. Witnesses appeared. Incriminating evidence was duly found.

Investigators learned Luka and Alexandra had behaved quite suspiciously at the office of a local newspaper where they had gone to place a notice about Andrei's disappearance. "[They] were completely composed, calm," a newspaper employee told investigators. "Something here wasn't right: the mother was too indifferent." The couple had "smiled strangely." A laundress claimed that Alexandra and her brother Fyodor had talked to her about Andrei's disappearance "with a smile." The overheated Kiev rumor mill produced a story that a man and woman resembling Luka and Alexandra had been seen hailing a cab, while carrying a big, heavy bag. In another version, the couple claimed the wrapped body was a sick boy they were taking to the hospital.

On June 3, the police arrested Fyodor. He, too, had an alibi, a coworker who swore they were together at Natalia's workshop. But at this point, of all the family members, he was in the greatest legal jeopardy. The day before the body was discovered, on March 19, he had been seen in Lukianovka covered in clay—exactly what would be expected if he had wriggled in and out of a cave. A boy testified that Fyodor had had him brush off his clothes. Fyodor claimed he'd soiled his clothes while sleeping in the street, presumably after going on a bender. The boy did confirm Fyodor was somewhat drunk, which was hardly exculpatory. Other witnesses also claimed Fyodor had acted suspiciously.

Once in custody, Fyodor, not surprisingly, again pointed the finger at his brother-in-law, Andrei's stepfather, Luka. More unexpectedly, he made a striking claim. He told Krasovsky he had found an important witness who had escaped the authorities' notice: a man who had seen someone resembling Luka near the caves on the morning of Andrei's murder. What was truly surprising was that Fyodor was telling the truth. Investigators confirmed the story.

Fyodor had tracked down the witness, a stove repairman, some weeks earlier. The man had told only a few people about the person he had seen while on his way to the Zaitsev factory to do a job at seven a.m. on March 12. But the story quickly spread in the Lukianovka anthill, making its way to Andrei's aunt Natalia, who told her brother about it. The man was known only by his nickname "Lapochka" (roughly translated, "Sweetie"), but Fyodor soon showed up at his door. His real name was Vasily Yashchenko; now he confirmed to the police that he'd seen someone near the Zaitsev factory on March 12 who struck him as suspicious.

Fyodor, having found a witness who he believed implicated his brother-in-law, decided to keep this information to himself, for purely self-interested reasons. According to a police report, "He ended his investigation and decided to say nothing about his conjectures, reasoning that you couldn't bring a dead boy back to life and the arrest of [Luka] would negatively affect the material situation of the family which he, Fyodor, would then have to support." But now that Fyodor found himself on the verge of being charged with murder, the witness he had discovered was his ticket to freedom. An excited Krasovsky restyled Fyodor from a suspect into a "colleague," as helpful citizens or informers were called, who would now aid in bringing his brother-in-law to justice.

However much Chaplinsky, the chief prosecutor, wanted to charge a Jew or Jews with the crime, he could not now ignore the suspicions of the famed detective he himself had helped put in charge of the case. In early June he reluctantly reported to the justice minister that "Nezhinsky's story could turn out to be truthful." Another development may also have made him hesitate. On June 6, Father Alexander Glagolev, a Kiev professor and leading Christian authority on the Jewish religion and rituals whose opinion Chaplinsky had solicited a month earlier, delivered his formal statement. Father Glagolev acknowledged "evidence of the hatred of Jews for non-Jews in the Talmud" but thoroughly dismissed the blood accusation. Echoing the judgment of the council convened by Holy Roman Emperor Frederick II in the very first such case in Fulda, he noted the age-old Jewish "prohibition . . . against the use of blood in any food" detailed in the Talmud. He emphasized that that proscription was "to my knowledge nowhere lifted, limited, or mitigated" in any known text and declared the very idea of a blood ritual "counter to the principles of Judaism, ancient and modern." He further implied that the ultra-pious Hasids were, if anything, less likely than other Jews to commit such an act of sacrilege.

Father Glagolev's lengthy contemplation of the case was no mere dry scholarly exercise. The killing had affected him deeply, and he concluded his statement with an unusual cri de coeur: "The horrible, blood-curdling murder of the innocent boy . . . stands before my mind as an insoluble mystery, one which perhaps can only be uncovered by the All-Seeing Eye!"

Sometime in late May or June, Evgeny Frantsevich Mishchuk, nominally Kiev's chief detective but now officially relieved of the case (the "secret" of Krasovsky's appointment had not remained so for long), sat himself down on an earthen bank near the Berner Estate in Andrei's old neighborhood of Lukianovka and lit a cigarette. He was out of uniform. He had dressed as nondescriptly as he could. In one pocket he had some caramels. For hours he had been roaming Kiev's impoverished, disreputable outskirts, sensing at every turn criminal dens and underworld hideouts where all sorts of fugitives, even wanted killers, took refuge. When he saw some children playing here, scampering up, down, and around the ruts, ravines, and caves near where Andrei's body was found, he hoped he had found the break in the case he was looking for.

Mishchuk was greatly troubled by the paths the investigation was taking. He no longer believed Andrei's family had anything to do with his murder, but Krasovsky had redirected the case toward them. Nor did he believe, as Chaplinsky avowed, that the Jews were responsible. Mishchuk was not a well-educated man. He had been expelled from a gymnasium for poor grades. But the idea that Jews were responsible for the crime, as Professor Sikorsky insisted, made no sense to him. Brandorf, the local prosecutor, considered Mishchuk "sluggish and incompetent." Krasovsky was certainly the better detective. But it was Mishchuk who at this point in the case had the superior intuition.

As he sat smoking, fingering the caramels, Mishchuk knew he had to wait and let the children come to him. He waited patiently, he recalled later, "while the children running past sometimes stopped to take a look at what this old fellow was doing." He gently struck up a conversation about what game they were playing and gave the children candy as they gathered around. When he sensed they were comfortable talking to him, he asked whether they were sorry that Andrei was gone, probing to see if they knew anything. Mishchuk found "the children were not greatly upset" by their playmate's death, lamenting that "children soon forget such moments." However hard he tried to draw out of them what they had heard among themselves or from their parents, "the children didn't understand what all the fuss was about and apparently had no greater interest than their games."

Had any stranger been seen with Andrei? The children didn't respond to his question, but they did volunteer their own fears. "Suddenly the children's tongues loosened," as they told of a notorious woman "in whose house all sorts of people were always hanging around, that there were parties, singing, noise, that at home their parents said it was a bad house, that they shouldn't go there . . . that she was shady, a fortune teller, that she knew spells, and was involved in all sorts of things and that all the people were afraid of her and would avoid her on the street . . . and that she was a thief and a killer." The children also said people mockingly called her "Cheberiachka."

———

In criminal patois, "cheberiachka," according to a contemporary dictionary of criminal slang, meant a "merry song with indecent subject matter." It was of a piece with Vera Cheberyak's other nickname, "Sibiriachka"—"the Siberian"—an apparent reference to her criminal acquaintances and the frosty region where they had served time in prison, or were destined to. Cheberyak's neighbors lived in dread of her. Questioned by the authorities, they called her "the lowest of the low," "a dark figure," an "evil presence."

Cheberyak was volatile and violent. Many a story about her ended with the words "and then she hit me in the face." She quarreled with her downstairs neighbor, Zinaida Malitskaya, the liquor store cashier, and hit her in the face in broad daylight. She hit another acquaintance "in her physiognomy," as the jocular Russian expression goes, for flirting with a man she considered hers. But such violence did not compare with the notorious and horrific act she had committed six years earlier—a crime that still haunted Lukianovka.

Cheberyak freely admitted to blinding her lover, a French accordion player named Pavel Mifle, by throwing sulfuric acid in his face. (He went on to become known as "the blind musician.") She matter-of-factly explained to acquaintances that she had retaliated after Mifle had hit her in the face. According to other accounts, she committed the act in a fit of jealous rage. Whatever her motivation for maiming her lover, she was tried for the crime and acquitted. Mifle testified in her defense, saying he had forgiven her, which apparently swayed the jury. After her acquittal, the relationship continued. Cheberyak would accompany Mifle to the clinic and to the French consulate, from which he received a tiny invalid's stipend of about fifteen rubles a month. She visited him frequently and sometimes had friends take food to his apartment two doors down from hers on Upper Yurkovskaya Street.

In her criminality and in her lying, Cheberyak was compulsive and impulsive. Her prevarications began with the name she went by in official documents: Vera Vladimirovna Cheberyak née Singaevskaya. She claimed to be twenty-nine years old, the daughter of a priest named Vladimir Singaevsky from Zhitomir, about a hundred miles west of Kiev, who died when she was six years old. In fact, her baptismal record shows the sacrament was administered on August 26, 1879, making her thirty-one years old in the spring of 1911. Court documents indicate her son, Zhenya, at first told police he was twelve. If his mother were truly twenty-nine, that would have made her a less than decent seventeen when she gave birth, which is likely why he later said he was eleven. He was actually thirteen, going on fourteen. But if the son had to remain a child so that the mother would not grow older, then she would see to it. As for her clergyman father, in the space on the certificate where her patronymic should have been, there was instead scrawled the abbreviation "illeg."—illegitimate. Cheberyak was born to Yuliania Singaevskaya, from a family of small landowners (a class somewhat above common peasants) and an unknown man. Court inquiries later established that Vladimir the priest from Zhitomir did not exist.

Cheberyak had a third nickname: "Verka Chinovnitsa," meaning "Verka the Civil Servant's Wife" ("Verka" being a diminutive of Vera). When Vera married Vasily Cheberyak, the son of a retired army captain some thirteen years her senior when she was only around seventeen, it must have seemed like a grand ascent. Unlike Andrei Yushchinsky's mother who, despite giving birth out of wedlock, was able to find a husband, Cheberyak's mother apparently never wed. Yuliania Singaevskaya gave birth to another illegitimate child—Vera's half brother Peter—by still another man. As the daughter of a single unwed mother with two children and no man to support them, Cheberyak must have endured a hard childhood. Vasily may have appeared a savior. But although he was a dutiful employee of Kiev's Central Telegraph Office, and steadily received promotions, he never made more than about forty-seven rubles a month. For Cheberyak—narcissistic, histrionic, emotionally and materially grasping, and magnetic to men, or at least a certain kind of man—simply to be "the civil servant's wife" would not do. Cheberyak set about creating a criminal gang that would serve as a source of income and sensual amusement.

The Frenchman Mifle was far from her only lover. She had many others, young men whom people noticed entering her home wearing one set of clothes and leaving wearing another. In the winter of 1910–1911, her gang included nineteen-year-old Mitrofan Petrov, who lived with her for a time and whom she referred to as her "lodger," eighteen-year-old Nikolai Mandzelevsky ("Nicky the Sailor"), and Ivan ("Red Vanya") Latyshev. She was said to be romantically involved with all of them. Cheberyak would try to pass off some of her gang members as her "brothers." Her half brother Peter (known as "Plis," which means "Velveteen") was also a member of her gang. But it was rare that the police weren't looking for Peter for one reason or another, and he usually made himself scarce in Lukianovka.

The Cheberyaks' three-room apartment, above the state liquor store, was the scene of wild, drunken carousing that scandalized the neighborhood. For some time Vasily Cheberyak had slept in one bedroom with the three children, while Vera kept the other bedroom for herself and whomever she was entertaining. Vasily, conveniently, spent little time at home at night, because he worked the graveyard shift at the telegraph office. He left in the evening and returned home in the early morning to sleep, often working additional shifts to earn extra money. On the infrequent occasions when he intruded, Vera's guests would drink him into a stupor so he could not interfere with their revelries (forensic chemical analysis of her home would find semen on the wallpaper). Vasily told a neighbor that he even suspected the young men slipped something into his drinks.

The police believed Cheberyak was behind dozens of robberies. Mishchuk, who had only been working in Kiev a few months, puzzled over why she had never been arrested, and discovered she was a police informer, selectively betraying her brethren to keep her own concern in operation. But her fortunes in crime apparently varied, and her high-living ways kept the family on the edge of a precipice. Mifle's mother, Maria, told the authorities, "Vera . . . would visit me, always wearing nice gold things and clothes. I would ask her where she got such things and she told me she bought them from her 'lads'—that is, thieves." A neighbor noticed that she wore a beautiful coat and changed her hats often. But others testified the family lived on the verge of poverty, amid shabby furniture, with Cheberyak sometimes complaining she had to stretch one day's dinner into three.

In the first months of 1911, Cheberyak's life began to fall apart. Perhaps she had grown more reckless, or her preternatural run of luck had simply run out. But that winter she stumbled from one farcical debacle to another. On February 18 she walked into the Gusin watch store on Lvovsky Street and sold a watch and chain for seventeen rubles. A day later, a customer noticed the watch, which had been stolen just days earlier from his mother's home. The storekeeper's wife began keeping an eye out for Cheberyak and, spying her a few days later, confronted her. Cheberyak of course denied any wrongdoing and, to demonstrate her unconcern, gave Mrs. Gusin another piece of jewelry for repair. Cheberyak, brashly overconfident, returned to the store on March 8. Mrs. Gusin called the police and Cheberyak was taken to the precinct. But Cheberyak somehow escaped and could not immediately be tracked down because she had given a false name, posing as the wife of a Colonel Ivanov.

On that very same day, Cheberyak was implicated in an entirely different crime. Some months earlier she had taken in a young woman who was down on her luck named Nadia Gaevskaya. Nadia at first believed that Cheberyak had befriended her out of kindness but to her irritation found herself treated as a servant. The relationship soured and, before the young woman left, Cheberyak sold Nadia a dress, saying it had become too small for her. On March 8, an outraged woman spotted Nadia on the street, recognizing the dress as her own—it had been stolen—and summoned the police. Nadia, in turn, accused Cheberyak, and the matter was turned over to a justice of the peace.

The next day, March 9, came the catastrophe: five members of her gang were arrested while entering a bathhouse, charged with the theft of two thousand rubles' worth of revolvers. Cheberyak's home was searched the following day, March 10, and though no evidence was found against her, her gang had been wrecked. She knew better than most that when the police targeted suspects, more often than not it was with the help of informers. Who had informed on her this time? Could it have been Pavel Mifle, at whose home she sometimes stashed stolen goods, or members of his family, whom she on more than one occasion complained "nursed a grudge against me"? Could it have been one of her beloved "lads"? Or could it been have been one of her son Zhenya's lousy friends?

It was just two days after the police raid that Andrei disappeared. Another week would pass before the two boys looking for treasure discovered his corpse in the cave. A neighbor who was a close friend of Vasily Cheberyak's noticed a striking change in Vera after Andrei's body was found. Her demonic self-confidence had deserted her. "She looked somehow upset, as if she had been blindsided by something," he recalled. "She walked around as if something had scalded her."

———

Detective Mishchuk had come to believe the trail led to Vera Cheberyak's doorstep. The sleuthing of Golubev, the right-wing hothead,
had luckily uncovered one genuine witness: Zhenya Cheberyak. Vera's
son told Golubev that he'd seen Andrei on the morning of March 12,
the day the boy disappeared, though he soon took back the story, and
denied he'd seen or met Andrei that day. Zhenya was questioned by
the authorities on May 11. This time the boy said he had seen Andrei
about ten days to two weeks before his body was found, but he did not
give an exact day. And he lied, saying Andrei had come by to play but
that he had refused.

A theory of the case was assembling itself in Mishchuk's mind. The
boy, it was clear, had seen Zhenya on the day he disappeared. Vera Cheberyak, it had been rumored, had taken advantage of the 1905 pogrom
to loot fabulous amounts of property during the chaos. He formulated
a hypothesis that Andrei's murder was committed "with the goal of
simulating a ritual murder and inciting a pogrom." That part of the
scenario could be considered wild conjecture. But he rightly believed
Cheberyak had to be considered a leading suspect and that intense
attention should be focused on her and her gang. For better or worse in
the Russia of 1911, detaining suspects in order to press them to confess
was standard procedure. But when Mishchuk recommended arresting
Vera Cheberyak, Chaplinsky, the chief prosecutor, scolded him: "Why
are you torturing an innocent woman?"

At the same time, Mishchuk began scheming against Krasovsky, just
as the other detective had feared. Mishchuk may have felt his intrigue
was justified, however. In a letter to the Kiev police chief on June 13, he
accused Krasovsky of attempting to suborn witnesses against Andrei's
stepfather. The chief of police forwarded the letter to the governor, who
sent it to Chaplinsky, who scrawled on it, "Relations between Krasovsky and Mishchuk are very bad." But no action was taken against Krasovsky who, strictly speaking, did not fabricate testimony, though he
would come very close to the line.

Krasovsky was now free to turn his attention to Andrei's family. He
prepared to exhume their delusions and bitter rifts and turn them into
his own theory of the case.

Nikolai Krasovsky believed the evidence against Luka was accumu-
lating. In June, a search of his workstation at the bookbinder turned

up clippings from right-wing newspapers about ritual murder, along with a slip of paper tucked into a book with notes on the anatomy of the blood vessels in the temple—the area of the skull where Andrei was stabbed some thirteen times. Krasovsky ordered Luka arrested on June 26. Also arrested were Luka's brother and, possibly to exert excruciating emotional leverage on the suspects, their blind father.

Krasovsky supervised as the police ordered Luka to dress in new clothes and try on various hats. A barber shaved Luka's beard, gave him a haircut (Luka noticed the barber paid particular attention to shearing the right side), and dyed his hair and eyebrows black. One of Krasovsky's deputies personally attended to curling Luka's mustache. When tears rolled down his face, the police raised their hands threateningly and told him, "Don't you dare cry, you so-and-so . . . your tears will make your mustaches unwind." The suspect was brought to the exact spot on a street bordering the area of the caves where the stove repairman Yashchenko said he had seen the man he described as "dark" and "dressed like a gentleman" (a description that in itself made it improbable the man was Luka). Despite the rather drastic makeover, Yashchenko still did not positively identify Luka as the man he had seen. Looking at him from one angle, he thought Luka might be the same person, but some facial features, particularly the nose, he said, were different.

Krasovsky was not about to let himself be defeated. The truth that he so strongly suspected lay hidden in Luka's guilt-ridden heart would be coaxed out into the open—with a small white lie easing its path. In Luka's presence, two "witnesses" (actually officers in civilian clothes) positively "identified" Luka as being at the crime scene. Shaken, at this point Luka said something like, "I'm obviously not going to avoid the gallows, but at least let my sick father go." These words were interpreted as a confession. Krasovsky believed he had his man.

The local prosecutor, Brandorf, was also a firm opponent of the "ritual" theory of the Yushchinsky murder. But he had reached a different and much more well-founded conclusion: that Andrei died at the instigation of Vera Cheberyak. Golubev, by identifying Zhenya Cheberyak as a witness, had unintentionally led the authorities to the mother. Everyone who had talked to Zhenya believed he lived in fear of his mother and that he knew more than he was telling. It was clear to all, even to Chaplinsky, that she must be investigated as a suspect.

In late May, Krasovsky and three other officers searched the Cheberyaks' home. The presence of a citizen witness was a part of standard procedure and the long-suffering landlord, Stepan Zakharchenko, was summoned to fulfill that role. Zakharchenko wanted nothing more than to remove the whole Cheberyak family from his property. He was tired of harboring this villainous woman and had had enough of her raucous, drunken parties. He didn't think much of her children either, who pilfered fruit from his orchard. What is more, he likely had recently learned Cheberyak had been chiseling money for years from his daughter, who ran a grocery store up the street, buying on credit and then paying back less than she had been charged. (His daughter inexplicably let Cheberyak maintain the account book.) His daughter had filed a complaint with the authorities, something Cheberyak probably did not yet know, and they were preparing to bring fraud charges against her. The landlord's relationship with Cheberyak was also fraught in one more respect that would grow in importance: he was friendly with Mendel Beilis.

As Zakharchenko went up the stairs to the Cheberyaks' apartment to join the police officers, Cheberyak's downstairs neighbor Zinaida Malitskaya followed him. She and Cheberyak had once been great friends, but their relationship had gone bad, as evidenced by their violent public quarrel some weeks earlier. (Cheberyak said Malitskaya had taunted her with a rumor she'd "spent the night" somewhere—she didn't appreciate the intimation that she was a loose woman.) Sensing trouble, Zakharchenko waved Malitskaya off, but she went up anyway, explaining that she wanted to witness the "big day." Upon seeing her, Cheberyak said, "What do you want?" Malitskaya said, "I came to see your big day." Cheberyak said, "Go away, you know I'm an anxious woman." Then she threw herself on Malitskaya and slapped her in the face. An officer pulled Cheberyak off and the search got under way.

While Krasovsky and two officers examined the premises, the third officer struck up a conversation with Zhenya and asked him about the murder. "He wanted to tell me something," the officer, a police supervisor named Evtikhy Kirichenko, recalled, "but suddenly stammered and said that he didn't remember." Kirichenko talked to the boy while sitting in a chair at the threshold between two rooms. Cheberyak was standing in the same room as Zhenya, across the threshold, off to the side but out of view. "When I asked Zhenya who killed [Andrei] I noticed that his face convulsed," Kirichenko reported. Leaning down in his chair, Kirichenko managed to catch sight of Cheberyak "standing and with her hand and with her whole body making threatening gestures." He and Zhenya caught the gestures at the same moment. Kirichenko, an experienced officer, was so overwhelmed that he broke his professional composure. It was as if he had come in touch with the "evil force," the woman the neighborhood children believed could cast spells. He immediately halted the conversation with Zhenya and rushed to a fellow officer to share his powerful intuition that this woman must have been involved in the crime. Nothing else, he felt, could explain the vision of sheer malevolence he had witnessed at the mention of the dead boy's name.

Brandorf had argued to Chaplinsky a number of times that Vera Cheberyak should be arrested but Chaplinsky had refused his request, as he had Mishchuk's. Brandorf felt he had no choice but to maneuver behind Chaplinsky's back to have Vera Cheberyak detained. He tried to convince investigating magistrate Fenenko, who shared his views, to act. But in the face of the opposition of his superior, Chaplinsky, and in the absence of clear evidence, the hypercorrect Fenenko would not take the risk.

As a last resort, Brandorf schemed to have Cheberyak detained by the Corps of Gendarmes, which had the power to take practically anyone into custody if he or she was deemed a possible threat to "state security." The powers of the Kiev Gendarmes had been further enhanced in anticipation of the upcoming official visit of Tsar Nicholas, along with Prime Minister Stolypin, at the end of August to unveil a statue of Nicholas's grandfather, Alexander II. The authorities were determined to clear the city of troublemakers. The deputy interior minister, General Pavel Kurlov, who had so decisively intervened to stop a pogrom in the wake of Andrei's murder, personally headed security for the visit. Nothing would be allowed to disrupt the majestic honor of the sovereign's presence in Kiev.

Therefore it attracted little attention when, on June 9, gendarmes led away one more potential troublemaker on the pretext that "suspicious persons, taking part in a political movement, gather at her home." In fact, the only people gathering at Vera Cheberyak's home were her young lovers and other assorted criminals. Brandorf had high hopes that he had the killer. "I firmly expected that if she sat in jail for a few days," he later testified, "the whole case would be solved."

Vera Cheberyak's husband, Vasily, also had high hopes—that Vera's arrest would finally change his luck for the better. His life with Vera—the long overnight shifts at the telegraph office, punctuated by the humiliating oblivion of drinking binges among her lovers, and now the constant fear of police raids—had made him a desperate man. The appearance of the gendarmes at his doorstep must have seemed like a deus ex machina. "I'll be free of her," he told a friend after his wife was arrested, "and I'll be able to start living a normal life."

But the hopes of both husband and prosecutor depended on an event that had not yet happened: a confession, or at least some slip, however small, under the pressure of hour after hour of questioning, which would implicate Cheberyak and her gang. Cheberyak possessed a fantastic and frightening capacity to intimidate, dominate, manipulate, and evade her accusers. (In her most recent such feat, she had beaten the rap in the matter of the stolen dress she had sold to her sometime boarder by somehow producing three witnesses—two female friends and a baker named Abramov—who swore she had come by it honestly.) But Brandorf and the senior gendarme officer, Lieutenant Colonel Ivanov, believed that Cheberyak would be a different, more vulnerable woman now that she was under arrest "as a matter of state security," a limbo where there were no lawyers and no means of appeal. While in confinement and under intense interrogation—something she had never experienced—they were confident she would crack.

Just as important, police could now question Zhenya Cheberyak out of his mother's earshot. In previous interrogations, the boy had clearly betrayed a desire to reveal the truth. With his mother safely behind bars, gentle questioning might loosen the bonds of the boy's fear. Indeed Zhenya, questioned a week after his mother's detention, did let slip some details that converged with what other witnesses were saying. He now admitted that Andrei had come by the Cheberyaks' house for some gunpowder. "I was afraid to tell you about the gunpowder in the last questioning because I thought that you would beat me for that," he admitted, "but now, when you explained that investigators can't beat anyone, I'm telling you the truth." And he confirmed that the last time he saw Andrei, the boy was without his coat, which was never found (a circumstantial detail that would grow in importance later in the investigation). But while he admitted that Andrei had visited him, he insisted that it was at two p.m., not in the morning, and denied that the day could have been March 12, the day his friend disappeared. The investigators were frustrated that Zhenya could not seem to break his mother's spell.

Zhenya, moreover, suddenly and suspiciously claimed to remember something that he had failed to mention in previous interrogations—and that implicated Andrei's uncle Fyodor. On the evening of March 12, he said he had been sent by his father to the beer hall to fetch two bottles and had encountered a "very drunk" Fyodor who, "seeing me, bent over and quietly said, 'Andrusha is no more, he's been stabbed to death.'" Questioned separately, his mother told a slightly different version of the story. Investigators found Zhenya's testimony to be contradicted by many witnesses. Cheberyak had probably planned for this testimony when mother and son would be separated. It was likely the story was a well-crafted but imperfectly coordinated lie to divert suspicion away from her.

A pattern had emerged: Vera Cheberyak invariably pointed the finger at the leading or most convenient suspect of the moment. After Andrei's mother was arrested, she was said to have spread stories about her abusive treatment of her son. When attention focused on the Jews, she avowed that they were the perpetrators. Now, when she believed Fyodor to be a prime suspect, she did what she could to pin the crime on him. The pattern would persist.

Cheberyak was held from June 9 to July 9 as a matter of "state security." But the security organs could hold her no longer without formal charges. On July 9 Brandorf found it necessary to have Officer Krasovsky arrest her formally for suspicion in Andrei's death. Her confinement could be kept secret no longer. Just five days later, she was released at the insistence of Chaplinsky after an indignant Golubev, greatly outraged that no Jew had yet been charged, demanded she be freed.

Little else is known about Cheberyak's five-week confinement. But the break the prosecutor and her husband both hoped for never came. She did not crack, and she returned home to her hapless husband who, far from being rid of her, would now be drawn further into her machinations.

Krasovsky had been on the scene when Officer Kirichenko had his unnerving encounter with Vera Cheberyak and must have been briefed

about it. But he ignored it, even though Kirichenko was one of his pro-
tégés. He continued to prosecute his investigation of Luka Prikhodko
with ruthless zeal. The tsarist justice system was not without checks
and balances, and Luka could have complained about any mistreatment he had suffered when he was brought in to be interviewed by
Investigator Fenenko. Asked later why he did not protest, Luka said,
"If they had asked me that night what my name was I couldn't have
told them."

The liberal press rejoiced at the discovery of the culprit—or rather
culprits, because it was assumed everyone in custody was guilty. "All
the information that the murderers have been found is now revealed,"
Russia's Morning opined. "Five [relatives] have been arrested . . . Two
of them belong to the most active ranks of the Union of Russian People." The Kadet newspaper *Speech* expressed the opinion that the relatives had imitated a ritual killing. The "whole fanatical gang" that had
"shamed the Russian people" had to be brought to justice.

But the case against Luka, if it ever can be said to have truly existed,
quickly fell apart. Alexandra had not been indifferent to her son's disappearance, as some witnesses claimed; she had fallen into faints and
frantically searched for Andrei throughout the city. The promissory
note did not exist. Andrei's father had given Alexandra seventy-five
rubles from the sale of the estate (including twenty-five for Andrei's
education); she filed suit in court for more but lost. Luka's alibi was
confirmed by his boss's neighbors. As for the slip of paper with the
description of blood vessels in the skull, Luka had tried to explain that
it fell out of a medical handbook given him for binding. The owner of
the book was found and confirmed the note had been written by him—
largely in Latin.

Krasovsky's instincts, for once, had failed him. He had fallen into
the trap that the great Hans Gross, the Austrian founder of the discipline of criminalistics, had cautioned about in his pioneering treatise of
the era, *Criminal Investigation*. The detective had resorted to "heaping
testimony on testimony," a path that invariably "will excite the babbler
to babble still more . . . encourage the impudent, confuse the timid, and
let the right moment slip past."

With the falseness of the accusation against the family exposed—
for the second time in three months—the Far Right was handed a tremendous propaganda advantage. (This is why a reconstruction of the
largely ignored prehistory of the Beilis case is critical to understand-

ing how it unfolded.) The credibility of the official investigation was shattered, and the liberal press—regarded as the Jewish press—made to look foolish. (It played into the Right's hands that some of the purveyors of misleading information, like the newspaper employee who claimed Alexandra and Luka had behaved suspiciously, were Jews.) How could anyone believe a simple artisan could write a note in Latin? Who could not have sympathy for the poor Christian mother who had been forced to miss her son's funeral and now had nearly lost her husband and brother?

Luka was released on July 14, after nearly three weeks in custody. Krasovsky had wasted his invaluable respite from right-wing agitation. Other investigators, lacking any concern whatever for the truth, were closing in on their preferred suspect.

By mid-July, Chaplinsky must have despaired of finding a way to charge a Jew with Andrei's murder and surely feared for his future advancement as he again came under sneering personal assault in the right-wing press. "Unfortunately, one cannot count on the Kiev prosecutor," an editorial in *Zemshchina* declared. "It is apparent that the interests of the Jews are dearer to him than justice." The *Russian Banner* slapped him indirectly, demanding that "the minister of Justice take a personal interest in the Yushchinsky case," implying that the chief prosecutor should be relieved of the matter. Chaplinsky, who was of Polish descent, had converted from Catholicism to Orthodoxy in his eagerness to prove himself a true Russian. For a man of such great, if hollow, ambition, his eye on a seat on the empire's highest court, the Far Right's attacks must have been distressing beyond measure. But fortune was about to provide him with an unlikely trio of saviors.

The first of them to appear—Kazimir "the Lamplighter" Shakhovsky and his wife, Ulyana Shakhovskaya—came to the authorities' attention in early July. The Russian writer Vladimir Korolenko described the couple as "poor, wasted shells." Ulyana was hardly ever sober. Kazimir was also a heavy drinker. They worked together, though it was a common sight in Lukianovka to see Ulyana staggering alone down the street in the evening, ladder over her shoulder, as neighborhood boys trailed behind, eager to help her light the 140 lamps on the couple's route.

The Lamplighters, as the couple was called, were the first witnesses to place Andrei in the vicinity of the cave on March 12, the day he disappeared. This made them the most important witnesses who had been discovered so far, though, for Chaplinsky's purposes, their initial testimony was of little use.

In his first deposition on July 9, Kazimir revealed how he had seen Andrei around eight in the morning on March 12, standing with Zhenya near the state liquor store, above which the Cheberyak family lived. He told of his last encounter with Andrei, how the boy had struck him playfully, but painfully, and how he had dispatched him with a crude insult. Ulyana had caught sight of Andrei with Zhenya slightly earlier but did not speak to him. Kazimir was emphatic that he had no idea what had happened to Andrei: "Where Zhenya and Andrusha went I don't know, only that since then I never saw Andrusha again."

Kazimir quite believably explained why he had avoided talking to the authorities for four months: "I myself am illiterate, I don't read the newspapers . . . I was afraid to get involved in this case because I have to walk the streets at night and early in the morning and people who didn't like my testimony might knife me." He hinted of whom specifically he might be afraid, saying, "You would be better off questioning Vera Cheberyak's neighbors. Those witnesses would know more than I do. They'll tell you what kind of person Cheberyak is. I myself heard she was a thief, but I can't tell you any more about her. For now I have nothing further to say."

In that "for now," leaving the door ajar, there was perhaps a hint of the pressure applied by Kazimir's lead questioner. Adam Polishchuk was one of two former Kiev police detectives Krasovsky had inexplicably retained as his assistants. Both of them had recently been cashiered from the force for assorted misconduct, including "consorting with criminals." Unbeknown to Krasovsky, Polishchuk was, in a sense, a double agent working undercover; he was cooperating with Golubev. He may have perceived in the case a path to rehabilitating himself through influential people. (He would, in fact, later be hired by one of the imperial security services and the Union of Russian People would arrange for his material reward.)

On July 18, Shakhovsky was questioned again, and his responses suggest he was trying to please his interrogators. "The place where Cheberyak lives is located next to the Zaitsev factory and is separated from it by a high fence. On March 12, you could pass from where she lived to the factory because the fence was badly damaged and parts of the fence were even missing . . . The factory grounds were managed by the clerk Mendel . . . I know that Mendel is on good terms with Cheberyak and would visit her home. For now I have nothing further to add."

At this point, the thinking of the would-be prosecution was taking a turn both logical and preposterous. Vera Cheberyak, they had reasonably concluded, could not be ignored as a suspect, and the Lamplighter himself was of the belief that she had something to do with the crime. Therefore, if the objective was to implicate the Jewish clerk, why not simply tie the two of them together? (This peculiar theory, unsupported by any evidence, would rise and then fade from view but strangely resurface during the trial as the prosecution became desperate to persuade jurors of their case.)

Shakhovsky was hinting at a criminal partnership of Beilis and Vera Cheberyak, but a conjecture would not be enough to implicate them in the murder. What was needed was an eyewitness, not mere circumstantial testimony. On July 19, Polishchuk paid a visit to the Shakhovskys' home, a bottle of vodka in hand. He worked on Ulyana as she drank herself into a near stupor. Polishchuk recognized he could not fabricate testimony outright. A witness was needed who would testify in court. He had to maneuver Ulyana into creating her own story. Surely she knew something? Surely she had heard something about Mendel? The operation was a delicate one, calibrating the dose of alcohol and the psychological pressure so that she would say the necessary words while drunk enough to be suggestible but not too drunk to speak. At a certain point, Ulyana uttered the desired words. Polishchuk reported, "Shakhovskaya told me directly that her husband knows everything and saw how Mendel, together with his son Davidka [actually Dovidke] led and dragged Andrei to the kiln."

At last Chaplinsky was close to obtaining the eyewitness testimony he needed. The next step was for formal depositions to be taken. But getting the alcohol-addled couple to agree on a single, consistent story soon proved to be beyond reach.

On July 20, Kazimir Shakhovsky was questioned a third time in the presence of Chaplinsky. He now came up with an entirely new and different tale. He himself had not witnessed Andrei's abduction by Mendel, he said, but he knew that Zhenya had:

I forgot to mention one important circumstance. Around the Tuesday after Saturday March 12, when I saw Andrei Yushchinsky together with Zhenya Cheberyak . . . I ran into Zhenya near my aunt's house . . . I asked Zhenya if he'd had a good time with Andrusha. He told me that it didn't work out with Andrusha because they were scared off the Zaitsev factory, not far from the kiln, by some man with a black beard who had shouted at them . . . after which they ran off in different directions . . . I have almost no doubt that the murder of Andrei Yushchinsky took place in a kiln of the Zaitsev factory . . . There lived there at that time one man with a black beard, specifically Mendel, the factory clerk . . . that's why this same Mendel must have taken part in the murder.

It was true that Zhenya, Andrei, and their friends liked to sneak onto the Zaitsev factory grounds to play on the clay grinders, carousel-like contraptions with a central pillar from whose apex extended a long rod attached at the other end to a pair of old carriage wheels. The children would take turns precariously riding astride the rod, while the others played the part of the draft horse, pulling the contraption round and round. But it was suspicious, to say the least, that Shakhovsky suddenly recalled this incriminating conversation.

Questioned separately the same day, Ulyana Shakhovskaya presented her own new and different story. No longer did she claim that her husband had witnessed the abduction. Instead, she declared she had an acquaintance—Anna "Volkivna," or Anna "the Wolf"—who told her she had witnessed the crime. Volkivna, whose real last name was Zakharova, was an alcoholic derelict whose moniker derived from her custom of sleeping outdoors in a place called Wolf's Ravine. She completes the drunken trio on which the initial case against Mendel Beilis was based. Ulyana's revamped testimony amounts to one drunk's retelling of another drunk's tall tale:

The day before yesterday I went out to light the lamps before evening and on the street I met my acquaintance Anna, nicknamed Volkivna. Volkivna, I remember, asked whether I knew anything about the boy's murder. I told her I saw . . . Andrusha on March 12 in the morning and didn't know anything else. Then Volkivna . . . told me that when Zhenya and Andrusha and a third boy went to play in the morning at the Zaitsev factory, they were frightened off by a man with a black beard who lived there, and what's more, grabbing him . . . he carried Andrei into the brick kiln. Zhenya and the other boy ran away.

This story still did not fully satisfy her questioners. After the deposition was read to her—Ulyana was illiterate—the record shows she spoke up again, with startling specificity. "I want to add," she said, "that Volkivna . . . told me that this person [the man with the black beard] was none other than the clerk of the Zaitsev brick factory Mendel."

Over the course of two days, then, the Shakhovskys had given three different stories implicating Beilis. First, Ulyana had claimed that her husband, Kazimir, had himself seen Andrei dragged off by a man with a dark beard. Second, Kazimir testified that Zhenya Cheberyak had told him he had witnessed the abduction by Beilis. Third, Ulyana asserted that her drunken friend Anna the Wolf had witnessed the crime—adding, doubtlessly under pressure, that the perpetrator was "Mendel."

That two witnesses had given three different and contradictory versions of events little troubled Chaplinsky, so eager was he for grounds to arrest Beilis. Chaplinsky allowed as how the testimony, taken piece by piece, was "not completely firm," but astonishingly found the stories taken together to be mutually reinforcing. Vladimir Korolenko the writer would point out the irony that initially the case would stand on the testimony of witnesses who could barely stand on their two feet.

Investigator Fenenko now found his prized integrity threatened, when Chaplinsky requested that he have Beilis arrested. Fenenko found the case against Beilis to be preposterous. But he could not defy orders—that would be insubordination, something his ethical code did not countenance. Fortunately, because Chaplinsky had given him what was formally not an order, but merely a request, he did his best to delay, telling Chaplinsky he needed three or four days to get the paperwork organized.

It is at this point that "Student Golubev," as he was invariably called, reenters the narrative. He had been the first one to identify Mendel Beilis as a suspect. Now he would make certain that the Jew was arrested. Chaplinsky recalled later that "an agitated Golubev came into my office and declared that all of Lukianovka knew about Shakhovsky's testimony and . . . that the people are preparing to deal with Beilis and Zaitsev on their own and organize a pogrom." Golubev was, more than likely, using this threat as a means of speeding up the arrest. But it was true that, while Mendel Beilis was unaware of it, word of Shakhovsky's testimony had quickly spread in Lukianovka, where nothing could be kept secret.

One of those who heard of it was a shoemaker named Mikhail

Nakonechny, a mainstay of the local gossip mill who, because he could read and write, had a side business filling out documents for local residents. Nakonechny would be one of the few heroes of the Beilis case. (His young daughter, as a star witness for the defense, would become its great heroine.) He could not have wanted to get involved in the entire affair because he knew Vera Cheberyak all too well—his wife had once had a violent confrontation with her. But he knew something that he could not keep it to himself: Shakhovsky had a grudge against Beilis.

By this time, Krasovsky's common sense and investigative abilities were returning to him. He had belatedly come to realize that the weight of the evidence indeed pointed to Vera Cheberyak and her gang. When he found out about Shakhovsky's testimony, and Beilis's impending arrest, he headed for Lukianovka to see what he could find out. There he ran into the distraught shoemaker.

"He came up to me, looking very upset," Krasovsky recalled. Nakonechny told him: "What filth . . . it's an absolute lie. Shakhovsky lives near the Zaitsev factory and has the habit of swiping firewood from [there] . . . He was called to account for the theft . . . and since it was Beilis who turned him in, he harbored a grudge against him."

By this point, though, the drive to take Beilis into custody was unstoppable. After Golubev raised the threat of a mob taking matters into its own hands, the histrionic head of the Kiev Okhrana, or secret police, Nikolai Kuliabko, contacted Chaplinsky, offering his help. Kuliabko appeared in the prosecutor's office and, "making a conspiratorial expression," as Chaplinsky described it, declared that he could detain Beilis using the enhanced powers granted him in connection with the tsar's impending visit. Chaplinsky told him that Vera Cheberyak should also be arrested, as Beilis's accomplice; at this point, he believed he could make a stronger case by treating them as a tandem. He confided that he was happy to have a pretext for Kuliabko's assistance. As the Okhrana chief recollected this critical meeting, the prosecutor urgently wanted him to arrest the pair as soon as possible in part because he was suspicious that the regular police were in the pay of the Jews:

> [Chaplinsky] explained to me that . . . Mendel Beilis and Vera Cheberyak were involved [in the crime] . . . It was being proposed to charge Beilis and Cheberyak, but in order to "prepare" the warrant, the investigative authorities needed two or three days, and there was

information that Beilis and Cheberyak might flee, and therefore it was necessary to promptly detain them. Chaplinsky went on to tell me that he did not consider it possible to entrust the detaining of Beilis and Cheberyak to the police . . . since it was bought off and therefore was entrusting [the arrests] . . . to me.

Chaplinsky reported to the minister of justice on July 21 that Vera Cheberyak was a suspect in the murder and that she should be detained. She "manifest[ed] exceptional interest in the course of the investigation," he wrote, "was collecting information about the facts the witnesses had related and there were rumors that she restrained witnesses from giving honest testimony, frightening them with the threat of reprisal." In particular, "her influence on the case was evident in how she constantly watched over her son Zhenya . . . apparently fearful that he might let something slip out," adding, "the boy gave the impression of knowing more than he told." Chaplinsky concluded: "Her detention might aid in the discovery of the truth."

Chaplinsky's report indicates he fully understood that Vera Cheberyak was, by all rights, the prime suspect in Andrei's murder. Yet he dearly wanted to charge a Jew with the crime. Unfortunately, the only halfway suitable Jew that could be found was a modest, hardworking, not terribly religious family man. Chaplinsky's initial solution—one that perhaps he thought ingenious—was to fasten the case against the Jew to Lukianovka's infamous Cheberiachka. Such was the strange beginning of what would soon become known as the Beilis affair.

At three o'clock in the morning, on July 22, 1911, a large detachment of police and fifteen gendarme officers under the command of Kiev Okhrana chief Kuliabko stormed the home of Mendel Beilis. The scale of the operation, suitable to the capture of an armed and dangerous underworld overlord, was risibly out of proportion to its humble and defenseless target. An immature and melodramatic Kuliabko was playing with his toy soldiers.

"Suddenly I heard knocking on the door—such knocking that I thought that there was, God forbid, a fire at the factory," Beilis recalled. "I jumped out of bed and ran barefoot to open the door. As soon as the door opened, approximately twelve men stormed in screaming loudly,

'Are you Beilis? You are arrested, arrested!' And they surrounded me from all sides. Stood themselves so firmly, exactly as if they were scared that I would break away from their hold and escape. I tried to ask, 'Why? What?'" A policeman told him he would find out soon enough and to move faster and get dressed.

Beilis was asked to account for all the money in his possession, presumably so the officers could not be accused later of stealing any of it. He had seventy-five kopeks. He was asked if he wanted to take the money with him or leave it with his wife. He said he wanted to leave it with Esther, who would need it more than he would, but he was not allowed to hand her the money himself. He had to give the coins to an officer, who then handed them to his wife. He was a prisoner now, subject to all the absurdities of "procedure."

The children had awakened and Beilis wanted to say good-bye to them, but the gendarmes forbade it. "'Come!' They yelled at me, and led me out of the home," he recalled. As he walked out of his house, he was handed over to four officers. Beilis did not know that procedure called for an arrested person to be marched down the street, not on the sidewalk. When he asked to walk on the sidewalk, an officer pushed him. "You walk here!" he sneered, "On the sidewalk he wants to go!" He was led on a winding route for nearly two miles down Kiev's nearly deserted streets until they reached the headquarters of the dread Okhrana where he entered into a nightmare that would destroy the life he had known and arouse the indignation of the world.

4

"Andrusha, Don't Scream"

At five o'clock in the morning, Mendel Beilis, escorted by a few gendarmes, arrived at the Kiev branch of the Okhrana. The rest of the contingent had stayed behind to search the home. After about an hour of waiting, Beilis heard the stomping of horses' hooves, followed by the clatter of spurs in the corridor. When the door to the room opened, he recognized the gendarmes who had been searching his house and felt somehow reassured to see the men were done with their work. When Nikolai Kuliabko, the Kiev Okhrana chief, entered, Beilis hoped that he would finally be questioned and clear up the whole matter, whatever it was. But Kuliabko only led him to another room, asked that he be brought tea and a roll, and immediately left.

"Remaining alone, I began to calm down from the sudden fear that had so confused me," Beilis later recalled. "I did not know what was happening or what they wanted from me." Though his tongue was "dry as hot sand," he could not drink the tea. The roll went untouched. "I was certain that as soon as they questioned me they would immediately see the mistake they had made, and would release me."

After three hours, Kuliabko entered. He had no formal role in the murder investigation—he was only holding the prisoner for a few days until his transfer to the police. So the personal command he took of the case was striking. For one thing, the Kiev Okhrana chief was well-known for his laziness. Repeated requests for information from St. Petersburg would pile up on his desk before he would respond. His ineptitude, too, was well-known. An official review had found his operation riddled with administrative deficiencies and staffed by ignoramuses. (Among other things, his top investigator, responsible for tracking revolutionary groups, did not know the meaning of the word "anarchism.") His brother-in-law was head of the imperial palace guard and Kuliabko had used that bureaucratic foothold to secure other influential patrons, including one whom he shared with the powerful deputy interior minister, General Kurlov, who blocked any attempt to demote him.

Within weeks Kuliabko's incompetence would lead to fatal results that would shake the empire and land him on the other side of the interrogation table. But at this early stage he seems to have perceived that the regime—in some sense, even its future—was to be invested in this peculiar case. Kuliabko, who was rumored to have his eye on a high post in the capital, apparently understood the fantastic gains to be made if only he could force a confession out of this poor Jew sitting before him in a tattered waistcoat.

"Well, did you drink the tea?" he asked.

"What do I need the tea for," Beilis said. "It would be better if you released me from jail, let me go to my wife and children. What do you want from me? I have committed no crime."

Kuliabko, perhaps taken aback by the prisoner's temerity, left the room without responding. When he returned, he handed Beilis a sheet of paper with questions written on it. Beilis was to write down his answers and then ring the bell. Kuliabko left Beilis alone with the large sheet of paper and a pen. Beilis made his way down the list:

Where are you from?
Who is your father?
What is your religion?
Do you have any relatives?
What do you know about Yushchinsky's murder?

When Beilis came to the last question he felt "the knife at my throat." He finally understood why he was there. He tried to console himself with the open-ended phrasing of the question. Perhaps he was only regarded as a possible witness. Because he was barely literate in Russian beyond the few words needed for the brick factory receipts, writing in the language came to him with difficulty. He wrote down his answers in Cyrillic letters whose gently curved pen strokes, like those of many a Russian Jew, bore a distinctly Semitic stamp. He wrote that he knew only what everybody knew, what he heard on the street. He rang the bell.

Kuliabko came in and examined the piece of paper, covered now with an alien scrawl. He told Beilis angrily that this would not do. The anger may have been feigned; he surely could not have expected an immediate written confession. The questionnaire was likely his idea of a psychological ploy.

"What do you know about Yushchinsky?"

Beilis shrugged. "What should I know? I only know that they found him dead."

"And who killed him?"

"How can I know?"

Kuliabko asked him the question repeatedly. "What do you know about Yushchinsky?" Beilis kept giving the same answer—that he knew nothing.

"Tell the truth."

"But this is the truth, that I do not know anything about it."

"Well, we will soon see about this," Kuliabko said. He left, slamming the door.

Beilis was again alone in the room.

> You can understand how bitter my heart was. I sit and think about the tragedy that had so suddenly fallen on my head, when I hear a cry from the corridor, a child's cry. I listen carefully, and my heart begins to tremble—I recognize the cry of my child Dovidke. Why is he here? What do they want from him? All of my limbs began to shake. I could not bear it and I began to bang on the wall.

Beilis's youngest son David (Dovidke) barely eight years old, had also been taken in the raid. Kuliabko was personally interrogating him. About a quarter of an hour later, the Okhrana chief entered with another boy—Vera Cheberyak's son, Zhenya.

"So you see," Kuliabko said, "I caught your son telling a lie. He told me that he had never played with Andrusha Yushchinsky and Zhenochka says that he did play with him." Beilis remained silent. He did not know what to say. Kuliabko then abruptly left the room with the boy, giving Beilis time alone for dark thoughts to gather.

> I again remained for a few hours with my bitter heart. The feeling that my son was held in captivity tortured me terribly. He was a little boy, a *pitsl* . . . and moreover still very weak. His cries, which I heard, stabbed me like a knife, and I could not calm myself down.

An even worse impression, that I will never forget, was made on me a little while later, when I saw him through the window of my room, which looked out to the corridor. I stood there and looked through the window; he was walking with one hand on the other, his head bent down. My heart shrunk terribly and again, even stronger, I began to bang on the wall.

Kuliabko reentered. "Why are you banging?"

"What do you want with my son?" Beilis said. He began, he recalled, "to cry and beg."

"Have no fear, we will not let any harm come to him," Kuliabko said, and then left Beilis alone to face his first night in prison.

The door opened and a woman brought in some food. "I do not want to eat," he told her, and asked her to give the food to his boy. The woman, who was a Christian, had tears in her eyes and told him that the boy had already been given some food.

"What is he doing there?" Beilis asked.

"Nothing, he is sitting on the bed," she answered, wiping the tears from her eyes.

Beilis reached into the torn pocket of his waistcoat for some loose change that he had neglected to hand over in the rush and confusion of the arrest. He tried to give the Christian woman the twenty kopeks, but she would not take them. He took comfort from this kind woman looking after his son, but he spent a sleepless night.

In the morning the Christian woman returned.

"Well, how is he?" Beilis asked her. "What did he do at night?"

"He slept with me," she answered, "but neither of us could fall asleep." Again she began to cry. After she left, hour after hour, Beilis jumped up at every creak in the corridor, running to the window, hoping to catch sight of his son. At around ten o'clock in the morning, Beilis heard voices through the wall. One said: "Do you know how to get home?" And immediately after that: "Take him away." Beilis rushed to the window and saw his son walking with a guard. This time he was not walking with his head bent but held high, a smile on his face. They were letting Dovidke go home.

Kuliabko, though, was not quite done with Beilis's family. The next day, Sunday, Beilis heard children's voices outside his door. Dovidke had been brought in for more questioning, along with Beilis's oldest child, Pinchas, who was thirteen. If the father did not confess, the Okhrana chief thought, then perhaps something useful could be extracted from the children. But though they must have been pressured to do so, the boys said nothing that would harm their father. Before they were allowed to leave, Beilis was given a few moments with them. He would not see any of his family again for many months.

"There is no insurance against prison or death." Beilis would write that this saying made perfect sense to him, being a Jew of his time and place. (His apparent misremembering of the Russian original—substituting the word "death" for "beggar's purse"—only made the saying more appropriately emphatic.) Until the moment of his arrest, he had thought himself quite secure in his adopted city. But as a Jew living in Kiev, part of him could not feel entirely surprised at being under lock and key.

The Russian Empire had been hostile to Jews for centuries. The first Cossack massacres of Jews had taken place in the mid-1600s, but the empire was home to few Jews until the end of the eighteenth century. Even the great Westernizer, Peter the Great, who was so open to new ways, could not bring himself to welcome the Jews. (Regarding their possible admission, he is reputed to have declared, "They are all rogues and cheats; I am trying to eradicate evil, not to increase it.") In 1727, Peter's successor, Tsarina Anna, issued a decree banishing the empire's small Jewish population. Periodic expulsions were the norm until Catherine the Great took the throne in 1762. It was Catherine's imperial hunger for large swaths of Polish land that made Russia home to the largest Jewish population of any country in the world. After the Third Partition of Poland in 1795, about a half-million Jews became Russian subjects. By 1900, that population had grown to more than five million, and Russia was the only country in Europe other than Romania that had not granted Jews equal rights. Jews were still almost entirely restricted to the Pale of Settlement, and even there they were barred from living in many towns, and in the countryside in general. Nor could they own land. But as Simon Dubnow, the pioneering chronicler of Russian Jewish life, wrote, "No place in the empire could vie, as regards hostility to the Jews, with the city of Kiev."

The city Mendel Beilis had called home for fifteen years was, uniquely, located in the heart of the Pale but was not part of it. Jews were permitted to live in towns and cities within a radius of hundreds of miles in every direction. But they were forbidden to live within the boundaries of Kiev itself without special permission. Legally speaking, Kiev was as "beyond the Pale" as were Moscow and St. Petersburg. In some ways, it was even more exclusionary. As the medieval cradle of Russian civilization, the "mother of Russian cities," Kiev occupied a special place in the Russian national consciousness, making Jewish "intrusion" seem all the more intolerable. Kiev was the only city in the empire that restricted its Jews to certain neighborhoods. These areas— not surprisingly, the city's least desirable ones—were often described as the empire's last existing "ghetto." Many poor Jews had no choice but to live in the infernal Plossky district, an industrial wasteland with no sewage system or running water whose residents packed themselves into the minimal gaps between the noxious factories and workshops. Sholem Aleichem dubbed Kiev "Yehupets" or Egypt, where "from time immemorial Jews have been as welcome to the people of the city as a migraine."

And yet, Kiev beckoned. For thousands of Jews like Beilis born in the poor shtetls, or Jewish towns, the city promised a better life. Here one might find employment, send one's child to a gymnasium where he could become a truly *Russian* Jew with better prospects, or even dream of making a fortune on the stock exchange where, as Sholem Aleichem wrote, "somebody heard . . . they make cheese pies from snow and fill sacks with gold."

A new life in Yehupets was often judged to be worth fearsome risks. For perhaps every ten or so Jews who lived there legally, there was at least one like the Sholem Aleichem character who "trembled like a thief, lay freezing in misery in an attic all night or curled up like a dog in a cellar." Kiev police were notorious for their nighttime raids, rounding up Jews, often whole families, suspected of residing in the city illegally. Even Jews who had the right papers might run afoul of some rule or find themselves expelled at the police's whim. "If they find the contraband, in other words Jews 'without the right of residence,'" Sholem Aleichem wrote, "they herd them like cattle to the police station and send them out of the city with great pomp, deporting them under guard, together with thieves" back to the Pale.

The months leading up to Beilis's arrest had been the most anxious time for Kiev's Jews since the pogrom of 1905. Even before the Yushchinsky murder sparked fear of another Black Hundred massacre, the police raids had intensified. The Yiddish newspaper *Haynt* reported in the spring of 1911 that the Kiev police had come up with an innovation, the *daytime* raid. The correspondent noted with irony the "progress" that signified. "For what purpose should people be tortured there at night and chaos be caused when the same can be done in the best way possible in broad daylight?" Large squadrons of policemen on horseback and on foot would storm Jewish stores, detaining all clerks and other employees en masse, and march them off "to the nearest police station with great cheer." Such scenes attracted little attention: "A few people gather in little circles, no larger than when a tailor displays a new suit and pants, or when a stray dog is captured."

But Kiev still embodied more hope than fear, a feeling that Sholem Aleichem elegiacally evoked:

> Where can a homeless young man go who dreams of achieving something in his life? Of course, to the big city. The big city is . . . a magnetic center for everybody who is looking for business, work, profession or position. A newly married man who has spent his wife's dowry; a husband who is disgusted with his wife; a man who quarreled with his father-in-law or mother-in-law or with his parents; a merchant who broke with his companions—where will all of them go? To the big city.

In Sholem Aleichem's grand, polyphonic drama of Jewish striving, Mendel Beilis's story fit into the most mundane plotline. He came to Kiev not to escape anyone or anything or for riches. He was not ambitious. He could have stayed where he was. He wanted only to work and raise a family. But the city's magnetic attraction was just strong enough to draw him into it after living his first two and a half decades in the Pale.

Mendel Beilis was born in 1873 or 1874, probably in the small village of Neshcherov, about twenty-five miles south of Kiev. His father, Tevye, was a pious, learned Hasid whom he revered. Mendel could not mention him without noting that the son was the lesser man. Beilis himself had little education, only a few years in a heder, or Jewish primary school. The first years of his life, during the reign of the "Tsar Liberator" Alexander II, who had freed the serfs in 1861, were a time of relative prosperity for Jews, who hoped the regime might grant them equal rights. Although emancipation never occurred, the government did relax residence restrictions and expand admission to secondary schools and universities. Alexander II's assassination by a bomb-throwing terrorist in 1881 abruptly ended any policy of accommodation. When his son, the reactionary Alexander III, took the throne, a wave of pogroms swept Ukraine. The number of victims by the next century's standards was small, no more than a couple of hundred. But as the first massacres of Jews in the Russian Empire in nearly 150 years, the pogroms traumatized the Jewish population.

Even more shocking than the massacres themselves was the official reaction to them. The government viewed violence against the Jews as evidence that the Russian people needed to be *protected* from the Jews. The "Temporary Rules" of May 3, 1882, known as the May Laws, imposed stricter limits on Jews' movement and commerce, marking the onset of a long-term decline in Jewish living standards. But the main effect, in historian Salo Baron's phrase, was to give local officials the ability to subject Jews to "administrative persecutions." (Most spectacularly, on the first day of Passover in 1891, all of Moscow's Jews, except for a few highly privileged ones, were expelled.) The labyrinth of anti-Jewish measures came to embrace some fourteen hundred statutes and regulations, supplemented by thousands of additional decrees and judicial rulings. The "Temporary Rules" would remain in effect until the fall of the Romanov dynasty in 1917.

Although Jews lacked equal civil rights, they bore equal civic responsibilities. Alexander III demanded of a foreign Jewish delegation, "Why do they [Russian Jews] evade military service?" In fact, contrary to legend (including, to some degree, Jewish legend), Jews did not evade the tsar's conscription any more than Russians did. And around the age of eighteen, Mendel Beilis was drafted into the Imperial Army.

He was sent some six hundred miles northeast to the city of Tver where, like 97 percent of Jewish recruits, he served in the infantry for the ludicrous salary of approximately twenty rubles a year. Life for all recruits was harsh. But Jews were more ruthlessly punished for minor infractions than their Russian comrades. All Jews were seen as potential deserters and closely watched.

Still, military service was not the catastrophe for a Jew it had once been. Alexander II had abolished the horrific "cantonist" system under which Jewish boys—officially no younger than twelve, but sometimes as young as eight or nine years old—were impressed into the army, often undergoing forced conversions to Russian Orthodoxy. The original twenty-five-year term of service had been reduced to about five, followed by nine years in the reserves. No attempts were made to convert Jewish recruits. It was impossible to keep kosher, but Jewish soldiers were allowed to gather in the regimental canteens and barracks to celebrate major Jewish holidays and were granted leave to attend seders and services in nearby Jewish communities. The more pragmatic Russian commanders even actively encouraged religious observance, sensibly seeing it as preferable to the traditional soldierly pastimes of whoring and drinking.

Military service did not strip Jewish recruits of their religion, but it did change the kind of Jews they were. For Mendel Beilis, as for thousands of other Jewish soldiers, the army was a kind of school. "The Jewish soldier underwent training, served, fought, and ate alongside the Russian Orthodox soldier," the historian Yohanan Petrovsky-Shtern has written. "His Judaism metamorphosed from a way of life into a creed, sustained by randomly observed rituals." In the melting pot of the army, Beilis's command of the Russian language improved. His social interaction with Russians increased his self-assurance. The degree of his religious observance relaxed. The army had prepared him for the big city.

Unlike Sholem Aleichem's parade of strivers, though, he did not rush there. He ended up in the profane domain of Yehupets only thanks to an unlikely chain of circumstances that hinged on his revered father's renowned piety.

A man of solid virtues, Mendel Beilis was never one to exert his will to shape his life. A current swept him into the army, and then to a woman named Esther, whom he married a year after his discharge. Her uncle owned a brickmaking kiln in a town about eight miles from Kiev, where he went to work. And, one day in 1896, opportunity came to him in the form of a letter from one of his cousins, who worked for the "sugar king" Jonah Zaitsev, offering him a job at the brick factory he was building in Kiev.

Before he was conscripted, Beilis had worked in a brandy distillery Zaitsev owned in another town. He had secured the job thanks to his father, Tevye, who, improbably, had been on friendly terms with Zaitsev, one of the region's wealthiest men, and had even been invited a number of times to the rich man's home. Years later, Zaitsev again took an interest in the son of his poor and pious friend, now dead, and must have felt it a good deed to give a decent job in the city to this young man starting a family.

Fifteen years later, Beilis was satisfied with his job as the factory's clerk and dispatcher. The pay was just forty-five rubles a month, plus rent-free lodging, and he worked at it six days a week. But he could pay for his oldest child, Pinchas, to attend a Russian gymnasium to which the boy had been admitted under the 5 percent quota for Jews. (Jews as a whole, by this time, amounted to about 15 percent of Kiev's population of 450,000.) David, just turning eight, studied in a heder. Out of six children, they had lost only one, the twin of their two-year-old daughter's. "I thanked the Lord for what I had," Beilis later wrote. "Everything pointed to a peaceful future."

Beilis's arrest on July 22 was supposed to have been kept secret until his formal transfer to the regular police, but the news soon leaked out. "Finally, it seems, the case is on the right path," the far-right newspaper *Zemshchina* reported approvingly days later. "The Yid Mendel Beilis, arrested in proposed connection to the crime, was subjected to a second interrogation by Investigator Fenenko." The report was overly optimistic. Vasily Fenenko, the investigating magistrate, had in fact refused to interrogate or arrest Beilis. A resolute opponent of the blood accusation, he believed Beilis to be innocent. Behind the scenes an intense battle was taking place over the prisoner's fate.

Prosecutor Grigory Chaplinsky was absent from the city when the arrest took place, having traveled two hundred miles to the estate of the minister of justice, Ivan Shcheglovitov, to confer about the case, which was taking on imperial importance. His conversion from Catholicism to Russian Orthodoxy and Russian nationalism seemed to be yielding the rewards to his career that he had hoped for. He had surely expected to spend the weekend basking in the minister's congratulations over his success in holding a Jew accountable for the Kiev boy's murder. But on July 23, Chaplinsky was handed a small slip of paper covered with numbers—a coded telegram from his office. Decoded, it read:

MENDEL CHEBERYAK ARRESTED MATTER OF SECURITY SHAKHOVSKYS
DENY TESTIMONY OF AGENT TOMORROW WILL QUESTION WOLF.

The message's form—unpunctuated, run-on, fevered—suited its alarming content. Mendel Beilis and Vera Cheberyak had been arrested as a "matter of state security." The Shakhovskys—the Lamplighters—were now denying or recanting what they had told "agent" Adam Polishchuk about the man with the dark beard, who was supposedly "Mendel." This meant the case, such as it was, had ceased to exist. The proponents of the anti-Semitic theory of the case were pinning their hopes on the forthcoming interrogation of the drunken derelict Anna the Wolf. The heavy-drinking Shakhovskys had not been formally deposed. Their stories had only been relayed in reports by Polishchuk, the renegade former police officer Krasovsky thought was working for him but who was actually doing the bidding of Golubev and the far-right Union of Russian People. The couple had indeed said the words Polishchuk had written down, but their stories were wildly contradictory and unreliable. And now the couple was being questioned in what was, for the prosecution, their most dangerous state: sober.

Hours after Beilis's arrest, Kazimir "the Lamplighter" Shakhovsky was formally questioned for the first time. He was confronted with the shoemaker Nakonechny's accusation that he had decided to "pin" the murder on Beilis because the clerk had accused him of stealing wood from the Zaitsev factory. Though he denied actually intending to frame Beilis, Shakhovsky admitted that Nakonechy's account of their conversation was essentially true. But more important, in this deposition he definitively denied his wife's claim that he had been an eyewitness to the crime. He declared, "I never told my wife that I saw Mendel drag Andrusha Yushchinsky toward the kiln since I did not see that."

Bibulous pilferer though he was, Shakhovsky sounds truthful in insisting that he had no desire to frame his neighbor. Under pressure to implicate Beilis, he had done something he knew to be wrong; now, step by step, he was going to make it right. Questioned again the next day, Shakhovsky went on to retract the story he had earlier told. He still maintained that he had run into Zhenya and that the boy had told him that he, Andrei, and some other children had gone to the factory to play on the clay grinders and had been chased off. But he retracted the essential part of his early claim: "About the man with a black beard,

Zhenya didn't tell me anything, I added that myself. I said that about the man with the black beard because I assumed that no one but Mendel could have been there to scare them off." He implied he had been pressured to say what investigators wanted: "The detectives [meaning, primarily, Polishchuk] were telling me about Mendel all the time . . . They talked about that so many times that I decided to add a little myself in my testimony . . . I have no grudge against Mendel. I only stated my supposition that he could have taken part in the crime." He then added, "You should ask Zhenya Cheberyak who probably knows about the whole thing but for some reason doesn't want to tell you the truth."

From the beginning, Shakhovsky had hinted at his belief that Vera Cheberyak was involved in the crime. Oddly, the hard-drinking Lamplighter, rather than any of the investigators, was apparently the first person to note an important circumstantial detail. When his wife had caught sight of the boy, she recalled him as holding his books. But when he had seen Andrei, a little later, on that street corner, the boy had no books and no coat. "I personally have no doubt that he left his books and coat at Cheberyak's apartment," Shakhovsky told investigators. "Where else could he have put [them]?" It took some courage for Shakhovsky to share his suspicions. Two days earlier the Lamplighter had run into Cheberyak on the street and she had threatened, according to a police report, to "deal with him in her own way."

Ulyana Shakhovskaya was formally questioned for the first time on July 22 or July 23, with similar results. She retracted most of her previous testimony, while revealing something of Polishchuk's interrogation methods. "To my previous testimony, I am adding the following: The day before yesterday . . . I, with Polishchuk, my husband and an agent drank vodka. From the vodka I drank I got so drunk that I definitely don't remember anything of what I told agent Polishchuk . . . My husband never told me that he himself saw Mendel and his son [Dovidke] drag Andrei toward the kiln." She still insisted that Anna the Wolf told her she saw "Mendel" carry Andrei off under his arm toward the kiln. But Ulyana allowed as how "telling me about this, Wolfie was a little tipsy." It later transpired that Polishchuk had sat drinking with the Shakhovskys from the time she got off work until three in the morning.

Ulyana also raised suspicions about Vera Cheberyak. She had run into her on the street on her way to give her deposition. Cheberyak complained that she, too, was under scrutiny and spat out, "Because of a shit like Zhenya, I am going to have to answer." The phrasing in Russian is ambiguous, with two possible meanings. "I am going to have to answer questions." Or: "I am going to have to answer for the crime."

Chaplinsky, the chief prosecutor, returned to Kiev around July 25. Had he been panicked by the telegram from headquarters? Had he at any point contemplated abandoning the tottering case and letting the prisoner go? Perhaps he hesitated for a few hours or a day. But when he sat down with Brandorf, the local prosecutor in direct charge of the case, and Fenenko, the investigating magistrate, he betrayed no doubt or indecision. He had settled upon a brilliantly simple tactic to deal with the Shakhovskys' inconvenient recantations: ignore them. Given enough time, he must have calculated, the prosecution would surely secure, in one way or another, the ballast of more "evidence." People would be found to fill the archetypal roles, especially that of the vivid and ingenuous eyewitness, successor to Thomas of Monmouth's maidservant who "saw the boy through a chink in the door." (In this calculation, Chaplinsky would prove correct, if only after an uncomfortably long interval.) The important thing was to keep in custody the only Jew on whom there was any chance of pinning the crime. Chaplinsky must have understood the flimsiness of the case. But he knew pursuing it was in the interests of his career, and he knew he had the backing of the justice minister, Shcheglovitov; in their meeting at his estate, Chaplinsky had surely conferred with him about how to proceed. The murder of a thirteen-year-old boy was now a priority of the imperial government.

The tsarist regime was not entirely lawless; a man could not be held by the Okhrana "as a matter of state security" for more than two weeks, which under certain circumstances was extendable to one month. When the time limit expired, the prisoner had to be handed over to the regular police and charged with a crime or set free. Chaplinsky, in any case, saw nothing to be gained by keeping Beilis locked up as a political prisoner. The whole point was to very publicly charge him with the bloodthirsty killing of a Christian child.

As Fenenko and Brandorf sat down with Chaplinsky to discuss what should be done with the prisoner, they knew that they had one point of leverage. Chaplinsky did not have the power to directly order Beilis officially arrested and criminally charged. Only Fenenko, as the investigating magistrate, could do that. Chaplinsky could dismiss Fenenko, of course, but that would cause a scandal, which he surely wanted to avoid.

Fenenko, true to his straightforward nature, simply told Chaplinsky that, in view of the clearly false nature of the testimony, it amounted to slander against an innocent man, and he would not order the arrest. Brandorf, more diplomatic and canny, tried to reason with Chaplinsky. He later recalled the scene:

> In order to prove the insufficiency of the basis for charging Beilis, I scribbled down on a piece of paper all the arguments laid out by Chaplinsky, and it added up to some kind of unbelievable assortment of suppositions and guesses, but no kind of logical framework of a pattern of evidence. When I read aloud this shameful, from my point of view, "indictment" and expected that it would . . . convince him of the impossibility of charging a person with murder on the basis of such information—let alone for a "ritual" purpose—the effect was the opposite . . . Chaplinsky found that on paper "it came out even better."

At this point, Brandorf stopped arguing. He did threaten to draw up a memo making the case for charging Vera Cheberyak that would be much more well-founded than the one against Beilis. But Chaplinsky, recalled Brandorf, "told me that he couldn't allow an Orthodox Christian woman to be charged in a 'Jewish' case." In this way, he let it be known that he was abandoning the outlandish theory linking Beilis and Cheberyak as partners in crime. Only the Jew would stand accused. The "Christian woman" would soon be released.

Nikolai Krasovsky had been marginalized in the case due to his unnecessary and disastrous detour into investigating Andrei's family. But he was belatedly regaining the form that had made him one of Russia's most respected detectives. Fenenko now brought him in to refute the allegations against Beilis. Krasovsky laid out the results of his investigation with complete objectivity. In a deposition on July 26, Krasovsky expressed his opinion that Pinchas Beilis was not telling the truth when he (for what would have been understandable reasons) denied knowing Andrei, finding that he had, in fact, played with Andrei and Zhenya a number of times. (There is no testimony in the record confirming they knew each other, though Andrei had a number of Jewish playmates.) He duly reported the unfounded rumors that Beilis and Cheberyak had been on intimate terms. More important, he reported that another search of Beilis's home and surrounding premises had turned up a bag of tools belonging to the factory harness maker, including several awls; Krasovsky had shown them to autopsy specialist Tufanov, who categorically determined that none of them could have inflicted Andrei's wounds. Krasovsky concluded: "I can present no information pointing toward the participation of Mendel Beilis" in the crime.

Though utterly convinced of Beilis's innocence, under pressure from Chaplinsky Fenenko did partially relent. He agreed to order Beilis's arrest by the police, but only on the condition that Chaplinsky give him a direct order in writing. Fenenko could have resigned—he was a man of some means, had no family to support, and could have managed without the government salary. But he decided the only result would be his replacement by a servile tool of the prosecution, and justice would be better served if he stayed on. At least, this was the explanation he gave later. But perhaps it was a rationalization; his very probity ultimately made him uncomfortable with an extreme act of defiance.

Chaplinsky did not immediately agree to Fenenko's condition. The investigating magistrate's pristine reputation meant his stamp of approval would add immensely to the case's credibility. This was something too valuable to give up without a fight. But Fenenko would not give in. The confrontation played out over four days. On July 29, Chaplinsky relented, informing the minister of justice that he was personally recommending Beilis's arrest. On August 3, with two days remaining in the two-week time limit for holding Beilis at the Okhrana, Chaplinsky gave Fenenko the formal written order he had demanded.

Fenenko had heard Chaplinsky argue his case, but he still may have been shocked at the written order's incoherence, twisted logic, and brazen fabrications.

Chaplinsky's order to Fenenko was nearly identical to his report to minister of justice Shcheglovitov. "The murder of Andrei Yushchinsky," the prosecutor informed the minister, "was committed by Jews for the purpose of obtaining Christian blood for the fulfillment of Jewish religious rituals." This judgment, he continued, "finds full confirmation in the conclusions of the Archimandrite Ambrosius and the distinguished professor in the department of psychiatry Ivan Alexeevich Sikorsky." (The contrary opinion of the distinguished theologian Father Glagolev goes unmentioned.)

In a parody of deductive reasoning, the order to Fenenko leads to the preordained result step by shaky step. The body was found near the Zaitsev factory, which was "under the supervision of the Jew Mendel Beilis." The factory contained "capacious kilns," which could serve as a "convenient place for commission of the crime." (No matter that Krasovsky and Fenenko examined the premises and concluded that the crime could not have been committed there.) The brick factory was "the only place in the area" with clay matching that found on the boy's clothing (contradicted by Krasovsky's analysis). Awls found at a Zaitsev factory workshop were "of the kind that inflicted all of the wounds" on the boy (already definitively dismissed by the pathologist). The security of the crime scene would have had to be ensured by someone. "Therefore"—the fatal word—"it stands to reason that the Zaitsev factory manager would have been in on the plan."

In both his report to the justice minister and in his order to Fenenko, Chaplinsky then slips in an astonishingly candid admission. Taken as a whole, the prosecutor concludes, "all the not completely firm testimony pointing toward Mendel Beilis . . . of Kazimir and Ulyana Shakhovsky, Adam Polishchuk and other witnesses, acquires the character of serious evidence against him." The only eyewitness testimony against Beilis, he is conceding, is "not completely firm"—a euphemism for untrustworthy, coerced, and recanted. (What he meant by "other witnesses" is a mystery, since there were none.)

Chaplinsky hides nothing. He admits the story that Kazimir Shakhovsky saw Beilis and his son dragging Andrei to the kiln was "not confirmed." He reveals that Anna "the Wolf" Zakharova had failed in her audition for the archetypal role of eyewitness to the terrible deed; she had "categorically declared under questioning that she told nothing to Ulyana Shakhovskaya and did not have any conversations about Yushchinsky's murder." And yet, he insists, "one cannot but come to the conclusion that Mendel Beilis took part in commission of the murder."

Fenenko, having received the order to charge Beilis, requested that the prisoner be brought to the courthouse. Unfortunately for the investigator, the arrest would not be merely a matter of signing an arrest warrant. His sense of duty required that he personally inform the prisoner he was being charged with a murder that both of them knew he did not commit.

Kuliabko did not question Beilis again after that first day at the Okhrana. He had, unsurprisingly, turned out to be an inept interrogator. Forcing a confession out of Beilis would have required genuine inquisitorial ability—the kind of guile and instinct for a prisoner's psychological vulnerability of a Krasovsky. Moreover, Beilis was discovering in himself a new kind of strength that Kuliabko's simplistic bullying, however agonizing, could not overcome.

Beilis was left alone, except when he was brought his meals, which he could not touch. He lost weight, and by the time Kuliabko appeared on the seventh day of his confinement he could barely stand.

"Well," Kuliabko said, "have you already considered your situation?" It was a final, feeble invitation to confess.

"I have nothing to consider," Beilis replied, "because I do not know anything."

That was their last exchange. That day, July 28, Beilis was transferred to a police precinct house. The mechanism for his criminal arrest and charging was being set in motion.

The premises in his new jail cell were a little brighter. A few Jews who had been detained in the regular police raids were held there and one of them, a tailor named Berkowitz, tried to comfort Beilis. Berkowitz had been brought in a month earlier when the police found one of his grown sons living with him, having come to the city to recuperate from an illness. The son was deported back to the Pale. Berkowitz was arrested for harboring an "illegal."

Every day the tailor's wife would bring him food and drink, and when she arrived Berkowitz persuaded Beilis to partake. Berkowitz told him he should remain strong and not lose hope. "Let us make a toast," he said, pouring them both some brandy. "*L'Chaim.* You will see that the Almighty will help." Beilis had no appetite, but he ate and drank one little glass of brandy and then another. He felt stronger and his mood lightened a bit, but then he remembered that he had had no word from home and no visits since that day when he had seen his

children. He wondered if his bosses or anyone from the factory was trying to help him. He got a piece of paper and wrote a letter to Dubovik,
the factory manager, and sent it off with Berkowitz's wife. At least he
could now be sure people would know of his situation.

Suddenly, Beilis was informed by a police officer that he was being
summoned to meet with the "investigator." He was unfamiliar with the
exact meaning of the word, but at the district court he was led into a
large room where he recognized Investigator Fenenko as the man who
had visited the factory a number of times after Andrei was murdered.
Also present was A. A. Karbovsky, who had replaced Brandorf as the
prosecutor in charge of the case.

Fenenko began by asking, "Did you know Andrei Yushchinsky?"
Beilis responded that while he may have seen him on the street, he did
not know him.

Fenenko and Karbovsky bandied about Jewish religious terms that
he did not know. Karbovsky, in particular, would consult a notebook
and ask him questions with words like *pidyon* (a ritual fee paid a rabbi
on behalf of a firstborn son) and *aphikomon* (the piece of matzo hidden
at the Passover seder) and *misnagid* (non-Hasidic Jew) to which Beilis
could only shake his head. His ignorance was unfeigned. (Questioned
after her husband's arrest, Esther Beilis told the authorities, "My husband is not at all religious . . . He even works very often on Saturday
and doesn't observe Jewish holidays since he's a poor man and we have
no time to celebrate anything, but have to work for our daily bread to
support the family.")

So when Fenenko asked, "Was your father a Hasid?" Beilis could not
understand why he was being asked the question, and it also somewhat
confounded him. He later confessed: "I must also tell you that I really
did not know, and it is still not entirely clear to me what a 'Hasid' is. In
my understanding, a 'Hasid' is a religious Jew who strictly abides by
all the laws, and dresses in long clothing. According to this understanding, all Jews in my opinion were divided into two types—'Hasidim,'
meaning, all religious Jews who wear long clothing, and non-Hasidim,
meaning today's Jews who wear short clothing, and do not abide by
the laws. And so, because my father, may he rest in peace, was very
religious, wore long clothing, and strictly abided by all the laws—I considered him a Hasid."

So to Fenenko's question, Beilis answered, "Yes."

"And you yourself?" Fenenko asked, "Are you also a Hasid?"

"This, as bad as I felt, caused me to smile," Beilis recalled. "Me a 'Hasid'?!" he thought. He replied that he was a simple God-fearing man but no Hasid by any measure.

A reluctant Fenenko was likely given his list of questions by Chaplinsky, whose line of inquiry was focusing on the supposedly nefarious Hasids or Hasidim. Hasidism had originated as an ecstatic, mystical Jewish movement in mid-eighteenth-century Poland and now constituted a large plurality of the region's Jews. The region's other main Jewish strain consisted of the *misnagdim* or *mitnagdim*—literally "opponents" of Hasidism—who propounded a more traditional form of the faith. By Beilis's time, the acrimony between the two groups had subsided, and in matters of religious observance their distinctions were minor. But the Hasidim would be portrayed by the prosecution as a sinister and secretive sect, "the men with black beards," who conducted the bloody and barbaric ritual.

Fenenko then asked him about a letter that had been found during the search of his home. The letter, which surely encouraged and relieved the prosecution, was from Jonah Zaitsev concerning the preparation of Zaitsev's yearly batch of Passover matzo. It turned out that for many years Beilis had overseen the production of Passover matzo for Zaitsev's family. At last, here was a direct connection between the suspect and the Jews' diabolical parody of the host made with Christian blood. Much would be made of this connection at the trial.

Beilis explained that one day, years ago, Zaitsev had offered him the opportunity to earn a few extra rubles by supervising this annual tradition—the baking and delivery of a ton of matzo for his large extended family and friends. He needed someone dependable and honest. For two weeks every year, Beilis supervised the baking of the matzo at Zaitsev's estate outside of Kiev, and its delivery on Passover eve, until the old man's death in 1907, when the tradition ceased. (Zaitsev's heirs were modern Jews in "short clothing," content to buy their matzo in a store.)

Fenenko asked whether he ever had to chase neighborhood children, in particular Andrei, away from the clay grinders. Beilis told him he had not. Over the next few days Beilis was questioned again a number of more times. "On the one hand, I felt encouraged [each time]," he would later write in his memoirs, "for if they desired to question me it was a sign that they wanted to know the truth. On the other hand I would become frightened of the wild questions they were putting, questions designed to confuse and entangle me."

On August 3, Beilis was brought in to meet with Fenenko alone at the courthouse. Fenenko, who must have been greatly distressed, looked lost in thought.

"I must send you to prison," he said. Beilis began to cry.

"Do not cry, Beilis," he said. Beilis recalled Fenenko saying the words "in a soft and heartfelt voice in which I felt compassion."

Beilis asked Fenenko why he would send an innocent man to prison. Fenenko said his investigation, still in progress, would reveal the truth, but in the meantime he was "obligated" to imprison him. He repeated again that "this is what the prosecutor ordered."

"Will I have to wear prison clothing?" Beilis asked.

Until now he had worn his own clothes. He later recalled the question with embarrassment: "Foolishness. That this is what I feared most of all at that moment. As long as I was in my own clothes, I saw myself as a free person who was arrested accidentally, and would soon be freed." On his last night at the police precinct, a veteran convict tried to comfort him. "In prison," he said, "it is much better. There at least you get some cooked food, while at the precinct you only get dry food." Uncomforted, Beilis spent a sleepless night.

As for Vera Cheberyak, who was also detained on July 22, little is known about her time as an Okhrana prisoner except for one exemplary episode. Cheberyak was probably held first at the Okhrana headquarters, but by the end of July she was transferred to a police precinct jail. On July 31, she had a new cellmate, Anna Darofeyeva, who had just killed her husband. Cheberyak might have seen in the forty-year-old Anna a kindred spirit or a woman in need of consolation (after all, in so many such cases, it was the man who had provoked the ultimate and decisive act). But instead, Cheberyak saw in Anna yet another potential mark.

Cheberyak struck up a conversation with Anna, telling her it had been her bad luck that her son, Zhenya, had known Andrei Yushchinsky, which had led her to come under suspicion in his murder. Cheberyak drew out the vulnerable woman about her own situation. She told Cheberyak she had no children, no family, no one to look out for her. As people often do when confronted by misfortune too immense to comprehend, Anna fixated on trivialities. The police had taken some things of hers and she was worried about what would happen to them. Cheberyak said she would help. She was sure she would be released soon, and she would take care of Anna's affairs. On a scrap of paper, Cheberyak had Anna draw up a document in her own hand. Anna, who must have been in a radical state of mental distress, thought she was giving Cheberyak permission only to take her things from the police station for safekeeping. In fact, in signing the paper, Anna apparently transferred to Cheberyak the right to dispose of all her worldly goods, such as they were.

Cheberyak was right to believe she would soon be released. Although nearly everyone involved in the case—from the upright shoemaker Nakonechny to the unscrupulous prosecutor Chaplinsky—sensed she was somehow involved in Andrei's murder, Cheberyak had never incriminated herself. As for that "shit Zhenya," as she had called her son, while she was locked up he had said nothing to harm her.

Cheberyak, though, still did not feel she was out of danger. It was about to become evident that the mother was in mortal fear of her son, and she would soon come under plausible suspicion of wanting him dead.

Knowing Cheberyak would have to be released in a few days, Detective Krasovsky set about wooing Zhenya while it was possible to question him outside of his mother's influence. He went to a bakery to buy some pastries and had them delivered to the Cheberyaks' home in the hope of putting the grateful boy in the right mood to open up when an officer paid a call.

The treats were surely welcome. By the time that Vera Cheberyak was whisked off to the Okhrana, the neighbors were becoming concerned about her children. They were growing thin. Their father, Vasily, had dearly hoped for his wife's removal from the family by the police, but the attention of the authorities had resulted in nothing but disaster. The destruction of Vera's criminal gang had deprived the family of much of its livelihood. Vasily was on his way to losing his job at the telegraph office. (He ascribed this to Krasovsky's machinations, later testifying that the detective had threatened, "I will ruin you," if he did not tell what he knew.) Zakharchenko, the landlord, had evicted the family from their apartment, forcing them to move. The children still sneaked into Zakharchenko's yard and stole fruit from his pear trees, no longer as a childish game but to stave off hunger.

In the first days of August, all three children fell ill. Vasily at first thought it was from eating green pears, but their symptoms quickly grew worse. Zhenya was taken to the hospital with dysentery. The boy was growing weaker with each passing hour; the doctor had almost no hope of saving him. Vera Cheberyak was released from jail on August 7 and, after signing for her cellmate's possessions on the way out, made her way to the hospital. It is not clear if the doctor told her that her son was, in all likelihood, dying, but he did tell her it would be better for her boy to stay where he was. She brought him home.

The eerie and unnerving scene that then unfolded would become part of the case's legend. It would become the focus of the wildest conspiracy theories and speculation. It would transfix the nation and serve as a linchpin of the defense. Though it may seem too contrived in its dramatic convenience to be credible, and as histrionic as a scene in a silent film (as indeed it would become in just a few months), it was witnessed by two men whose motives were unimpeachable, for neither wanted to undermine the blood accusation.

When Krasovsky heard that Zhenya had been taken home, he immediately sent Polishchuk and another officer to watch over him. "In his delirium he kept saying Andrusha's name," Polishchuk reported, in an account recorded three days later. "Sometimes it seemed to Zhenya that Andrusha was catching him, and he cried, 'Oh, Andrusha, don't catch, don't catch; at other times [it seemed to him] that Andrusha was firing [from his gun], and then he began to cry: 'Andrusha is firing, firing,' and then . . . he cried: 'Andrusha, don't scream.' "

Polishchuk's account continues: "When Zhenya occasionally came to, his mother took him in her arms and gestured to the detectives: 'Tell them, dear son, so that they won't harm either your mother or you, since we both don't know anything about the Andrei Yushchinsky case,' to which Zhenya answered: 'Leave me alone, mama, it's painful for me to remember that.' " His mother prodded him: "Tell them, little one, that I have nothing to do with it."

Polishchuk also noticed a contradictory impulse. When Zhenya started to say something, his mother did something strange and disturbing: she bent over him and covered his mouth with kisses. It seemed clear to Polishchuk that she wanted to prevent him from talking. When he questioned her about this, she said it was difficult for her son to talk and she didn't want him troubled.

Present to administer the final sacraments was Father Fyodor Sinkevich, a leader of the right-wing youth organization Double Headed Eagle who would soon become its chairman. Cheberyak later claimed that Zhenya had requested that she summon him, but Sinkevich did not know Zhenya. It is all but certain that inviting Sinkevich was Cheberyak's idea. She must have nurtured a hope that this leading right-wing clergyman would bear witness as her son offered her a dying exoneration.

Sinkevich could see that the boy was near death. "I gave him communion, then made to leave, when the boy called out to me, 'Father,'" Sinkevich later testified. "I approached him with a tender feeling and asked, 'What is it, my child.' He didn't say anything. Then he called out 'Father' again. I again asked 'What is it, my child.' He again said nothing, and however hard I tried with soothing words to encourage him to say what he wanted to, he didn't say anything." Sinkevich later shared his impression with the court: "It seemed to me that he wanted to say something but for some reason couldn't bring himself to. It made the impression of some kind of complicated psychological process going on."

Cheberyak had followed the young priest into the room, so quietly he did not notice her until he happened to turn around. He formed a sense that Cheberyak, standing behind him and facing the bed, was trying to communicate something to the boy wordlessly.

After he left the boy's bedside, Sinkevich had a conversation with Cheberyak in which she said something quite striking. They talked about the Beilis case and, while he could not remember everything she said, he did recall her saying, "They are wrongly accusing the Jews." Cheberyak was clearly in the midst of her own "complex psychological process." Just a few months earlier she had told the authorities she believed the Jews had something to do with the crime. Now, she inscrutably needed to tell a leader of the city's anti-Semites that her previous avowal was not true. Perhaps it was a momentary pang of conscience seeping through her twisted and tormented psyche under the unbearable stress of the moment. She would change her mind one final time about whom to implicate in the murder—with dramatic consequences—in time for the trial.

Zhenya died on August 8, the day after he was brought home from the hospital. A few days later his eight-year-old sister, Valentina, died. Only nine-year-old Ludmila survived. Andrei had been in Zhenya's thoughts in his final moments but, if the dying boy knew anything about the identity of the killer, he took it with him to the grave.

Did Vera Cheberyak have something to do with her son's death? Polishchuk told Fenenko he suspected her. Of course, she was locked up at the Okhrana when the boy fell ill, but perhaps she had somehow gotten the message out and had the deed done.

Others also believed the children had been poisoned but, depending upon their political beliefs, they singled out different culprits. The liberal paper *Contemporary Word* pointed the accusing finger at the Far Right: "It is well-known that the Union of Russian People has taken this matter in hand. Is it any wonder that, as a result, there has occurred a new crime?" The far-right paper *Zemshchina* implicated the Jews, noting that "during the investigation of Dreyfus, that lowly traitor, eleven witnesses in turn, one after the other, fell victim to sudden death." The "elimination" of a witness, the paper said, "constitutes the usual method of the bloodthirsty [Jewish] tribe." Although the coroner's official microscopic analysis found the bacteria causing dysentery in Zhenya's body—clear evidence of a natural death—the accusations persisted willy-nilly. It was said that "a large amount of cuprous poisons" had been found in the boy's bowel—or that death came from one of those insidious toxins that leave no trace.

In the aftermath of her children's deaths, Cheberyak's emotional and financial circumstances could not have been more desperate. She raised what money she could. She sold the things she had filched from Anna Darofeyeva, the murderess she had duped. (A dismayed Anna received a postcard from Cheberyak in jail informing her that her things had been sold for three rubles, of which she never saw a kopek.) Meanwhile, with the children just a few days in their graves, Cheberyak suddenly emerged as everyone's favorite villain. Cozying up to Father Sinkevich had bought her no immediate goodwill on the right. The Black Hundred press had begun to implicate her in Andrei's murder, a collaboration that they may have felt their Jewish murder conspiracy logically required. Cheberyak had conspired with the Jews to kill Andrei, and now they had killed Zhenya as well. "It turns out she was close to a certain Yid," *Zemshchina* noted, apparently with Beilis in mind. "How could Zhenya remain among the living? After all, he could let something slip out." Certainly, a reporter of any political stripe knew Vera Cheberyak made fantastic copy. *Zemshchina* dramatically reported on August 17: "[Zhenya's] death was not an unexpected event for his neighbors, for they often heard how the mother threatened the boy: 'If you let your tongue go loose I'll kill you like a dog. I'll strangle you with my own hands, if you let out so much as a squeak.'" (Whether true or not, to anyone who knew her the quotation sounded utterly believable.) The focus on Cheberyak as a Jewish accomplice would turn out to be a brief detour. Right-wing reporters would soon opt for a more streamlined version of events, as the prosecution had, with both Andrei and Zhenya the victims of the Jews alone, ceding the lurid fascinations of Lukianovka's evil presence to the progressive press.

But now Cheberyak prepared to take steps to defend her honor. As a grieving and slandered mother, she readied herself to make a personal appeal to the very highest authority in the empire. For in a few days, as if by divine coincidence, the imperial sovereign, Tsar Nicholas II, was arriving in Kiev.

5

"You Are a Second Dreyfus"

At nine o'clock in the morning on August 4, 1911, Mendel Beilis departed the police precinct for the provincial prison about two miles away where he would spend more than two years of his life. He was accompanied by a single officer. It was an act of remarkable negligence, for Beilis was now the most important prisoner in the Russian Empire. This ordinary man who had never pretended to be anything else had become an irreplaceable figure in a drama at the highest levels of the regime. Tsarist officials, moreover, were already realizing that this case was sure to draw the attention of the world. With the success of a show trial dependent on his continued survival, the authorities should have treated the health and safety of Mendel Beilis as a matter of high importance. Yet here he was, walking down the street, virtually unguarded, a target for any fanatical avenger of Andrei, the Boy Martyr, who had supposedly been killed by this Jew for his blood.

On the other hand, the negligence was perhaps not so remarkable; the lax security was just another symptom of a wider systemic disorder in the tsar's realm. Strangely for a quasi-police state, the empire's security organs never developed a true culture of professionalism; they were rife with incompetence. Before the month was out, this deficiency would bring about a deadly debacle in the very heart of Kiev that would shock all of Russia and profoundly affect the life of Mendel Beilis. But on this summer day, as he walked along, looking like anyone else in his own clothes, the disregard for his safety amounted to the small gift of a final human hour before the prison gates closed behind him.

The officer escorting him, unlike the gruff crew that had taken him from his home thirteen days earlier, was a kindly fellow who insisted they take the trolley. At some point Beilis's neighbor Stepan Zakharchenko, who was Vera Cheberyak's landlord, boarded the trolley car. He wore his Union of Russian People badge, with an image of Saint George slaying the dragon set beneath a cross and the imperial crown, over the motto, "For Faith in Tsar and Fatherland." The badge marked him as a "true Russian," a Black Hundred sympathizer. But when he noticed Beilis, he came over and embraced and kissed him. "Do not be scared," Zakharchenko told his neighbor. "Have no fear, we will all take care of you . . . All of us in Lukianovka know that you are innocent. We will do anything that we can for you. We will not permit an innocent person to rot in prison. Have no fear, have no fear." When Zakharchenko got off the trolley, the two men parted warmly.

Beilis and his guard disembarked at the Lukianovka market, and from there it was a brief walk to the prison. On the way, the officer bought ten pears from a fruit stand and, to Beilis's surprise, offered them to him. Beilis tried to refuse, but the officer insisted, stuffing them into the prisoner's pockets. "Don't worry, I bought them for you," the officer told him. "We know that you are innocent, that you are suffering for nothing."

The compassion of these two Christians—Zakharchenko and this officer—gave Beilis hope and left him greatly moved. He could see the officer was moved as well. If such men could see he was innocent, he thought, then maybe he would soon be freed.

The feeling lasted only until he reached the prison.

In the waiting area he joined fifteen new arrivals. They knew exactly who he was. "They all surrounded me and looked at me as if looking at a wild animal," he recalled. "I saw how they crossed themselves and heard them saying, 'That is Yushchinsky's murderer.'" Until now, Beilis had comforted himself with the thought that sometimes a mistaken accusation happens. Maybe someone had falsely denounced him. Whatever the case, the error would eventually be recognized and corrected. But now people were calling him a murderer to his face, and with such certainty, with such a look in their eyes.

Then came the moment he had so feared. In the police precinct he had been allowed to spend one last night in his own clothes. Now he was led off to a room where he had to strip naked and put on his prison garb. As he tried to take off his boots, he felt he was going to faint. A guard came over and took them off for him. The rough black shirt he put on chafed his skin. After he got dressed an old man approached him and told him to sit down. The old man turned out to be a barber who cut his hair and beard. Then Beilis was taken to the quarantine ward where new inmates spent their first month of imprisonment.

When the door to the quarantine ward was opened, Beilis was hit with a strong, dank, nauseating gust of wind that reeked of human filth. Before him was a large room with black tar-covered walls and barred windows. He stood at the door in a state of confusion, transfixed by the forty or so men in the room. "I see them pushing. They are shoving each other. They are hitting each other, they are cursing each other," he recalled. One man was singing. Another was telling a dirty story. The room was bare of furniture, without a single chair or anything else to sit on.

Moments after he entered the room there was a great commotion as a voice cried, "Dinner!"

He had noticed four or five pails filled with slop lying on the floor—the men had been waiting for the cue to begin eating. The pails contained enough food for everyone, and each one was big enough for several prisoners at a time to eat from, but there were only three spoons. The meal call triggered a wild scuffle as the men fought over who was going to eat first. After some time, and not a few bruises, the winners emerged, a truce was agreed to, and the men, tired from the fighting, formed a line. Each took a set number of spoonfuls before passing the spoon to the next man. Sometimes a man tried to sneak an extra spoonful or two and another scuffle would break out. Beilis could not bring himself to eat the disgusting slop and watched the scene from a corner he had found to sit in. Mealtime only grew more unpleasant after a cellmate found a piece of a mouse in one of the pails, displaying it to all, not in complaint, Beilis later wrote, "but to deprive others of their appetite and get more for himself."

After dinner came "tea," which appeared to be just hot water. A prisoner who looked Jewish to Beilis came up to him, making signs with his hands. The man, who was apparently mute, offered him a dirty piece of sugar. Beilis thanked the man with words and gestures but managed to put aside the gift covertly without eating it.

Everyone here, too, knew what the charges were against him, but after his initial anxiety at the hostile reception in the waiting room, and the raucous antics that had greeted him here in the quarantine cell, he found that his fellow convicts actually treated him quite well—in fact, with a kind of rough-and-ready fair-mindedness. These men—many of them, no doubt, hardened criminals—did not assume that anyone was guilty as charged. They would judge for themselves, and in the ensuing days Beilis would undergo a kind of trial. The quarantine cell became an impromptu courthouse and jury room devoted to "the Beilis case," as the matter came to be known, inside the prison walls and worldwide. The defendant watched as his fellow prisoners held conversations about the case and argued about it. Beilis seems to have stayed in his corner, not speaking up. But if the prisoners had read or been influenced by the debate in the lively local and national press (over what was then "the Yushchinsky case"), it would have given them plenty of ammunition for both sides. *Kiev Opinion,* the city's leading liberal daily, with many Jewish staffers, was predictably anti-regime and opposed the blood accusation. Black Hundred papers like *Russian Banner,* on the other hand, railed against Jewish bloodsuckers, both figurative and literal, and would soon express great satisfaction at Beilis's arrest. Most interesting was the *Kievan,* which, while anti-Semitic, stood for what it saw as principled conservatism, condemning the blood accusation as superstitious slander.

It is striking to think that the first considered public debate about Mendel Beilis's guilt took place in this fetid quarantine cell, anticipating the scenes about to erupt in barrooms, at dinner tables, and in drawing rooms across the empire, as well as in the State Duma. Even if Beilis himself said little, the prisoners must have weighed the evidence as they remembered it from the press as well as from Kiev's prolific rumor mill. Perhaps a Jewish inmate or two dared to contribute his expertise. Many of his fellow prisoners knew a thing or two about the darker side of human nature and how to sniff out a liar. Eventually, Beilis recounted, the prisoners reached their verdict:

> They concluded that I am innocent, and that the entire story about blood in matzo is no more than a made-up story. One of the convicts came up to me and said: "You are a second Dreyfus!"
> I asked him: "What is a Dreyfus?"

Beilis knew nothing of the world-famous case of the Jewish army officer in France who, based on fabricated evidence, had been falsely accused of treason in 1894 and sentenced to life imprisonment on Devil's Island. The affair had deeply divided the French Republic, inspiring a whole movement of "Dreyfusards" devoted to freeing Dreyfus and exposing the conspiracy and cover-up at the highest levels of the French government. Dreyfus had been freed only in 1899, thanks

largely to the efforts of the writer Émile Zola, and not officially exonerated until 1906. Beilis's cellmate tried to explain to him who Dreyfus was:

> "This," he says to me, "was also a person who was arrested for noth-
> ing. The entire world, however, took up his cause. Do not be scared,
> your truth will also be revealed."
>   "What do I care about this Dreyfus," I say, "as I must suffer in the
> meantime?"
>   "Yes, yes," he says to me, nodding his head, "in the meantime you
> must suffer."

On August 25, around the same time as Beilis was receiving his infor-
mal exoneration from his cellmates, Vera Cheberyak answered a knock
at her door. As the month drew to a close, Cheberyak had every right
to expect breathing space in which to mourn for her son and daughter
in peace. The pathologists' report had shown the children had died of
natural causes. The yellow press could insinuate whatever it wanted,
but there was no chance she would be charged in their deaths. As for
Andrei's murder, she had been detained and questioned about it for
nearly six weeks in total, but she had said nothing to harm herself—
and neither, as much as she had distrusted him, had her late son. What
was more, she had only recently been released on the order of the chief
prosecutor, Grigory Chaplinsky, himself; she now had a network of
high-level protectors who would not allow her to be held for the crime
because it conflicted with their plan to charge a Jew. But when Cheberyak, dressed in black, opened her door, she was confronted by a
police officer who declared the unthinkable: she was under arrest for
the murder of Andrei Yushchinsky.
    The arrest, it turned out, was the work of Evgeny Mishchuk, Kiev's
widely disrespected chief of detectives, who had been foisted on the
city's police department the previous year thanks to his St. Petersburg
connections. Vasily Fenenko, the capable and fair-minded investigating
magistrate, shared Mishchuk's suspicions about Vera Cheberyak. But
as a detective, he regarded Mishchuk to be totally inept. Fenenko was
astonished to receive a telephone call around one p.m. informing him
that Mishchuk was boasting of success where his detractors had failed:

he was claiming to have literally unearthed proof that Cheberyak was behind Andrei's murder. A cache of evidence had been found buried on Yurkovsky Hill in Lukianovka. Fenenko was to proceed there immediately.

Fenenko arrived to find Detective Mishchuk strutting the scene with an unbearably self-satisfied air, proclaiming that Andrei's missing belongings had been found and the case solved. He had received a letter from an anonymous informant telling him the exact location where Andrei's belongings were buried, along with evidence that, according to the anonymous letter writer, implicated Vera Cheberyak. Officers had dug up a package wrapped in yellow paper. So sure was Mishchuk of its contents that, even before having it opened, he had ordered Cheberyak and a member of her gang arrested.

The package now lay in the courtyard of a nearby building, ready to be opened in the presence of witnesses, including Fenenko. An officer peeled away the paper to reveal a white cloth sack. Wrapped in the sack were some burned remnants of clothing, including suspenders, and two metal spikes. The officer then reached into the bag and pulled out the torn pieces of a letter, the contents of which had nothing to do with the crime. But Vera Cheberyak's name was mentioned in the letter, as was the name of a member of her gang. The incriminating evidence had, it seemed, been carelessly left in the sack by the perpetrators. With an arrogant and victorious look on his face that infuriated Fenenko, Mishchuk declared, "Ritual murder in the twentieth century doesn't happen." Mishchuk was correct. Jewish ritual murder did not occur in the twentieth century, or in any other century for that matter. But he had not succeeded in ensnaring the killers. Instead, he had fallen into a trap.

Mishchuk was not the most competent detective, but he was still a threat to the conspiracy to charge a Jew with Andrei's murder. Though he had been shunted aside, he was still chief of the investigative division of the Kiev police force. He was unyielding in his opposition to the blood accusation (for which he must be given credit). The proponents of the blood accusation had to find a means to get him out of the way. Their plot would play on his arrogance, his unwarranted self-confidence, and his justifiable suspicions about the identities of the killers. In the weeks after Andrei's murder, a petty criminal named Semyon Kushnir had offered his services to Mishchuk as an informer.

It was Kushnir who had passed along the anonymous letter pointing to the location of the buried cache of supposed evidence. Since the letter confirmed what Mishchuk already believed to be true, he did not doubt its authenticity.

When Nikolai Krasovsky arrived, he pushed his way through the large crowd that had gathered around Mishchuk's find. It took just one glance to relieve him of any concern that his despised rival had solved the case. The metal spikes were each the diameter of a small candle and nearly a foot long. Neither one, he was sure, could have served as the murder weapon, which had been thinner in diameter and far shorter. As for the burned clothes, among the shreds of quilted fabric supposedly from Andrei's coat he noticed a piece that looked like a flounce from a woman's garment.

Later that evening, Fenenko consulted the autopsy specialist who confirmed that the long spikes could have had nothing to do with the murder. As for the clothing, Andrei had never worn suspenders and the ones that were found were, in any case, those of an adult. What was more, the package was determined to have been in the ground only two or three days. This had all been a crude fabrication.

Mishchuk was dismissed from his post and he and three other officers were arrested on charges of falsifying evidence. Kushnir later confessed to drafting the supposedly anonymous letter. It was never established on whose orders he was acting, but the scheme may well have originated high up in the chain of command, possibly with Grigory Chaplinsky, though it is also possible that the hoax was perpetrated by criminals hoping for a reward and that the prosecutor merely exploited the opportunity to eliminate the troublesome detective. In any case, Chaplinsky took an extreme measure in indicting Mishchuk. Kiev's governor, A. F. Giers, was against bringing charges, but Chaplinsky threatened to wage bureaucratic war against him by blocking appointments to key posts. There was never a genuine investigation as to who was behind the fabrication as the case against Mishchuk went forward.

Despite Chaplinsky's efforts, Mishchuk and his codefendants would be acquitted of all charges a year later by a panel of independent-minded judges in Kiev, which took about ten minutes to come to a decision after hearing witnesses who contradicted themselves or were discredited on the stand. Under the Russian justice system, though, a not-guilty verdict could be appealed, and the prosecutor exercised his privilege, citing several dubious technicalities. The appeals court voided the guilty verdict, basing their decision on a discrepancy between the original panel's summary verdict, which stated the defendants were "not guilty," and the same panel's explanatory opinion, which stated only that the charges were "not proven." It then took the virtually unheard-of step of remanding the case to a court in a different city. The authorities were clearly counting on a more submissive panel of judges coming to an opposite decision. On retrial by the Kharkov court, Mishchuk was convicted and sentenced to a year in prison. His conviction would send a signal: this is what would happen to opponents of the blood accusation.

For the high officials determined to charge a Jew with the murder of Andrei Yushchinsky, Krasovsky was a far greater threat than Mishchuk. But Krasovsky was too clever to fall for a crude trap. His enemies would need to devise a different and even more brazen scheme to get him out of the way. But that lay months in the future.

Meanwhile, Krasovsky had regained his footing as an investigator. He had spent days meandering along Lukianovka's streets, dressed in the clothes of a simple workingman, striking up conversations with anyone who might have seen or heard something about the case. From a night watchman he first heard a story circulating in the neighborhood that filled in the critical piece missing amid the suspicion surrounding Vera Cheberyak: a motive.

The story existed in two versions, differing about the timing, but with the same core. One day Andrei had decided to cut school and he, Zhenya, and a third boy had gone out near the caves to cut off some switches from the shrubs there. Andrei's switch had been the best, longer and more flexible than Zhenya's. Zhenya had demanded that Andrei give it to him. Andrei had refused, and the two boys had quarreled. Zhenya had told Andrei, "If you don't give me yours, I'll tell your aunt that you didn't go to school, and you came here to play." Andrei had supposedly answered, "And if you tell on me, I'll write to the police that at your mother's thieves are constantly hiding and bringing stolen things." Zhenya, the story went, had gone home and told his mother.

In one version, the quarrel had taken place some days or weeks before Andrei's disappearance. After hearing Zhenya's story, two of

Cheberyak's cohorts had supposedly said that Andrei needed to be "quieted down," so he wouldn't blab and that if necessary, he needed to be "rubbed out." Nothing had come of that, at first. Then, on March 9, came the arrest of four members of Cheberyak's gang and, a day later, the search of Cheberyak's home by the police. Now the hunt by the gang for the informer was on. Suspicion turned to Andrei. When he knocked on Zhenya's door on March 12, Cheberyak and her gang took advantage of the opportunity to do away with him.

According to the other version of the story circulating in the neighborhood, the boys' quarrel had taken place on the very morning Andrei had disappeared. In that case, the gang may have assumed that, if Andrei was talking about betraying them, then perhaps he had already done so. Panicked and angry, Cheberyak's men had not needed a well-thought-out reason to take their revenge. After Zhenya ran off, Andrei had made his way back to his friend's house, carrying his switch, perhaps to make up with his friend. There he'd been confronted. Then: shouted accusations, the boy's frightened look, conclusions quickly drawn, and action taken.

Krasovsky had his men canvass Lukianovka for witnesses, attempting to trace the story back to its source, but the mysterious third boy proved elusive. Still, the essence of the story sounded plausible, though if Andrei was indeed killed for being a stool pigeon, his death was doubly tragic. Police records note the name of the informer behind the March 10 police search: it was not Andrei, but Evgeny Mifle, brother of Pavel, Vera Cheberyak's blind lover. The Mifle family was determined to see Cheberyak put behind bars. In the end, the search had resulted in no charges against her for robbery or selling stolen goods. But her gang's ensuing frenzy of suspicion may have led to a far more horrible crime.

Only a few hours after Cheberyak was arrested, she was just as suddenly released. Such outrageous treatment at the hands of Kiev's chief detective must have made her even more determined to make a personal appeal to the tsar to restore her good name. Nicholas took with great seriousness the thousands of petitions he received from ordinary citizens requesting his mercy and intervention in matters large and small; he spent hours each week personally reviewing them. He treasured this duty because with each plea he took in his hands, he felt the age-old, mystical bond between tsar and people come to life.

In just four days Tsar Nicholas II was due to arrive in Kiev on an official visit. Cheberyak must have felt blessed that her appeal could be conveyed to the tsar here, in her native city, rather than having to forward it to the capital. Amid her endless misfortune, the tsar's visit surely seemed an unearthly piece of good luck, and she intended to take advantage of it.

General Pavel Kurlov, assistant minister of the interior and head of the Corps of Gendarmes, was already in Kiev to supervise the extensive security precautions in advance of the tsar's arrival. A few months earlier, from his desk in the capital, he had saved the Jews of Kiev from a pogrom in the aftermath of Andrei's murder by dispatching a timely order to protect them. His mission remained the prevention of disorder of any sort in the city, with the supremely important priority of ensuring the safety of the sovereign emperor. Unfortunately Kurlov, at the worst possible time, was in an impaired state, laid up in his hotel suite with back pain. Desperate for relief, he summoned the fashionable doctor of Tibetan medicine Peter Badmaev, who treated much of St. Petersburg high society, including members of the court and Duma leaders, for all manner of complaints (in particular, venereal diseases and impotence) with exotic herbal infusions and "arousing powders." Typically for the era, even such a trivial thing as being treated for an aching back was bound up with court intrigue. Badmaev was a would-be rival of the imperial couple's beloved, madly charismatic holy man, Grigory Rasputin.

Rasputin himself would be present in Kiev during the tsar's visit and available to come to the aid of the royal heir, the sickly seven-year-old Alexis, should he be stricken with one of his hemophilic episodes. Nicholas and Alexandra regarded Rasputin as a gift from God. The court physicians had proven powerless to stop their son's excruciating bouts of internal bleeding; the desperate parents had no doubt that only the man they referred to as "Our Friend" had the power to relieve the boy's suffering. For his part, Prime Minister Peter Stolypin, who also served as interior minister, viewed Rasputin as a mountebank and a threat to the reputation of the monarchy. During the past year, the press had published article after sensational article about the "semi-literate" and "depraved" Siberian peasant and "spiritual quack" who had become a favorite in "certain court circles"; the newspapers had even featured lurid stories of innocent women he had defiled. After compromising pictures of him were brought to the tsar's attention, Rasputin left the country in March 1911, at Nicholas's prodding, on a long pilgrimage to the Holy Land. Stolypin had tried, unsuccessfully, to banish him from the capital permanently. But by August Rasputin had returned home and was again in the imperial couple's embrace. Theirs was a deep emotional and spiritual bond that could not be broken. During the years of their intense relationship, Rasputin addressed Nicholas and Alexandra as "Papa" and "Mama" (ostensibly because they were the mother and father of the Russian people). To the tsar, Rasputin was a "good, religious, simple-minded Russian" and the sovereign treasured their frequent and lengthy conversations. "When in trouble and assailed by doubts," he once confided, "I like to have a talk with him and invariably feel at peace with myself afterward." Their dialogues could combine the spiritual with the political, which surely worried Stolypin. In fact, just two weeks before coming to Kiev, Nicholas had entrusted "Our Friend" with a mission of state importance: to evaluate a possible candidate to relieve Stolypin of his secondary post as minister of the interior. Rasputin told the gentleman that the tsar had sent him "to look into your soul." While the story sounds implausible—that this poorly educated, physically filthy, licentious "holy man" would be entrusted with such vital government business—Rasputin was almost certainly telling the truth.

The two charlatans, Rasputin and Dr. Badmaev, would later form a partnership, helping install one of the doctor's patients, Alexander Protopopov, who was rumored to suffer from advanced syphilis, as the empire's final, half-mad, interior minister. But in August 1911 the two men were at odds. Badmaev schemed in vain to supplant Rasputin as healer to the tsarevich Alexis. Rasputin reputedly mocked Badmaev, saying, "He has two infusions. You drink a little glass of one, and your cock gets hard; but there's still the other: you drink a really tiny glass of it, and it makes you good-natured and kind of stupid, and you don't care about anything." Perhaps the bedridden general Kurlov ingested one that made him "kind of stupid"—there were rumors that Badmaev's potions contained substances stronger than herbs. A more serious impairment to his security efforts in Kiev, however, was Kurlov's near-total lack of previous experience in police work. Owing his ascent largely to the patronage of the empress, Kurlov, like so many other tsarist officials, could himself be counted as a kind of charlatan.

Still, the security preparations for the imperial visit appeared impressive. The authorities in Kiev had made a massive effort to round up undesirables. Large numbers of people deemed suspicious had been arrested, with the police invoking the government's emergency powers to keep them in custody. Along parts of the tsar's route to and from the city, security officers were stationed every dozen yards. Three hundred buildings along critical routes within the city had been searched "from roof to cellar."

The imperial train, with its eleven dark blue, gilt-trimmed cars, arrived in Kiev on August 29. The tsar was accompanied by the empress Alexandra and the couple's "most august" children: their four daughters—Olga, Tatiana, Maria, and Anastasia (OTMA as they dubbed themselves)—and their youngest child, the tsarevich Alexis. Prime Minister Stolypin and members of the cabinet had arrived earlier and were there on the platform, along with local dignitaries, to greet the imperial family.

Among those at the station was Father Fyodor Sinkevich, the priest who had been present at Zhenya Cheberyak's deathbed. He delivered a few words welcoming the tsar in the name of Kiev's monarchist organizations such as Double Headed Eagle. As he addressed the tsar he may have already had in his possession the "most humble petition" from Vera Cheberyak and been looking for an opportunity to pass it on to the sovereign. The suspicious scene the priest had witnessed three weeks earlier as Zhenya lay dying had done nothing to undermine his belief that a Jew had killed Andrei for his blood. Cheberyak's plan to enlist Father Sinkevich as her protector had succeeded. In the petition, Cheberyak expressed bewilderment as to why suspicion fell on her in the matter of Andrei Yushchinsky's murder. As one who had led an "irreproachable life of toil" and "in the name of the sufferings of a mother deprived of two of her children," she pleaded with the tsar to reveal the names of the people persecuting her, so that she could "once and for all be rid of this matter."

From the train station the imperial carriages proceeded along the three-mile route to the physical and spiritual heart of the city, the magnificent St. Sophia Cathedral, dark green and white, its thirteen golden domes shining. The streets, brightly decorated with banners welcoming the sovereign, were lined with worshipful, cheering crowds. Such demonstrations of affection were expected and encouraged; Nicholas took deep satisfaction in public displays of adoration by the common people. But Kievans had been warned not to throw flowers in the path of the tsar's carriage: any flying object had to be treated as a bomb. A contingent of students who had been deemed reliable had strewn a token stretch of one thoroughfare with blossoms. When Nicholas and his family arrived at the cathedral, where Andrei Yushchinsky had once studied at the religious school, they were anointed with holy water by the metropolitan, and the tsar's week of official activities began.

At some point in the next two days, Tsar Nicholas was briefed on the Yushchinsky investigation. The tsar had likely received his first briefing on the case from justice minister Ivan Shcheglovitov in St. Petersburg on May 18, probably a summation of the results of his deputy Liadov's mission to Kiev. It was then that Nicholas may have first heard mention of the poor Jewish brick factory clerk. There is no record of any other briefing on the case between May and the tsar's arrival in Kiev. While the tsar was an ardent reader of the right-wing press, during the languid days of August he may not have paid close attention to news of the investigation and not known of the purported break in the case.

For Grigory Chaplinsky, the chief prosecutor, the meeting with the tsar was surely one of the greatest moments of his life. He had only a few minutes with the sovereign, but he required just a few words to sum up his progress. Dimitry Grigorovich-Barsky, at the time a senior prosecutor, who later became an attorney for Beilis, witnessed this key meeting. He later gave an account that might seem to stretch credulity but was confirmed decades later in a document from the archives of the Ministry of Justice. Chaplinsky told the tsar, "Your majesty, I am happy to report that the true culprit in the murder of Yushchinsky has been found. It is the Yid Beilis."

If Nicholas responded verbally, it was not recorded; but upon hearing this news Nicholas bowed his head and crossed himself.

Nicholas did not like Jews. He believed they were exploiters of poor and vulnerable Russians and fomenters of revolution and likely agreed with this father, Alexander III, who wrote in the margin of a report on the wretched state of Russian Jewry, "We must not forget that it was the Jews who crucified our Lord and spilled his precious blood." While he did not directly provoke violence against the Jews, he sympathized with the Black Hundreds and was grateful for their support in suppressing "bad elements" in the populace during the 1905 revolution. In December 1905, he not only gratefully accepted the badges presented to him and his son by a delegation of the Union of Russian People, both he and Alexis wore them for years. (On one occasion, when Nicholas gave an audience to the editor of a Black Hundred newspaper, the man dandled the tsarevich on his knee. Seeing the badge on the man's chest, the little boy pointed to his own and said, "I'm a Unionist too!")

On the one hand, Nicholas's attitude toward the Jews was unremarkable for his time and among his circle. Even his most forward-looking officials, like former prime minister Sergei Witte, believed Jews to be either revolutionaries or capitalist bloodsuckers. Or, strangely enough, both. As the eminent historian Hans Rogger pointed out, an odd feature of tsarist anti-Semitism was that both the most reactionary and progressive officials shared the assumption that "Jewish money . . . would join with Jewish misery for a common assault on the regime." The striking aspect of the regime's policy, according to Rogger, was "the way reality and delusion combined to shape action." Even such sophisticated men as Witte, and perhaps even Stolypin, sincerely believed that the all-powerful "leaders" of Russian Jewry could manipulate their five million coreligionists into doing their bidding. The oft-expressed notion that the regime cynically used anti-Semitism as a means of deflecting popular anger is largely a misconception. In fact, tsarist officials truly saw the Jews as a monstrous, multi-tentacled threat. The "Jewish question" was for them a real and pressing problem, not a political ploy.

On the other hand, Nicholas's hostility toward the Jews had an especially extreme aspect that confounded even his closest advisers.

While many officials shared a belief in the worldwide Jewish conspiracy and the mythical union of Jewish capital and the revolutionary movement, most of them understood the reality of Jewish poverty in the Pale of Settlement and the counterproductive nature of many anti-Jewish governmental restrictions. Many people in authority shared the understanding that Jewish discontent was a threat to public order that needed to be defused. A reasonable policy, in their view, would require some harsh measures to deal with the "Jewish threat" but would also involve significant accommodations.

In October 1906, when the horrific year of revolutionary violence had abated, Prime Minister Stolypin felt the time had come to allevi-

ate or eliminate some of the hundreds of anti-Jewish measures established by the government. Many of the edicts, he believed, were merely
irritants that could even inflame Jews, especially Jewish youth, toward
revolution. In a private conversation he told a journalist, "The Jews
throw bombs. And do you know the conditions under which they live
in the Western parts [of the empire]? Have you seen the poverty of the
Jews? If I lived under such circumstances perhaps I too would start to
throw bombs."

Stolypin was no liberal. During and after the revolution of 1905, he
had thousands of alleged revolutionaries and opponents of the regime
summarily executed by field courts-martial without due process of law.
The nooses from which they were hanged were dubbed "Stolypin's
neckties," and decades later railway cars for transporting prisoners were
still called "Stolypins" in Russia. But he was an ambitious reformer who
famously declared that, given twenty years of peace, he would transform the country. His mission was to create a state based on the rule
of law, which would remain an autocracy, to be sure, but with a well-
educated populace and a thriving new class of independent farmers.
"I am fighting on two fronts," Stolypin confided to the renowned British historian of Russia Bernard Pares. "I am fighting against revolution, but for reform. You may say that such a position is beyond human
strength and you might be right." Part of his plan to create a law-based
state was, to a degree, normalizing the situation of the Jews.

After a series of contentious meetings in the early fall of 1906, the
Council of Ministers sent a very modest packet of reforms to Tsar
Nicholas for his approval. One measure, for example, would grant to
Jews who had worked as artisans or merchants for a certain period of
time outside the Pale of Settlement the permanent right to live there.
Another called for special fines on families of Jewish draft evaders to
be abolished. In a report to the tsar, Stolypin laid out at length the
pragmatic arguments for improving the lot of the Jews. He clearly had
every expectation that the tsar would approve of the measures because
he noted in his report that only those who have "a general feeling of
intransigent hostility toward Jewry" could oppose them.

Nicholas took nearly two months to reply. On December 10, 1906,
Stolypin received the tsar's extraordinary response. The tsar had
decided to reject the contents of this ministerial "journal," as it was
called, in its entirety:

I am returning to you the journal on the Jewish Question without my confirmation. Long before its submission to me, I thought about this day and night. Despite the most convincing argument in favor . . . an inner voice more and more firmly repeats to me that I do not take this decision upon myself. So far my conscience has *never* deceived me. Therefore, I intend in this case to follow its dictates. I know that you, too, believe that "the heart of the Tsar is in the hands of God." So be it. For all those whom I have placed in authority I bear awesome responsibility before God and am ready at any time to account to him.

The emphasis on *"never"* is in the original. The tsar believed his "inner voice" was infallible. And, in this instance, the voice dictated that he should take no action to alleviate Jewish suffering, even though his ministers believed the situation undermined the stability of the regime. Stolypin's personal reaction went unrecorded, but he was surely shocked. The moderately conservative Vladimir Kokovtsov, an ally of Stolypin who was finance minister at the time, wrote in his memoirs: "None of the documents in my possession shows so clearly the Tsar's mystical attitude toward the nature of his imperial power as this letter." The "inner voice" episode also provides a kind of key to the regime's mysterious decision to pursue the case against Mendel Beilis.

The decision to prosecute Beilis was the product of two mentalities or sets of perceptions: the generally held belief in the menace presented by the Jews combined with Tsar Nicholas's personal belief in the divine nature of his power and his mission on earth. Nicholas was a true believer in the myth of the *Tsar-Batiushka,* or saintly "Little Father Tsar." Fundamental to the myth was the precept that the tsar's authority came from God and from the personal bond between tsar and people. Nicholas's recent predecessors had believed in this spiritual dictum, in principle, but Nicholas lived it out with unique intensity and relied on it as a guide to action. Nicholas more than once expressed his aversion to his rationalist ancestor Peter the Great, the legendary Westernizer who, in his view, heedlessly "stamped out all the pure Russian customs." Nicholas had an abiding nostalgia for an idealized Russia, before Peter's reign began in 1682, when the connection between tsar and people was thought to have been close and pure. A part of that bond, for Nicholas, was shared hatred of the Jews.

It has been argued that the Beilis case was part of a political agenda by certain officials. It was, supposedly, a way of derailing a bill in the Duma to abolish the Pale of Settlement or, more generally, as the historian Orlando Figes put it, "to exploit xenophobia for monarchical ends . . . to mobilize the 'loyal Russian people' behind the defense of the tsar and the traditional social order." But the bill on the Pale had died in committee several months earlier, in February 1911, before Andrei's disappearance; it never had any chance of passing. Nor did the regime ever actively use the Beilis case to rouse the population on behalf of Mother Russia. In fact, the record shows that the government was fearful of popular involvement straight through to the end of the trial. Another motive explaining the prosecution of the case, pressure from the Far Right, is also unconvincing; the Far Right was a creature of the regime, heavily dependent on it for secret funding and, in any case, divided by vicious infighting, with the Union of Russian People having split into three rival organizations. The government was quite able to defy the Far Right when it desired.

In pursuing this mad venture, then, the tsar's personal ideology, not politics, was the necessary condition, the indispensable factor. Left to themselves and their generic anti-Semitic prejudice, the tsar's ministers would have somewhat moderated the regime's anti-Jewish policy. The tsar, however, had demonstrated his belief that his divine mission dictated the Jews' unrelieved oppression. Thus the high officials who backed the Beilis case were motivated not by the desire to mobilize the people or to pursue a political agenda but to please the tsar and so advance themselves.

For political expediency in service to the tsar's beliefs, there is no better example than the career of Ivan Shcheglovitov, the justice minister throughout the Beilis case. A former chief prosecutor of the State Senate, as the Russian supreme court was called, he had been one of the empire's most distinguished jurists. He was regarded by none other than Oskar Gruzenberg, Russia's most prominent Jewish defense attorney (and future head of Beilis's defense team), as a man of unimpeachable integrity. Shcheglovitov, during his years as a prosecutor, law professor, and major architect of judicial regulations, was known as something of a progressive, even interceding more than once to commute the sentences of people convicted of political crimes. In his forties, however, Shcheglovitov was suddenly infected with an overpowering case of political ambition. He set his sights on becoming the minister of justice and left the Senate for a lesser position in the Justice Ministry, calculating that he would succeed in rising to the top post, which he did in 1906—whereupon, as former prime minister Witte succinctly put it in his memoirs, he "destroyed the courts." Shcheglovitov did his best to obliterate the hard-won independence of the judiciary—the one institution that Russians could point to with pride as striving toward Western standards, forcing out judges and prosecutors deemed politically unreliable and sending out his minions to harass and intimidate officers of the court into producing verdicts the regime desired. Gruzenberg was shocked, writing in his memoirs that "Shcheglovitov's moral transformation was not so much a decline as a roaring avalanche." Shcheglovitov became known by the nickname "Vanka Cain" ("Johnny Cain") after a legendary eighteenth-century brigand who duped the state into making him a powerful police official but used his post to unleash a massive crime wave.

A man of great intellectual sophistication, Shcheglovitov was probably no more anti-Semitic than the average Russian official and had even helped Gruzenberg win a lenient sentence for a Jewish vigilante convicted of trying to kill a notorious instigator of pogroms. Now, in 1911, only one motive could explain why such a man would support a ritual murder trial: self-interest. This, in turn, could only mean that he believed he was doing what the tsar wished him to do.

True, the tsar's wishes were often hard to discern. And, at this point, officials may have relied merely on his single brief gesture of crossing himself at the mention of the suspect or a meaningful nod to a minister during one or another briefing. But it stood to reason that a man who believed a divine whisper urged him to persecute the Jews was likely to welcome an endeavor that sought to prove their fanatical malevolence. Nicholas's "inner voice" had not changed its counsel since his 1906 veto of the pro-Jewish measures. Just two weeks before his visit to Kiev, the tsar had signed yet another anti-Jewish restriction, one that limited trade by Jews east of the Urals, sternly instructing his ministers, "Everything needs to be done to prevent the Jews from taking over Siberia."

One powerful figure, however, was unquestionably appalled and unsettled by the Beilis case. In early September, as the brick-factory clerk neared the end of his stay in the quarantine cell, his best hope of avoiding prosecution lay in the possibility of intervention by the prime minister, Peter Stolypin. Stolypin was a fervent Russian nationalist. Like all senior tsarist officials, he was an anti-Semite, but he was not a racist. That is, he did not see the Jews as an irredeemably evil race. Rather, he saw the Jews as a political and social problem, one that could be dealt with, if only the tsar allowed it, by political means. No record exists of Stolypin's opinion of the Beilis case, but it is inconceivable that he believed that putting a Jew on trial for killing a Christian boy would be in the interests of the regime. Such a public spectacle could only needlessly alienate the Jews even further. Stolypin, moreover, was greatly worried about the impact of Russia's anti-Semitic excesses on the empire's image abroad and on its foreign economic interests. He was specifically concerned in the fall of 1911 about an intense lobbying campaign—the first of its kind in history—led by the American financier Jacob Schiff calling for the abrogation of the Russo-American commercial treaty of 1832 as punishment for Russia's anti-Jewish policies. A ritual murder case could only give the backers of this campaign more ammunition.

A pragmatic anti-Semitic supporter of Stolypin's later said the prime minister would never have let the Beilis case go forward. During the past year, Stolypin had shown his political fortitude by attempting to banish the "Mad Monk" Iliodor as well as Rasputin, both favorites of the tsar's. He had stood up to the Far Right in a major confrontation dealing with the organization of local governments in the western provinces, so he may well have succeeded in thwarting a foolish endeavor that the tsar had not explicitly endorsed.

When he was briefed on the case in Kiev, Stolypin could only have grown more alarmed. But any action to forestall the prosecution of Beilis would have to await his return to St. Petersburg, an event that depended on his continued existence, which in turn depended upon the efforts of his subordinate and political enemy, General Kurlov, who was in charge of all security precautions, as well as the Kiev Okhrana chief, Nikolai Kuliabko. Stolypin needed around-the-clock protection to stay alive. In his five years in office, he had survived some seventeen attempts on his life, including a spectacular bombing of his home that killed twenty-seven people and wounded two of his children. Kurlov arranged for Stolypin to be protected by a twenty-two-man security detail, but an aura of impending tragedy would overtake the prime minister's visit to Kiev, thanks to an outburst by his nemesis Rasputin.

The erratic and charismatic holy man was said to have a gift for prophecy, supposedly predicting the calamitous sinking of the Russian fleet in the war with Japan in 1905. He could also, it was said, predict the fates of individuals, whether they would fall ill, and how their lives would unfold. Seldom were his prognostications riddles to be unraveled; they were direct and verifiable. On the day the tsar and his entourage arrived in Kiev, his prophetic urge concerned the prime minister.

Barred by Stolypin from appearing in public with the tsar, Rasputin stood among the crowd of ordinary people on the street, watching the imperial family and the attending dignitaries pass by on the way to the cathedral. As Stolypin's carriage passed, Rasputin exclaimed, "Death is following him! Death is riding behind him!" Rasputin reputedly spent the night tortured by the vision and was heard muttering about it over and over as he tossed in his bed. It was an eerie omen, though one that Stolypin, had he known about it, would certainly have shrugged off. No one was more fatalistic about his future than the prime minister himself. The first line of his last will and testament, drafted years earlier, read, "I want to be buried where I am assassinated."

The main event of the tsar's visit to Kiev, the unveiling of a monument to his grandfather Alexander II, took place without incident. So did a number of other outdoor events, which were thought to present the greatest security risk. The command performance of Rimsky-Korsakov's *Tale of the Tsar Saltan* at Kiev's Municipal Theater on September 1 was deemed to be thoroughly secure. The identities of all the guests were vetted. Only those possessing a special pass—the rarest of the twenty-six types issued for the Kiev events—were allowed to enter the theater. The Kiev Okhrana chief, Kuliabko, the man who had arrested Mendel Beilis six weeks earlier, was present to supervise security.

The tsar and two of his daughters, accompanied by the Bulgarian crown prince, occupied the Kiev governor-general's parterre box, the closest one to the stage. (That evening the empress Alexandra, as was so often the case, was indisposed and did not attend.) The first row of the orchestra was reserved for the highest officials, and Stolypin sat in seat number five, between the governor-general, F. F. Trepov, and the minister of the imperial court, Baron V. B. Fredericks. When the lights went up during the intermission, the prime minister stood up and leaned on the barrier of the orchestra pit. As he conversed with Baron Fredericks and another dignitary, a slim young man slipped into his row, stopping within five or six feet of him. The young man pulled a pistol out of his pocket and fired two shots. One bullet hit Stolypin in the hand and the other found its mark in the right side of his chest, shattering one of the orders hanging from a ribbon on his jacket. Kiev's governor, A. F. Giers, described the scene:

> At first he did not seem to know what happened . . . With slow and deliberate movements he placed his hat and gloves on the barrier, opened his jacket and, seeing his vest heavily soaked with blood, waved his hand, as if wanting to say, "It is all over." Then he sank heavily into his seat and said clearly and distinctly . . . "I am happy to die for the Tsar."

Nicholas had been in the drawing room with his children and immediately returned to his box when he heard the shots. Before being taken to the hospital, Stolypin, Nicholas later wrote his mother, "slowly turned toward me and crossed himself with his left arm."

The prime minister had been left totally unguarded. Not an officer was to be found within a hundred paces of him. Before the assassin could get off a third shot, he was set upon by a crowd of four dozen gentlemen in evening clothes who pushed him to the ground and beat him in the face with their opera glasses, egged on by the spectators' cries of "Kill him!" Nicholas expressed regret, apparently with utter sincerity, that the police did not allow the crowd to beat the man to death.

Stolypin was, of course, attended to by the best physicians in the city, including Dr. Nikolai Obolonsky, dean of the medical department of the Kiev's St. Vladimir University, who had performed an autopsy on Andrei Yushchinsky. At first the doctors had a good deal of hope that the prime minister might survive. After three days, though, he took a turn for the worse, and he died on September 5, 1911. Damage to his liver had turned out to be more severe than first believed. The main damage to the organ, it was determined, had been done mostly not by the bullet but by fragments of the Order of St. Vladimir of the Third Degree awarded him by Nicholas, which had been driven into his body. Prime Minister Stolypin had truly died for his service to the tsar.

The shooting of Stolypin triggered new fears of a pogrom: the prime minister's assassin—a twenty-four-year-old anarchist, law school graduate, and sometime secret police informer named Dimitry Bogrov—turned out to be a Jew. (In an act of staggering gullibility, Kuliabko had let Bogrov, whom he believed to be his agent, talk his way into the theater by claiming that he could prevent an attempt on the prime minister's life.) Born into a prosperous and highly assimilated family, Bogrov was Jewish only in the ethnic sense, but in the aftermath of the assassination, that indisputable identity was all that mattered. Black Hundred agitators riled up crowds with incendiary speeches. The day after Stolypin's death, a gang of twenty thugs threw stones at Jewish students and assaulted Jewish merchants on Alexander Street with knives. Thousands of Jews jammed into Kiev's train station hoping to flee the city.

As it happened, investigating magistrate Vasily Fenenko, temporarily putting aside the Beilis case, was called upon to interrogate the assassin. Bogrov's motives are not entirely clear, but his primary intention was likely to restore his honor after having been unmasked as a police informer. His anarchist comrades had recently discovered his treachery and confronted him, demanding that he prove his loyalty. (Such dramatic scenes were not uncommon: the revolutionaries' ranks were riddled with informers.) Only a spectacular terrorist act that put his own life at risk would do. Bogrov had killed Stolypin, in part, to expiate his guilt over betraying his comrades, knowing that they would surely kill him if he did not follow their instructions. Bogrov also spoke bitterly to his interrogators of the regime's intolerable treatment of the Jews, so his ethnic roots may have played a role in the assassination, as well. On a deeper psychological level, though, Bogrov—who was executed just eleven days after firing the fatal shot—may be judged one of the era's numerous romantic suicides. During the last anxious years of the Romanov dynasty, the self-inflicted deaths of disillusioned young men and women had become an epidemic, a fashion, and a fixation, with morbidly curious readers opening their morning papers to find news of the most creative final expressions of despair, often cast as acts of social protest. ("Let my drop of blood fall so that the moment will draw nearer when the sea floods its banks and compels you to come to your senses," read a precocious fifteen-year-old boy's famous letter.) Bogrov was of this affectedly world-weary ilk. In a letter to a friend some months earlier he declared himself to be "depressed, bored, and lonely" and with "no interest in life," which he saw as "nothing more than an endless series of cutlets" he would have to consume. After being exposed as an informer, he could have fled abroad but chose not to. He entered the Kiev theater of his own free will, knowing there would be no escape. At least his chosen path to self-annihilation would ensure that the entire society felt a disorienting shudder.

Russia's new prime minister, Vladimir Kokovtsov, was determined to stop any anti-Jewish violence. He assured a delegation of concerned Jews that "the most decisive measures" would be taken to stop a pogrom. He made good on his promise. Three Cossack regiments were dispatched to predominantly Jewish neighborhoods in Kiev, and nearby governors were ordered to use force if necessary to stop pogroms in their regions. Tsar Nicholas approved all of the new prime minister's actions; he, too, wanted no disorder. Within a few days, the threat of violence had passed.

The country was left to ponder a scandal. How could it be that Dimitry Bogrov had been able to enter the theater, armed, and with a valid pass, and shoot the prime minister at virtually point-blank range? Rumors immediately began that Stolypin had been killed by a right-wing conspiracy with the collusion of the secret police. Colonel Kuliabko was sentenced to a prison term for negligence, but he was the only official punished. General Kurlov was known to have schemed extravagantly against Stolypin, even having the prime minister's mail opened in the hope of finding compromising material. But the tsar terminated an investigation of Kurlov, ensuring that speculation about a conspiracy to assassinate the prime minister would never be laid to rest.

Mendel Beilis knew nothing of politics, assassinations, and fatal blunders, or worse, among men with important titles. To him, all powerful men were simply part of the undifferentiated class of "the bosses." Beilis did not understand what a personal disaster the death of Russia's most powerful boss was for him. Stolypin was likely the only man in the empire who could have helped him. His successor, Kokovtsov, was a decent enough man but not nearly of the same stature; he was a caretaker, not someone to fight political battles. It was bad enough for Beilis that Stolypin was dead, but Stolypin had met his end at the hands of a Jew. The right-wing press, which had vilified Stolypin during his lifetime, deified him now. The newspaper of the Union of Russian People,

Russian Banner, even asserted that Stolypin had been killed by a Jewish conspiracy because he had refused all attempts to bribe him to cover up the ritual murder and leave Mendel Beilis unpunished. If it had ever been possible for the government to drop the case, it was unthinkable now. Bogrov's fatal shot all but assured that Mendel Beilis was going to stand trial.

The world of revolutionaries was as far removed as could be imagined from that of Mendel Beilis, as he awaited his imminent transfer from the quarantine cell to the general prison population. But with Stolypin's death, help would have to come from the most unexpected places. It was from the shadowy and treacherous realm inhabited by men such as Bogrov that two prospective saviors would, astonishingly, emerge.

As for Vera Cheberyak, her "most humble petition" to the tsar, pleading with him to help clear her of suspicion in Andrei's murder, was passed on to the sovereign on September 4, before his return to St. Petersburg. No record exists of any response. Cheberyak, bereaved and besieged, set about gathering all her wiles to deflect suspicion from her door.

6

"Cheberyak Knows Everything"

In mid-September 1911, after spending a month in the squalid quarantine cell, Mendel Beilis was led off to his new quarters. Bidding goodbye to the men who had, in a manner of speaking, acquitted him of Andrei Yushchinsky's murder, he was led to another large cell, which housed about thirty men. If the men of cell number five were like his previous cellmates, then things might still be tolerable, he hoped, at least in terms of human companionship. And at first some of the men were friendly toward him. Two of his fellow prisoners were Jews, one a robber, the other a merchant named Eisenberg who had been imprisoned due to an irregularity with a promissory note. Beilis had grown tired of talking about his predicament, so when Eisenberg asked what he was in for, he told him he was a horse thief.

Weighing on Beilis the most was that he had not seen or heard from his family for nearly two months. The prison authorities did not allow him to send or receive any letters, nor were they required to. Under the Russian legal system, until there was an indictment, a prisoner had very limited legal rights and could not even be represented by an attorney. Was anyone trying to help him? Beilis had no idea. Maybe there was nothing to be done and he would remain in prison forever. His only connection with his family came through the food packages he received every Sunday, but the strongest prisoners wrested the packages from him and left him little or nothing. Of the prison food, all he could bring himself to eat was the bread ration.

Beilis's most immediate concern was his feet. As a former infantryman who had endured many a long march in the cold, he knew that scrupulous care of one's feet—with good-fitting boots, and the regular changing and cleaning of foot wraps (socks were unknown)—had to be strictly observed. (The tsar's army made it clear that a soldier's feet were his own responsibility. On being drafted, he was issued a few pieces of leather and had to make his boots himself or, as most recruits did, take them to a cobbler at his own expense.)

But in his intense state of worry, Beilis couldn't stop pacing the cell hour after hour, and the exposed nails inside the crudely made prison shoes dug into his soles. Walking became an agony. One day, about a week after his arrival in the cell, he noticed the lone chair across the room was empty. He crawled over to the chair and pulled himself onto it. The moment he sat down, a prisoner—one of the men who, until now, had treated him kindly—approached him and said sharply, "Stand up, let me sit down!" Beilis told him his feet hurt and he could not move. The man punched him hard in the face, drawing blood. Beilis screamed and the other prisoners gathered around him. On the verge of passing out, he heard some of the prisoners saying to each other that the assault was an "analysis." An "analysis," he was about to learn, was prison jargon for the testing of a new prisoner to see if he could be trusted. The men who had been nice to him had just been sizing him up. Would he take his blows and remain silent? Or would he turn informer? The greatest sin in jail was to complain to "the bosses." If he held his tongue, he would be considered a "brother." If he told, he was a traitor and might be killed unless the prison authorities removed him in time.

His cellmate Eisenberg, agitated, rushed up to him, and explained that he must say nothing. "You do indeed see," he said softly yet firmly in Beilis's ear, "what kind of people are here. They are convicted criminals, murderers. Act as if nothing happened," he advised. "Stay silent, the pain will go away." Beilis managed to stop crying from the pain. Someone brought him some water and he washed the blood off his face, but he could do nothing about the swelling.

Later, when a guard saw that Beilis had been punched and demanded to know the culprit, Beilis said nothing. But another prisoner, perhaps a naive new arrival, pointed to the man who had hit Beilis and said, "Him."

"Why did you hit him?" the guard shouted.

"Why did he murder a Christian child?" the man retorted.

"And you yourself saw this?" the guard asked.

The guard led Beilis and his assailant toward the prison office, punching the man a few times. Along the way, other officers punched him and he was thrown down a flight of stairs. Despite what the man had done to him, Beilis worried that the man might break his neck.

Even though Beilis himself had, by all rights, passed his "analysis"— he had kept his silence—the warden considered it unsafe to leave him in cell number five. He was transferred to cell number nine, the "informers' room"—known as "the monastery"—for prisoners who were in danger of being killed by their fellow inmates. In the monastery he would be safe from attempts on his life, but his new home would prove to hold other dangers.

If the Beilis family can be said to have been lucky in something, it was that fate had chosen the right brother to be sent to prison. Mendel and his older brother, Aaron, were opposite in physique and temperament. Aaron was a rangy and dapper six-footer. Mendel was of medium height and a little plump—at least before his arrest—and dressed shabbily. Aaron was in a turbulent and unhappy marriage, while Mendel had a placid and satisfying family life. Aaron was caustic, combative, worldly, and intensely interested in politics. (He likely had a better education than Mendel, with their father making the common choice to concentrate the family's resources on one son.) Aaron worked on Kiev's stock exchange—one of the strivers out of a Sholem Aleichem story. Mendel was an agreeable sort with no ambition other than to secure his children a good education and a better life. He could, as he was finding out, stoically endure hardship—harsh interrogation, near starvation, even a bloody "analysis." Aaron, who never could hold his tongue, would likely not have lasted a day in prison. Aaron was not close to his brother. The two men inhabited different worlds and saw each other only a few times a year. But Aaron would prove the right man to fight for his brother's freedom.

In mid-September, soon after the assassination of Prime Minister Stolypin, Aaron took Mendel's wife, Esther, for a consultation with Arnold Davidovich Margolin, one of Kiev's best-known defense attorneys. The thirty-four-year-old Margolin was famous for his work as an advocate for victims of pogroms and for defending Jews who had organized armed self-defense units to fight against the Black Hundred marauders. An ardent Zionist, he served as the president of the Russian branch of the Jewish Territorial Organization, devoted to creating a Jewish national home in a place other than Palestine. (The group believed a return to the ancestral homeland was an unrealistic goal and explored the possibility of settlement in, among other places, Uganda and Angola.) Margolin was also the son of one of Russia's wealthiest men. His father, David Margolin, was a self-made multimillionaire who owned two shipping companies and a number of sugar refineries and factories in the Kiev region. The younger Margolin was as well connected as any Jew in the city. He was someone who could marshal the support of Kiev's Jewish grandees.

In explaining Mendel's predicament to Margolin, Aaron likely communicated his somewhat condescending attitude toward his brother. He did not appreciate Mendel's simple virtues. To Aaron, his brother was a person without much initiative, someone "who had always worked for others." He more than once implied that Mendel had been taken advantage of by the Zaitsevs who, he felt, paid him poorly. Aaron was agitated. The main thing he wanted Margolin to know was that his brother was a simple man with little education who did not know his rights. He and Esther wanted action to speed Mendel's release from prison.

Margolin did his best to calm them down. He shared the prevailing belief in Kiev's elite circles that, despite the unpleasantness of the prime minister's assassination by a Jew, the Yushchinsky matter would be cleared up in a few days and Mendel Beilis would soon be released. He sincerely could not believe that the regime would go forward with a trial for ritual murder. He also explained to Aaron and Esther that, at this point, there was little of a practical nature he could do. Under the Russian justice system, a defense lawyer had no role until the preliminary investigation was concluded, the indictment handed down, and the defendant bound over for trial.

Margolin did not share with Esther and Aaron that he still had some small concern that this strange case would go forward. In any event, he was not one for complacency. Beilis's release could not be taken for granted and he set about organizing a defense, in the unlikely event that one should become necessary. He arranged a meeting with Vasily Fenenko, the investigating magistrate, whom he knew quite well. Fenenko was eager to talk, and what he told Margolin was at once reassuring and worrisome. Fenenko wanted it known that he believed Beilis to be innocent, and he asked Margolin to inform Jewish leaders privately of his view of the case. It was a matter of his honor, the magistrate implied. "The evidence against Beilis is laughable and absurd,"

Fenenko emphatically told Margolin, according to the latter's memoir. "I am convinced he will be released within a few days." He told the defense attorney that he believed the murder was the work of a gang of professional thieves. Fenenko, reasonable man that he was, still could not believe the case would go forward.

Margolin found it troubling that Beilis had been arrested over Fenenko's extreme objections. He quickly secured the consent of Kiev's Jewish leaders to form a defense committee. Members included Rabbi Shlomo Ha-Cohen Aronson, Kiev's leading "spiritual rabbi" (as opposed to the official "crown rabbi" whose salary was paid by the state); Mark Zaitsev, the son of Jonah Zaitsev, founder of the family's sugar refining business; Dr. G. B. Bykhovsky, the senior physician of the Zaitsev hospital; and three lawyers, including Margolin. One of the committee's first actions was to send a telegram to Russia's leading Jewish defense attorney, Oskar Gruzenberg, asking him to come to Kiev as soon as possible. Gruzenberg was best known for his political cases. He had defended the revolutionary Leon Trotsky, a leader of the 1905 revolution (he was sentenced to internal exile, from which he easily escaped) and represented the writer Maxim Gorky when he was accused of inciting armed insurrection. Among his fellow attorneys, he was greatly respected for his courtroom skills in appeals cases, which required the most airtight arguments based on fine points of the law. For this new case, he had unmatched practical experience, having successfully defended the Vilna barber David Blondes, who had been accused of attempted ritual murder a decade earlier. Gruzenberg came to Kiev and met with the defense committee to discuss a course of action should Beilis be formally charged with murder. In the following weeks, in the fall of 1911, he traveled to Kiev periodically to consult on the case.

Gruzenberg and Margolin respected each other greatly but had a fundamental difference from the beginning over how to proceed. Margolin was chronically frustrated by what he regarded as the passivity of Jewish leaders in the face of threats from outside. They "were very honorable men," he later wrote in his memoir, "but rather indecisive and timid whenever it was a question of showing some initiative in defending Jewish interests" against tsarist acts of repression. Margolin favored an active defense on all fronts—in public and behind the scenes. Gruzenberg, on the other hand, was confident that, if worse came to worst, no jury would convict a defendant, even a Jew, based on such preposterous evidence as existed. "In truth," Gruzenberg later wrote in his own memoirs, "I was most concerned about the Jews doing something foolish." In his book he refrained from mentioning his colleague's name, but when it came to foolishness that could wreck the defense, it was Margolin who most worried him.

The deep differences between Gruzenberg and Margolin over the case may have stemmed from their different backgrounds and relationships toward their Jewishness. Gruzenberg was as Russified as a Jew could be without actually converting to Russian Orthodoxy. A decade older than Margolin, he was born in 1866 in the Ukrainian city of Ekaterinoslav (now Dniepropetrovsk) but grew up in Kiev before moving to St. Petersburg to practice law. He had an intense and lifelong love of the Russian language and culture. (The opening line of his memoirs, written decades after the trial: "The first word that reached my consciousness was Russian.") He had no comparable affection for Jewish culture. Gruzenberg's father, a well-to-do merchant, had been an ardent follower of the *Haskalah,* or movement for Jewish enlightenment, that sought to modernize Judaism and Jewish life. The son could not speak Yiddish and had little religious education. But his father also enjoined him never to abandon his Jewish heritage. By adulthood, the mixed imperative had left Gruzenberg spiritually stranded, conflicted, and bereft of a sense of belonging. He did not feel a connection to the Jewish people and expressed antipathy to religiosity in general, disliking its "theatrical character."

It would take two traumatic experiences to awaken Gruzenberg's sense of obligation to the Jewish people. When he was a student in Kiev, his home was raided in the middle of the night by policemen looking for Jews living in the city illegally, without residence permits. By the time of the raid, his father had died, the family had run out of money, and his mother was living in his household. Gruzenberg's papers were in order, but his mother's were not, or so the police insisted. The poor woman was led off to the police station and spent a night in jail. Gruzenberg managed to obtain her release and avert her deportation to the Pale of Settlement thanks only to the intervention of a wealthy acquaintance.

The incident ingrained in Gruzenberg a determination to fight autocratic tyranny—but it took the funeral of his first child, who died in infancy, to bring him to a feeling of special responsibility toward his people. Years later he still recalled with distaste the pious Jews, his supposed brethren, who descended on his home after his son's death and took possession of the body. "Strangers," he called them, "wearing long sidelocks and dressed in long robes, dirty with grease." He found these men, and the ritual they imposed on him and on his son's body, unnerving and almost grotesque. Yet, to his confusion, he was struck with a profound sense that these men had a claim on him that could not be denied. "Along with my child," he wrote, "they had also taken my soul." He asked himself why it was he felt these religious men had a claim on him. He began to read books about Judaism and at first decided that while the Jews have suffered, so have all peoples. He considered himself to be an enlightened man, above national feeling, but then found himself asking whether such an attitude was not a kind of egoism. In this moment of self-examination he came to understand a simple truth: Jews needed to help their fellow Jews. If they did not, then very likely no one else would, and they would be lost.

Margolin, too, struggled with his religious and national identity. He later summed up his early years: "Jewish background and synagogue; Russian [native] language and school; Ukrainian village and song . . . I was tossing in pain for a long time, trying to find a synthesis of these impressions and feelings." But Margolin's father—who, like Gruzenberg's, was one of the *maskilim,* adherents of the *Haskalah*—more successfully balanced enlightenment and religion. The son attended a Russian gymnasium, but the household was strictly observant; Margolin studied Hebrew and at the age of thirteen read from the Torah in his synagogue as a bar mitzvah. At the same time his affection for his city and for Ukraine ran deep. "I loved my native city Kiev, from my earliest days," he recalled, "loved the Dnieper, the Ukrainian village with its housetops of straw, the cherry trees, and the golden yellow fields of the country." By adulthood he had resolved his inner contradictions, and his various cultural attachments lived in harmony. Unlike Gruzenberg, he was entirely comfortable in his modern Jewishness. Though a thoroughly secular man, he maintained a lifelong affection for his religion, the sight of any synagogue always stirring in him a deep feeling of connection.

No one could say that Gruzenberg did not fight for Jewish rights, but he did so strictly within the conventional bounds of his profession. His weapon was his mastery, as he put it, of "the iron whip of the law." Margolin, on the other hand, was by nature an activist. Law was just one weapon in his arsenal. He was coming to the conclusion that Mendel Beilis needed more than an ordinary defense. It was not enough to show that the defendant was *not* the culprit. "It was necessary," he later explained, "to respond to the prosecution not with a defense, but with an offensive." Margolin decided he must turn detective and find the real killers.

Vera Cheberyak did not know of Margolin's plan, but she had reason enough to feel cornered. The sneering references to her in the pro-Beilis press had not abated; her name had become a byword for villainy. ("Vera Cheberyak, a woman of a certain reputation," the *Kievan* referred to her with delicate scorn.) Now that her gang was mostly in jail or under police surveillance, she had been deprived of her capacity to intimidate. People were willing to testify against her. She was under investigation for at least four crimes, including robbery, fencing stolen goods, and fraud, and she was fearful that her friends—if they ever truly were her friends—would go to the police and inform on her about more of her crimes. When she learned that an acquaintance was going to be questioned by the police, she tested the woman's reliability in an unusual way. She took her to a store and asked her to pick out a pair of gloves. Then she asked her: "If I took those gloves, if I stole them, would you tell on me?" The woman said no, she wouldn't. "And if they beat you?" Cheberyak asked. The woman admitted that then, yes, she might. "You," Cheberyak told her, "are a bad friend."

Above all, Cheberyak was concerned that some way would be found to tie her to Andrei's murder. Of some comfort was the fact that her archenemy, Nikolai Krasovsky, was gone from the scene. His temporary assignment in Kiev had been allowed to lapse on September 8, and he returned to his post in the city of Khodorkov. Krasovsky did not fight to stay on the case. He did not want to see an innocent man in jail but had lost the heart to deal with the case any longer, having proved all too correct in his original prediction that the case would cause him nothing but trouble. But he was mistaken in believing that his departure from Kiev would bring an end to the intrigues against him. Within a few months he would be drawn into the case again, as he was compelled to struggle for his own freedom as well as that of Mendel Beilis. But for now he savored the relief of returning home to his quiet provincial post.

Krasovsky's able protégé, Officer Evtikhy Kirichenko, was still on the case in Kiev and actively pursuing Cheberyak. Kirichenko could not get out of his mind the chilling image of Cheberyak possessed by rage and fear at the mention of Andrei's name as he questioned her dying son, Zhenya. Kirichenko went back over ground that he and Krasovsky had previously covered, reinterviewing people who might spark fresh leads. Within a few weeks he turned up the piece of the case against Cheberyak that had been missing: a witness to the crime.

Or at least a witness of sorts. Zinaida Malitskaya lived directly below Vera Cheberyak at no. 40 Upper Yurkovskaya Street. She and Cheberyak had once been friends, but their relationship had devolved into intense mutual hatred. Kirichenko had witnessed the two women's antagonism in May when Cheberyak assaulted Malitskaya for taunting her when her home was searched. At the time, he had talked to Malitskaya briefly and she had told him she had something to say about Cheberyak, but she ended up being questioned by another investigator, to whom she only said that Cheberyak was "a dubious person" and that she had little doubt she would end up at hard labor. Kirichenko was nagged by a sense that Malitskaya might know more than she was telling. On November 10, he questioned her again. This time she revealed that, on a morning some days before Andrei's body was discovered, she had heard suspicious noises overhead. Kirichenko immediately arranged for a formal deposition of her to be taken by Investigator Fenenko.

The layout of Malitskaya's ground-floor apartment, which adjoined the state liquor store she ran, was exactly the same as that of the Cheberyaks'—a vestibule with a kitchen and a small room on the left, another small room on the right, and a large room at the back. She had no difficulty pinpointing the location of every footstep above her, she said. On the morning in question in March, at around eleven a.m., when her store was empty of customers, she took a moment to step into her apartment. Overhead, she heard Vera's front door slam and then a few footsteps resound near the door. She claimed she could recognize the footsteps of all the Cheberyaks and she was confident the woman at the door was Vera Cheberyak. Then, she said:

> I clearly heard the quick, light steps of a child going from the door of the large room in the direction of the small room on the right side of the vestibule. Then I heard the quick steps of a number of adults

going in the direction of the same door [of the small room] where I heard a child's steps going. At the beginning I clearly heard a child crying, then a child's squeak, and finally some kind of commotion. I thought then that something unusual and strange had happened in Vera Cheberyak's apartment.

The steps of the adults around the boy, after they had caught up with him, were clearly audible. The boy's steps whispered only a brief while on the floor before fading out. She had the impression that a child had been grabbed and something had been done with him, but she had not seen any reason to be especially alarmed. Malitskaya said she then went back to her store and complained to a woman customer about the noise upstairs. The Cheberyaks were always making noise, she said. The woman told her that she saw the children leaving the house earlier, so she thought Malitskaya might get some peace. Malitskaya was puzzled about why, then, she had heard a child upstairs.

Fenenko knew there were problems with Malitskaya as a witness. She hated Cheberyak and fought with her, but then it was hard to find anyone in Lukianovka who knew Cheberyak and had not. She had waited months to come forward with her story. She explained she had been afraid of Cheberyak and guessed the police would eventually figure everything out, but her husband told her she had an obligation to tell what she knew. Her husband, Fyodor, backed up her story, telling Fenenko he had told her weeks earlier to reveal what she had heard. Fenenko went to Cheberyak's old apartment with another officer and verified that footsteps and muffled voices really could be heard downstairs. Malitskaya seemed credible to Fenenko, which strengthened his conviction that Cheberyak and her gang were behind Andrei's murder.

Beilis's path to "the monastery," cell number nine, had been harrowing, but if the price was being punched in the face, then it was almost worth it. With only fourteen men, the cell was less crowded, his fellows were of a less crude sort, and the living conditions were somewhat better than in cell number five. The sense of menace was gone and Beilis even made a friend. Ivan Kozachenko was a gaunt fellow of thirty with whom he appeared to have quite a bit in common. Kozachenko told Beilis that he, too, was an army veteran and an innocent man, though his alleged crime—robbery and assault—was of a conventional sort. Before he had fallen on hard times, he said, he had for two years been an officer in the Kiev police force's investigative division. Over the next two months, Beilis and Kozachenko spoke often. Beilis told him of his unbearable anxiety that nothing was being done to gain his freedom. Kozachenko listened sympathetically. If it weren't for this kind man, Beilis was sure, he would be losing his mind.

Kozachenko had fair hope of an acquittal, which meant Beilis now had someone who might be able to help him on the outside. Kozachenko agreed to contact Beilis's family if he was released. For now, Kozachenko volunteered to help Beilis smuggle out letters. He knew that one of the guards took letters for a few kopeks and offered to act as a go-between. Beilis could not believe his good fortune and, indeed, should not have believed it: Kozachenko was a police informer.

Kozachenko had been placed in Beilis's cell at the request of Lieutenant Colonel Pavel Ivanov, deputy chief of the Kiev Gendarmes, who was in charge of the agency's investigation into the Yushchinsky murder. An acquaintance described Kozachenko as a swindler who would pick your pocket as soon as look at you. But Kozachenko was not an especially successful crook. Before landing in prison he was homeless and went about in tattered clothing, eking out the occasional ruble by selling wild game birds.

Later, not without reason, some observers and historians would assume that from the beginning Ivanov's intent was to manufacture evidence against Beilis. The truth was more haphazard. Ivanov was, at this point, pursuing the investigation honestly. He did not believe that Beilis was guilty. The planting of an informer might, if anything, have aided in Beilis's exoneration (though that was not Ivanov's goal). But this was not how matters worked out. In mid-November, after Kozachenko obtained a slip of paper and a pencil, Beilis dictated a brief note to his wife in his broken Russian while another prisoner wrote it down, correcting the grammatical mistakes. (Presumably Kozachenko demanded the letter be written in Russian, rather than have Beilis write it himself in Yiddish, so that he would know what was in it.) In the note Beilis inquired after Esther's health and that of the children. Then he asks "whether anyone is doing anything for me" and pleads, "How long will I have to suffer unjustly?"

Kozachenko took the letter to the guard who, after receiving permis-

Andrei Yushchinsky's
bloody shirt.

The cave in Kiev where
Andrei's body was found.

Front page of the *Double Headed Eagle*, the organ of Vladimir Golubev's right-wing youth group. The bottom lines, under Andrei's autopsy photo, read: "Christians, guard your children! On March 17 the Yid Peisach begins."

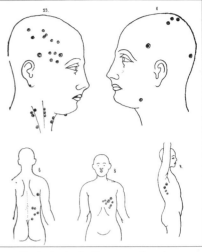

Pathologist's diagram showing Andrei's four dozen wounds.

Andrei Yushchinsky in his coffin.

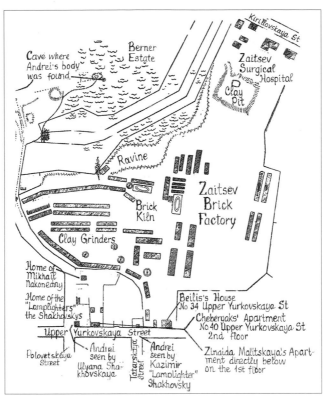

The crime scene and its environs
(a translation of an official map made for the court).

The "Lamplighters," Kazimir and Ulyana
Shakhovsky. They were among the last
people to see Andrei Yushchinsky alive.
*(Russian State Film and Photo Archive at
Krasnogorsk/Abamedia)*

The home of Vera and Vasily Cheberyak,
down the street from that of Mendel Beilis's
family. The Cheberyaks' apartment is
on the upper right.

Кто убійцы? Загадочное дѣло объ убійствѣ мальчика Андрея Ющинскаго. Однако журналисту С. И. Браазулю-Брушковскому, личными арестовать и содержится въ тюрьмѣ еврей Бейлисъ, котораго обвиняютъ въ убійствѣ ...

Вѣра Чебырякъ.   Петръ Сингаевскій (Плисъ), братъ Вѣры Чебырякъ, извѣстный профессіональный воръ, бывшій мясникъ.   Борисъ Рудзинскій.   Иванъ Латышевъ, извѣстный среди воровъ подъ кличкой «Ванька Рыжій».

The headline reads "Who Are the Killers?"
FROM LEFT TO RIGHT: Vera Cheberyak; her half brother,
Peter "Velveteen" Singaevsky; Boris "Borka" Rudzinsky;
and Ivan "Red Vanya" Latyshev. Months later, Latyshev would jump
out a police precinct window to his death. *(Collection of Vladimir Belko)*

Zhenya Cheberyak, Vera's son.
He was also Andrei Yushchinsky's best friend
and one of the last people to see him alive.

Vera Cheberyak.

Nikolai Krasovsky, flanked by his two assistants,
Alexei Vygranov *(left)* and Adam Polishchuk *(right)*.
Polishchuk would betray Krasovsky and join the
conspiracy to frame Mendel Beilis.

Vladimir D. Nabokov, father of the
novelist, liberal political leader,
and journalist who reported on the trial.
*(Central State Archive of Film, Photo and
Audio Documents, St. Petersburg)*

Vladimir Golubev, who first pointed to Beilis
as a suspect. *(Russian State Film and Photo
Archive at Krasnogorsk/Abamedia)*

Mendel Beilis leaving court in May 1913,
the rolled-up indictment in his hand.
(Collection of Vladimir Belko)

The Beilis family during the trial.

Aaron Beilis, Mendel's brother.

Minister of Justice Ivan Shcheglovitov.
(Central State Archive of Film, Photo and Audio Documents, St. Petersburg)

Nikolai Maklakov, minister of the interior and brother of Beilis's attorney Vasily Maklakov.

Grigory Chaplinsky, Kiev's chief prosecutor and architect of the case against Beilis.

Vasily Maklakov, member of the Russian parliament and of the Beilis defense team. *(Central State Archive of Film, Photo and Audio Documents, St. Petersburg)*

Arnold Davidovich Margolin, Beilis's first attorney, who made it his mission to find the real killers.

The defense team.
FROM LEFT TO RIGHT: Dimitry Grigorovich-Barsky, Nikolai Karabchevsky, Oskar Gruzenberg, and Alexander Zarudny.

sion from the deputy warden, changed into civilian clothes and delivered it to Esther Beilis. Esther was overjoyed to hear from her husband. She was illiterate so she ran to get a neighbor to have the note read to her and to dictate a letter in response. She gave it to the prison guard along with fifty kopeks for his trouble. The deputy warden deposited the fifty kopeks in a collection box for the prisoners, examined Esther's letter, and gave the guard permission to give it to Beilis. The guard handed it to Kozachenko who, no doubt desiring to keep his "friend" in a state of nervousness, did not pass it on to him.

Having received no response, Beilis sank into despair. (If he had gotten Esther's brief note, it would not have brought him much comfort. She said nothing about any efforts to help him. "Do not worry," she wrote, "God will provide and you will be freed. God knows the truth that you are in prison for no reason.") By November 22, the four-month anniversary of his arrest, he had not received a single communication from anyone in the outside world. But Beilis still felt hopeful because Kozachenko had been acquitted and was about to be released. Beilis hastened to dictate another letter, a longer one, this time transcribed by a helpful nobleman who had been jailed on fraud charges. The letter read:

My dear wife, the person who will give you this note served in prison with me . . . I ask you to welcome him as one of our own. If it weren't for him I would have been lost long ago. Do not be afraid of this man, he can help you a great deal in my case. Tell him who is testifying falsely against me. Go with him to Mr. Dubovik [the factory manager]. Why is no one doing anything to help me? . . . I've been suffering here for four months, and it is clear no one is doing anything. Everyone knows I am here unjustly as if I am a thief or a murderer. Everyone knows I am an honest person . . . I feel that I cannot endure it anymore if I have to stay in prison any longer. If this man asks you for any money, give him some for expenses . . . Is anyone doing anything to get me out on bail? These enemies of mine who testify falsely against me are getting revenge on me because I didn't give them firewood . . . All the best to you and the children.

Kozachenko asked Beilis to sign the letter himself and write a few words to make it clear the letter was from him. Taking the pencil, Beilis squeezed in at the bottom of the page a postscript in his ungrammatical Russian: "I am Mendel Beilis don't worries you can depends on this person as on me." Beilis read over the letter several times before turning it over to Kozachenko who folded it, wrapped it in a handker-chief, and placed it in a side pocket of his jacket. When it was time for Kozachenko to go, Beilis started crying and pleaded with him to "do something" to help get him out of prison. Kozachenko promised that he would and told him not to worry, that in two or three weeks he would be free.

Kozachenko had no intention of turning over this letter to the authorities, likely because he was hoping to extract money from the Beilis family for his supposed assistance. Desperate to secure his help, Beilis, according to a cellmate's later testimony, had impulsively offered to pay his friend's hundred-ruble legal bill. Being an independent con man was looking to be more lucrative than being a police informer. But as Kozachenko was being processed for release, a guard asked him if he was taking any notes from prisoners. He told Kozachenko he would frisk him, so there was no point in hiding anything. As Kozachenko reached into his pocket and turned over the letter, his imagination began working.

Why Kozachenko did what he did next is not entirely clear. He liked to make up stories and was a convincing liar; even the criminals in cell number nine believed him when he said he had been a policeman. He may have been afraid that attempting to smuggle out the letter would get him into trouble, so to turn the situation to his advantage he would say what he thought the authorities wanted him to say. Moreover, he was of a type that Beilis in fact would encounter fairly rarely in prison: a visceral Jew-hater. A longtime acquaintance later recalled going on a walk a few years earlier with a very drunk Kozachenko in their home village when they came upon a Jewish wedding where children were running around. Kozachenko started hitting them. Then he started going after the adults, threatening that the Christian villagers would soon "stir up a riot against them." Both fear and hatred must have swirled in his mind as his way to the prison exit was blocked and he was led off to explain the presence of the contraband letter.

By the time he reached the warden's office Kozachenko had con-cocted the core of his story. The missive might seem harmless, he explained, but it was in fact a letter of introduction to the Jewish cabal whose mission was to obstruct the investigation. He was then delivered immediately for questioning by Investigator Fenenko. Kozachenko explained how the letter had come to be written and how Beilis had entrusted him to deliver it to his wife. Then he made a horrifying claim: Beilis had enlisted him to poison two witnesses in the case, "the Lamplighter," Shakhovsky, and a man who went by the nickname of "Frog," whose name he did not know. "I expressed my agreement," Kozachenko said, "but, of course, I would not have done that since I don't want a Yid to drink Russian blood." Beilis had instructed him to dispatch the two men using vodka laced with strychnine, Kozachenko declared. The strychnine would come from the Jewish Hospital adjoining the factory grounds. He said that Beilis had told him that the Lamplighter had to be eliminated because he had seen him with Andrei Yushchinsky. Beilis had not explained what he had against "Frog." Kozachenko would initially be given three hundred or four hundred or even five hundred rubles for his expenses, but if he succeeded in his deadly mission, "they would give me money enough to last for my entire life, and the money would be given to me by the entire Jewish nation."

One part of his wild statement did ring true. Beilis, he said, had told him he was sure "that if he were convicted, then the whole Jewish nation would suffer." Beilis was indeed coming to understand the larger importance of his case and that the honor of the Jewish people depended on what happened to him and how he conducted himself. It was a thought that would sustain him in prison and, it is no exaggeration to say, save his life. And the first time he expressed it may have been to this false friend.

Kozachenko was then questioned by Lieutenant Colonel Ivanov, who headed the Corps of Gendarmes' independent investigation into the murder. Ivanov undertook to check the veracity of Kozachenko's story. He deputized Kozachenko as a "colleague" and sent him out to the Zaitsev factory, where he could present himself as Beilis's former cellmate and gather information. Ivanov had Kozachenko followed, and he questioned him upon his return from each of his forays. Eventually, Ivanov caught Kozachenko in a clear lie: he had invented a meeting with Aaron Beilis that had not happened. Ivanov brought in the agents who had tailed him and confronted him. "I screamed at Kozachenko," Ivanov later testified, "and said that I would immediately send him to prison. Kozachenko fell onto his knees, started crying, and said, 'Forgive me, I made it all up.'" In conversations with others about the incident, Ivanov explicitly declared that Kozachenko confessed that his whole story about Beilis had been a fabrication.

Ivanov immediately called Fenenko and told him that Kozachenko's testimony was false. He asked if he should deliver a report, but the chief prosecutor, Chaplinsky, intervened, saying no report was needed, that everything would be sorted out during the investigation. In fact, Chaplinsky had no intention of disregarding Kozachenko's accusations. The deposition remained in the record, never formally retracted. This testimony was, of course, as Chaplinsky had said about the alcoholic Shakhovskys', "not completely firm." But that was not a serious problem in the mind of the prosecutor. Chaplinsky believed that a solid case could be made out of less-than-firm building blocks if enough of them could be found. It did not matter that one part of the story made no sense—"Frog" (the shoemaker Nakonechny) had given testimony that was favorable to Beilis. He reported to justice minister Shcheglovitov that if the Shakhovskys' testimony gave sufficient cause for Beilis's arrest, then Kozachenko's strengthened the case enough to proceed with the indictment.

Kozachenko was never punished for his perjury, but Beilis suffered severely for trying to smuggle out the letters. Two days after he bade Kozachenko farewell, the door of his cell opened and a guard called his name. Beilis was told to get his things. He felt a surge of hope. Was he finally being freed? Maybe his friend had managed to help him already. "I thought perhaps God Almighty was having mercy," he recalled, "but wait, it was too good to be true." Instead, he was summoned to the prison office, where he was confronted with the letters he had written. For the violation of prison rules, he was punished with solitary confinement. His new cell, as he recalled in his lengthy interview after the trial in the Yiddish newspaper *Haynt,* was "simply a grave for living people," dark, cold, and totally bare:

> A cold shiver ran through me. I began to walk around, back and forth—in order to warm up a little. But it did not help. I felt the tips of my fingers freezing. What saved me a little was only the small lamp which stood on the iron-forged table, with which I warmed my hands the entire night. And just imagine that in such a room, better said a grave, I would have to stay for the entire winter. They did bring me a mattress the next day; however, the cold and darkness

were unbearable. I felt just like an animal in a cage. Entire days I paced from one corner to another. I longed for some nice light. I literally climbed the walls and managed to reach the tiny little window which was high up and took a look at the light of the world.

In November, the attorney Arnold Margolin made what small steps he could toward helping Beilis. He had Aaron write a letter to his brother instructing him to file a motion for dismissal of the case and request testimony from expert witnesses—including pathologists and a noted Hebraist—who could refute the case against him. (The authorities never delivered the letter, but it was unlikely that Beilis would have been capable of acting on the advice in any event.) Margolin and Gruzenberg drafted a petition on behalf of Beilis's wife, Esther, requesting a prompt conclusion to the preliminary investigation. But the investigation dragged on, an indictment grew more likely, and, for Margolin, the need to identify the real killers grew more urgent. The ever-cautious Fenenko, who had already taken an uncharacteristic risk by secretly talking to Margolin, could offer no concrete assistance. Margolin knew he had to venture somehow into the criminal underworld. But he was stymied about finding a way in.

The attorney's unlikely entrée to the criminal lower depths appeared in the somewhat absurd figure of a journalist named Stepan Brazul-Brushkovsky. For some weeks Brazul (as he was usually called) had been conducting his own private investigation into the Yushchinsky murder. He was, in a way, the mirror image of the young right-wing leader Vladimir Golubev, who had first proposed Mendel Beilis as a suspect. Brazul, too, was an amateur for whom the case had become an obsession. His colleagues at *Kiev Opinion* mocked him for it. But he was a liberal and, being married to a Jewish woman, quite literally a philo-Semite. As a journalist, he was a journeyman of modest reputation. As a detective, he was inept and laughably gullible. But his investigation would improbably, even farcically, lurch toward revealing a plausible scenario for Andrei's murder.

Brazul knew Krasovsky from his days as Kiev's chief detective. He had approached him over the summer and tried to persuade him they should work together on the Yushchinsky case, but Krasovsky was, not surprisingly, uninterested. They remained in touch, however, and Krasovsky confided to Brazul his frustration at the arrest of an innocent man. He could not share any specific information, but he gave Brazul one piece of advice. "I'll put it simply," he told him. "The whole case, the whole riddle lies with Vera Cheberyak. Focus yourself on Vera Cheberyak, and the case will be cracked." Brazul, who could be dense, apparently failed to understand what Krasovsky was trying to tell him: that he believed Cheberyak was behind the crime. Brazul understood him to mean only that Cheberyak had useful information. Still, on that assumption, he began to focus on her with single-minded intensity.

Brazul took the opportunity to introduce himself to Cheberyak at Zhenya's funeral and express his condolences. When the young journalist contacted Cheberyak again sometime in mid-September, she did not know quite what to make of him—or how to take advantage of him. That would take time to figure out. Meanwhile, she accepted his invitations to go out to eat and drink with his friends, which would at least allow her to enjoy some fine free meals. As they met over the next few weeks, she talked a great deal about her dead children, who she was sure had been poisoned by someone. Her husband had been let go from his job at the telegraph office, and she had to work, picking up the odd client as a midwife and "healer." (She had taken some classes in midwifery as a young woman but never completed the course.) The rest of her time was taken up by the endless summonings of investigators. She was being persecuted, she said, by Fenenko and Lieutenant Colonel Ivanov, who unjustly suspected her of involvement in Andrei's murder. She complained of feeling hounded and harassed. She was exhausted. "I'm a woman," she told him. "I have a little girl, I need to be home." Blind to her scheming nature, Brazul may have been unduly moved by her plight.

For two months, Cheberyak continued to deny her involvement in the crime and said nothing of what she might know about who had killed Andrei. Then, on November 29, according to Brazul, she told him that, while she didn't know who the culprit was, she was in a position to find out. She suggested that there was truth to the original theory that Andrei's stepfather and uncle had been involved. Brazul believed her. A colleague who joined Brazul for one of these evenings told him bluntly, "This is a woman who always lies. She lies even when she's telling the truth. And if she's talking in her sleep, then while she's talking she probably also lies." Brazul ignored the warning. He continued to insist Cheberyak was not involved in the crime but could find the killer.

On December 1, Brazul dropped by Vera Cheberyak's house and was surprised to find her lying in bed, "half dead," as he recalled, her head wrapped in bandages. "That's it," she told him, "yesterday I really got it good." Cheberyak said that she had been coming home at night when two men assaulted her, one of them beating her with an iron "chocolate bar." (Cheberyak's speech was always peppered with criminal slang.) Bandaged and bloody, she now revealed to Brazul what she said were her true suspicions regarding who had killed Andrei. The night that she was ambushed, it had been too dark for her to see her attackers, but she was sure that one of them had been Pavel Mifle, the lover she had blinded six years earlier by throwing sulfuric acid in his face. She was certain he had organized the vicious assault because he knew that she was trying to find out who had killed Andrei. Cheberyak said she had told Mifle she was going out to buy candles that she would use to divine the murderer's identity—the villain's face, she told him, would appear before her in the candles' glow. Upon hearing that, she claimed Mifle said, "Don't you start divining." Mifle had to have been involved in Andrei's murder, she claimed to Brazul, along with Andrei's stepfather, Luka, and others, including Mifle's brother and mother, but she explained that she had to go to a prison in the city of Kharkov to talk to a convict who had more information. To Brazul, this all made perfect sense.

Brazul felt he was in possession of valuable, sensational information. As it happened, he also knew Margolin well. They had worked together at two of Kiev's progressive newspapers. Margolin regarded Brazul with a mixture of admiration and condescension, remarking that "his work was notable for its quixotic character, in the best sense of the term." When his friend told him that he was on the trail of Andrei's killer, Margolin was skeptical. Brazul was honest and well intentioned, but he was no detective. So Margolin at first refused when Brazul suggested setting up a meeting with Cheberyak, but Margolin did visit Fenenko to share what Brazul had told him. "No sooner than I had mentioned the name of Cheberyak," Margolin recalled, "than Fenenko repeated literally the same words I had heard from [Brazul]: 'Cheberyak knows everything about this case.'" Fenenko was still tight-lipped about specifics, but Margolin correctly understood that he meant Cheberyak was not just a witness who "knew" things but rather was an accomplice to the crime.

Fenenko's office was in the building of the Kiev Circuit Court and

Margolin had some other business to take care of at the court that day, December 3. As he passed Fenenko's office again, someone pointed out "a small, thin restless figure" waiting to be interrogated. It was Vera Cheberyak. "The upper portion of her head and one eye were bandaged," Margolin recalled in his memoir of the case. "It was sufficient, however, to see only that one eye to gain an idea that she was a dangerous woman. She was casting feverish, hateful looks in every direction, scrutinizing everybody suspiciously." Margolin, like so many people who crossed Cheberyak's path, appears to have been overwhelmed at the mere sight of her, by the malevolence her physical presence conveyed. Margolin had not intended to get personally involved in the investigation. In the event that Beilis was indicted, he would be one of the defendant's attorneys, so it would only be prudent to keep his distance from potential witnesses. But now his fascination with Cheberyak was beginning to overpower his caution.

The next day Margolin told Brazul that he would meet with Cheberyak, though only if measures were taken to protect his identity. As it happened, he was going on business to Kharkov, about three hundred miles east of Kiev, and could meet with Cheberyak there. Margolin later claimed, unconvincingly, that he merely wanted to avoid having Cheberyak find him in Kiev and pester him, but he must have known that what he was about to do carried tremendous risks: it could lead to the unmasking of Andrei's killers and exonerate Beilis. Or it could end in catastrophe for the defense, lending credence to the idea that cunning Jews were secretly conniving to pin the case on a Christian woman.

Kiev's Jewish leaders maintained their wariness, as Fenenko found when he officially deposed Margolin's father, David, who was the vice chairman of a group known as the Representation for Jewish Welfare of the Kiev Executive Authority. (The very name of this body, as cumbersome in Russian as it is in English, suggested that Jews were an alien presence, requiring something in the nature of a foreign mission to their own government. Indeed, Jews were officially classified by the regime as an "alien" people.) Rumors had apparently reached the authorities that certain Jews might be meddling in the case. Fenenko, almost certainly on orders from above, questioned the elder Margolin about whether this allegation had any basis in fact. The industrialist, in all sincerity, assured Fenenko that no such unofficial investigation was being conducted and that he himself would oppose such an effort because the matter was the responsibility of the proper authorities. But Fenenko himself had by this time lost faith in the authorities, felt powerless to resolve the cases, and was, in fact, encouraging the elder Margolin's son to do whatever he could to push the investigation forward and prevent an innocent man from being indicted.

Arnold Margolin arrived in Kharkov by express train on December 7 and checked into a suite at the luxurious Grand Hotel where he presented his internal passport, which all citizens needed for travel, copying down the requisite information in the register, including that he was "of the Jewish faith." Brazul arrived on a different train with Cheberyak, having treated her to a first-class compartment, and secured her a room in the somewhat less-grand Hotel Hermitage. Accompanying them was a former police officer, Alexei Vygranov, disguised in a university student's uniform, who had been Krasovsky's assistant and was now helping Brazul with his investigation.

Margolin was given to mocking Brazul's pretensions to be a detective, but his own efforts to conceal his identity were remarkably clumsy. He received Cheberyak in his own rooms at a hotel where he had registered under his own name. Brazul presented the esteemed gentleman to Cheberyak as a member of the Kharkov city Duma, failing to explain why a resident of the city would be staying in a hotel.

The meeting lasted a little less than an hour. Cheberyak, according to Margolin, immediately took charge of the conversation. She removed her bandage, displaying to all the gash on her head, and claimed she had been beaten by Pavel Mifle, who had poisoned her children, and declared her determination to get revenge on him. (Her story varied—she had also told Brazul that Mifle's mother, Maria, had poisoned the children.) She presented herself, in Margolin's words, as a "noble avenger," declaring, "I am prepared to let myself perish but I will destroy Mifle." She repeated what Margolin had already heard from Brazul—that Andrei had been killed by his stepfather, his uncle, Mifle, and others, and that she was planning to meet with a prisoner in Kharkov who had more information about the crime.

On their return to Kiev, Margolin and Brazul compared their impressions. Brazul believed that Cheberyak's story, if not entirely true, had a great deal of truth in it. True, she never met with her supposed informant in Kharkov, about whom she had been frustratingly vague, but that did not necessarily undermine her story. Margolin, on the other hand, was emphatic in his conviction that Cheberyak's story was a total lie. He came away from the Kharkov trip confident that Cheberyak had been directly involved in Andrei's murder. Cheberyak, he felt, had the demeanor of "a person who was being hunted, who sensed danger" because investigators were on her trail. But in concocting a convoluted lie, had Vera Cheberyak possibly let slip part of the truth about Andrei's murder? During their meeting, Margolin had mostly kept his silence, but he did probe Cheberyak about the supposed motive behind Andrei's death. Why, he asked, had Andrei been killed? Andrei, Cheberyak claimed, had been eliminated by Mifle's villainous "gang of thieves." But why, Margolin pressed. Because, she said, the boy knew what they were up to: he was a "dangerous witness."

During a visit to Kiev around this time, Gruzenberg got wind of Margolin's involvement with Brazul and was greatly displeased. He told Margolin that he was taking unnecessary risks. "Why place our untarnished case in jeopardy?" he argued. The accusers lacked credible evidence. They "would welcome the opportunity" Margolin was affording them to declare that the witnesses for the defense were tainted and their testimony the product of a Jewish lawyer's conspiracy. The trial would not settle their argument. Decades later Margolin would still be insisting that his "offensive" tactics had been a boon to the defense, while Gruzenberg continued to maintain that the consequences of the amateurish investigation had been disastrous.

What is indisputable is that the courtroom confrontation between Arnold Margolin and Vera Cheberyak would become a sensational highlight of the trial. Cheberyak, of course, could not have known that the clandestine meeting in Kharkov would lead to a headline-making moment around the world some two years hence. But before she returned to Kiev, she had taken steps toward turning the secret trip to her advantage. She was not going to give the important gentleman she had met any chance to deny their encounter. She removed a poster from the wall of her Kharkov hotel room and wrote her name on the wallpaper. She also mailed a postcard to her husband to prove the date she had been there. The rare missive to Vasily Cheberyak from his despised and dreaded wife read, "Thank God, everything is fine."

Toward the end of December, it became clear to a despairing Fenenko that he had failed to thwart the effort to indict Beilis for the murder of Andrei Yushchinsky. He had been confident that, in the course of his investigation, the absurdity of the charges would become so over-whelmingly self-evident that the case would be dropped. But now Chaplinsky stepped up the pressure on him to declare his investigation complete, a legal requirement before an indictment could be drafted. The prosecutor undoubtedly desired to start off the new year with a case that would gain him national renown.

Chaplinsky, however, was still concerned by the scantiness of the evidence, which he himself had more than once admitted was "not com-pletely firm." More evidence quickly had to be found—or fabricated. To this end, there now emerged the strange partnership that would shape the entire case. Grigory Chaplinsky, chief prosecutor of the Kiev Judi-cial Chamber, would work in concert with Vera Cheberyak, the ter-ror of Lukianovka and leading suspect in Andrei's murder. Later they would meet and conspire. At this point, though, the collaboration was unspoken, arising naturally to fulfill the needs of the ambitious official and the criminal sociopath. In these days, the week before Christmas 1911, each of them executed a separate and mutually reinforcing plan to firm up the case.

On December 20, Vera Cheberyak sent off her hapless husband, Vasily, to Investigator Fenenko with a new story to tell. Vasily was now completely in Cheberyak's thrall. He would do whatever she wanted. Just a few months earlier he had longed to see her arrested. Now he was prepared to relate whatever lies she instructed him to tell in order to deflect suspicion away from her.

As he sat down in front of the investigator, Vasily did not rush to tell his new story. He was of noble stock and, though poorly paid (16 rubles 50 kopeks a month), he was proud of being a civil servant, which gave him elevated standing among the meaner denizens of Lukianovka. His self-esteem, dependent on such minuscule differences in status, was in need of shoring up. Even with Zhenya and Andrei in their graves, it was important to him to express his disdain for his son's friend. His Zhenya, he said, had indeed played regularly with Andrei Yushchinsky, but the friendship, he wanted it known, was "a state of affairs that I did not like at all." Andrei's family were "simple people," he explained, "and I did not want *my* boy to go around with *that* kind of boy." Having made sure to place his dead son on a higher plane than the boy's dead friend, he proceeded to recount the tale his wife had given him.

In the preceding nine months, questioned repeatedly by investigators, none of the Cheberyaks—not Vasily, not Vera, not any of their three children—had mentioned Mendel Beilis. Now, however, Vasily made a dramatic claim. Several days before the discovery of Andrei's body, he said,

> Zhenya came running into the apartment . . . and he told me that he had been playing with Andrusha Yushchinsky on the clay grinder in the Zaitsev brick factory and that Mendel Beilis had seen them there and chased after them.

Mendel Beilis's sons, he said, were standing nearby, laughing. Zhenya, in this new account, did not say he saw what happened to Andrei but, thanks to Vasily Cheberyak's new assertion, the prosecution would now be able to argue that while Zhenya had escaped the clutches of the Jew, Andrei had not. Chaplinsky could feel relieved that he at last had a relatively respectable-looking witness who ensnared Beilis in a story that put him under suspicion.

Chaplinsky still faced a nagging problem in the autopsy reports, which lent little support to the ritual-murder theory. The first autopsy, performed by the city coroner, A. M. Karpinsky, failed to confirm the ritual-murder scenario in any way; its results were consistent with a brutal, senseless murder. A report on the second autopsy, which was delivered on April 25, found that the primary cause of death was "the body's almost complete exsanguination," or loss of blood (a dubious conclusion, as noted earlier, likely reflecting pressure from Chaplinsky, and one that would be vigorously contested by the defense). Still, in the report there was no definitive confirmation that the goal of the crime had been to drain the body of blood.

Fenenko was almost surely ordered by Chaplinsky to bring in for questioning Dr. Nikolai Obolonsky and the anatomist N. N. Tufanov, who had performed the second autopsy. Fenenko was compelled to ask both men an entirely unwarranted and speculative question: "If blood was extracted from Yushchinsky's body, from what wounds would it have been most convenient to gather it?" On December 23, the specialists obliged by responding: "Given that the most profuse bleeding was in the left temple region . . . and also from the right side of the neck . . . one must assume that it would have been most convenient to collect blood from Yushchinsky's body from these wounds, if blood actually was collected." This was rather flimsy stuff, but better than nothing. At least the experts had been coaxed into considering the draining of blood as if it were a possible scenario.

The year closed with an event that would change the course of case. On December 31, 1911, Nikolai Krasovsky found himself disgraced, when he was suddenly and summarily dismissed from his position for supposed misconduct as a police official in Khodorkov. Some years earlier, it was alleged, he had detained a peasant named Kovbasa without sufficient cause. (Suddenly the tsarist authorities were getting finicky about improper detentions.) Krasovsky's enemies had not been content to let the detective quietly resume his former life; the officials fomenting the blood accusation had decided to exact their revenge, stripping him of his livelihood and reputation. Yet as acts of revenge go, this one was remarkably counterproductive. Krasovsky previously had no intention of resuming his involvement in the most frustrating case of his career, but he now felt himself compelled to do so. He set about planning his return to Kiev to reclaim his good name by proving the case against Andrei's killers.

7

"Who Is a Hero?"

For Mendel Beilis the new year got off to a promising, if painful, start. On January 4, 1912, in his seventh week of solitary confinement, a guard opened the door and told him to get ready to leave his cell. The investigator wanted to see him. They were taking him to the courthouse.

Kiev was in the midst of a brutal cold spell, and during Beilis's long walk down the city's streets in tattered shoes with holes in the soles, his already badly ulcerated feet became frostbitten. He limped into Vasily Fenenko's office in terrible pain but was elated to learn why he had been summoned: the investigation, Fenenko told him, was nearly complete. Beilis himself was the final witness. Upon hearing the news, he thanked God that his ordeal might soon be coming to an end. Five months earlier Fenenko had, with such heartfelt sorrow, sent him to prison, but assured him that his investigation would reveal the truth. Now Beilis was filled with hope. He understood that charging him, of all people, with "ritual" murder made no sense at all. "I am a completely unreligious Jew," he told Fenenko in his brief deposition. "I always work on Saturdays . . . I only go to Synagogue once a year, on the Day of Atonement." Regarding the one new substantive claim against him, he formally denied that he had ever told his former cellmate Kozachenko to poison any witnesses. Then he was led away on the long, agonizing walk back to the prison, returning to his cell, he later remembered, "with frozen feet . . . and a happy heart."

Fenenko, though, was appalled that the end of his investigation had resulted not in the dropping of the case but in Beilis's imminent indictment. The day after their meeting, he signed the final page of the sheaf of depositions and reports and sent it off to the prosecutor's office. No rational or honest prosecutor would indict a man based on the material contained in those pages, but by now Fenenko knew he had lost his battle against the fomenters of the blood accusation and had no choice but to let the machine of the criminal justice system grind into its next gear. Beilis, however, was simply happy that the process had finally moved on to the next step.

When he returned to his cell Beilis removed his shoes and saw that his feet were badly swollen. He showed them to a guard, who told him to just wait until they got better, but his feet got worse by the minute. Finally, another guard barked at him to get up and hurry to the infirmary, in another building. But Beilis could not walk. The guard, annoyed, just kept shouting, "Move on!" Beilis was paralyzed by pain. Finally a prisoner found some rags and bound them around his knees: Beilis crawled on them across the snow and ice to the infirmary. There he was welcomed to a kind of heaven. A compassionate physician's assistant gave him his first real bath in months and prepared a bed with fresh linens. Beilis slept thirty-six hours straight.

He awoke, unfortunately, to the ministrations of someone far less kind. Mendel Beilis would meet relatively few aggressive anti-Semites during his years in prison, but the doctor who operated on his feet was one of them. "Well, now you know for yourself what it feels like to be cut up," the physician said as he punctured and drained the sores in what seemed to Beilis an intentionally leisurely fashion. "You can imagine how Andrusha felt when you were stabbing him and drawing his blood." After the excruciating procedure, Beilis remained in the relative bliss of the infirmary for several days, but he was released before his feet were fully healed. Apparently an important person was coming from St. Petersburg to inspect the facility and it would not do to present the most infamous prisoner in the empire laid up in bed with bad feet.

On January 10, Beilis's attorney, Arnold Margolin, received word from his sources that his client was to be indicted for the murder of Andrei Yushchinsky. Margolin believed that the defense had to launch an offensive against the prosecution's case immediately—do anything possible to undermine or perhaps even forestall the indictment. But Kiev's Jewish leaders were unwilling to take any action other than to print up some academic tracts arguing against claims of Jewish ritual murder. Margolin felt frustration and contempt for these timid men, so fearful of being accused of "meddling" or "provoking" the regime that they would do nothing to stop a case that threatened every Jew in the empire. "Under the circumstances," Margolin wrote in his memoir of the case, "inactivity seemed to me to be nothing less than criminal." With a certain arrogance, but not without justification, he complained that any necessary measures "involving not only real but merely imaginary personal risk were graciously left exclusively to myself."

But what action could Margolin take? The young attorney had to admit that the available ammunition for an offensive was meager. He resorted to the only weapon he had: his bumbling journalist friend Stepan Brazul-Brushkovsky. Margolin encouraged Brazul to go to the authorities with his theory of the case, based on what Vera Cheberyak had told him, implicating her blinded former lover, Pavel Mifle, and others in Andrei's murder. Margolin was certain that Brazul's theory was wrong. Cheberyak, he believed, was not merely a helpful source, as Brazul thought, but was complicit in the crime. No matter. In deploying Brazul, he felt he was at least drawing attention to Cheberyak, with the potential result that someone would get spooked, something would shake loose, and the real killers would be revealed.

On January 18, Brazul submitted an affidavit to Investigator Fenenko and went public in the newspapers with his account of Vera Cheberyak's accusation that Andrei had been killed by a "gang of thieves" that included Mifle, Andrei's stepfather, his uncle Fyodor, and others, to keep him quiet about their supposed crimes. Brazul's scenario seemed absurd to everyone but him and did nothing to slow down the process of indicting Beilis. But the blank shot did have an immediate effect of some consequence: it unleashed a mother's rage. When Maria Mifle heard that that the woman who had maimed her son now dared to accuse him of murdering a child, she was determined to get revenge. She had information that could put Vera Cheberyak behind bars, and now she was going to use it.

Maria Mifle's son Pavel had recently shared a secret with her. When his former paramour was escorting him to the French consulate to receive his invalid's pension, he noticed she was taking a roundabout route. When he asked why, she confessed it had to do with the near disaster the previous March, when she had been arrested for selling a stolen watch and chain to a store and had barely managed to flee the police precinct after giving a false name. Fearful she would be recognized, she made sure to give the store a wide berth. Three days after Brazul's story broke, Maria Mifle went to the police. (Only later did her son agree to testify.) They arrested Cheberyak on January 25 and called in Mrs. Gusin, proprietress of the Gusin watch store, who identified her as the "Mrs. Ivanov" who had sold stolen goods to her. A few weeks earlier, Cheberyak had also been charged with another crime—defrauding her local grocer. Now, for the first time since she had thrown sulfuric acid in Pavel Mifle's face six years earlier, Vera Cheberyak was in serious danger of going to prison.

Margolin was pleased. Just as he had hoped, Brazul's story put Cheberyak under the authorities' further scrutiny. This, he believed, could only be to the good.

Meanwhile, on January 30, Beilis was again roused from his cell for another excruciating walk to the courthouse to receive his formal indictment. Beilis was overjoyed to catch a glimpse of his wife and children, who were in the courtroom—it was the first time in six months he had laid eyes on them, though he was not allowed to speak to them and was taken back to prison without being able to do more than turn his head and wave.

After returning to his cell, he spent entire days intensely studying the document he had been handed. "Menahem Mendel Tevyev Beilis," he read, "is indicted for entering into an . . . agreement with other persons unknown to deprive Andrei Yushchinsky of life, and in a torturous manner." He found the charge understandable enough, though horrible, but many of the words were unfamiliar to him. He knew what a "law" was, but what was an "article"? As Beilis would often say later, prison was a "good school." Eventually he would feel himself to be quite a *zakonnik*—or man well versed in law. But he did understand the most important thing: the court had set a trial date the seventeenth of May. It was a long time to wait, but he started to feel much better. He could count the days now with a sense of purpose. And, more good news, Margolin had arranged for him to have weekly visits with his family.

On February 12, Beilis was led into the visitors' chamber at the prison and locked into one of its wire cages as his wife, children, and brother Aaron were brought in to see him. The noise and commotion in the large room were so intense that he and Esther could hardly hear each other. He was shocked at her appearance—now that he could see her up close, she appeared years older than when he had last looked in her eyes seven months earlier. They spoke little and could do little more than cry and touch each other's hands through the small gaps in the wire mesh. Because their conversations were monitored, they were allowed to speak only in Russian, which made communication frustratingly awkward; Esther could barely speak the language and Beilis only imperfectly. Still, seeing his family greatly lifted his spirits. He ate and slept better and felt much healthier. He knew it was important that he maintain his strength as best he could in this hellish place where six or seven convicts a day died of typhoid fever. He viewed every day he survived as a victory.

Now that Beilis was officially an indicted prisoner, his lawyers were finally able to take action on his behalf, filing reams of petitions, motions, and lists of witnesses to be summoned. Margolin visited him in prison and reassured him that everyone knew he was innocent and that the indictment only reinforced that belief. Indeed, the indictment was pathetically feeble and unconvincing, at times even comic in its candor ("[The witness] Ulyana Shakhovskaya recounted her story in a drunken state . . ."). The document reads more like an exoneration until the point in the narrative where Vasily Cheberyak finally appears with his story of how Zhenya and Andrei were being chased by Beilis the clerk from the Zaitsev brickworks. Then the informer Kozachenko materializes with his tale of the defendant promising him untold Jewish lucre to poison the "Lamplighter" and "Frog." No mention is made of Kozachenko's admission to Lieutenant Colonel Ivanov that he had made everything up.

The indictment was most notable for a striking omission: nowhere in it was there a direct accusation of ritual murder. Margolin and his colleagues puzzled over why this might be so. Most likely, they concluded, the prosecution was acting out of strategic considerations; the skeleton, so to speak, of the ritual murder charge was undeniably there. While Professor Sikorsky's pronouncement about "the revenge of the sons of Jacob" was nowhere mentioned, the indictment did quote his judgment that the crime was marked by "slow blood loss" and "the extraction of blood," which were referred to together as a "goal" of the crime. Moreover, the indictment, with no pretext, notes Beilis's role in preparing the Zaitsev family's matzo and that Beilis's father had been a pious Hasid. The inclusion of all this material made no sense unless the prosecution was planning to use the blood accusation, if only in an underhanded way. With such a weak case, Margolin guessed, the prosecution had decided that it was better to avoid direct mention of the ritual-murder charge and let the jury, as he put it, "read between the lines." He was likely correct about the prosecution's strategy at this point. In fact, in April the court even ruled against allowing expert testimony on Judaism on the grounds that the prosecution was not making religion an issue in the case. Within months, however, the state would change course, deciding to embrace the medieval myth fully and—although it would deny doing so—put the Jewish religion itself on trial.

As the first anniversary of Andrei Yushchinsky's murder approached, Vladimir Golubev, head of the Kiev right-wing youth group Double Headed Eagle, found himself surprisingly frustrated. He had arguably done more than anyone to create the case against Mendel Beilis, having first brought the name of this Jew to the attention of the authorities. But he had ended up marginalized, his organization under close official supervision, unable to participate actively in the case. Now that Beilis was indicted, he could do little more than fret that the boy-martyr's death was not being acknowledged with proper solemnity. On the day before the anniversary, as police officers stood close by, a small group of about thirty Black Hundreds gathered at Andrei's grave. Aside from the chanting of prayers, the gathering was quiet—the authorities had forbidden any speeches for fear of provoking anti-Jewish violence. On March 12, the day of the anniversary, a requiem for Andrei was held at St. Sophia Cathedral without incident. All this left Golubev greatly distressed. The commemorations were perfunctory, he felt; the whole city should have joined in mourning. When he heard that a nationalist organization was holding a ball that very night, he grew enraged. He stalked into the ball, mounted the stage, and began loudly reproaching the dancing couples for enjoying themselves on such a sacred day. The revelers refused to be conscience-stricken and Golubev refused to break off his rant. The police had to be called, and he was escorted from the premises. Little more would be heard of him until Beilis's trial, when the prosecution would welcome his amateur detective work and febrile rage.

When Margolin told Beilis that everyone believed him to be innocent, he himself had no idea just how right he was. At the upper levels of the empire's security apparatus, the opinion was unanimous: the defendant was innocent and Tsar Nicholas's regime was courting political disaster by pursuing the case. Astoundingly, no police official, of either high or low rank, ever even pretended to consider Mendel Beilis seriously as a suspect.

On January 28, two days before the indictment was handed down, Colonel Alexander Shredel, head of the Kiev office of the Corps of Gendarmes, wrote a report to his superior in St. Petersburg, a vice director of the national Department of Police. After dismissing Brazul's outlandish scenario, Shredel let it be known that his office's secret investigation "gives a firm basis to propose that the murder of the boy Yushchinsky occurred with the participation of [Vera] Cheberyak" and members of her gang. On February 14, in a follow-up report titled "Personal. Top Secret. Deliver Directly to Recipient's Hands," he wrote that in spite of Beilis's indictment, the Kiev Gendarmes' investigation was still continuing under the direction of his subordinate, Lieutenant Colonel Ivanov, and was still "chiefly concentrated around . . . Vera Vladimirovna Cheberyak and criminals directly connected to her." He named seven of her gang members as suspects. Ivanov's investigation would soon narrow down the list of perpetrators to three: Vera's half brother Peter "Plis" ("Velveteen") Singaevsky, Boris "Borka" Rudzinsky, and Ivan "Red Vanya" Latyshev. The investigation, Shredel declared, was operating on the assumption that Andrei "was the unwilling witness of a criminal act of this gang whom 'it was necessary to do away with out of fear.'" The last phrase was in quotation marks, meaning it was apparently a verbatim quote from testimony by a witness cited in a previous report that has unfortunately been lost. The full range of the testimony on which Ivanov based his judgment will never be known, but it is clear he had little doubt about who the real killers were.

Regarding the strength of the charges against the Jewish prisoner accused of killing Andrei, Shredel made a harsh and strikingly candid judgment. "The indictment of Mendel Beilis," he wrote, "given the inadequacy of the evidence against him and the widespread interest in this case, which is becoming known throughout almost all of Europe, may occasion a great deal of unpleasant consequences for officials of the judicial branch and completely justified reproaches regarding the conduct of the investigation, the hastiness of the conclusions and even their one-sidedness." On March 14, along similar lines, he warned:

"The . . . evidence against Beilis, as is now becoming clear, will completely fall away in the course of trial testimony."

As for the prosecutors (as opposed to police officials), a peculiar episode in the spring of 1912 casts light on their own private doubts about the defendant's guilt. Among the local Black Hundred leaders offering to assist the prosecution was Grigory Opanasenko, chairman of the Railroad and Cabdrivers' Division of the Russian National Union of the Archangel Michael, one of the larger far-right organizations. The prosecution paid his theories of the case serious attention, in particular the notion that the draining of Andrei's blood was achieved with the help of highly insidious "special instruments" peculiar to the Jews. (The theory was, in the end, never adopted.) On April 29, Opanasenko sought out a key member of the prosecution team, A. A. Karbovsky, to inform him of an eerie rumor. "Yushchinsky's ghost is appearing to the perpetrators of the crime and demands their clothing," he had heard. "They do not sleep at night and are ready to confess." Karbovsky, apparently in all seriousness, set about trying to confirm whether Andrei's restless spirit had been seen calling upon anyone at the witching hour. Opanasenko did not name the haunted men but must have had in mind Beilis and his supposed black-bearded accomplices. But in a striking indication of his personal beliefs about the case, Karbovsky seemed to question everyone about this apparition except Mendel Beilis and, as far as is known, not a single Jew. Most tellingly, he paid a visit to a prison where he queried two members of Vera Cheberyak's gang doing time there for robbery. One was Ivan Latyshev, whom the Kiev Gendarmes had identified as one of Andrei's likely killers. Both convicts answered the prosecutor's strange question in the negative, with Red Vanya declaring: "I have had no alarming dreams and suffer from no hallucinations."

With the arrival of spring, both Kiev and Beilis's spirits began to thaw. The poorly heated cell became a little more habitable. He no longer awoke, as he had sometimes, to find his hand frozen to the wall. He was given an occasional cellmate, which relieved his solitude. (One of them, a Russian peasant, was quite a decent fellow who Beilis decided, probably correctly, was not an informant.) Most of all, he was happy about the progress toward his May 17 trial. On April 7 a panel of prospective jurors was selected. When he was summoned a few days later to the prison office for a visit with Margolin, Beilis had no reason to expect any bad news. During their meetings, Margolin invariably said something to make him feel better. "You will be victorious," he would say, and reassure him that he would not have to wait long. Now, when Beilis casually asked if there was anything new, Margolin got right to the point: the trial was being postponed, with no new date assigned. "I felt like a bullet was shot in my head," Beilis recalled. "I thought that I would go insane." He had been counting the days and the hours, and now the clock had stopped.

Margolin explained that an expert had fallen ill and the trial could not begin without him. An "expert"? Beilis had learned what an "investigator," a "prosecutor," and a "juror" were, but he was yet not enough of a *zakonnik* to know what an "expert" was. But he knew it sounded serious. Margolin tried to reassure him that this was a minor setback. The trial would still happen soon. Beilis began to cry and accused Margolin of not wanting to tell him that things were going badly. Margolin tried to calm him down. Professor Sikorsky, a key prosecution witness, had, in fact, taken ill. But Beilis returned to his isolation cell feeling "like a live body in a grave."

Beilis recalled this as the very lowest moment of his years in prison. Adding to his torment, under the system's absurd rules, as a prisoner without a trial date, he had his family visitation rights suspended. He was utterly alone again. For the first time he thought of suicide. "'Rather than such a life,' I thought to myself, 'Death is better.' And I certainly would have done it, as these were minutes when life became unbearable." But as his thoughts darkened, he found unexpected comfort in his identity as a Jew and in the religion that had been a marginal presence in his life since the day he had left for the army some twenty years earlier. He had come to understand that his case was not just about him but about the Jewish people as a whole:

> "Well, if this is so," I said to myself, "then my death will leave a stain on the Jews. Because if I commit suicide, the Jew-haters will certainly say that I myself caused my death because I saw that I am not able to prove my innocence, or that the Jews did it to me in order that the truth would not be exposed." And this truly did prevent me from taking this terrible step, and gave me strength and courage.

Comforting words from his youth, long dormant, came to him now:

> I myself am not a great scholar of Jewish books. But from heder
> [primary school] I still remembered some verses and words which
> remained in my memory. I remembered the verse *"eyzehu gibor*
> *ha'kovesh et yitsro"* [Who is a hero? He that conquers his evil incli-
> nation]. And this verse constantly floated in front of my eyes when
> the terrible thought of suicide would arise. "One must be a hero,"
> I thought to myself, "by restraining the evil inclination and indeed
> live."

Drawing on the power of that Talmudic saying, Beilis began to eat
and sleep better; maintaining his own well-being was a way to spite
his people's enemies. He resolved to live to see the day when the truth
would be revealed.

As Beilis sat alone in his jail cell, murmuring long-forgotten prayers,
he could take solace from something else as well. Civilized opinion was
rallying to his cause. He was indeed becoming "a second Dreyfus."

The first mention in the West of Andrei Yushchinky's murder came
from Reuter's news agency. At the end of April 1911, the agency—with
no editorial comment—telegraphed to its subscribers a translation of a
sensational article about the case from the Russian far-right press. (A
sample: "In bygone days the Chassidim used to crucify their victim,
but later they considered it sufficient to drive nails into various parts
of his body . . .") Credulous editors published the article in a half-dozen
provincial newspapers in Great Britain and Northern Ireland, and
it also served as the basis for a few reports in American papers. The
London-based *Jewish Chronicle* expressed outrage "that an agency of
the reputation and standing of Reuter's should aid in circulating these
infamous slanders." Dr. Herbert Friedenwald, secretary of the American Jewish Committee, accused the Russian government of ginning up
the ritual murder charge "as a pretext for starting a pogrom" or, even
more insidiously, with the goal of inciting the Russian populace in order
to demonstrate that the regime had the power to *prevent* a pogrom if
it so desired. (The speculation was off the mark—even at that early
stage of the affair, the regime sought to avert anti-Jewish violence.)

Friedenwald declared the case to be another reason to support the committee's campaign for the abrogation of America's commercial treaty with Russia.

For well over a year, Friedenwald's statement was the last of any note by an American public figure about the case. Once news of the accusation against Mendel Beilis seeped into the West, the worldwide protest movement in his defense began not in the United States or Great Britain, but in Germany. The realm of Kaiser Wilhelm II was initially the most hospitable soil for an effort to defend a Russian Jew. France and Great Britain were allies of Russia; together, the three countries constituted the Triple Entente, an alliance whose goal was to counter German power. The French and British foreign ministries avoided any issue that might unnecessarily upset the Russian government. Public opinion in France and Great Britain ran strongly against the kaiser's regime; to press judgment unduly on Russia exposed a critic to the charge of undermining the entente and being pro-German. W. T. Stead, one of the greatest British journalists of the era, took Jewish anti-Russian activists to task for this very reason. "No one has ever accused me of anti-Semitism," he wrote in one of his final articles before he boarded the RMS *Titanic* in April 1912, for a voyage in which he would be one of the 1,514 casualties. "I owe too much to the authors of the Old and New Testaments . . . I am all the more bound to warn my Jewish friends that they may give dangerous impetus to anti-Semitism if they persist in subordinating the interests of general peace to pursuit of their vendetta with Russia." Stead, a renowned humanitarian and champion of civil rights, was no reactionary, but as the historian Maurice Samuel acerbically observed, "One cannot help wondering how he saw a vendetta of the Jews against the Russian government rather than the reverse."

Launching the pro-Beilis movement, then, was a politically complex maneuver. Jewish leaders in Western Europe, much like their Russian counterparts, faced their own sensitive, tactical decisions when it came to defending their brethren. Fortunately, Western European Jews had two remarkable leaders—one German, one British—of superb sophistication in the ways of diplomacy, the press, and public opinion. Dr. Paul Nathan was a philanthropist and head of the Hilfsverein der deutschen Juden, or Aid Society of German Jews. Lucien Wolf led the Conjoint Foreign Committee of the Board of Deputies of British Jews and the

Anglo-Jewish Association. He was also a diplomatic correspondent for leading British newspapers and editor of Darkest Russia, a weekly chronicle of the plight of the Russian Jews. The two men, who were close friends, were sometimes referred to in jest, but not inaccurately, as "the ministers of foreign affairs" of German and British Jewry. No one could accuse Nathan and Wolf of timidity, but they were careful to formulate the pro-Beilis effort as a movement of outraged Gentiles. This was not to be seen as a "Jewish" protest. They solicited no Jews to sign the open letters they organized.

The public advocacy for Beilis took off following Beilis's indictment in the spring of 1912. Nathan launched the effort, coordinating the first open letter, denouncing the "unscrupulous fiction" of the blood libel. Published on March 19, 1912, it was signed by German as well as Austrian and Danish religious leaders, scholars, politicians, and writers, including Gerhart Hauptmann, who would win the Nobel Prize in Literature that year, and novelist Thomas Mann. Ten days later an open letter in France condemned the "absurd" and "libelous" charge against Beilis, signed by 150 luminaries including the future Nobel literature laureate Anatole France. The text of each letter was diplomatically fine-tuned: the German version was addressed to humanity at large, making an appeal in the name of civilization, while the French signatories, taking the tone of colleagues counseling a valued ally, were careful to call themselves "friends of Russia."

The ebullient Margolin would have enjoyed explaining to Beilis how the greatest men of the age were denouncing the Russian government because of what it was doing to him. Perhaps Beilis had heard of Sherlock Holmes, whose name had already entered the Russian and even Yiddish lexicon as a synonym for a great detective? His creator, Arthur Conan Doyle, had signed the open letter that had been published in the *Times* of London along with some 240 other notables. Among the luminaries signing the British letter were the archbishops of Canterbury and York; the primate of Ireland; the Speaker of the House of Commons and leading members of Parliament, including Labour Party leader J. Ramsay McDonald; numerous professors at Oxford and Cambridge universities; and eminent writers such as Thomas Hardy, H. G. Wells, and George Bernard Shaw.

Dated May 4, 1912, the *Times* letter declared, "The question is one of civilization, humanity and truth. The blood accusation is a relic of the days of Witchcraft and Black Magic, a cruel and utterly baseless libel on Judaism, an insult to Western culture and a dishonor to the Churches in whose name it has been formulated by ignorant fanatics." The letter warned that there was "grave reason to fear" that the revival of the incendiary charge could provoke violence and "endanger many innocent lives."

That the British signatories declared themselves to be "animated by the sincerest friendship for Russia" did nothing to mollify the Russian government. Baron Heyking, the Russian consul general in London, indignantly responded in a letter to the *Times* of London on May 10, 1912. "The accusation of ritual murder is not at all leveled against Judaism and the Jewish people as a whole," Heyking wrote, "but only against the accused, who is believed to belong to a small secret sect carrying the Talmudian teaching to the extreme of ritual murder." He insisted: "That secret sect must not be confounded with the Jews at large." But the baron, in defending the honor of his government, unin-tentionally gave the game away. He was apparently unaware that, offi-cially, the defendant was at this point *not* accused of ritual murder; in fact, the court had explicitly ruled to the opposite effect when it excluded the testimony of expert witnesses on the Jewish religion as irrelevant. But the baron, like everyone else, understood perfectly well that the heart of the case was the blood accusation. And, even as he denied it, he made it clear that "the Jews at large" stood accused. His letter clearly implied that if the horrific rite was inherent in "the Talmudian teach-ing," then every Jew must share in the guilt.

Through an intense exercise of personal will, Mendel Beilis had retained his grip on his sanity, but his initial, sickening intuition about the delay in the trial was utterly correct. His stay in judicial purgatory would be longer than anyone anticipated—thanks in part to his obvious inno-cence, which was proving to be a serious nuisance to the government.

"The trial will undoubtedly end in the exoneration of the defendant due to the impossibility of factually proving his guilt," Kiev governor A. F. Giers to wrote an Interior Ministry official on April 19. When the defendant was set free, he feared, "[it] would make an extremely dis-tressing and unpleasant impression on the Russian population." Among the Jews, his acquittal would "arouse indescribable jubilation and joy."

This was, in other words, a formula for disorder, violence, pogroms. The governor did not dare suggest dropping the case, however. He was worried exclusively about its timing. Elections to the Duma were taking place in the fall. Any disorder at that time would be most unfortunate. He respectfully recommended that the trial be postponed until after the elections. Informed of the request, justice minister Shcheglovitov immediately agreed. Beyond his recognition of the impact of the trial, what is notable about Shcheglovitov's decision is that the man in charge of the imperial judicial system, the prime backer of the case, believed that Mendel Beilis would in all likelihood be acquitted.

The trial would ultimately be delayed far into the next year. The postponement transformed the case, providing all parties the gift of time. It gave the prosecution time to manufacture new evidence. It gave Vera Cheberyak time to scheme. And it gave Margolin and Brazul, aided now by Nikolai Krasovsky, formerly the chief detective on the case, time to take the offensive.

In March 1912, Krasovsky returned to Kiev unemployed, disgraced, and determined to regain his reputation. The previous fall, with sorrow and relief, he had washed his hands in frustration of this cursed case. Then on New Year's Eve 1911, he had been shocked to be summarily dismissed from his post as a provincial police officer. Now it seemed that his fate, like that of Mendel Beilis himself, depended on unmasking the real killers of Andrei Yushchinsky.

Krasovsky had held from the beginning that, in the absence of physical evidence, the only way to crack the case was to coax someone into confessing. Exactly how he was going to accomplish this he had no idea. He was no longer a police officer; he could not arrest a suspect, bring him in, and interrogate him in the hope the person would break. He would have to find a way to penetrate Vera Cheberyak's gang and trick one or more of the perpetrators into confessing.

Arnold Margolin was glad to have the renowned detective working on his side. But now that he was officially Beilis's attorney, he acted more cautiously than he had previously, keeping himself one step removed from the investigative work and using two of his liberal lawyer colleagues as intermediaries, even as he stayed deeply involved in Krasovsky's efforts. With Margolin's covert help, Krasovsky and

Brazul formed a somewhat uneasy partnership. The detective had his doubts about the journalist. When they met, Krasovsky berated Brazul for failing to consult with him before going public with his preposterous theory that the blind Mifle was behind the crime. (Perhaps Krasovsky had forgotten that he had brushed off Brazul's first offer of collaboration some months earlier.) But now Brazul had finally come to the conclusion—correctly, in Krasovsky's view—that Vera Cheberyak was not merely someone who had information about the murder but was herself complicit in the crime.

Over the next several weeks, Krasovsky formulated a plan that at first blush seems outlandish: they would penetrate the gang with help from the treacherous Russian revolutionary underground. Krasovsky and Brazul quickly settled on two young revolutionaries they thought they could recruit to their cause. Amzor Karaev was a twenty-five-year-old anarchist-communist of noble birth. By nationality an Ossetian from the Caucasus, he had served four prison sentences, including three and half years for possession of explosives. Flamboyant, violent, and mercurial, he has been described as a character straight out of Dostoyevsky. His fellow radical, Sergei Makhalin, was a twenty-one-year-old aspiring opera singer and agricultural college dropout who had been arrested three times for political crimes, including for an "expropriation"—as revolutionaries called their robberies—when he was just sixteen years old. He belonged to no party and had no ideology other than hatred of the regime and a desire to enlighten the masses; he gave free classes on urgent questions of the day, with the hope of imbuing in the common folk, as he put it, "the spark of truth."

It might seem absurd to turn to two such figures to exonerate a Jew wrongly accused of a murder believed to have been committed by professional criminals. But while Krasovsky's plan was audacious and risky, it had a cunningly persuasive rationale. The Russian revolutionary underground and the criminal underworld overlapped. In fact, one so shaded into the other that it was sometimes difficult to know who was a radical and who was a criminal. Contemporaries called it "the seamy side of revolution." As one anarchist leader lamented, too often "the bomb-thrower expropriators . . . were no better than the bandits of southern Italy." The revolutionary movement, of course, had a strong intellectual contingent, which included men such as Stolypin's assassin Dimitry Bogrov or, to name two much better-known figures, the future leaders of the Bolshevik revolution, Vladimir Lenin and Leon Trotsky. The "seamy" and intellectual contingents converged as well, but the criminal crew did much of the dirty work, especially the armed robberies that funded the movement. In this period the future Soviet supreme leader Joseph Stalin was the pistol-packing, bandit revolutionary par excellence, organizing and taking part in numerous bank robberies and holdups in his native Georgia. Karaev, like Stalin, was from the Caucasus, where revolutionary cells were most likely to act like traditional bandit gangs.

But not just any revolutionary figure would do for the task that Krasovsky had in mind. He needed a man who was both in good standing in the underworld and would be taken seriously by the public and, possibly, a jury. In the spring of 1912, this was not an easy brief to fill; being a revolutionary no longer had the righteous glamour it previously possessed. Just a few years earlier, in 1905 and 1906, throwing a bomb or stealing from the state or the plutocrats earned one a halo of romantic allure. Assassinations of tsarist officials—an average of about ten per day in those years—earned the sympathy, if not open approval, of respectable liberals. By 1912, however, disillusion had set in. The regime had collected itself and crushed the revolutionaries. Revelations that leading radicals had secretly been police informers tarnished their popular appeal. The recent assassination of Prime Minister Stolypin struck even liberals who detested him as a senseless atrocity.

In Amzor Karaev, Krasovsky and Margolin believed they had a rare man who retained the charisma of the revolutionary outlaw. Karaev was idolized by his fellow convicts for his bravery and brazenness in standing up to prison authorities. He was famous, in particular, for one extraordinary incident. One day, several years earlier, he had complained to a prison guard of a toothache and asked to see a doctor. The guard mocked him and refused his request. In protest, Karaev emptied the contents of a kerosene lamp on the floor. For this offense he was convicted, unjustly, on charges of attempting to escape. When Karaev saw the guard again he stabbed him to death. Karaev was charged with murder, but a jury acquitted him, and he returned to prison a hero. The verdict might seem like a surprise, and little is known about how the jury reached its conclusion, but until about 1907 much of the Russian public, and even quite a few officials, were highly sympathetic to the revolutionaries, which sometimes allowed liberal lawyers to obtain surprisingly lenient sentences if not outright acquittals. With his radical swagger and lawbreaking reputation, Karaev certainly seemed like the kind of man who could gain the confidence of Vera Cheberyak's confederates. The question was how to persuade him to come to Kiev and take part in the emerging plan.

Brazul approached Makhalin, an acquaintance of his, and told him of the scheme. Like Krasovsky, Makhalin had his doubts about Brazul, whom he considered a "frivolous" person, but he signed on to the plan. He had known Karaev in prison and he sent him a cryptic letter to his home in his native Ossetia, saying he had an important matter to discuss and it had to be in person. Karaev agreed to come to Kiev.

When Karaev arrived in the city, and Makhalin dropped by his hotel room to explain why he had summoned him, Karaev's initial reaction was apoplectic. He was enraged that Makhalin had made him travel thousands of miles to hear such a proposal. "You want me to conduct an investigation?" he said, in Makhalin's recollection. "How dare you!" He was offended at what he took to be an enticement to violate his criminal code of honor. Karaev took out his pistol and started waving it around—a gesture he resorted to when he felt a point needed emphasis. Makhalin tried to calm him, telling him that they should just sit down and have a sensible talk. Karaev put away the gun and listened as Makhalin assumed the earnest tone he employed when teaching his free classes to the poor. He explained to Karaev that, in his view, the Beilis case was "introducing poisonous anger in the masses" and it was necessary to do something about it. Makhalin understood the powerful hatred underlying this case; as a boy, he later testified, he had witnessed a pogrom, an experience that had helped turn him into a revolutionary. Karaev felt himself being persuaded by Makhalin's appeal to his conscience. As an anarchist-communist, he could only despise all discrimination based on race or religion. The pair then met with Krasovsky, who at first concealed his identity, presenting himself as "Mr. Karasev," a gentleman who had taken an interest in the Beilis case and was helping with the investigation (an assertion that was more or less true). Karaev took three days to think things over and then informed Makhalin he would take part in the plan to prove the innocence of the poor Jewish brick-factory clerk.

Karaev, Makhalin, and Krasovsky would all later provide accounts of how the plan was executed, with all of them agreeing on all important details. Their versions would closely correspond to the one offered by Vera Cheberyak's half brother, Peter Singaevsky, except for those details that incriminate him. Those discrepancies would set the stage for a dramatic confrontation at Beilis's trial, as Cheberyak and Singaevsky faced their accusers in open court.

Singaevsky was key to the plan because he was the only one of Andrei's suspected killers not in jail at the moment, except for Cheberyak herself. Karaev quickly turned to his vast network of criminal connections to find a way of meeting Singaevsky and gaining his confidence. It turned out the two men had a mutual acquaintance, someone Singaevsky trusted: Lenka, nicknamed Ferdydudel, a barber with underworld ties. On April 19, Ferdydudel tracked down Singaevsky in a bar and told him that the notorious outlaw Karaev wished to meet him. The small-time crook must have been awed by Karaev's interest in him, and over the next several days Karaev loosened him up, taking him to restaurants to eat and, especially, drink. As a pretext for their meetings, he invented a story about needing some "good men" for a big robbery, a "wet job"—Russian criminal slang for murder—that involved killing as many as ten people for a prize of forty thousand rubles in loot. Would his new friend be able to help? Singaevsky was interested and lamented that his good comrades "Red Vanya" Latyshev and Boris Rudzinsky were in jail on robbery charges. In passing, he mentioned that some people were trying to "pin" the murder of the boy Yushchinsky on them.

Karaev felt he was getting somewhere, but Singaevsky still acted as if he knew nothing about Andrei's murder. He was an utterly dimwitted fellow, and disappointingly cautious. After four days Karaev met with Krasovsky and Brazul to brief them and discuss how to proceed. They devised a clever ruse to pressure Singaevsky to open up about the crime. Karaev would warn him that he and his half sister, Vera, were going to be arrested for Andrei's murder. On the afternoon of April 24, he took Singaevsky out to a criminal haunt, the restaurant Versailles, and broke the bad news: he had learned from "his man" in the Gendarmes that Singaevsky and Vera were about to be charged with Andrei's murder. In fact, he said, the warrants had already been drawn up.

According to Karaev, Singaevsky panicked and began to talk. His first reaction was that the two *shmary,* "floozies," who had seen something had to be rubbed out. "Measures" had to be taken. The "floozies" Singaevsky had in mind were two sisters, Ekaterina and Ksenia Diakonova, who would go on to play a dramatic and at times bizarre role at the Beilis trial. They were good friends of Vera Cheberyak's who, Krasovsky had long suspected, knew more than they were telling. For weeks, he had been conducting his own parallel covert operation, patiently working to win the women's confidence. He had managed to secure an introduction to them through an acquaintance and, posing as a Moscow gentleman, took them out almost daily to restaurants and the theater, talking at first of everything but the Beilis case. Finally, when they felt comfortable enough to open up to him, Ekaterina revealed that she had knocked on Cheberyak's door on the day Andrei had disappeared, sometime in the morning or perhaps early afternoon. When the door opened she said she saw Singaevsky and Rudzinsky running from one room to another while Red Vanya covered something with a coat in the corner. Ekaterina asked what that pile in the corner was. Cheberyak said it was just some "junk," slang for stolen goods. Ekaterina had a sense something was not right. The sisters also revealed an important material fact. They told Krasovsky that at Cheberyak's they would often play a game called Post Office that involved writing little notes to one another. The game was played with pieces of perforated paper—very much like ones found near Andrei's body.

If Singaevsky was about to confess, Karaev wanted there to be another witness. Karaev took him back to his hotel room, where they met with Makhalin, whom he introduced as a trustworthy criminal comrade. Karaev pretended to be desperately upset about his new friend's situation, at one point pulling out his gun and beating himself on the head with it in feigned frustration. Singaevsky again cursed the "floozies" who had figured out that he had something to do with the crime. His mind veered from one desperate measure to another. They should kill the Diakonova sisters, Lieutenant Colonel Ivanov, and Officer Kirichenko, Singaevsky said, or break into the Gendarmes' office and steal the case files. Karaev picked his moment and, gesturing to Singaevsky, said, "There's the real killer of Yushchinsky."

Singaevsky replied, "Yes, that was our job." The gang's business had been ruined, he said, "because of the bastard."

Makhalin had to quickly decide the best way to get as detailed a confession as possible. He told Singaevsky that he wanted to help him, and it would be good if he told as much as possible about the circumstances of the crime.

"There's nothing to tell," Singaevsky said. "We grabbed him and dragged him to my sister's apartment."

"Who do you mean by 'we'?" Makhalin asked.

"Me, Borka, and Red Vanya," Singaevsky replied, He added that Vanya was a good guy but wasn't good for a wet job; he'd thrown up after the murder.

Why had the job had been so messy? Karaev asked. Why hadn't they gotten rid of the body?

Singaevsky answered derisively, "That was dictated by Rudzinsky's ministerial brain." He told them now it had been a bad idea to leave the body so close to his sister's house. They should have dumped it in the Dnieper, Singaevsky said, or put it in a basket and disposed of it somewhere on their way to Moscow, where they had fled the day after the crime.

Singaevsky, quieting down, stopped talking about desperate "measures" and said he needed to send a message to Boris Rudzinsky. He did not specify what the message was, but presumably it concerned Andrei's murder. There would be an opportunity to get word to him, Singaevsky said, when Borka was escorted from prison to the investigator's office at the courthouse on April 27. The only way to communicate with him would be through the secret sign language Russian convicts had developed to talk among themselves. Karaev was fluent in it, and now Singaevsky asked him to sign a message to his friend. He would tell Rudzinsky that Singaevsky would leave a note for Borka in the outdoor latrine at the courthouse. This scheme pleased Krasovsky and his partners; they now had the chance of obtaining an incriminating piece of written evidence in the perpetrator's own hand. On the appointed day they stationed themselves near the building's entrance. Krasovsky and Brazul lurked near the outhouse ready to grab the note. Karaev managed to catch Rudzinsky's eye, and they began conversing in signs, but the guards, sensing something was up, hustled the prisoner away before Karaev could get his message across, and Singaevsky departed without leaving the note.

Still, the operation as a whole had been a tremendous success. Margolin and members of the Beilis Defense Committee decided that Brazul should deliver a written affidavit relating Singaevsky's confession and the revelations of the Diakonova sisters to Lieutenant Colonel Ivanov, the head of the Gendarmes' investigation. Brazul would make a further claim in the affidavit—that the mysterious letters implicating the Jews and signed by "a Christian," which were sent to Andrei's mother and the pathologist days after the body was discovered, were written "at the dictation of Vera Cheberyak" and that the handwriting matched that of a member of her gang. The affidavit was delivered into Ivanov's hands on May 6. On May 30, the results of Brazul's investigation were revealed in the Kiev newspapers and reprinted in papers across the empire. The stories created an unbelievable sensation. "Brazul's Declaration," as it was called, threw the prosecution into a state of chaos.

The defense demanded that the indictment be thrown out and the case remanded to the magistrate for a new investigation. Chaplinsky, the chief prosecutor, passionately resisted at first. His communications that May reveal a man in a deep state of anger, even emotional crisis. The case that was to make his reputation was falling apart. The high post in the capital that he craved was slipping from his grasp. He complained that his refusal to reopen the investigation in the face of new evidence was "arousing an outcry in the Yid press." Yet he had to concede that it was not just the Jews who were against him. "Many influential people at the present time," he noted with disapproval in a letter to an official, "are unfavorably disposed to the staging of a ritual murder case in court."

He was dismayed to hear such an opinion expressed even by people he might otherwise respect. On May 23, Lieutenant Colonel Ivanov recommended to Chaplinsky that Vera Cheberyak be arrested and asked his approval to move ahead and bring her in. Chaplinsky reported to the justice minister that Ivanov "regarded [the evidence] as completely sufficient material for the indictment in the murder not of Mendel Beilis but Vera Cheberyak, Latyshev, Rudzinsky and Singaevsky." Chaplinsky added, without any explanation or justification, that he had denied Ivanov's request. On May 28, Chaplinsky wrote in unusually personal terms to deputy justice minister Liadov, the man whose mission to Kiev had signaled the regime's backing of the case a year earlier. "An onslaught is being conducted [on me] from all sides," he complained, seeking to convince him to terminate the Beilis case. "I, of course, am not going to take this bait," he concluded defiantly, "and chase my well-wishers away."

In resisting the "well-wishers" pushing him to quash the case, he had the full backing of justice minister Shcheglovitov. On June 8, the minister summoned Chaplinsky to St. Petersburg to consult over how to deal with the disastrous turn that the Beilis affair was taking. The two men reconsidered their strategy and decided that delay would work in their favor. They would take the opportunity to rid themselves of the pathetically weak indictment and begin the investigation afresh in the hope of strengthening the case against the accused.

On his return to Kiev, Chaplinsky announced that he was dropping his opposition to withdrawing the original indictment and agreed to have the case remanded back for reinvestigation. On June 19 the Kiev Judicial Chamber acceded to the request. The case was now back to where it had been almost exactly eleven months earlier when Beilis had been dragged from his home in the middle of the night. The court rejected a defense motion for Beilis to be freed on his own recognizance. He remained in prison, in a state of legal limbo, again an unindicted prisoner with limited legal rights.

Chaplinsky had great hopes for the new investigation. He had pushed aside the troublesome Vasily Fenenko, who had fought him at every step, and appointed a new, compliant investigating magistrate who was enthusiastic about making the case against a Jewish suspect. The chief prosecutor was heartened by two important developments that he knew about and the defense did not. First, Vera Cheberyak had formulated a promising new scheme to impugn the integrity of the defense and incriminate Mendel Beilis. Second, he knew that Brazul's vaunted "independent investigation" was booby-trapped like an anarchist's bomb: for Karaev and Makhalin, those supposed star witnesses for the defense, were not what they appeared to be.

Makhalin and Karaev were indeed revolutionaries. They presented themselves as classic specimens of the genre: Makhalin, the leftist of the high-minded sort, and Karaev, the radical outlaw. Yet these young men were also commonplace among the denizens of the revolutionary world in one other respect. Makhalin was registered in the files of the Okhrana or secret police under the code name "Deputy." Karaev was known to the secret police under the rather obvious "Caucasian." The two men had been—inevitably, one is tempted to say—informers.

The previous fall, Karaev had come under suspicion by his anarchist comrades of working for the Okhrana. His friend Makhalin, whose treachery was still undiscovered by his fellow radicals, organized an internal investigation that assuaged the cadre's suspicions—raising enough doubts about Karaev's alleged perfidy that no one felt confident enough of his guilt to kill him.

Karaev, smarting from the mistrust of his fellow revolutionaries, reacted much like Stolypin's doomed assassin Dimitry Bogrov, who had been exposed by his comrades as an informer. He was looking for a way to cleanse his reputation. In the Beilis investigation he believed that he had found what he needed—except his would not be a suicidal act like Bogrov's but instead one of regeneration. He would emerge alive, his honor restored, ready to bask in renewed adulation.

At the time Karaev had nearly been unmasked, he was in fact no longer working for the Okhrana. Although he had been receiving one hundred rubles a month for his services and appeared to earn his pay by supplying reliable information, he was let go for behavior judged too unseemly even by Okhrana standards. According to a department report, the information he provided was of serious interest but turned out to be the product of "the methods of the agent provocateur and his inclination to blackmail." In other words, Karaev had not just tipped off the police about crimes that others had planned; he had entrapped his comrades, luring or coercing them into criminal schemes and setting them up to be arrested.

The prosecution thus had information that could destroy the credibility of these two key defense witnesses. Who would believe the story of two professional informers who had every incentive to lie, who indeed had lied for a living, at least one of whom had been dismissed in disgrace? But would the prosecution be able to use this top secret information in court? It was a question that would be debated intensely behind the scenes and resolved only at the last moment, as the witnesses took the stand.

Vera Cheberyak, in the wake of Brazul's devastating declaration, decided to cast her lot definitively with the prosecution. Chaplinsky may have wanted to build a case without relying on the notorious villain of Lukianovka, but now he needed her. When it came to credibility in court, Cheberyak surely had her shortcomings, but compared to the witnesses he had, which at present numbered three well-known drunks, she amounted to a gift.

Reacting to Brazul's report, Chaplinsky's chief deputy, A. A. Karbovsky, searched frenetically for some way to strengthen the case, reinterviewing key witnesses. On May 14 he questioned Cheberyak. In seven previous depositions to Investigator Fenenko, she had never mentioned Mendel Beilis or said anything about Zhenya and Andrei visiting the Zaitsev factory. In December, her husband, Vasily, had suddenly recalled that Zhenya told him that he and Andrei had been chased away by Beilis, but Vasily did not clearly implicate him. Now, fourteen months after Andrei's death, Vera suddenly recalled that her son had directly accused Mendel Beilis of the crime. She told Karbovsky:

About a week after Andrusha's funeral Zhenya told me that he and Andrusha . . . and other children . . . on March 12, 1911, played at the Zaitsev factory . . . At that time Mendel Beilis jumped out with his sons and other Jews. Beilis's sons ran after Zhenya and Mendel himself chased Andrusha. Zhenya ran away . . . and saw, in his words, that Mendel Beilis grabbed Andrusha . . . and dragged him to the [brick] kiln."

The role of the prosecution in sculpting Cheberyak's testimony remains a matter of speculation. On June 2, in an unusual step for a man of his position, Chaplinsky had a personal conversation with the witness and had her questioned again by another prosecutor. The historian Alexander Tager, who reviewed three of her depositions in which she recounted her new story, noted substantial inconsistencies among them, suggesting that the prosecution helped shaped her account. Only the final version was made public.

On May 30, Vera Cheberyak came to prosecutors with another striking story. She revealed that, in December of the previous year, the journalist Brazul had taken her to Kharkov to meet with some sort of gentleman for a strange talk about the Yushchinsky case. She described the man as "a Jew, very plump, slightly balding, with bulging eyes and a slight lisp." It did not take long for the authorities to figure out that this was Arnold Margolin. In her telling, during the meeting she was offered a forty-thousand-ruble bribe to admit to Andrei's murder. (She was never clear on whether it was Margolin or another participant in the meeting who made the offer.) She was told she could be spirited out of the country to enjoy her new wealth, but even if she had to stand trial, the best lawyers in the empire would have no difficulty securing her acquittal. Thanks to Cheberyak's allegation, Margolin now had to admit to his meeting with her, which he had wanted to keep secret. He denied the fantastic story of the bribe, but with the state moving to disbar him for his alleged interference in an official investigation, he had no alternative except to resign as Beilis's attorney. Gruzenberg was livid at his colleague's recklessness. The Black Hundreds, not to mention the prosecution, could point to Margolin's escapade as proof of a Jewish conspiracy to cover up the hideous ritual. This was a disaster for the defense.

The authorities' next target for harassment was Brazul. In early July, Vera Cheberyak slapped Brazul with a lawsuit claiming injury to her reputation. She also filed libel suits against several newspaper editors who had printed his charges against her. Given the volume of the paperwork and the rapidity with which it was filed, it is inconceivable that Cheberyak mounted this effort on her own; the suits were undoubtedly organized by Chaplinsky's office to bolster her credibility as a witness.

The prosecutor and his superiors then turned their attention toward neutralizing Nikolai Krasovsky, who had for so long been such a nuisance. Krasovsky was unemployed, but he was a free man and a threat. In the eyes of the public he was still the great detective who had cracked so many unsolvable cases and was now receiving encomiums in the liberal and enlightened conservative press for revealing the true killers of Andrei Yushchinsky. This could not stand. On July 17 he was confronted by police officers and read a list of charges against him. He was now criminally accused of improperly arresting the peasant Kovbasa, the purported offense that had gotten him fired from the police force. He was charged with destroying official paperwork regarding his assessment of an unpaid tax in the amount of sixteen kopeks from a citizen in 1903. (The implication was that he had pocketed the money.) Most absurdly, he was being investigated for stealing a winning lottery ticket while conducting a search (whether of a person or someone's premises is not clear). The man who people were calling the Sherlock Holmes of Russia was under arrest.

As Krasovsky spent his first night in jail, his coinvestigators knew they, too, were in danger. Sergei Makhalin had the good sense to flee the city. Amzor Karaev, never one to flinch, rashly remained in Kiev and on August 13 the police arrested him as well. The exact pretext is unknown but, like Krasovsky, his true crime was undoubtedly that of challenging the blood accusation.

By the end of the summer, the prosecution acquired one more exciting addition to its case: a self-proclaimed eyewitness to the crime— nine-year-old Ludmila Cheberyak. Almost exactly a year earlier Vera Cheberyak had pleaded with her dying son Zhenya to absolve her of Andrei's murder, but the boy had failed her, with his last words earning her only more suspicion. Now the mother offered up her one surviving child to the prosecution to exonerate her by condemning another. Perhaps the girl would succeed.

Vera Cheberyak must have been sufficiently self-aware to realize that her testimony alone would likely not be enough to convict Mendel Beilis. She was a notorious figure. People recognized her from her picture in the paper and harassed her on the street. On one occasion in mid-July of 1912, a passerby pointed her out, one thing led to another, and soon a large crowd of people was screaming, "Yushchinsky's murderer!" as it chased after her. She had to duck into a courtyard and hide there until the mob dispersed.

Unlike her mother, Ludmila could play the archetypal role of the virginal eyewitness. Unlike the pure maidservant in Thomas of Monmouth's twelfth-century account, she would not claim to have seen the evil deed "through a chink in the door" but rather to have witnessed the crime in broad daylight. The case would be much the stronger with an innocent girl prepared to point her finger at the bestial Jew in the dock as the man who had killed her young friend.

Ludmila had been questioned on May 14, 1912, separately from her mother. In that affidavit, which was kept secret from the defense, she said nothing to incriminate Beilis. But when she was questioned by the new investigating magistrate, Nikolai Mashkevich, three months later, on August 13, she suddenly told the story that made her the prosecution's dream witness. She now claimed to have gone with Zhenya, Andrei, and other children to play on the clay grinders at the Zaitsev factory on March 12, 1911, the day Andrei disappeared. Mendel Beilis and two other Jews had chased after the children. (In this tale, unlike her mother's account of Zhenya's story, Beilis's sons go unmentioned.) Beilis, she testified, "caught Zhenya and Andrusha by the hands and started dragging them away, but Zhenya broke away and ran away with the rest of us, but Andrusha was dragged away by the Jews somewhere." That, she said, was the last she saw of him.

The case against Menahem Mendel Tevyev Beilis, such as it was, was now complete. Beilis would have to maintain the patience and restraint of a hero for far longer than his attorneys had ever expected. If he thought of every day he survived in prison as a victory, then his victories would be many. He would have to wait more than a year for his chance to stand before the court and tell the judge, the jurors, and the world: "I am not guilty."

8

"The Worst and Most Fearful Thing"

One evening, as the new year of 1913 approached, Mendel Beilis was sitting alone in his cell (in one of the intervals when he had no cellmate) when he heard the approach of footsteps and several voices, and then a woman outside his door saying, "It would be curious to see this rascal." Immediately there followed the grinding of the thirteen locks on his door, as each was opened in turn. The sound always unnerved Beilis, making him feel obsessively as if someone were hitting him on the head from behind over and over.

A guard opened the door and the woman and a man in a general's uniform stepped in. "What a terrible-looking creature," the woman said. "How fierce he looks."

The general was interested in Beilis as more than a sideshow attraction and started up a conversation. He began by telling Beilis that he might soon be set free. "On what grounds?" Beilis asked.

The general said that the tercentenary jubilee of the Romanov dynasty was approaching and, to demonstrate his mercy, the tsar would issue a broad pardon for convicts. If only Beilis would "tell the truth"— that is, confess—things would go well for him, he was sure.

Beilis answered that he didn't need a pardon; he needed exoneration. He would not leave prison until he was declared innocent. Beilis grew enraged, though his impression was that the man was sincerely trying to give him some "good advice." (The general and the lady, to all appearances, were a pair of curiosity seekers with no sinister motive— certainly the lady's presence was no aid to any scheme.) However, even if his advice was well meaning, the general was quite wrong, as were hopes among the Jewish population that the tsar would soon set Beilis free. The impending festivities did not improve Beilis's chances for release. In fact, his trial would serve as the climactic public spectacle of a year dedicated to the greater glory of the House of Romanov.

Tsar Nicholas was indeed looking forward to the tercentenary celebrations as he greeted New Year's Day 1913 at the Grand Palace at Tsarskoe Selo, the "Tsar's Village," south of St. Petersburg, where he spent as much time as he could. He disliked the capital. "Peter's City" was too modern for his taste and, he felt, inauthentic and inorganic to Russia. Tsar Peter had, as Nicholas once put it, recklessly uprooted "healthy shoots" of the Russian way of life along with the weeds. Nicholas belonged in Moscow, the true heart of the Russian Empire. Once a tiny medieval principality just six hundred square miles in size, Moscow had grown into the enormous realm over which he now ruled. Residing in Moscow was not a practical possibility for the Russian sovereign; the machinery of government had been established in St. Petersburg for some two centuries. But in Tsarskoe Selo, Nicholas erected a perfect replica of an old Russian town as the headquarters for the Cossack squadrons of his Personal Convoy and Imperial Rifles, who went about in seventeenth-century costume. Here Nicholas could commune with the glorious Muscovite past.

Dressed in the contemporary uniform of his Cossack guardsmen (Nicholas loved uniforms and had closetsful of many different kinds), he faced a New Year's Day dominated by tiresome official duties, as he personally received official good wishes from scores of notables, including nearly every official of the foreign diplomatic corps all the way down the ranks to the third secretary of the Persian mission, Mr. Hassan Han-Gaffari. As a teenager, Nicholas had found this duty so painful the first time that he had virtually run away from it. Nicholas's mother, the empress Maria Fyodorovna, had once scolded the young Nicholas to mind his manners in such situations, writing him in a letter, "Above all, never show you are bored." Nicholas had since developed stoic endurance in the face of his tedious ceremonial responsibilities.

As the new year began, Nicholas had reason to worry about the condition of his realm. The years 1910 and 1911 had mostly been marked by domestic tranquillity, with the significant exception of Prime Minister Stolypin's assassination. But 1912 had witnessed the revival of mass social unrest. In April 1912 soldiers had fired on a crowd of peaceful demonstrators at the Lena goldfields in southern Siberia, killing five hundred miners. The massacre sparked a relentless wave of strikes that had drawn in some seven hundred thousand workers to date and was only escalating.

However, if Nicholas found himself feeling worried or bored as one dignitary after another bowed before him, he could find relief in pleasanter thoughts. The year 1913 was to be a special year for him, his family, and all of Russia. It was to be a year of celebration, of deeply meaningful reflection on Russia's past that would reaffirm the everlasting, mystical bond of tsar and people. In the coming months Nicholas and his family, together with all his subjects, would commemorate with the grandest of ceremonies the founding of the Romanov dynasty.

The coronation in 1613 of the current monarch's ancestor Michael, the first Romanov tsar, had brought an end to the Time of Troubles, a calamitous fifteen-year period that had left Russia leaderless, beset by famine, ensnared in two wars (with Poland and Sweden), and combating numerous internal rebellions that left Moscow largely burned to the ground. Many observers had compared the Revolution of 1905 to the Time of Troubles; as for Nicholas, he seemed to draw spiritual inspiration from the challenge presented by the massive disorder. He saw himself as the heir to Michael and the other Romanov tsars, not just in lineage but in resolve and historic import; like them, he had faced wars and uprisings and would become one with the people as their God-given commander, leading Russia back on a course to greatness.

As recently as the late nineteenth century, Peter the Great, who ruled from 1682 to 1725, had been regarded as the indisputable founding figure of modern Russia. He was the great Westernizer, the giant of a man who had delighted in roughly shaving off the beards of the retrograde noble class of boyars, forcing them to cast off the old ways. Nicholas's father, Alexander III, who took the throne in 1881, initiated a movement toward a nostalgic premodern vision of Russia, one that demoted Peter the Great and even disparaged him as un-Russian. (Alexander, quite conscious of the symbolism, was the first tsar in two centuries to wear a full beard.) Nicholas would now make the break with Peter even more explicit. The celebrations would proclaim: modern Russia was born not with Peter's Westernizing reforms but with a uniquely and deeply Russian event: the divinely inspired decision of the Zemsky Sobor, or Assembly of the Land, to select Michael as the first Romanov tsar on February 21, 1613.

Leading up to the 1913 jubilee, the regime launched an unprecedented effort to burnish the cult of the past using modern means of pub-
licity. The departures from tradition—even in the name of upholding
it—caused consternation among some of its guardians. New Year's Day
1913 saw the issuance of the first-ever postage stamps bearing portraits
of the tsars, including the reigning one. Some befuddled postmasters
balked at defacing Nicholas's image with a cancellation stamp, which
seemed a sacrilege. In the official organ of the Holy Synod, the soiling
of the tsar's image with a postmark so sickened one bishop that he
was moved to despair. Was he still in Russia, he asked "or has the kike
come and conquered our tsardom?" Some traditionalists were appalled
as the imperial court for the first time authorized the mass production
of various knickknacks—commemorative medallions, posters, decorative boxes, even pencil cases—bearing the tsar's image. But progress, at
least of this backward-looking sort, could not be stopped.

One uncontroversial innovation was the first-ever official biography
of a living tsar. During the month of January, Nicholas took time personally to go over the proofs of *The Reign of the Sovereign Emperor
Nicholas Alexandrovich,* authored by Andrei Elchaninov, a major general and military academy professor who was a member of the tsar's
suite or retinue. Nicholas must have been greatly pleased by the book's
central metaphor; it perfectly expressed his image of himself. "Thousands of invisible threads center on the Tsar's heart," Elchaninov
wrote, "and these threads stretch to the huts of the poor and the palaces
of the rich. And that is why the Russian people always acclaim its tsar
with such fervent enthusiasm."

The strongest of threads connected Nicholas to the Black Hundreds, which he knew to be fomenting the blood accusation and the
case against the Jewish clerk. That bond was never on more exalted
display than it was in St. Petersburg on February 21, 1913, as the tercentenary celebrations began. A thirteen-hundred-member contingent
of the two largest far-right organizations, the Union of Russian People
and the Russian National Union of the Archangel Michael, marched in
official religious processions through the streets of the city, then massed
in front of the Kazan Cathedral, waving their overtly political banners
during an outdoor church service in honor of the anniversary. No one
could doubt that these extremists enjoyed the favor of the tsar. Their
causes were the tsar's causes, including their intense anti-Semitism.

Nicholas had become the first Russian ruler to convey clearly to the *narod,* the common people, his belief in the existence of Jewish ritual murder. He never articulated this message in words but conveyed it through unmistakable ceremonial symbolism—by so visibly supporting the Black Hundreds, as on this day—and through the actions of his officials in the notorious Kiev murder case.

Another invisible thread, of exactly the benign sort Nicholas's biographer Elchaninov had in mind, had once connected Tsar Nicholas to Mendel Beilis. Beilis, a veteran of the tsar's army, had labored in a factory whose profits supported a hospital founded in honor of Nicholas and Alexandra's marriage and dedicated to doing good works. With Beilis's arrest that thread had been severed. But his indictment represented a new sort of bond, indeed a strange sort of dependence, between the imperial sovereign and the lowly prisoner, as he lay in his cell, louse-ridden, shivering himself to sleep every night in his second winter in prison.

The ultimate cause of Beilis's nightmare lay in Nicholas's mystical self-image. This is why the historian Hans Rogger declared that "no purely rational explanation [of the Beilis case] seems to 'make sense.' " Its "rationale" was intuitive and unconscious—nonrational, if not irrational. The true motive behind the prosecution of Mendel Beilis was the same as that of the freshly minted stamps, the mass-produced souvenirs, and General Elchaninov's gaudily laudatory tome: to strengthen the bond between the ruler and his people. That effort, Nicholas believed, was the surest way of warding off a new Time of Troubles. In a sense, Mendel Beilis had once again been drafted into the service of the tsar.

Nicholas was abetted by his ministers, who acted out of careerism but, more deeply, by the need, in Rogger's words, to "supply the ingredients for a missing faith." Their staging of the affair was part of "the search for a principle, for a common belief that would rally and bind together the disheartened forces of unthinking monarchism." Given Nicholas's deficiencies as a ruler, "they had only anti-Semitism and the notion of universal evil, with the Jews as its carriers, to make sense of a world that was escaping their control and their intellectual grasp. To give visible proof that ritual murder had been committed would confirm such a version of events, give it body and reality."

The jubilee gave Nicholas a welcome excuse to escape the capital on a pilgrimage into the heart of Russia that would conclude in his beloved

Moscow. As for Mendel Beilis, during the first months of 1913 he felt himself going nearly out of his mind from the endless delays in his case. "Generally speaking, the life of a prisoner in jail is hell," he wrote in his memoirs, and his seemed an all-too-genuine hell, a torment without end. He was plagued by nightmares. "The usual kind of nightmare," he wrote, "was that I was either led to execution or being chased after, choked or beaten. I would awake, shuddering with fear." He noted, in bitter irony, "I felt a sort of relief in finding upon awakening that I was still in jail—and not in the torture house of my dreams." Six times a day he was roughly strip-searched by a team of five guards. Frequently the guards had to undress him because his fingers were so numb from cold that he could not unbutton his own clothes. The guards would taunt him, without much imagination, often repeating the same line, "You liked to stab the boy Andrusha, to draw his blood. We will do the same thing to you now."

Beilis was not aware of it, but by the late winter of 1913, events were in fact moving forward toward his trial. The investigating magistrate, Nikolai Mashkevich, was close to completing the work that would serve as the basis for the second indictment of Beilis in the murder of Andrei Yushchinsky. The period of the late winter and early spring of 1913 was also crowded with other important developments that would influence Beilis's fate: several court cases involving Nikolai Krasovsky and Vera Cheberyak, and the sudden deaths of two men, including one of Andrei's suspected killers.

Krasovsky, a key witness for the defense, had spent the better part of a year under relentless judicial assault. He had been arrested in mid-July 1912; after his release six weeks later, he went through endless hearings and at least two trials. The state had pressed a total of five charges against him. (The original charge—that he stole a winning lottery ticket from someone during a search—appears to have been dropped.) On February 5, a court acquitted him of improperly destroying official correspondence regarding the assessment of an unpaid tax of sixteen kopeks. Krasovsky's wife finally found the missing papers in a trunk they had packed for their journey back home from Kiev; they were duly forwarded to the proper authorities and Krasovsky was exonerated. He was also acquitted in the case of his alleged illegal detention of the peasant Kovbasa and on three other charges whose exact nature is not known. Over half a year's time, the state had tried to destroy Krasovsky and it had failed.

February 8 brought more good news for the defense. Vera Cheberyak, the prospective star witness for the prosecution, was convicted of forgery in a fraud case involving her local grocer and sentenced to eight months in prison, later reduced to five. The conviction was an indignity to her in three respects. For the first time in her life she had been found guilty of a crime: the infamous Cheberiachka was now, officially, a crook and a convict. Second, the crime of which she was convicted was unworthy of her reputation. This was the woman whose den of thieves reputedly organized spectacular robberies—the woman who, according to rumor, had so filled her apartment with plunder during the Kiev pogrom of 1905 that she fueled her hearth with bolts of silk fabric looted from Jewish stores. The charges that finally brought her down were pitiful: the jury found her guilty of making seventy-six erasures in an account book of money she owed, changing "1 ruble 73 kopeks to 1 ruble 19 kopeks; 2 rubles 13 kopeks to 13 kopeks ... 70 kopeks to 10 kopeks," and so forth. The swindle netted her only a few dozen rubles. And Vera Cheberyak suffered a third humiliation: she lost her name. In the course of the proceedings the court discovered her true origins. She was stripped of the patronymic "Vladimirovna," to which she was legally not entitled. The woman sentenced to prison in court documents was recorded as "Vera Illegitimate Cheberyak." She was now branded with the same middle name that had haunted Andrei Yushchinsky to the end of his life.

The death of a witness is almost invariably an inconvenience but, for the Beilis prosecution, the demise of Dr. Nikolai Alexandrovich Obolonsky represented an opportunity. Obolonsky, the dean of the medical department of the University of St. Vladimir in Kiev who had performed the second autopsy on Andrei, died suddenly from pneumonia on March 14. The doctor had always been less than satisfactory to the prosecution. He would not affirm—even, it appears, under some pressure—that the motive of Andrei's murder was to extract blood. When he was asked leading questions, he complied by speculating what might have happened "*if* blood was collected" but would go no further. He was too distinguished a physician to be replaced as a witness without cause; this was, after all, the man who had been called upon to help try to save the life of Prime Minister Stolypin.

Now the prosecution was free to search for an expert who would say exactly what was necessary. On March 26, Chaplinsky, the chief prosecutor, directed Mashkevich, the investigating magistrate, to solicit the opinion of Dr. Dimitry Kosorotov. Kosorotov, who was a professor of medicine, rendered his opinion expeditiously just two days later. "The pattern of the wounds does not give a basis for concluding that the chief goal was the infliction of torture," the doctor wrote. "The wounds are grouped mainly in those places where one could feel for the veins of the major arteries." His conclusion: "The wounds were inflicted with the goal of collecting the greatest quantity of blood for purposes of some sort." This was the first time that a pathologist had explicitly rendered such a judgment. The city coroner, Dr. A. M. Karpinsky, who had performed the original autopsy, had found no signs at all pointing to the extraction of blood. Dr. Obolonsky and his colleague, the anatomist Tufanov, had, at best, only hinted at such a motive. Dr. Kosorotov now obliged by forging a vital link in the case for the prosecution. Still, if the goal of the crime had been the extraction of blood, then why? The doctor made a show of scientific propriety by refraining from speculation. It would be left to other experts to explain to the jury exactly what constituted the "purposes of some sort."

Toward the end of March, Mendel Beilis was summoned to the office of Mashkevich, the investigating magistrate, who told him that the investigation had been completed. Fourteen months had passed since Beilis had taken that excruciating walk across snow and ice to hear very similar news from Mashkevich's predecessor, Vasily Fenenko. But where Fenenko was deeply ashamed of his involvement in the case, Mashkevich had no such qualms. The investigator read aloud portions of the record to familiarize the defendant with the evidence. For the first time Beilis heard about Brazul, the Diakonova sisters, Malitskaya, and others. "He reads and reads," Beilis recalled of the investigator, "and my head simply began to swim." Disoriented, he found himself casting his eyes about the room as if searching for answers. When Mashkevich finished his presentation, he told Beilis he was turning the material over to the prosecution. Beilis still did not fully understand the judicial process and again became overly optimistic that the whole case might soon be coming to an end. He looked forward to giving Esther the good news. But, while he was visiting with his wife, the assistant prosecutor, Karbovsky, who always monitored their conversations, interrupted Beilis to explain that the end of the investigation did not at all signal the conclusion of the case against him. The investigation would be followed by the indictment, which would take time to draw up; then, after more preparation, came the trial. Esther began to cry. As Beilis, crestfallen, prepared to return to his cell, Karbovsky offered him a cigarette. When Beilis accepted it, Karbovsky made a strange remark, asking with a smile, "Aren't you afraid I might try to poison you?" Puzzled, Beilis responded, "Why would someone want to poison me?"

The meaning of the mysterious remark became clear a short while later when one of his attorneys, Dimitry Grigorovich-Barsky, came to visit. The attorney told Beilis he had an important request that he knew would be hard on him: he had to stop receiving food from home. The Black Hundred newspapers were claiming that the Jews planned to poison him out of fear that he might confess and reveal the truth of the blood accusation. The defense team was concerned that someone on the Far Right would actually try to poison him, to make the conspiracy theory about the Jews appear to be true, as well as to avert the embarrassment of a potential acquittal. Beilis immediately agreed to the request and, on his own initiative, tried to eliminate all chance that he would be poisoned. He had been receiving his food alone, in his isolation cell. Now he petitioned to take his meals with the other prisoners. The prison authorities refused the request, telling him, "If you want to eat, eat what you are given—if not, you can starve. No special privileges for you."

Beilis feared angering his guards, who would kill a prisoner on the slightest provocation. In general, he tried to be as accommodating as possible. But now he responded with a courageous act of defiance: he declared a hunger strike. For three days, the guards slipped the tray with his meals through an aperture in the door of his cell and each time when they took it away the food was untouched. Prisoners who did not eat for three days had to be examined by a court officer, so on the third day Karbovsky appeared. He reiterated to Beilis that he could not get special treatment. To Beilis's surprise, however, the authorities shortly relented and soon he was eating with his fellow prisoners again from a common pot. The food was nearly inedible and at mealtimes he could force down barely enough to keep himself alive. He was living his life half-starved, but he had won a small victory.

Later that month, though, Beilis failed to carry out one of his attorney's other crucial instructions—causing a near disaster for the defense. Grigorovich-Barsky had asked him to request a copy of the entire preliminary investigation—hundreds of pages of reports and depositions. Under Russian law, only the defendant himself could submit the request. Beilis did so and the next morning Mashkevich called on him at the prison. He asked Beilis if he was sure he wanted to make this request, warning that it could delay the trial by several months. The idea of more delay was simply unbearable and threw Beilis into a panic. Of course, Mashkevich might be trying to scare him, but what if he was telling the truth? Beilis figured that if the defense really needed the documents, it would find a way to get them. So he told Mashkevich that he was changing his mind. He withdrew his request.

A few days later, on March 31, Beilis's wife and brother came to visit him. Even though the visits were monitored, Aaron remained true to his abrasive self. Karbovsky noted with indignation in one report that Aaron "allows himself ironic comments about the investigation" and cited one of Aaron's sarcastic witticisms. "They are looking for a Jew with a black beard," Aaron told his brother, "and you grew yourself a beard, didn't you?"

During this visit, Aaron asked his brother if he'd ordered the copies. When Mendel said no, Aaron started screaming at him. "Mashkevich says something to you and you refuse the copies?!" Aaron told him he shouldn't listen to anybody's stories. A copy of the preliminary investigation was the basis for preparing the defense. "The devil knows what's in it!" he shouted. The defense had to find out soon. And did his brother understand that this was not an ordinary case but a "political" one? Aaron would not stop screaming. Karbovsky summoned a guard and had the man escorted from the prison. He noted that further visits by Aaron would be "undesirable."

Aaron had been somewhat unfair to his brother, who well understood his was no ordinary case, but in his anxiety had let himself be tricked. When Beilis finally ordered the copies, it caused no delay in the case. But he would have to wait six more months for his day in court.

———

In these eventful weeks, the prosecution lost one witness, Dr. Obolon-sky, and came out the better for it. The defense also lost a witness, albeit a hostile one, for whom there was unfortunately no replacement. On the night of March 28, 1913, Ivan "Red Vanya" Latyshev was caught after breaking into the fabric store of the brothers Gorenstein on Konstanti-novskaya Street, trying to make off with six hundred rubles' worth of silk. Latyshev, who had been in and out of jail for the past two years, was known to the police as a breaking-and-entering specialist and a member of Vera Cheberyak's gang. He was also, according to Krasov-sky and Brazul's investigation, one of Andrei's three killers. When Latyshev was brought into a precinct office on the robbery charge, it seemed like a routine arrest. But when an investigator mentioned that he recognized his picture from newspaper stories about the Yushchin-sky case, Latyshev apparently grew spooked. He dashed for a window, opened the shutters, and stepped out onto a drainpipe. Whether he was trying to escape or kill himself cannot be known for certain, but he managed to land on the roadway headfirst, as if in a dive. He died of his injuries hours later at the hospital. Latyshev had once insisted he had had "no alarming dreams" and "no hallucinations" about Andrei. But he was the one who reputedly had thrown up after the murder, lacking the stomach for a "wet job." Perhaps he had been hounded by guilt, or was pursued by fear of the boy nicknamed Domovoi, after the creature known to haunt people's nights.

On May 24, a mild spring day, guards took Beilis to the courthouse where he was handed his new indictment, which was some forty-two pages long. He rolled it up into a cylinder and clutched it in his hand as he was taken back to prison. By now he understood that this was only the beginning of a lengthy process that would lead to his trial.

After Beilis received the indictment, Oskar Gruzenberg, now his primary attorney, came to visit him for the first time. Beilis asked Gruzenberg to just tell him the truth. He was already used to disappointments, he said. What were his chances at his trial? Beilis's first attorney, Arnold Margolin, had always tried to rally Beilis's spirits with optimistic talk during their visits, assuring him he would eventually be freed. Gruzenberg was given to speaking more straightforwardly. "Certainly it is not going badly," he told Beilis. "Everyone does indeed see that you are innocent. However, one cannot know what can happen." Gruzenberg then related a story about one of his brothers, who had been perfectly healthy but had come down with some sort of illness. The doctors had laughed it off, telling him it was nothing, but he never got better and eventually he died from the illness. "It is the same with trials," he told Beilis. "No one can know how it can sometimes turn. There is no basis at all on which to convict you, and we can all certainly hope that you will be freed. However, no lawyer can say with certainty that the sick man will get better. That is the truth."

Gruzenberg was careful not to raise his client's hopes, but the new indictment did give the defense reason for optimism. The document was four times longer than the previous indictment, but the case against Beilis, in the attorneys' opinion, was still ridiculously weak. The most significant change had nothing to do with the evidence against the defendant. In the first indictment, Jewish blood lust was hinted at but not overtly mentioned as a motive—the prosecution, as Margolin put it, made you play a game of "blind man's buff." In the new indictment, the prosecution played no games. No ambiguity remained: the state had fully embraced the blood accusation.

The prosecution made two assertions. First, it averred that Jewish ritual murder was a reality, not a myth. Second, it claimed that the murder of Andrei Yushchinsky was a hideous example of this diabolical practice. The indictment cited two witnesses in support of both assertions. The first witness was Dr. Ivan Sikorsky. The new indictment now quoted his judgment, made in May 1911, that Andrei's murder showed all the signs of the "vendetta of the sons of Jacob." Sikorsky, whatever one thought of his racial or religious views, was unquestionably an eminent and respectable figure. The other witness affirming the blood accusation, Father Justin Pranaitis, was, most assuredly, not respectable in the least.

That the prosecution was relying on Pranaitis was an indicator of its desperation. Pranaitis was a Catholic priest from Lithuania who lived in the Uzbek city of Tashkent, in Central Asia. The lead prosecutor, Oskar Vipper, told a newspaper after the trial that Pranaitis had been chosen "because among the Russian Orthodox clergy there were no such resolute, steadfast men." The state, in fact, could not find a single suitable expert among the Russian Orthodox clergy or lay scholars of religion to testify to the reality of ritual murder by the Jews.

This disappointment was foreseeable. While the regime was highly anti-Semitic, the religious and cultural roots of the blood accusation in Russia were, in fact, rather shallow. The myth sprang preeminently out of the Catholic tradition; it was, as the noted historian John Klier put it, a Catholic "import" to Russia, amounting to "learned behavior" on the part of Russians. Certainly, many ordinary Russians believed in it and many Russian Orthodox priests expressed their belief in it in their sermons and even in church publications. Moreover, rumors of ritual murder had played a role in instigating some pogroms. But the Russian Orthodox Church, as such, had never advocated for the myth; its theologians did little to spread it and, on occasion, even denounced it.

The most active propagators of the blood accusation in the Russian Empire were Roman Catholics or Eastern Rite Catholics, also called Uniates. The most notorious and influential of these was the flamboyant charlatan Hippolyte Liutostansky, a Polish Catholic priest who had been defrocked for sexual misconduct (he had ended up contracting syphilis), and then converted to Russian Orthodoxy, taking vows as an Orthodox monk before leaving religious orders to write such works as *The Question of the Use by Jewish-Sectarians of Christian Blood for Religious Purposes in Connection with Questions of the General Attitudes of Jewry to Christianity*. Quite literally a buffoon, he performed comical "Jewish sketches" in a St. Petersburg tavern, fabricated claims that prominent Jews had offered him a hundred thousand rubles to suppress his work, was sued by his own publisher for defamation, publicly renounced his anti-Semitic views and denounced pogroms, then later claimed that the Jews had intimidated him into his renunciation, and resumed his anti Semitic career.

Liutostansky seems a figure impossible to take seriously, yet many respectable people embraced his lurid pseudo-scholarship unblinkingly. He was likely an influence on Pranaitis, who was of the same ilk, if not quite as colorful. Pranaitis had written a pamphlet in 1892, in Latin, entitled, *Christianus in Talmude Iudaeorum sive Rabbinicae Doctrinae de Christianis Secreta (The Christian in the Jewish Talmud, or the Secret Rabbinical Teachings Concerning Christians,* published in English as *The Talmud Unmasked).* The work attracted little notice at first, but by the time of Andrei's death it had been translated into

Russian, and leading far-right figures were citing it in support of the ritual murder charge. Pranaitis had written that he was sure he would be murdered by the Jews for revealing the truth about them, but in the intervening twenty years no one had obliged by fulfilling the prophecy. He was in fine health in December 1912 when he was invited to testify for the prosecution.

Pranaitis, a graduate of the St. Petersburg Theological Seminary, had once even been considered for an appointment as a bishop. Still, despite his credentials, the prosecution had reason to be uneasy about him. In December 1912, after Pranaitis had been deposed in the Beilis case, the government's Department of Religious Affairs circulated a memorandum advertising "disagreeable" information about his past. In 1894, Pranaitis took a painting to the St. Petersburg workshop of a craftsman named Avanzo to have its frame gilded. After the painting suffered accidental damage, Pranaitis claimed it was the work of the Spanish master Murillo and the property of a Roman Catholic cardinal; he demanded three thousand rubles as compensation. He and the trusting Avanzo settled on a payment of a thousand rubles. But it soon was exposed that Pranaitis had made up the story. The painting was no Old Master, and Pranaitis was going to pocket the money himself. He was apparently not criminally charged, but he was banished from the capital to a provincial parish. In 1902 he ended up in Tashkent, in the Central Asian region then called Turkestan, where he angered the authorities with what they regarded as unlawful proselytizing using "rather cunning methods." The regional governor-general's office found that his "fanaticism could incite religious and national enmity between Russians and Poles in Turkestan."

Pranaitis was a flawed choice for testifying to the truth of the blood accusation, but the state could find no better alternative. Liutostansky, then in his late seventies, was still alive, but the prosecution must have judged him too seedy. It had no choice but to overlook the sins of the priest from Tashkent.

In the indictment, the prosecution was careful to limit the blood accusation to Jewish "fanatics" and unenlightened Jews, and not seek to condemn the entire Jewish people outright. The conventional line of sophisticated Russian anti-Semites, this distinction was transparently deceptive. Judeophobes most often pointed their finger at the Hasids, from whose supposedly backward ranks the bloodthirsty fanatics came. But accusing the Hasids was little different from condemning Jews as a group. The Hasids were not merely a sect of Judaism; they constituted one of its two major branches in Eastern Europe, with millions of adherents. Moreover, if such a large portion of Jewry was inclined toward ritual murder, the question naturally arose: How could the so-called sophisticated Jews not know about it? As much as the state would deny it, at the Beilis trial all Jews would stand in the dock.

As for the remainder of the indictment, the defense could feel somewhat relieved. The prosecution was still relying on the contradictory, admittedly drunken testimony of the Lamplighter couple, the Shakhovskys. The major new contributions to the prosecution's case were the testimony of a notorious criminal, Vera Cheberyak; her daughter, Ludmila; and Beilis's ex-cellmate, the informer Kozachenko—which is to say, a sociopath, her frightened child who had obviously been coached into providing a false eyewitness account, and a lowlife police informer. All three would surely be vulnerable on examination in court.

But the defense had its own vulnerabilities. The major one, in Gruzenberg's view, had been entirely avoidable—namely, Margolin's decision to meet secretly with Vera Cheberyak. He had always believed that, in doing this, Margolin had acted foolishly and recklessly. Now his opinion was confirmed by the vigor of their opponents' attacks upon Margolin. The prosecution devoted a whole section of the indictment to the disastrous Kharkov adventure and Vera Cheberyak's charge that, during a meeting at which Margolin was present, she had been offered forty thousand rubles to confess to Andrei's murder. Margolin, having been forced to resign as defense counsel, would have to testify as a witness, which in a sense would put the defense itself on trial. Margolin had given the prosecution raw material it could use to spin stories about a Jewish conspiracy dedicated to shrouding the truth.

Gruzenberg might have felt a bit heartened had he known that two members of the judicial panel that approved the indictment wrote a minority opinion, not made public at the time, arguing that the case should be quashed. N. Kamentsev was the chairman of the panel, composed of members of the Kiev Judicial Chamber, the region's highest court. L. Ryzhov was the panel's rapporteur, assigned to examine the evidence and deliver a report to the panel. Thus, the two members most familiar with the record of the investigation had found the case laid out in the indictment "unconvincing in its totality," its supposed facts "hardly trustworthy," and had contended that no reasonable jury could base a guilty verdict upon it. In conclusion, they wrote: "The investigation of Mendel Beilis should be terminated." But these courageous jurists were outvoted seven to two.

On May 25, the day after the indictment of Mendel Beilis became public, Tsar Nicholas made his gala entrance into Moscow, parading down Tverskoy Boulevard on horseback. He rode alone, twenty yards in advance of his Cossack guardsmen, dismounted on reaching Red Square, and strode across it, passing through the Spassky or Savior's Gate into the Kremlin. He had reached the final destination of his pilgrimage in honor of his ancestor Michael, the first Romanov tsar.

Prime Minister Vladimir Kokovtsov was struck by "the absence of any real enthusiasm and the comparatively small crowds" that had greeted the tsar during his journey around Russia. The same impression of public apathy troubled others as well. Anna Vyrubova, the empress Alexandra's closest confidante, remarked on "the undemonstrative masses of people" at the opening festivities in St. Petersburg. "No enthusiasm was evident anywhere," lamented a senior court official in a personal letter. "We clearly live in those times when faith and love for the Tsar and fatherland have died out."

Nicholas, however, expressed only satisfaction at the popular response he received. He had been inspired by his journey through the real Russia that he so deeply loved. The tour had first taken him and Alexandra to the medieval towns of Vladimir and Suzdal, wellsprings of Russian civilization, east of Moscow, and then north to the upper Volga region. There they had sailed down the river to Kostroma, the city where the sixteen-year-old Michael Romanov had learned of his selection by the Assembly of the Land as the new tsar. At the Kostroma monastery, the abbess Martha blessed Nicholas using the very same Mother-of-God icon with which Michael had been blessed in 1613.

Notwithstanding any apathy his ministers and courtiers might have perceived, the celebrations reinforced Nicholas's belief in his divine mission. "Now you can see what cowards those state ministers are," Alexandra told a lady-in-waiting after her husband had bowed his head to the final, massive gathering at the Kremlin. "They are constantly frightening the emperor with threats of revolution and here—you see it yourself—we need merely to show ourselves and at once their hearts are ours." Prime Minster Kokovtsov recalled in his memoirs that from this time forward Nicholas became more and more convinced that he could do everything by himself "because the people were with Him, knew and understood Him, and were blindly devoted to Him."

In this jubilee year, Nicholas had resolved to reestablish the full measure of his autocratic power. The public adulation that he perceived only bolstered his confidence in his mystic mission. He regretted the democratic concessions he had made in 1905. He would do his best to take them back and restore the natural order. Nicholas now considered dissolving the Duma or stripping it permanently of its very modest legislative power. That fall he wrote his interior minister that a bold move to emasculate the Duma would be "in the Russian spirit." In the end, Nicholas's wiser advisers prevented him from taking these extreme measures. But the tsar was still bent on demonstrating, in every way possible, his rejection of Western democratic and legal norms that he believed were alien to his people.

Given the open and zealous chauvinism of the monarch himself, the prosecution of Mendel Beilis amounted to a powerfully symbolic act. "The belief or non-belief in ritual murder," the historian Richard Wortman argues, "drew a clear line between those who shared [the tsar's] views and those who hoped to set the Russian monarchy on a Western course"—the course he had rejected. Moreover, as the trial would make clear, the case served to undermine the courts, the one Russian institution that, in principle, fully conformed to Western standards (thanks to reforms introduced by his grandfather Alexander II) and for which Nicholas therefore felt contempt. And, finally, the case signaled the tsar's belief that the Black Hundreds, and the officials allied with them against the upstart Jews, were in harmony with the "Russian spirit."

The tsar had resolved to rule exclusively according to the divine, purely Russian dictates of what he called his "inner voice." The cult of the seventeenth century, and the imperative to purify the autocracy of any Western taint, would obsess Nicholas until the final day of his reign as Russia's last tsar.

By the spring of 1913, the European movement in support of Mendel Beilis was gathering strength. The previous year had seen petitions signed by illustrious men who were filled with moral indignation but offered little factual evidence to refute the ritual murder charge. Now some of the world's most eminent physicians were taking up Beilis's cause.

The new season saw the publication in Germany of a book of medical opinions by fourteen specialists from across Western Europe who would go on to present their conclusions at an international conference in London at the end of July. Their prime target was their once respected colleague, now a star witness for the prosecution, Professor Ivan Sikorsky. One after the other, the doctors vented their ridicule. Professor Ernst Ziemke, dean of the College of Medical Jurisprudence in Kiel, Germany, declared, "He without a doubt . . . is governed by considerations arising from unbridled fantasy . . ." "One does not know what to be more surprised by, the naivete or the tendentiousness," said Professor August Forel of Zurich. Professors Julius Wagner-Jauregg (a future Nobel laureate in medicine) and Heinrich Obersteiner of Vienna wrote, "On becoming acquainted with his conclusions it even seems doubtful that the author is a psychiatrist at all." All were outraged that Sikorsky had exploited his legitimate scientific reputation for despicable ends. Sikorsky was rebuked by the London conference as well as by congresses of physicians in Vienna and St. Petersburg in the fall.

Perhaps the most valuable report supporting Beilis's cause was delivered by three British physicians who focused not so much on Sikorsky or the mythical nature of the charge as on a simple question: What story did the four dozen wounds on Andrei's body tell? Drs. Augustus J. Pepper, William Henry Willcox, and Charles A. Mercier forcefully made a key anatomical point: "The wounds inflicted by the killers were not of the sort that would cause strong external bleeding." If such bleeding were the goal, "a completely different kind of weapon would have been used." A killer who wanted to drain a body of blood and collect it in a vessel would hardly go about it with an awl that could inflict only puncture wounds. The obvious weapon of choice would be a knife that could neatly open up a vein or an artery. (Such a method, they pointed out, was, after all, well known to the Jews: the Jewish butcher, or *shoket,* severed vessels in the neck with an extremely sharp blade.) "It appears to us quite impossible that the boy was killed for the purpose of collecting blood," the doctors concluded. The crime was nothing more than a "coarse, brutal murder, committed by a person of unsound mind."

In the United States, the effort in support of Mendel Beilis got off to an oddly slow start. With nearly three million Jews, America was second only to Russia in Jewish population. The American Jewish community, by all rights, should have been the natural leader in the worldwide movement to free Beilis. The country's most influential Jewish organization, the American Jewish Committee, had been founded in the wake of the pogroms of 1905–1906 out of concern for the plight of Russian Jewry. In January 1911, the committee had undertaken its unprecedented public campaign, led by the financier Jacob Schiff, to persuade the U.S. government to abrogate the Russo-American Treaty of 1832 governing commercial relations between the two countries. The pretext of the campaign was that American Jews were subject to discrimination by Russia in the issuance of visas, but it was clear to all that its real purpose was to punish Russia for the way it treated its own Jews and pressure the imperial government to grant them equal rights. Within a year, the effort succeeded in convincing a reluctant President William Howard Taft to abrogate the treaty, over the objections of the State Department. The victory heralded the arrival of American Jews as an effective interest group that, when it chose to, could compete on an equal footing with other ethnic lobbies at the highest levels.

Yet right up to the trial in the fall of 1913, the American Jewish leadership failed to take action in the Beilis affair. An editorial in America's oldest Yiddish paper, *Yidishes Tageblat* (Yiddish Daily News), lamented, "The blood libel in Kiev is shocking in and of itself; however, in addition, it has also emphasized our powerlessness and to what extent we lack real leadership and an acceptable plan of action." It was indeed true that Jewish political power in America was still nascent, with the treaty abrogation campaign an exceptional effort and singular success. A few Jews served in the House of Representatives in 1913, but the country had no Jewish politicians of national stature. In the first decades of the twentieth century American Jewish leaders were still wary of acting as an ethnic interest group and rarely lobbied for specific legislation. America's Jews sought to be seen as Americans first. Jewish leaders were highly ambivalent, for example, about Zionism—the ideal of creating a Jewish state. Schiff was especially adamant that participation in the Zionist movement was irreconcilable with being a good American. (His attitude and that of other Jewish leaders would begin to change by the end of World War I.) Louis Marshall, the committee's president and a prominent attorney, was cautious about taking up

Jewish causes without profound and prolonged consideration. He was often heard to say about his fellow Jews something of this sort: "We are always talking too much about Jews, Jews, Jews, and we are making a Jewish question of almost everything that occurs."

Jewish leaders were just as wary, or perhaps even more so, of being perceived as interfering in domestic affairs as in foreign ones. By remarkable coincidence, in fact, in the summer and fall of 1913, the American Jewish community was coming to grips with a homegrown case of a Jew wrongly accused of a child's murder. The case of Leo Frank was a study in the committee's hesitancy to intervene.

Leo Frank was sometimes called the "American Dreyfus," but a Russian observer perhaps more aptly called him the "American Beilis." The superintendent of an Atlanta pencil factory, Frank was accused of murdering a thirteen-year-old employee, Mary Phagan. Unlike Beilis, Frank was from a well-to-do family and, as a prominent member of the Jewish community, served as the president of the Atlanta chapter of the B'nai B'rith. Beyond the difference in their socioeconomic status, the cases of the two men were quite similar, even eerily so: flimsy circumstantial evidence, unreliable witnesses, outrageously prejudicial state conduct, fear of mob violence, and a star witness for the prosecution who was a leading suspect in the murder. (The case even had its own Krasovsky in the world-famous private detective William Burns.) In August 1913, after a monthlong trial, Frank was convicted and sentenced to death. Anti-Semitism was only one factor in the conviction. Class and regional resentment also played a role. The prosecution portrayed Frank, a New Yorker with an Ivy League education, as a rich northerner who preyed on poor southern womanhood. Anti-Semitism came to the fore after the verdict was handed down when a rabble-rousing Georgia politician, Tom Watson, organized a bigoted campaign against Frank's appeal, demanding that "the filthy, perverted Jew of New York" be put to death. The Frank case shocked America's Jews and led to the formation of the Anti-Defamation League of B'nai B'rith.

The American Jewish Committee turned its attention to the Frank case only after the verdict was delivered. Jacob Schiff was in favor of involving the group in the case and starting a defense fund for the appeal. Louis Marshall was opposed to public action on the not unreasonable grounds that perceived Jewish interference could only harm Frank's chances in court. In the fall of 1913, the committee decided for the time being to work behind the scenes, soliciting contributions for the defense and attempting to persuade southern newspaper editors to run articles questioning Frank's guilt. The next year, Marshall changed his mind and took charge of the defense, arguing Frank's case, unsuccessfully, before the Supreme Court. In August 1915, after Georgia governor John Slaton commuted the death sentence to life imprisonment, Frank was kidnapped from prison and lynched by a group of vigilantes among whom were many prominent Georgia citizens, including a former governor.

In the fall of 1913, that horrific final act lay two years in the future. As committee members pondered the Beilis and Frank cases, they were similarly hesitant about how to handle them. The record of the one committee leadership meeting devoted to the Beilis case, held only when the trial was nearly over, captures the scattered state of their thinking. Judge Mayer Sulzberger, the committee's first president, argued against casting any campaign as rallying to the support of an individual. "The entire issue," he held, "was one between the Russian government and the Jewish nation." The only correct strategy, in his view, was to "leave Beilis out of the picture altogether." Beilis the man must be completely absent from any campaign to save him. (Exactly what he meant by this in practice is not clear.) He cautioned that the tsarist regime's enemies were not necessarily allies in this matter. "The Russian Revolutionists," in his view, "would undoubtedly prefer that Beilis should be convicted," as it would allow them to accuse the regime of "a new crime." All present thought it advisable to lay the groundwork for public action in the event Beilis was convicted. But only Rabbi Judah Magnes, one of the era's great Jewish organizers, expressed the opinion that the broad mass of American Jews should be more outspoken about the Beilis case. The Jews ought to be given a chance to express themselves," he argued. "In this country, the Jews have been very quiet in this matter." By which he appeared to mean, too quiet.

Ordinary Jews, in fact, were deeply interested in the case, as evidenced by the rush of numerous Yiddish theater troupes, including Kramer's Comedy Theater, to stage plays about it in time for the trial. "It seems that we can expect a theatrical Mendel Beilis epidemic," the New York–based Yiddish newspaper, *Di Varhayt* (The Truth) reported disapprovingly two weeks before the trial began. The eruption of dramas started with the smaller theaters, vaudeville houses, and music halls, where spectators might be treated to a Beilis performing a duet with Gruzenberg in jail, and by a Vera Cheberyak who broke out into a song and dance routine. At least two dramatizations of the Beilis story included a romantic subplot involving Beilis's daughter and one of his attorneys (though in real life the eldest daughter was only five years old).

The "epidemic" quickly infected the most prominent Yiddish actors and producers, with six major productions announced in New York alone, and with others scheduled in Philadelphia, Boston, Chicago, Cleveland, and other cities. The shows competed in their presumption, each one contending that it had the "true" or "real" Beilis rendition. The People's Theater in Chicago boasted that its *Mendl Beylis, der idisher martirer* (Mendel Beilis, the Jewish Martyr) was "the greatest sensation, the greatest drama of the twentieth century." Jacob Adler, known as "the Great Eagle" and the most celebrated Yiddish actor of his generation (and father of the famous method-acting coach, Stella Adler) also betrayed no modesty. "The voice of the people is the voice of God," the advertisement for his theater declared. "The people want me, Jacob Adler, to play Mendel Beilis."

Di Varhayt, dismayed at all the tastelessness, tut-tutted at the "sin of trying to make a few dollars" off serious events that should not be staged. In the coming weeks, that sentiment would be expressed dozens of times over in the Yiddish press, which was virtually unanimous in expressing horror and shame at what it saw as the exploitation of a tragedy for the Jewish people. But however crude and crass the Beilis shows were, they amounted to the first mass expressions of outrage in America against the barbarous spectacle in Kiev. It would take some time for any Jewish leaders to match the interest and sense of urgency of the common folk.

In July, Beilis received word that after more than a year of delays, the court had finally set a new trial date: the twenty-fifth of September. He had a wait of more than two months ahead of him, but having a definite day to look forward to settled his mind. "It is this not knowing why, when and what that is the worst and most fearful thing, the thinking and waiting every day, every minute for liberation, and the same thing for entire years, day after day, one night after another—this is terrible, this is unbearable, one can simply become insane," he recalled. In the weeks before the trial, he felt better physically. He ate better, somehow swallowing more of the prison food. Even on the nights leading up to the trial, when he might have been nervous, he slept soundly.

Beilis might have slept less well had he known of the ordeals that his quartet of would-be saviors—all of them key witnesses for the defense—were enduring in those same weeks. Nikolai Krasovsky was unemployed, with no means of supporting his family. Though the persistent detective had been exonerated of all of the criminal charges against him, he was still reprimanded for "failure to observe formalities" in the matter of detaining the peasant Kovbasa. His arrest of that fellow, for belonging to an illegal political organization, had been justified, at least according to the standards of Russian law at that time. That the police later saw fit to rearrest Kovbasa did nothing to help Krasovsky, who remained banned from serving on the force.

Still hanging over the head of the journalist Stepan Brazul-Brushkovsky was an accusation of criminal libel by Vera Cheberyak, which threatened to land him in prison. However, the state had wisely moved to postpone the libel proceedings until after Beilis's trial. After all, what if Brazul won? A victory would strengthen his credibility and tarnish a star prosecution witness. It apparently took some time to find a suitably absurd charge to lay Brazul low in time for the trial. In July, an army officer lodged a complaint with the authorities, swearing that he had witnessed Brazul in a Kiev public park rising to his feet the first two times the national anthem was played and remaining seated for the third. Brazul was charged with lèse-majesté—affronting the dignity of the emperor—and sentenced to a year in a fortress, standard punishment venue for political prisoners, where strict solitary confinement was the rule.

After his arrest in July 1912, the anarchist Amzor Karaev had been sentenced to five years of exile in a remote village in south-central Siberia thirty-five hundred miles from Kiev. He had sworn in an affidavit that Vera Cheberyak's half brother, Peter Singaevsky, had confessed to him his role in the murder of Andrei Yushchinsky. As a witness duly subpoenaed by the defense, the state was duty bound to deliver him to the courtroom. But on August 30, Karaev wrote a letter to Krasovsky informing him that he was convinced the prosecution would make every effort to keep him from testifying. He was determined to come to Kiev on his own: in other words, to leave illegally. Escape from exile was relatively easy in tsarist Russia. It would have been much easier had he not written a letter to a man who he should have realized was almost surely under police surveillance. (Sometimes it seems as if Karaev was not completely sane.) The letter to Krasovsky was, of course, intercepted and the secret police had Karaev arrested for planning to escape.

Only Sergei Makhalin, Karaev's partner in attempting to hoodwink a confession out of Singaevsky, had a relatively easy time of it, having made himself scarce by leaving Kiev. He had come into a modest legacy from his grandfather, enabling him to give up tutoring. He devoted himself now to his operatic training and indulging his taste for dandyish getups, which would attract much attention at the trial.

Very early on the morning of September 25, the racket of the thirteen locks came as sweet sounds to Mendel Beilis's ears. A guard opened the cell door and took him to the prison office. There laid out for him was his old blue suit, which he had not seen for two and a half years. He was taken aback by the powerful effect the sight of it had on him. In the worn pieces of cloth he saw his freedom. A guard told him to don the suit, which he did gladly. Everyone was suddenly friendly toward him. The guard helped him on with his clothes and the prison officials escorted him to his carriage, Beilis recalled, "as if they were accompanying a groom." It felt as if something magical had happened.

"Mr. Beilis," the warden told him, "go in good health, and do not forget us." The prison officials were calling him "Mister," treating him like a human being. This was unexpected. Perhaps, he thought, this was a good sign. He was led to a coach surrounded by a dozen policemen on horseback. Beilis joked that anyone else would have to pay two hundred rubles for such royal treatment, but they were giving it to him for nothing. Everyone laughed.

Once inside the coach he looked out the window. Large numbers of people lined the streets the entire way to the courthouse. At first the crowds frightened him, but he was soon moved to tears. People cheered, doffed their hats, and waved handkerchiefs. Most were university students, but there were hundreds of others—men, women, children. He had heard that people supported him, but this was the first time he had seen it with his own eyes. They were everywhere straining to catch sight of him, looking out of their windows, even on rooftops. Some, it was true, were not well-wishers: he could recognize a good number of Black Hundreds by their badges. The entire route was lined with mounted Cossacks, to ensure that there was no disorder. When the crowds surged too close to the coach, the Cossacks drove them back, snapping their whips.

The carriage drew up to the courthouse on St. Sophia Square, across from the thirteen-domed cathedral where Andrei Yushchinsky had once studied, hoping to become a priest. Beilis jumped out, telling the driver, "I will pay you on my way back." Again, people laughed. He was led through long corridors to a room that he was disappointed to find was only a waiting area for prisoners.

After a short while, a tall man with a beautiful head of gray hair, theatrically swept back, entered the room. Nikolai Karabchevsky was widely regarded as Russia's foremost defense attorney. He had joined the defense team the year before, but Beilis was meeting him for the first time. Like everyone who met Karabchevsky, Beilis was struck by his imposing physical appearance. "It was as if a strong light had penetrated the room," Beilis would say. Karabchevsky introduced himself but did not move to shake his hand, explaining that the authorities had ordered the defense team to stay at least three steps away from the defendant. It was outrageous, but they had to obey the rule for now. The attorney made sure Beilis was brought cigarettes and a meal from the court restaurant. Greatly fortified, Beilis remained in the waiting room for three hours until a small door opened and his guards led him into the courtroom. The trial was at last about to begin.

9

"Yes, a Jew!"

At around noon on October 25, 1913, Mendel Beilis, surrounded by guards, found himself in an oblong courtroom, with large windows on one side, big enough to seat two hundred people. Behind the judges' bench, draped in crimson, sat four robed men, one of them with a magnificent gray beard parted in the middle to form two downy wings. Above, in the gallery, the four dozen Russian and foreign journalists fortunate enough to receive passes sat cramped together at tiny lecterns.

"A place can scarcely be found on the globe where people who know how to read are not aware of the Beilis case and do not have an opinion about it," observed Vladimir D. Nabokov, a prominent liberal opponent of the regime (and the father of the novelist), who covered the trial for the newspaper *Speech*. Indeed, Mendel Beilis, dressed in his comforting old blue suit, approached the dock as the defendant in what was now undoubtedly the most notorious trial of the young century. In fact, the only legal case of the age to rival Beilis's in worldwide attention and perceived significance had been that of another Jew, the French officer Alfred Dreyfus, who had been accused of passing secrets to the Germans, and whose identity as a Jew had been the primary source of contention around the justice he received.

Dreyfus's two trials for treason, in 1894 and 1899, had occurred behind closed doors, but the proceedings against Beilis were public, attracting 150 news organizations, most of them foreign. At the main telegraph office, forty employees had been hired and extra lines installed to handle the increased traffic, but at the courthouse the facilities were inadequate. The acoustics were poor and, despite rumbling electric fans, the ventilation miserable. No matter the weather outside, the courtroom was oppressive and the air fetid. More than one witness would faint during the trial. Court was in session twelve to fourteen hours a day, seven days a week, with a half-day break on Sundays the only respite.

Beilis exchanged a few words with his attorneys, men he had been told were the best lawyers in the land. Surely, he thought, they would not let him perish. Then he was seated in the dock, perpendicular to the right side of the judge's bench, and looked at the jurors, directly opposite him, across the width of the room. His heart sank. He had imagined the twelve men who would judge him would be people like his attorneys—educated and respectable citizens. But before him he saw mostly simple peasants, with bowl haircuts, some even wearing caftans tied at the waist, the traditional village garb. These were the ones who would decide his fate? Even apart from any prejudices they might have, how could they possibly understand the learned testimony of university professors? In Russian courts, verdicts were decided by majority vote. (A tie would mean acquittal.) Just seven of these men could destroy his life.

The composition of the jury stunned the liberal press, too. All adult males were eligible for jury duty, but Kiev was a university center, and a jury this uneducated was unheard of. In all, seven of the jurors were officially classified as "peasants." Two were "townsmen" or "petty bourgeois" (the estate to which Beilis himself belonged and which included ordinary working folk). Three were "officials," a category that encompassed nearly anyone who worked in a government office and held a pen.

The jury had almost certainly been rigged, at least as much as was possible, primarily through restricting which citizens were allowed onto the panel from which the final twelve were chosen. The previous year, the justice minister had sent out a secret order that the regime's opponents—"strangers to the high aims of justice"—should be expunged from the jury rolls. In practice, this meant excluding many educated citizens. For the Beilis trial, someone had apparently taken that directive to an extreme. The thirty-three-member panel had only four people of any education. No direct evidence of jury-rigging ever surfaced, but in other panels chosen in the courthouse at the same time, the educated contingent was about three times as great.

What is certain is that, after the panel was selected, interior minister Nikolai Maklakov made an illegal and risky move: he ordered the secret police to put all prospective jurors under surveillance. Eight days before the trial began, the chief of the imperial Department of Police, Stepan Beletsky, sent a coded telegram to the Kiev authorities ordering the Kiev Gendarmes to place the panel "under the closest, most careful, and most competent observation" and gather information "for judging [their] state of mind." A senior agent in Kiev warned his superiors that the effort was futile and, if discovered, would surely cause a public scandal. He was ignored. The initial surveillance in fact yielded no useful material. But when the twelve final jurors were sequestered in courthouse apartments for the trial's duration, the interior minister had twenty-three agents, some of them masquerading as court pages, keeping them under close watch and listening in on their conversations.

Mendel Beilis's five-member defense team, which worked pro bono, were the greatest collection of Russian legal luminaries ever assembled to defend a single man. The head of the team, and its only Jewish member, was Oskar Gruzenberg. The leadership role was somewhat unsuited to his temperament. He admitted in his memoirs that "my bellicose character and my inability (or rather my unwillingness) to smooth off the sharp edges frequently made me unbearable." He had often been threatened with disciplinary action after an altercation with prosecutors and judges and was so intemperate that he had once penned a grossly insulting letter about a minister of justice that was certain to be opened and read by the police (the letter was addressed to a prisoner). His colleagues in the bar emphatically agreed that he could be quarrelsome and domineering, but he was undoubtedly a great attorney and one of the few who had experience with a ritual murder accusation, having successfully defended the Vilna barber David Blondes a decade earlier.

Gruzenberg would share the greater part of the cross-examination duties with Nikolai Karabchevsky, who was not merely an eminent attorney but a national celebrity. At sixty-two, he was still an attractive man, carried himself like a romantic hero, and enjoyed a legion of female fans. The court enthusiasts known as "legal ladies" would take in his trials as they would the theater, so transporting did they find his orations. Gruzenberg thought Karabchevsky was overrated as an orator, but he had achieved some astounding victories, with a special genius for defending admittedly guilty clients in sensational murder cases: a man obsessed with a prostitute whom he killed in a rage when she refused his offer of marriage; a young woman who shot to death her sadistic lover; an Armenian who fatally stabbed the Turk who had massacred his family after running into him in a coffeehouse years later. (The two men were acquitted, and the woman got off with a token sentence.)

Karabchevsky loved receiving large fees but gave much of his money away, had a strong social conscience, and represented many clients pro bono, including Jewish victims of pogroms, in civil suits. He defended the most violent opponents of the regime. His most stirring moment was surely his summation in the 1904 trial of Egor Sazonov, who had assassinated the brutal and widely despised interior minister Viacheslav Plehve. Karabchevsky boldly attacked Sazonov's victim, essentially arguing that killing a butcher such as Plehve could not properly be considered murder. "And grasping the bomb with trembling hands," Karabchevsky declared, "[Sazonov] believed that it was not so much filled with dynamite and fulminate of mercury, as with the tears, sorrow, and calamity of his people. And when the shards of the bomb exploded and scattered, it seemed to him that it was the clanking and breaking of the chains which had been binding the Russian people." That a political moderate like Karabchevsky could so passionately defend a terrorist is a striking indication of the progressive elite's profound alienation from the regime. The court, which reacted to his speech with public hostility, may have been more like-minded than it let on. It spared Sazonov the noose, sentencing him to a life of hard labor.

Some of Karabchevsky's gifts were, unfortunately, of limited use in the trial about to get under way in Division 10 of the Kiev Circuit Court. The great attorney was a virtuoso of melodramatic rhetoric that bewitched enlightened judges and cultured jurors steeped in Russian and world literature. (His summation in defense of the Armenian killer quoted Gibbon.) To win over this jury, he would have to adjust his natural style.

The third attorney, Alexander Zarudny, was a small, bearded man of fifty who appeared so unimposing that a friend once joked that one had to look closely to notice him. Yet he was renowned for his tireless work defending political prisoners. Gruzenberg likened him to a one-man rescue team who raced along icy and dangerous legal roads from one political case to another. The two men had defended members of the revolutionary 1905 St. Petersburg Soviet, including its leader, Leon Trotsky. Zarudny, though unprepossessing, was quite capable of making himself noticed. He would have a secondary role in the questioning in the Beilis case but would regularly explode with cries of "Objection!" and "I request this be noted in the record!" His objections were meant to keep the prosecution off balance and help lay the grounds for an appeal, should one become necessary, but his demeanor risked alienating the jury. Gruzenberg found him to be a brilliant orator at his best, but uneven, while Karabchevsky likened Zarudny's arguments to moves in chess that skipped over squares, forcing the listener to strain to sort out the speaker's logical steps.

Soon to arrive from St. Petersburg was perhaps the most intellectually brilliant member of Beilis's legal team, Vasily Maklakov. A prominent advocate for revolutionary defendants, Maklakov was also a member the Duma, where he belonged to the Kadet or Constitutional Democratic faction that sought to transform Russia into a state based on the rule of law. Maklakov personified the extreme division rending the upper levels of Russian society: his younger brother, the reactionary and anti-Semitic Nikolai Maklakov, was the minster of the interior actively conspiring to convict Mendel Beilis. (The brothers lived on neighboring estates but, not surprisingly, had not spoken in nearly two decades.) At forty-four, Vasily Maklakov was one of a younger breed of attorneys who adopted a more plainspoken style than his elders. By the end of the trial some would think Beilis's freedom hinged on the effectiveness of Maklakov's summation.

Rounding out the team was the respected Kiev attorney Dimitry Grigorovich-Barsky, who had often visited Beilis in prison. He had something of a personal interest in the case. As a prosecutor, he had been involved in the failed effort to convict Vera Cheberyak in the blinding of her former lover, Pavel Mifle, seven years earlier. He would now have a chance to face her again and, if not convict her, then at least hold her accountable for an even more terrible crime.

The prosecution was composed of far less eminent figures. Technically, there was only one prosecutor, Oskar Vipper. A thin, tense greyhound of a man, Vipper was an assistant prosecutor of the St. Petersburg Judicial Chamber, the capital's highest court. Why he had been especially selected for this case is not completely clear. Gruzenberg thought Vipper lacking talent, but the *Kievan,* which opposed the case, rated him as moderately competent.

Vipper was joined by Georgy Zamyslovsky, a far-right-wing member of the Duma, and Alexei Shmakov, a notoriously and proudly anti-Semitic attorney and Moscow city council member, who decorated his study with pictures of Jewish noses. Shmakov was the author of some of the most popular Russian works on the supposed global Jewish conspiracy, most recently *The International Secret Government (Revised and Expanded Edition),* in which he wrote, "In the world there exist not fifteen million Jews . . . but *one* Jew copied *fifteen million* times." The two men were technically "attorneys for the civil plaintiff," representing Andrei Yushchinsky's mother, but they functioned as co-prosecutors (and will be referred to hereafter as the "civil prosecutors"). Under Russian law, a criminal trial and a civil suit for damages could be combined. The two attorneys were seeking five thousand rubles (about a decade's worth of his old salary) from the virtually penniless defendant.

Surprisingly, both Gruzenberg and Beilis's original attorney, Arnold Margolin, had something of a soft spot for Shmakov, whom they very generously credited with a misguided but genuine sort of integrity. For Margolin, the corpulent, elderly Shmakov "reminded one of a clumsy, sulky bear" who was "fair and honest in his fashion." Gruzenberg wrote in his memoirs that Shmakov "was not by nature a malicious man . . . but rather one who had been completely possessed by a blind anti-Semitism." As for Zamyslovsky, they simply found him "exceptionally vile," a careerist and conniver who believed that he could turn fame from the Beilis case to his professional and material advantage.

As for the four members of the judicial panel, only its impressively bearded chairman, Judge Fyodor Boldyrev, was of any importance. Karabchevsky had a low opinion of him—in fact, he had been making fun of this very man for most of his life without realizing it. Decades earlier Karabchevsky had been faced in a case by an insecure and incompetent prosecutor whom he remembered only as "Fedya" (the diminutive of Fyodor—the equivalent of "Teddy"). Before that trial, Fedya's wife had paid Karabchevsky an unexpected call, imploring him to go easy on her husband and perhaps even give him a few pointers so he could at least give a respectable performance against his already celebrated young opponent. After that, Fedya had entered the lexicon of Karabchevsky and his circle. As in, "Could you believe that Fedya today?" Or, "That fellow was quite a Fedya." But he had lost track of the real fellow entirely until one day he realized that the chief judge in this strange case was, astonishingly, the Fedya of legend.

Boldyrev, somewhat inexplicably to outside observers, had been drafted for the case from a provincial court in the small city of Uman, about a hundred miles south of Kiev. His main qualification arose from a secret report assuring the authorities of his "firmly right-wing convictions." Unbeknown to Karabchevsky and Gruzenberg, justice minister Ivan Shcheglovitov had promised Boldyrev the chairmanship of Kiev's highest court, the Judicial Chamber. Boldyrev surely understood that the promotion was contingent upon his satisfactory conduct of the case. As the trial approached, a police agent reported that the judge was said to be in a highly anxious state "and had even undergone a special course of hydrotherapy." Given the stakes for Boldyrev, his anxiety was understandable. The treatment seems to have been effective. Throughout the proceedings, Fyodor "Fedya" Boldyrev maintained his august judicial demeanor.

By the time Beilis sat himself down in the prisoner's dock, hope had left him. He stayed motionless for quite a while, staring at the jury. Then he turned to his left, glancing at his wife, Esther, in the front row, dressed in black, her head wrapped in a black lace scarf. From time to time he lifted his spectacles to wipe away tears with a handkerchief.

The first two hours were taken up with maddening technicalities and bickering. The defense and prosecution teams argued over where they would sit. The defense objected when the prosecution was placed too close to the jury. The prosecution objected when it was seated next to the defense, complaining that the defense would overhear its conversations. Waving his hand contemptuously, Karabchevsky told them, "Your conversations interest us little." The session could not begin until all witnesses were present, but Ulyana Shakhovskaya, the Lamplighter's wife, was not to be found. The police tracked her down, roaming the streets drunk, and dragged her into court. At 2:28 p.m. a bailiff finally shouted, "Court is in session!"

The judge began by questioning Mendel Beilis.

"What is your name?"

"Menahem Mendel Tevyev Beilis."

"How old are you?"

"Thirty-nine."

"How many children do you have?"

"Five."

"Your place of permanent residence is Kiev?"

"Kiev."

"Are you a Jew?"

Observers remarked that Beilis now spoke up noticeably, answering the question more loudly than the judge had asked it. "I did not recognize my own voice when I answered," Beilis wrote later. He felt himself almost shouting:

"Yes, a Jew!"

The question about religion betrayed no special prejudice. The judge questioned all the witnesses in similar fashion and each was sworn in by a clergyman of his or her faith—Jews by a rabbi, Catholics by a Catholic priest, and so forth. The judge reprimanded the rabbi for adding, after swearing in his first witness, "May your testimony shed light on the truth." The words were not relevant to the oath, the judge admonished. Thereafter the rabbi hewed to the oath as written.

Vera Cheberyak, small and thin, wearing a fashionable hat with yellow feathers, attracted the most attention. Impressions of her vary. Some found her beautiful, some not. All found her compelling. Nabokov, writing in *Speech,* described her as "dark-complexioned, with thick sensuous lips and an energetic chin." Hers was an ordinary face, one you might pass by without giving a second glance, yet somehow also one you would never forget. Many commented on her distinctive, sharp body movements and large, dark, constantly darting eyes ("beautiful, restlessly wandering" in one mesmerized reporter's description). When she was called to the witness stand—literally a stand, as all witnesses, unless infirm, stood while testifying—the judge asked her, "Have you ever been convicted of a crime?" For once, Cheberyak looked cowed. She lowered her head and said nothing. The judge took the gesture as an affirmative response and it was entered into the record that she had been convicted of defrauding her local grocer and sentenced to a prison term. From the defense's point of view, it was a good start—at least the jury would know this witness was a criminal.

By the end of the session, which ran late into the evening, the proceedings were already taking a physical toll. Vera Cheberyak had fainted and several child witnesses had also collapsed, from hunger (the court had neglected to make provision to feed them). Beilis recalled that by the time he was led out of the courtroom, he himself was "near to fainting from boredom and exhaustion."

Upon returning to his cell, he found it pleasantly altered. Instead of a dirty mattress on the floor, there was now a nice cot. Moreover, he recalled, "all the guards acted like old friends." Apparently the order had been given to treat him better and ensure he presented himself as a robust defendant. The regime knew the world was watching.

The next morning Beilis's journey from prison occasioned far less commotion than it had on the first day. Out of the small window of his carriage, unobstructed by crowds, Beilis could see the unreeling ribbon of pastel-painted plaster facades—yellow, blue, green, red, pink—of the low two- and three-story buildings so characteristic of Kiev and other cities in the empire. A final turn brought the conveyance back to the courthouse, an irregular pinkish brick polygon four stories high, occupying the better part of a city block. As if by an architect's oversight, it lacked a grand entrance to impress the beholder with the power and authority of justice. The guards led Beilis in through one of its nondescript doorways and up stairs and down dimly lit corridors to the courtroom where, after more than two years of waiting for this moment, he would finally make his plea.

Beilis sat nervously in the dock, his back to the row of windows, so strangely incapable of providing ventilation, but offering a beautiful view of the "many-tiered honeycomb" of the city, as the writer Mikhail Bulgakov called it, with the leaves just turning color, against the clear blue sky. He didn't know where to put his hands, kept wiping his sweaty palms, squinted frequently at the crowd, and could not restrain his tears. Russian trials provided for no opening statements by the prosecution and defense. Instead, the indictment was read aloud. One of the assistant judges read it slowly, in a strong, clear voice that overcame the bad acoustics. Beilis, though he had read the document many times, listened attentively.

Then chief judge Boldyrev turned to Beilis and asked him: "Do you admit your guilt in conspiring with other persons unknown, with the

premeditated goal, out of motives of religious fanaticism, for ritual purposes, to deprive Andrei Yushchinsky of his life on March 12, 1911 . . .
gagging him, and killing him . . . by inflicting forty-seven wounds on
his head, neck and torso with a pointed instrument, causing injuries
to veins in the brain and neck, arteries in the left temple and injuries
to the dura mater [the outermost brain membrane], the liver, the right
kidney, the lungs and heart—which injuries, accompanied by painful
and prolonged suffering, resulted in the almost complete draining of
blood from Yushchinsky's body?"

Beilis responded, "No, I am not guilty. I was a soldier, then I earned
my living by honest work and raised my children. Suddenly I was
taken, arrested, held in prison. Why I do not know. Nothing was . . ."
Boldryev interrupted him, saying explanations were not appropriate
at this time but that he would be free to speak his piece later and even
question witnesses.

Beilis had been able to control himself during his plea, but as his
attorneys argued with the judge, he put his head to his knees and
erupted in loud, deeply resonant sobs. The passionate wailing filtered
through the still air all the way up to the gallery where it was heard as
a dull room-filling drone. Beilis's sobs would punctuate the proceedings every few days. The eruptions could come at any moment—during
testimony by a witness for the defense or for the prosecution or a dispute over a procedural matter. The judge would ask the defendant if he
needed some time. Beilis would invariably say no, to please let things
proceed. His sobs visibly discomfited the judges and court officers.
They brought tears to the eyes of some spectators. But the noted Yiddish writer S. Ansky, who covered the trial, wrote, "It is clear that Beilis
is not a broken man." He wore an "expression of suffering—but not of
a timid or submissive person, but of an indignant one."

The first witness was Andrei's mother, Alexandra Prikhodko, a
woman of about thirty-five, her long hair plaited in a braid. Given her
mistreatment of her son, her testimony was poignantly double-edged,
honest grief mixed with unspoken regret. "Andrei was illegitimate.
Did you love him just as you did your other children?" the prosecution asked. "More than any of them," she answered. Andrei's maternal
grandmother, Olympiada Nezhinskaya, notably refused to say anything against the Jews. It seemed Andrei had a Jewish friend, Gershik
Arendar. "Did you take any notice of the fact that he was friends with

a Jewish boy?" the prosecution asked. "No," she answered. Had she asked the police if "maybe the Jews killed him?" Again, no.

The initial witnesses were wholly irrelevant to the question of Mendel Beilis's guilt. After a few days, the left-wing activist Vladimir Bonch-Bruevich, writing in *Kiev Opinion,* mockingly declared, "We must inform our readers of an exceptionally important and interesting piece of news: Beilis has ceased to be the defendant!" Beilis's odd status as a nonentity at his own trial was one of the most widely commented on aspects of the proceedings. Nabokov's colleague at *Speech,* Stepan Kondurushkin, noted that one could sit in the courtroom for hours on end, even a whole day, without knowing who was on trial. One of the two police officials filing daily reports noted: "The trial is making a strange impression: over the course of three days, no one is interested in Beilis."

Also prominent in the first days was the testimony of a series of squirming police officers who tried to explain away their mishandling of the crime scene. It often seemed, many observers noted, as if the Kiev police were on trial. Andrei's mother, stepfather, and grandmother recounted in detail their weeks of torment at the hands of detectives Mishchuk and Krasovsky. The prosecution broadly hinted that some sort of Jewish conspiracy was at work in misleading the police.

A series of Andrei's friends and schoolmates, bashful, stammering boys tugging at their trousers and the hems of their jackets, spoke of their friend. Gershik testified how Andrei had shared his fantasies about his real father, who would surely call for him one day. He also told of how he had once given his friend the best possible present, a toy gun that used gunpowder and could shoot real bullets (ones you had to cast yourself out of melted lead). When cross-examining Gershik's father, Gruzenberg brought up that Russian children often played with Jewish ones on the streets of the Slobodka suburb. "And none of them disappeared?" he asked. To which the man replied, of course not.

The prosecution made much of an old Jew named Tartakovsky who roomed with the Arendars and was said to be devastated by Andrei's death. An old man with no family took a shine to a young boy and was stricken with grief at his murder—something was suspicious here. As for the poor man's subsequent death from choking on a bone during a meal, the prosecution hinted at a Jewish cabal.

Zarudny popped up with continual objections, which had their intended effect. Vipper, the state prosecutor, would try to adopt a sarcastic and haughty air but often looked jumpy, unnerved, and even disoriented. Shmakov, on the other hand—fat, slow-moving, with an old man's muttering tone—maintained his sarcastic composure. "Every time I say something about Jews Mr. Zarudny asks for it to be entered into the record," he cracked at one point. "So the whole record is going to be scribbled over entirely with Jews!"

On the morning of the third day, people swarmed Kiev's newspaper stalls. The most sensational event of the trial's opening phase had occurred not inside the courtroom but outside it, in the form of the lead article on the front page of the *Kievan* by the paper's editor, Vasily Shulgin—a full-blown attack on the prosecution. Demand for copies colossally outstripped supply. Newspaper sellers made a killing as customers paid a ruble just to read the issue while standing at the stall. The defense bought an early copy for three rubles. The price quickly went up to five. By evening the issue had been confiscated by the government and copies were going for fifteen rubles.

Shulgin was one of the most intriguing figures in the entire Beilis affair: a brilliant journalist, a member of the Duma, an uncompromising opponent of the blood accusation, a convinced monarchist, and a die-hard anti-Semite who believed the Jews were a pernicious, exploitative force that needed to remain suppressed. He also thought the trial was an offense to anyone's sense of justice. He thundered:

> The Beilis indictment is not simply an indictment of one man, but an indictment of an entire people for one of the most heinous of crimes, the indictment of an entire religion for one of the most infamous superstitions . . .
>
> One doesn't have to be a lawyer, but need only have some common sense, to understand that the Beilis indictment is mere prattle which any defense attorney could break down without even trying.

Shulgin attacked chief Kiev prosecutor Grigory Chaplinsky for removing Detectives Mishchuk and Krasovsky from the case for their refusal to hunt down a man merely because he was a Jew. "The entire police force," he wrote, "terrorized by the actions of the judicial chamber's prosecutor, realized that anyone who uttered a word . . . other than what the authorities wanted to hear . . . would immediately be thrown in prison." Risking prosecution for criminal libel, he concluded, "We assert that the prosecutor of the judicial chamber, Privy Councillor Grigory Gavrilovich Chaplinsky, intimidated his subordinates and choked off all attempts to cast light on the case."

Shulgin had shockingly accused the regime of conspiring to convict an innocent man. Accounts of the article, though not the full text, were printed in papers across the empire. This was the "*J'accuse*" moment of the Beilis case. Unlike Émile Zola's famous broadside in the Dreyfus case in France, it did not exactly fuel a movement. But it did have an enormous impact on educated public opinion. "Look at what Shulgin says . . ." was a trump argument for those trying to convince their friends that the prosecution of the brick-factory clerk was a travesty of justice.

The Beilis case had become a dangerous rallying point for opponents of the regime. After Shulgin's article came out, the security apparatus stepped up efforts to harass the press, ultimately punishing 102 papers. Six editors were arrested, thirty-six issues of various papers were confiscated, three papers were closed for the duration of the trial, and forty-three were fined a total of 12,850 rubles. The punishments, invariably "for an attempt to inflammatorily influence the public," were all illegal because none of the material targeted was inflammatory, a fact tsarist officials admitted in secret communications. Moreover, the punishments inflicted were haphazard and ineffectual. (What, really, could be achieved by fining Nabokov, coeditor of *Speech,* a hundred rubles?) The attacks on the press were part of a larger—and largely futile—attempt to maintain public order. Russia was in the middle of an escalating wave of strikes, which would continue for another eleven months until the first shots of the Great War. Countless groups of striking workers adopted pro-Beilis resolutions. A demonstration of several thousand workers in Warsaw—Poland was then part of the Russian Empire—had to be broken up by the police. Strikes of Jewish workers in support of Beilis broke out in Vilnius, Riga, and Minsk. University students across Russia held one-day protest strikes. At St. Petersburg University, following Shulgin's example, right-wing students posted a letter declaring that, although they considered the Jews to be "a harmful nation," they could not support "the unjust charge of ritual murder."

As for violent attacks on Jews, there were scattered incidents, but the regime—greatly concerned, in general, with suppressing all violence—was quite successful in preventing anti-Jewish retribution. The trial was a moral assault on the Jewish people, but Jews were relatively safe from bodily harm—for the time being.

The trial of Mendel Beilis was, both literally and figuratively, a messy and disorderly affair. With the passing days, cigarette butts, spittle stains, and other rubbish accumulated in the hallways. (Visitors ignored the numerous "Please Do Not . . ." signs staring reproachfully from the walls.) Inside the courtroom, witnesses for the defense and prosecution were often mixed together in no sensible pattern, called in no particular order, and even for no apparent reason. (In the Russian system, witnesses were called by the judge, who did the initial questioning, and were not identified to the jury as testifying for one side or the other.) Quite a few prosecution witnesses were asked only, "Do you know anything about this case," said no, and were excused. On the evening of the fourth day, September 28, amid a run of wholly irrelevant witnesses, the judge called to the stand Mikhail Nakonechny. The erratic course of the trial had abruptly brought it to one of the strongest witnesses for the defense and perhaps the only one whom Beilis's supporters could rightly call a hero.

Nakonechny, nicknamed "Frog," was a shoemaker with seven children who lived not far from Beilis, at the opposite end of the same courtyard as Vera Cheberyak. He more than anyone else had done his part to exonerate Beilis. Two years earlier, when he had heard that the lamplighter Kazimir Shakhovsky was incriminating Beilis, he immediately informed the authorities that he had heard this man vow to "pin the crime on Mendel." Shakhovsky himself admitted that this damning account was truthful. Tall and neatly dressed, Nakonechny looked nothing like a frog; he had a side business as a kind of poor man's attorney, filling out legal petitions for the illiterate and giving them advice in the bargain. All who saw him testify commented on the righteousness and sincerity that he projected.

Zamyslovsky, the prosecutor and esteemed Duma member, tried hard to confuse the poor Lukianovka shoemaker into a contradiction or at least unsettle him, but Nakonechny could not be intimidated. When his opponent said accusingly, "So you are a *professional petitioner*"—implying he was the clever sort who made up stories to fit the occasion—Nakonechny replied humbly that professionals appear in court, whereas "I consider myself a craftsman." When Zamyslovsky tried to interrupt him, Nakonechny cut him off. "Let me finish," he said. "My heart is anxious, and I want to make sure to keep nothing from the court." When Zamyslovsky did speak, the shoemaker batted back his sneering insinuations. "So it seems you greatly *troubled yourself* to inform the investigator about everything regarding this case?" Zamyslovsky said sarcastically. "I didn't 'trouble myself,'" Nakonechny responded. "But I have a grain of decency and I considered it my obligation to say what I knew because an innocent man might suffer." At the words "innocent man," Beilis broke down, but the questioning continued.

Nakonechny performed a great service to the defense by explaining clearly for the first time why the story of Beilis dragging off Andrei defied all common sense—something the defense had not yet had an opportunity to do. After Zamyslovsky mentioned the scenario, Nakonechny, almost screaming, said, "If that had happened, all the children would have raised such a cry that not an hour would have passed before we, the whole street, would have known about the boy's disappearance."

The prosecution should have objected, and the judge should have cut him off; this was merely the witness's opinion, however well founded. But his dignity and passion cowed the court into letting him speak. Leaving the witness stand, Nakonechny fell on his fourteen-year-old daughter Dunya's shoulder and cried. She, too, would be an important witness, coming face-to-face with Vera Cheberyak's daughter in one of the most dramatic moments of the trial.

Her own testimony was several days off, but toward the end of the fourth day Vera Cheberyak managed to enter the trial in the most unexpected manner. Amid a run of useless prosecution witnesses, a woman named Daria Chekhovskaya stood to testify to the good character of Andrei's mother. Asked the general question, "What do you know about this case?," the woman stunned the courtroom. In the waiting room, she said, she had heard Vera Cheberyak trying to intimidate a young witness. The two women had been sitting on the same bench, back-to-back, when she heard Cheberyak call over one of Zhenya's old playmates. "She started to coach him," Chekhovskaya testified.

"She told him: You tell the court, 'All three of us went to the factory—Zhenya, and Andrusha and me. They chased us. We ran away and they grabbed Andrusha' . . . Say that you broke free from Beilis's arms, and Andrusha was left behind. Say that he [Beilis] grabbed him and dragged him off." According to Chekhovskaya, the boy told Cheberyak he wouldn't say any of that. The prosecution tried to insinuate that the woman was lying. "You were called to testify about the mother and now you offer us this bit of news!" Vipper snapped. But he could not shake her testimony.

The stage was set for an "eye-to-eye" confrontation, a provision of Russian trials when witnesses contradicted each other directly. The judge would give Vera Cheberyak a chance to call the boy a liar to his face.

The fifth day, according to *Speech* correspondent Stepan Kondurushkin, "could justifiably be called 'the day of the black beards.' " To prove that Beilis and various other dark-bearded men were responsible for Andrei's murder, the prosecution first turned to Kazimir and Ulyana Shakhovskaya, the Lamplighters. The hard-drinking couple had already given half a dozen different versions of their stories to investigators, contradicting themselves and each other, and finally recanting most of their testimony. Kazimir, an alcoholic wreck of a man, spoke haltingly and frequently got tied up in his own words. Attorneys for both sides had trouble getting sense out of him. He stuck by part of his story—that Zhenya had told him that someone had chased the boys away from the Zaitsev factory. But otherwise his testimony was less than helpful to the prosecution.

"Did the detectives tell you to testify against Beilis?" the judge asked.

"The detectives gave me vodka to drink. They took us and told us to say this and that."

"Did they ask you to testify against Beilis?"

"Yes." [. . .]

"Why were there so many changes in your testimony? Did they coach you?"

"Of course."

"Did [the detectives] give you both [him and his wife] liquor until you were drunk?"

"Yes, until we were drunk."

Ulyana, a woman with watery eyes and a perpetually confused smile, simply gave the impression, the *Kievan* reported, "that she was not playing with a full deck." Did the derelict Anna the Wolf really tell her she saw a man in a black beard carrying off Andrei? "Yes," she whispered. But pressed on what Anna had really told her, she said, "I don't remember, she was too drunk, and I couldn't make out what she said." Did the detectives tell her to testify against Mendel? "Yes, yes." Did she say anything against him? "No, I didn't."

The day's final witness was Vladimir Golubev, the volatile leader of the right-wing Kiev youth group Double Headed Eagle. It was he who had first brought the man he called "the Yid Mendel" to the attention of the authorities as a suspect in May 1911. If not for him, it was nearly certain, the defendant would not be sitting in the dock. Golubev impressed Beilis as looking like some sort of outlaw, which was a more correct intuition than he probably realized.

Golubev, while useful to the prosecution, was also dangerous. He had spent the past year and a half under the authorities' watch—alternately coddled and scolded. The chief prosecutor, Grigory Chaplinsky, would consult with him about the case. But Golubev also had to suffer what he must have considered continual petty indignities. The police fined him ten rubles for placing an unapproved notice in his group's newspaper announcing a public requiem for Andrei. Another issue was confiscated due to an inflammatory article about the case and a poem seen as calling for a pogrom. All this was humiliating. Had he not kept his word—for more than two years—not to incite a pogrom? The authorities, however, were right to be concerned. By the late summer of 1912 his desire to shed Jewish blood had begun to overwhelm him. Until then, Golubev seems to have been more a talker than a doer. But on the night of September 5, 1912, he and about ten of his comrades set out for the largely Jewish Podol neighborhood armed with iron bars and rubber truncheons. They shouted, "Beat the Jews," and "Take that for Stolypin"—it was the first anniversary of the assassinated prime minister's death—as they struck several Jews (as well as one Russian student, apparently by mistake). Pursued by police, they rushed off to the vicinity of the Choral Synagogue, where they beat a few more Jews. Just after midnight, Golubev hit a Jewish student on the head. There the police caught up with him and his crew and they were arrested. But he was never charged with a crime and so, when he gave his oath to the court, he could honestly claim a spotless record.

Testifying ought to have been the greatest moment of his young life. He had been waiting for it for so long. No one could censor him. His every word would be taken down and published in full in the morning papers—even the liberal papers. But his gait was shaky, his face pale. The witness did not at all live up to the grand role of instigator of the case that now gripped the world. He looked so ill that the judge told him he could postpone his testimony until the next day if he wished. "No, I can talk," Golubev said, and then promptly fainted and fell to the ground.

A refreshed Golubev testified the next morning. He mainly restated his reasons for suspecting the brick-factory clerk, while sprinkling his remarks with the word "Yid" (*zhid*) and its adjectival variant (*zhidovskii*). Guided by the writings of the pseudo-scholar Hippolyte Liutostansky, he had quickly concluded that the crime followed the pattern of "Yid ritual murders." He canvassed the Lukianovka neighborhood to find out "whether the boy Yushchinsky had any relationships with Yids." He implied that Detectives Krasovsky and Mishchuk must have been in the pay of the Jews. With his confident manner, he was probably the best prosecution witness so far. But under cross-examination by Gruzenberg, he let slip one item of great significance for the defense. A few weeks after Andrei's murder Golubev had been the first person to question Zhenya Cheberyak about the last time he had seen his friend Andrei. At that time, Golubev admitted, Zhenya had said nothing about playing with him on the clay grinders at the Zaitsev factory or about being chased by men with black beards. According to Golubev, Zhenya had told him that he and Andrei had played in a field, bought lard at a store, then dropped by Zhenya's house and—here is the key detail—Andrei left without his coat. Andrei, this account clearly suggests, had left his coat in the Cheberyaks' apartment. It was never found. The defense did its best to hint at the obvious conclusion: whoever knew what had happened to Andrei's coat knew what had happened to Andrei.

Golubev also offered some unintended comic relief. At one point he assured the court that the defendant came from a line of tzaddiks, or wise men, and "was respected because he was a tzaddik" himself. Beilis, for once, erupted in laughter.

Around one p.m. on this, the sixth day of the trial—September 30, 1913—the judges, the jury, the attorneys, and selected witnesses, including Golubev, exited the courthouse and piled into twenty-five carriages and automobiles. Accompanied by policemen on horseback, the vehicles snaked toward Lukianovka to survey sites relevant to the case. As a safety precaution, the defendant traveled in his coach along quiet side streets. Two years, two months, and eight days after his arrest in the middle of the night, Mendel Beilis was going home.

The day was cold and windy. Overhead, storm clouds threatened. As the convoy arrived in Lukianovka, the smell of smoke pervaded the air—somewhere nearby a building was on fire. But nothing could keep away the curious. A reporter noted that they loitered "by houses, in doorways and in windows . . . children, women, workers and prostitutes." Shooed away by the police, they would reappear minutes later a few steps down the street.

Beilis observed everything through the tiny window of his carriage. When the judge asked if he wished to be present during the examination of the various sites to be visited, he said, "Yes, yes," and stepped onto the ground of his old neighborhood. Seeing some familiar faces, he doffed his cap and bowed.

At Vera Cheberyak's old building, two boys were recruited to perform a test. They went up to her apartment on the second floor with a policeman and re-created Andrei's supposed screams. One could indeed hear what was going on upstairs, which meant that the Cheberyaks' downstairs neighbor, Zinaida Malitskaya, could have discerned Andrei's final cries and the shuffling of feet overhead. ("They were like a dancing couple," she testified in court, "as if they were doing a step, first in one direction and then in the other.")

As Beilis walked the familiar streets, the crowd grew larger and noisier. The police could not keep the people away. Beilis was bowing often now. People shouted excitedly, "Beilis! Beilis!" He smiled, with tears coming to his eyes. The procession stopped at his former home at the edge of the Zaitsev factory. Did Beilis want to go into his old apartment? "I want to, I want to," he said, tearing up again. After examining the premises, where his family no longer lived, the party proceeded to the factory, surveying the famous clay grinders and the kiln into which the "men with black beards" had supposedly dragged their victim. "Everything is the same!" Beilis exclaimed.

In fact, however, one thing had changed. Two years earlier, when Detective Mishchuk had visited Lukianovka in search of witnesses, he had been disappointed that Andrei's playmates had refused to talk about their dead friend. They had seemed to want to forget him. But Vladimir Korolenko, who covered the trial for the national newspaper the *Russian Gazette,* had found it easy to strike up a conversation with some children, evoking a flood of memories. "Of course, we knew him!" they said. "How many times we played with him on the clay grinders together!" "When we played with toy soldiers, he always returned everything, never stole any." (Unlike Vera Cheberyak's Zhenya, who would steal and then say, "That's mine.") "He was very handy. He knew how to cast toy cannons in sand molds." "He was such a good boy!" Now, everyone wanted to talk about Andrei.

At the cave where the boy's body had been found, the shrub-strewn incline was so steep that weaker members of the party had to link arms with a steadier partner. The cave was lit by a flashlight, which observers said cast a spooky glow. The jurors entered it one at a time, each shaking the dust off his clothes as he came out. Now it was raining, and by the time they reboarded their vehicles, the court procession was drenched. Vipper the prosecutor fretted he might fall ill and cause a delay in the trial. Beilis got into his coach for the ride back to prison, his homecoming at an end.

On the morning of the trial's seventh day, the judge summoned Anna "the Wolf" Zakharova, and a flabby barrel of an old woman dressed in rags shambled toward the bench. Anna, according to Shakhovskaya (in at least one version of her story), had said she'd seen Andrei dragged off by a man with a black beard. In a sworn deposition, the old woman had denied she'd seen or said any such thing. Yet as she reached the witness stand, the prosecutor rose to his feet with an air of hopeful confidence.

The testimony reads like a cross-examination by the defense, even though the prosecutor asked all but the first question, which was posed by the judge.

"What do you know about this case?"

"I don't know anything."

"Did you tell Ulyana Shakhovskaya that on the 12th of March you saw how a boy at the Zaitsev factory was grabbed by a man with a black beard?"

"No, I didn't tell her that."

"Where do you sleep at night?"

"Wherever I can."

"Do you drink?"

"I drink a little." *(Laughter in the hall)*

"Did the detectives question you?"

"Yes. I said that I didn't say anything, I didn't know anything."

"So Ulyana [Shakhovskaya] made up everything?"

"Yes, she made it up herself."

"And do you like to babble when you drink?"

"No, I don't like to."

Twice during her testimony, to the laughter of the audience, Anna started wandering away from the stand, only to be steered back by a bailiff. Vipper, irritated, wrapped up his examination.

"Do you prefer to be silent or to speak?" he asked.

"I like to be silent more," she said.

"There you go!" he said, pouncing as if she had betrayed the truth. The witness, he implied, had been pressured into silence. The defense declined to ask any questions, considering it unnecessary. The judge called Shakhovskaya to the stand for an "eye-to-eye" confrontation with "the Wolf." The two women started heatedly gibbering at each other, again to titters from the crowd. When the court was done with her, Anna shuffled off, crossing herself with great relief. In the wake of Anna the Wolf's testimony, the correspondent for the *Times* of London wrote, "The last of the prosecution's patchwork evidence against Beilis, derived admittedly from thieves and drunkards, has thus disappeared and it seems incredible that the imperial authorities will allow this nauseous case to proceed further."

At this point in the trial, the incredulous spectator could rightfully ask not only how the case could go on, but how the prosecution could conduct the case in such a way as to inevitably attract ridicule. The prosecutors were reasonably intelligent men. The case was closely supervised by justice minister Shcheglovitov who, whatever his flaws, was a highly sophisticated jurist. In its discovery procedures, the Russian judicial system was fairly thorough; all the key witnesses had been deposed in advance, sometimes on multiple occasions. The prosecution *knew* what Anna the Wolf and the Lamplighters would say, yet relied on them nonetheless.

In the history of the blood accusation, the prosecutors of Mendel Beilis stand out for their fumbling inability to craft a convincing narrative of guilt. Critics invariably called the Beilis case "medieval," but the comparison was misleading. Ritual-murder prosecutions of centuries past often achieved a kind of persuasive power. The twelfth-century monk Thomas of Monmouth, the originator of the ritual-murder myth, set a high standard; in *The Life and Miracles of Saint William of Norwich* he builds his case against the Jews quite compellingly. In its narrative art, the work is something of a masterpiece. For pure storytelling, the 1475 trial of twenty-three Jews for the murder of little Simon of Trent overwhelms with its brutal logic, as the prosecutors extract ever more detailed confessions from the accused. (The torture inflicted upon each defendant—hoisting by the arms tied behind the back with a device called a strappado—was legally sanctioned and noted in the transcript.) In the Tiszaeszlar trial of 1882–1883 in Hungary—the first ritual-murder case of the modern era in a Western country—interrogators coerced a detailed account of the crime out of a supposed eyewitness, the thirteen-year-old son of a synagogue sexton; the boy's narrative of the killing of a fourteen-year-old girl was so convincing that an honest deputy prosecutor, Ede Szeyffer, concluded that it was a lie only a full month into the trial, at which point he convinced the court to free the fifteen defendants.

As for the Beilis case, minister of justice Shcheglovitov confidentially acknowledged its flimsiness to more than one person. But there was never any question of dropping the case. The minister looked upon the thinness of the evidence against the defendant as but a challenge to be overcome. Conversations he had in the year or so leading up to the trial document how he groped toward a novel and cunning solution.

A meeting with an old acquaintance in mid- to late 1912 captures Shcheglovitov when he was at his most uncertain and even pathetic. When the acquaintance, a government official named Vladimir Talberg, scolded him for backing a case that rested on such a "shaky foundation," he did not dispute the assessment. But he insisted that "long experience" had taught him that even in a "hopeless" case, "the talent of the chief judge," as well as the prosecutor, aided by "unexpected turns of events," could result in a conviction. He was, in other words, counting largely on biased conduct from the bench and blind luck.

By the summer of 1913—that is, two or three months before the trial—Shcheglovitov seized on the hope that the problem lay not in the evidence but the failure of the prosecution to make the most of it. He complained that Kiev's chief prosecutor, Grigory Chaplinsky, had let him down. Surely, he thought, a competent investigator could firm up the case. To that end, he summoned Arkady Koshko, the chief of detectives of the Moscow police, to St. Petersburg to review the entire case file.

After a full month of work, Koshko met with the minister again to brief him on his conclusions. Koshko's memoir sheds unusual light on the minister's thinking. "The investigation was conducted improperly, one-sidedly and, I would say, in a biased manner," Koshko recalled telling the minister, to his extreme irritation. The detective saw no evidence that Beilis was guilty, nor any convincing reason to believe the crime was ritual in character.

After listening to Koshko's presentation for a few minutes, the minister interjected, "I can see that at the impending trial the Jews will have no better defender than you!"

"I am not at all defending the Jews," Koshko replied. "I am just reporting to Your Excellency my completely objective opinion."

Shcheglovitov then took another tack, whose significance Koshko did not fully understand at the time. "Let us assume for a moment that Beilis is innocent," he said. "Isn't it obvious to you that this was ritual crime?"

"No, it is not at all obvious," Koshko replied.

The minister told Koshko, "I have never doubted it [the crime's ritual character] for a minute, based on the irrefutable conclusions of the great authority, Father Pranaitis," the prosecution's expert witness on the Jewish religion. For some time the detective and the minister argued over this point—whether the evidence pointed toward a ritual murder, irrespective of Beilis's guilt. As they sparred, the minister demonstrated great familiarity with the work of the Tashkent priest.

"I hope that the verdict of the jurors will shake your philo-Semitic views," the minister said, concluding the conversation, pointedly without extending his hand: "Good day, sir!"

Shcheglovitov's remarks to Koshko were the first hints that the state had come up with an innovative insurance policy against the failure to convict the defendant. The minister's attempt to separate the issue of Beilis's guilt from that of the ritual nature of the crime would become the heart of the prosecution's strategy. Judge Boldyrev, it was decided, would ask the jury to consider two questions separately. The first question would be straightforward: Was the defendant innocent or guilty of the murder of Andrei Yushchinsky? The second question would, in effect, ask the jury to decide whether Andrei Yushchinsky had been killed as part of a Jewish ritual. (The exact wording of the question, which had yet to be worked out, would be indirect, but unmistakable in its implication.) The jury would be free to find Mendel Beilis not guilty, but the prosecution's argument would lead it to answer the second question affirmatively. Treating the issue of the blood accusation separately from the guilt of the defendant appears to have been historically unprecedented. Whoever thought of it, perhaps Shcheglovitov himself, had hit upon an ingenious maneuver.

The prosecution, then, felt an unusual level of comfort in putting on a case against Beilis that it understood was highly flawed. It knew that it would still have a chance at a favorable verdict, even if the jury found the defendant not guilty. On this matter the prosecution was surprisingly candid. Not long before the trial began, Beilis's attorney Vasily Maklakov ran into civil prosecutor Georgy Zamyslovsky in the halls of the Duma, the parliamentary body in which they both served. Maklakov told Zamyslovsky that he thought the prosecution's case was weak. "Let him [Beilis] be acquitted," Zamyslovsky replied. "What's important to us is to prove that this was a ritual murder."

Still, the prosecution had hardly given up on getting a murder conviction against Mendel Beilis and condemning him to a life of hard labor. It knew that it had two illicit advantages over the defense: it was receiving daily intelligence reports on the sequestered jurors, and it had an active ally in Judge Boldyrev. For the first five days of the trial, the judge, perhaps out of concern for his reputation, had conducted the trial in an impartial manner, repeatedly admonishing prosecutor Vipper for his procedural infractions. "The judge often interrupts the prosecutor," a police agent telegraphed in a report to St. Petersburg at the end of the fifth day, "That severely unnerves him." The judge's conduct of the trial, the agent noted, greatly dissatisfied Kiev's chief prosecutor, Grigory Chaplinsky. Someone, probably Chaplinsky himself, must have had a talk with Boldryev because the next day the agent reported that the judge and Vipper had "made up." By the eleventh day, another agent noted approvingly that "the judge skillfully directs the attention of the jurors to the details [of the prosecution's case] . . . and subtly but unmistakably guides witnesses who become confused to the right path."

Boldyrev was aware of the illegal surveillance of the jurors, approved of it, and, with Vipper and Zamyslovsky, avidly listened to reports of their private conversations. His bias in favor of the prosecution would become more and more apparent. But only at the end of the trial would it become clear to what extreme lengths Judge Boldyrev would go to maximize the chances of a conviction.

Unaware of these machinations, after a long court day was over, the exhausted defendant looked forward to laying himself down on his nice new cot; but as he slumbered his trial went on. All over America Mendel Beilises were taking to the stage, putting themselves in the dock with great flair, lending the proceedings the fine dramatic form they lacked in real life. "The Mendel Beilis epidemic," anticipated with such distaste by a dyspeptic critic, was intensifying. The Yiddish productions played to packed houses of spectators who cheered Gruzenberg, hooted at the prosecution, and cried at the woes of the defendant, who was invariably tortured without mercy. The Yiddish press expressed outrage and embarrassment at the plays, denouncing them as *"shund"*—trash, cheap melodrama. "The audience sheds rivers of tears," one dismissive critic wrote of a New York production. "Every woman soaks seven handkerchiefs . . . and every man three."

But the plays spread the news. Many productions left the denouement unresolved, adapting to events as they developed, amounting, in the words of one historian, to "three-dimensional newsreels." And they were precocious expressions of a wave of public protest only now gaining momentum in the country.

One of the few to grasp this point was an editorial writer in the New York–based Zionist newspaper *Dos Yiddishe Folk* (The Jewish People). The popularity of the plays, the author argued, "shows once more the nationalism and deep Jewishness of most of our people . . . It is this

feeling that has given us sufficient strength to withstand the many enemies who rise up in every generation to annihilate us." The author was
far more perceptive than the ostentatiously high-minded critics. They
failed to pick up on what the popularity of the vulgar plays said about
American Jews: their sense of solidarity, their commitment to justice,
and their potential for collective action.

With the Yiddish theater acting as a kind of raucous chorus, a massive grassroots movement in support of Beilis had belatedly begun
sweeping the United States. The American Jewish Committee, America's leading Jewish lobbying organization, remained wary of public
protests as possibly counterproductive. (So, too, establishment leaders
in Europe. In Germany, the *Jewish Chronicle* reported the assimilationists to be "furious" at the Zionists for organizing pro-Beilis rallies.
In Great Britain, Lucien Wolf, known as the Jewish community's "minister of foreign affairs," wrote that he favored "discreet diplomacy,"
arguing in a private letter that the "protest meetings or other Jewish
agitation on the Blood Accusation will only play into the hand of the
anti-Semites.")

The American Jewish Committee organized a letter of protest from
prominent Christian clergymen, which it hoped the State Department
would deliver to St. Petersburg through proper channels. But around
the nation, countless Jewish congregations and local Jewish organizations began taking action on their own, spontaneously holding rallies
and petitioning the White House. They were joined by many local and
state governments and a variety of Christian and other groups. The New
York and Wisconsin state legislatures passed resolutions condemning
the trial. The House of Deputies of the Episcopal Church called on the
Russian Orthodox leaders to declare the ritual-murder charge against
the Jews to be false. The New York Esperantists pledged to instigate a
worldwide protest movement and drafted an open letter, in Esperanto,
for distribution throughout Europe. The success of the Esperantists
was rather limited, but in America the pro-Beilis movement would cul-
minate in some of the largest mass protests of Jews and greatest upsurge
of Jewish-Christian solidarity the country had yet seen.

As the eighth day of the trial began, the courtroom was overflowing, the
seats filled with "elegant women and girls of Kiev society, clergymen,

military men, officials," the *Kiev Opinion* contributor Bonch-Bruevich said in a dispatch. "Lorgnettes, binoculars (though forbidden) . . . and a sea of feathers in women's hats, flutter, shake and obstruct one's view." Every court officer with an excuse to be present sat in a row behind the judges' bench, their gold buttons gleaming. The crowd was not simply excited, according to one *Kievan* reporter, it was ravenous. All the spectators wanted to be able to say that they had been there for the testimony of the notorious Vera Cheberyak.

As opening acts, the witnesses preceding her that day were cast to perfection, maintaining the interest of the audience but not upstaging the dark diva herself. Mendel Beilis made one of his periodic cameo appearances. He never took the stand during the trial, but he did exercise his right under Russian court procedure to give an "explanation" on a specific matter, describing how he had supervised the baking and delivery of matzo for his employer Jonah Zaitsev, an activity that the prosecution presented in the most sinister light. Beilis explained there was no ritual for the production of matzo, just a rabbi present to ensure that the crew observed the rules of kosher baking. "These are just illiterate Jews," he told the court. "They roll out the matzo, and then might start eating bread and drinking tea. And that's strictly forbidden. So [the rabbi] is watching so that . . . they don't do that." A reporter noted that Beilis spoke more loudly than he had on previous occasions and "with a great deal of gesticulation." He would still weep from time to time but was becoming more comfortable in the courtroom.

Then Detective Krasovsky's former assistant, Adam Polishchuk, an elegantly dressed young man with a crew cut and short beard, took the stand. Krasovsky had once trusted him, but now Polishchuk was a full-fledged participant in the effort to convict Beilis. Asked his profession, he told the court that he worked for the secret police. When Krasovsky had hired him, he had been an unemployed police officer; presumably his new job was a reward for the service he was about to provide.

Polishchuk, startlingly, proceeded to accuse Krasovsky of murdering Vera Cheberyak's two children with poisoned pastries, in contradiction to the pathologists' report that conclusively proved that they had died natural deaths of dysentery. As for the defendant, Polishchuk suggested that Mendel Beilis had murdered Andrei in league with the hay and straw dealer Faivel Shneyerson, who took his meals at the Beilises' home. (The prosecution, in essence, made an unindicted coconspirator out of Shneyerson, a young man who was supposedly of the noble line of Lubavitcher Hasidic wise men.)

But Polishchuk, prodded by the defense, made his greatest impression with his description of Zhenya Cheberyak's deathbed scene. In August 1912, while still working for Krasovsky, he had been assigned to watch over the gravely ill boy. Because his original deposition was part of the record, he could not lie about this key episode. He said nothing willingly, forcing the defense to dig for every detail. But even in his halting rendition, the story was chilling. Nothing could blunt the eeriness of how Zhenya's final thoughts turned to his dead friend, or the attempt by his mother to persuade her dying boy to exonerate her ("Tell them, little one, that I had nothing to do with it") and her apparent fear that he would say something to incriminate her, as she silenced him by covering his mouth with kisses.

Eleven-year-old Ludmila Cheberyak, Vera's only surviving child, her chestnut hair divided in two braids that reached nearly to her waist, directly preceded her mother on the stand. She possessed not only her mother's large eyes, dark brows, and long eyelashes, but the same ability to spin tales. She struck observers as having unnatural poise for one so young, yet somehow maintaining an air of childish innocence as she told the nightmarish story of the children's jaunt to the Zaitsev factory and how Beilis and two other Jews had supposedly chased them.

The defense had earlier argued the whole story had to be false because, in the fall of 1910, the Zaitsev factory management had put a complete stop to the children's visits to the clay grinders by erecting an impassable wooden fence. The fence was the subject of endless testimony. The defense probably got the better of the argument, but negatives are notoriously hard to prove and it was a challenge to rule out the possibility that the children had ever found a way through the fence, which made Ludmila's testimony crucial.

"We were playing on the clay grinders," the girl told the court. "After a while the factory manager Mendel"—prosecution witnesses always seemed to give Beilis a promotion—"started chasing us and the others chased us as well." Her story was well wrought (undoubtedly with the help of her mother and perhaps the prosecution), as if to insulate her from cross-examination. She did not assert that she herself had seen Beilis grab Andrei. Such an account would have opened her to an aggressive line of questioning from the defense. She said she had only heard Andrei scream as she and the other children were chased off. However, she said her younger sister, Valia, now conveniently deceased, had seen Mendel grab Andrei: "She screamed and told me, 'Andrusha, Andrusha, they dragged him off.'"

The judge then called for an eye-to-eye confrontation between Ludmila and the shoemaker Nakonechny's daughter Dunya. Ludmila claimed that Dunya had been playing with her and the boys when the Jews chased after them. When Dunya took her place beside her former friend at the witness stand, she lost no time calling her a liar.

> Judge: "Did you play with that girl on the clay grinder . . . did Beilis chase you away?"
> Dunya: "That never happened."
> Ludmila: "We were chased then."
> Dunya: "Who ever chased us? Think again, and then let's see you lie."

Ludmila started to cry. "Girl, why are you crying?" the judge asked. She answered, "I am afraid." The prosecutor asked for it to be entered into the record that the girl cried and said she was afraid. He was setting up a main argument of his summation—that a Jewish conspiracy had bribed witnesses to support Beilis, or else had intimidated witnesses into retracting incriminating testimony or maintaining their silence.

Vera Cheberyak strode to the stand in an eye-catching black velvet hat with a wide brim, trimmed all around in yellowish-orange faux ostrich feathers, from which rose a sort of feather pom-pom that bobbed distractingly as she moved. Beilis looked at her intently, maintaining his gaze the entire time she testified. Witnesses were supposed to face the judges at all times so, seated where he was, about a dozen feet directly to the right of the stand, Beilis could stare only at her profile, perhaps focusing on her nose with its small bump and its slight but definite bend to one side. As more than one observer noted, it seemed at this moment as if there were two defendants in the courtroom. Was the real perpetrator sitting in the dock or standing before the judges? Or, a skeptical reporter asked, was he perhaps somewhere else, laughing at the whole farce?

Cheberyak began with a request to the judge that betrayed both her self-awareness and her anxiety. "Would you be so kind as to read aloud my previous testimony?" she asked, meaning her prior statements to investigators. "After all," she said, "I cannot remember everything." She clearly was hoping for assistance in her effort to avoid contradicting herself or to smooth over her inconsistencies as best she could. But the judge had no choice but to say no. Previous statements could be read back only after the witness had begun testifying and if one side or the other pointed to a possible discrepancy between different versions. "Whatever you remember," Judge Boldyrev said, "that is what you will tell the court."

She started off well enough, though, the words pouring out of her in a steady and forceful stream. After the judge's usual opening question, her testimony fills seven columns of small print in the transcript, save for one brief interruption. As with her physical appearance, descriptions of her voice are contradictory—it was said to sound both "metallic" and "melodic," with an unusual range, hitting high notes and then descending so low the sounds seemed to growl from deep in her chest. (One correspondent compared her to the famed mezzo-soprano Anastasia Vialtseva, beloved for her virtuoso renditions of gypsy songs.)

She spoke well, but perhaps too well, too fluidly. To one correspondent, she seemed to speak "as if she were running away." She described the key scene vividly—how Beilis and the other Jews ran after the children at the brick factory, how Zhenya barely escaped, leaving Andrei behind. It was all very compelling, but suspiciously well-performed for a secondhand account. (She was supposedly only relating Zhenya's story, after all.). It struck one reporter that only two kinds of people describe scenes so vividly: eyewitnesses and liars.

Cheberyak recounted her story of the trip with the journalist Stepan Brazul to Kharkov in December 1911 and how Arnold Margolin, or one of his confederates, offered her the enormous sum of forty thousand rubles to confess to Andrei's murder, and how she would be spirited out of the country or defended by the best lawyers in the land who would secure her acquittal. Nearly as important for the prosecution was another story she told: how she had sent Zhenya to buy milk from Beilis not long before Andrei disappeared, and how the boy supposedly returned, pale with fear, saying two Jews dressed in strange black garments had run after him, but he had gotten away. One of the Jews was old, the other tall and young. According to Cheberyak, her son said one looked like the hay and straw dealer, Shneyerson, the supposed

Hasid of the noble line, and the other could have been Shneyerson's father. (When Shneyerson testified, he turned out to be a rather surly, self-confident, and clean-shaven young man who did not at all look the part of a nefarious Hasid.)

After the prosecution was done, Gruzenberg began an orderly cross-examination, addressing this potentially most dangerous witness with no hint of confrontation in his voice and in an almost soothing tone. Vera Cheberyak was an impressive witness as long as no one asked her any real questions. Gruzenberg began with a very simple one.

"Were you questioned many times by the investigators?"

"Yes, many times," she said, though she couldn't remember how many.

From that one exchange everything followed. Gruzenberg was leading her step by step until she stood over a trapdoor.

So she had been questioned a number of times. When, Gruzenberg asked her, had she first told the authorities Zhenya's story about Jews grabbing Andrei at the factory? She insisted that she had first told investigating magistrate Fenenko the story in June 1911, even though there was no record of that.

But in that deposition of June 24, he calmly asked, "did you not tell the investigator that Zhenya did *not* go [out with Andrusha to play]?"

"I don't remember," she said.

"And didn't the investigator question you again, in July?" Gruzenberg asked. In fact, he asked, hadn't the investigator questioned her several more times?

Again: "I don't remember."

Gruzenberg then asked the judge to corroborate the dates on which Vera had been questioned by Investigator Fenenko. After some shuffling of papers, the judge responded: "On April 22, June 24, July 11, July 26, and December 3, 1911." Gruzenberg interrupted, "Excuse me, your honor, but she was also questioned September 13."

"Absolutely correct," the judge said, "September 13," making a total of six times.

Then Gruzenberg had the judge confirm the devastating fact: in every one of her six depositions in 1911, Vera Cheberyak had said that Andrei had come to ask Zhenya to go out and play but Zhenya had refused. The records showed that the first time she asserted the two boys had gone out to the Zaitsev factory and that Beilis had chased after them was in her deposition of July 10, 1912, fourteen months after the murder. It seemed no coincidence that her new story came only a few weeks after Brazul had accused her of being involved in the crime.

But had she ever mentioned Mendel Beilis in any of those depositions in 1911?

The record showed she did do so once, on July 26, four days after they had both been arrested simultaneously. (It will be recalled that prosecutors at first seriously considered charging them as a tandem, but Vera Cheberyak was released two weeks later.) She had told investigators that, come to think of it, there was reason to suspect the Jewish clerk. She herself had no firsthand information, she said, but Andrei's aunt Natalia had told her she had had a *dream* in which Andrei was stabbed to death by Jews!

Did the witness remember telling the investigator this rather odd story, which notably made no mention of Zhenya, clay grinders, or Jews with black beards? "It seems maybe I did," Cheberyak said, "but I don't remember exactly."

The trapdoor had been sprung. Taking his turn at questioning the witness, Karabchevsky made sure Cheberyak would find no way to climb back out. His cross-examinations, unlike his flowery summations, were elegantly simple. Her husband, Vasily, had testified that Zhenya had told him about the Jews who had chased and grabbed him and Andrei at the Zaitsev factory immediately after it happened, on March 12, 1911. Zhenya had supposedly run in panting and in terror. Did her husband tell her about that? Yes, she said. But she didn't react in any way, share it with anyone? "I didn't pay it any attention," she responded. "I didn't attach any significance to it."

Karabchevsky wisely refrained from following up, letting the absurdity of the answer speak for itself. Even the simplest peasant juror would wonder: How could any mother possibly be so indifferent to the attempted kidnapping of her own child and the disappearance of his friend?

It would be unfair to Vera Cheberyak to allow her disastrous performance to impair her reputation as a virtuoso liar. The courtroom was not her natural habitat, and she had simply told too many contradictory stories over too long a period of time, all of which were in writing, with every page of every deposition signed by her. She had no explanations for her shifting accounts, other than saying "That's what Zhenya told me" at a particular time, or "I don't remember."

The public may have felt cheated at the diminished and intimidated

Cheberyak it had witnessed. But it got a glimpse of the real Vera Cheberyak two days later, when she was put into the eye-to-eye confrontation with the boy Nazary Zarutsky, whom she had allegedly tried to coach in the waiting room. The boy confirmed the earlier witness's story that Cheberyak had told him to say he had been with Andrei and Zhenya, even though it was not true. "Look me in the eyes. How dare you lie!" Cheberyak shrieked.

"The boy suddenly shrank," a reporter wrote. "His face, small like an apple, winked and twitched in fright." Finally the crowd could see the woman who dominated, who bullied, who terrorized. The defense was about to erupt in an objection, but Judge Boldyrev beat them to it. However favorable he was toward the prosecution, this display was too much for him. "Don't you dare intimidate the witness!" he barked at Cheberyak.

In one of his daily reports to St. Petersburg, a secret police agent inexplicably struck an optimistic note about this damning turn of events. "Although the testimony of Cheberyak herself is of dubious reliability," he wrote, "the chances for the prosecution have slightly increased." But civil prosecutor Alexei Shmakov scribbled down a harsher verdict in his notebook: "She has given herself away, the lying bitch. And that is all there is to it."

10

"We Have Seen the Killer"

The eleventh day of the Mendel Beilis trial began unusually late, at twelve thirty in the afternoon, giving the jurors a welcome break. This session promised to feature two exotic witnesses subpoenaed by the prosecution—a pair of Jews from Western Europe hinted to be two of the "men with black beards"—unindicted accomplices in Andrei Yushchinsky's murder. However, the essential player in the day's proceedings was not a witness or even a human being, but Mendel Beilis's cow. The trial, peculiar from the outset, was growing even stranger.

The cow, of course, could not testify for herself, but she had already been testified *about* in such detail that she had become a compelling, even pivotal character. She had been acquired by Beilis to provide milk for the family along with some excess he could sell to bring in a few rubles. She had fallen into a ravine and broken her leg. The leg had apparently healed (the extensive testimony on this score is, frankly, contradictory), but she became a money-losing burden to her owner. With the approaching winter, feed had become too expensive and Beilis insisted he had sold her off in September 1910 to pay off his debts. The prosecution sought to prove that assertion was a lie.

The astounding amount of time spent debating the fate of a cow was due entirely to Vera Cheberyak. She had claimed that, shortly before the murder, she had sent her son, Zhenya, to buy milk from Beilis and he reported that there he had seen two Jews, dressed "strangely" in long black garments. The prosecution asserted that these men were likely accomplices of Beilis in killing the boy. The story's credibility hinged on the bovine's whereabouts in March 1911. The prosecution was obsessed with proving the cow had still been part of the Beilis household.

———

The testimony was revolving more and more around Cheberyak—to bolster her credibility in accusing Beilis, prove her a liar or even culpable in Andrei's death, or clear her of any involvement. As she sat in court day after day, her hat feathers fluttering, she increasingly overshadowed the defendant whose presence was becoming, as one observer remarked, "an annoying formality." Even tangential matters related back to her, as was the case here.

The dispute over the cow started fittingly with a Mrs. Bykov, whose name derives from the Russian word for bull. The persistent questioning—"Mrs. Bull, what do you know about the cow"—caused some amusement. What she knew was that the Beilises did not have a cow by early 1911. In fact, she remembered having helped out Beilis's wife, Esther, by buying milk for her.

State prosecutor Oskar Vipper was not pleased with her testimony. "What do you think happened to Beilis's cow?"

"They probably sold it."

"Was there ever a case when a cow of his died?"

"There was."

"Now you say it died and earlier you said they sold it. There you go!" His sarcastic tone suggested this witness could not be trusted.

The next to take the stand was an old man named Vyshemirsky, who had lived two doors down from Beilis on Upper Yurkovskaya Street. Beilis was glad to see this familiar face. Vyshemirsky was a cattle trader from whom Beilis had bought livestock over the years and a freelance carter who often hauled bricks from the Zaitsev factory. Vyshemirsky was someone Beilis knew well, someone he trusted. The judge started off by asking him what he knew about the case.

"I don't know anything. I only know from what people tell me," Vyshemirsky answered.

The judge then asked, "From which people?"

Vyshemirsky took a long pause. He was someone from whom nothing unusual could be expected. But Beilis, knowing him so well, picked up on something unusual in his demeanor. He later recalled that he wondered why Vyshemirsky was taking so long to gather his thoughts, and felt a brief moment of unease.

From whom had Vyshemirsky heard things? "From Ravich," he answered the judge. "He told me that his wife dropped by Vera Cheberyak's and she saw a body there around the same time as the boy was killed."

The story that Vyshemirsky said he had heard from his friend Amerik Ravich caused an immediate uproar. A body in Vera Cheberyak's apartment? Where had this tale come from? It was nowhere mentioned in the reams of preliminary depositions. Outraged and suspicious, the prosecution demanded to know if this man's testimony was truly a surprise to the defense. The defense insisted that it was indeed.

Adele Ravich had supposedly seen the body, wrapped in a carpet, in the Cheberyaks' bathtub. Her husband confided the story to Vyshemirsky as the couple prepared to leave the country. Amerik Ravich said Vera was afraid the authorities would get him and his wife to talk about what they knew—and so she gave them the money for tickets to America.

While "the body in the carpet" seized the public's imagination, it curiously did not much affect the trial. A *Kiev Opinion* reporter half-seriously suggested that Vyshemirsky's story was not nearly inventive enough to galvanize a trial in which the bizarre had become routine. "In any normal trial, it would have brought the proceedings to a halt, occasioned a reassessment," he wrote, but under the circumstances, both sides treated the revelation as a nuisance. Vyshemirsky—a plain-spoken and reluctant witness—did appear to be telling the truth about what Ravich had told him. But had Ravich, or his wife, fabricated the story? The couple had indeed suddenly left for America the previous year.

Both sides willingly left the witness's sensational story behind, and the questioning veered back toward the more comfortable territory of the cow and its whereabouts in March 1911. To civil prosecutor Zamyslovsky's final question, "Was the cow black or spotted?" the witness pled ignorance.

The testimony about the cow was the prelude to the appearance of the two Jews from abroad, Yakov Etinger and Samuel Landau. The prosecution had strongly intimated that "Etinger and Landau"—they were invariably referred to in tandem—had been the two "strangely dressed" Jews that Zhenya had supposedly seen on the milk run to the Beilis household.

Landau, who was in his late twenties, was a cousin of Mark Zaitsev's, son of Jonah, the founder of the family brick business that employed

Beilis. Etinger, in his early thirties, was Zaitsev's brother-in-law. Landau lived in Germany and Etinger in Austria-Hungary.

The pro-Beilis spectators greeted their appearance in the courtroom with a soft chorus of satisfied laughter: Could any pair have been more comically miscast for their supposed roles? These fashionably dressed young men were impossible to imagine as black-mantled, fanatical Hasids of the "noble" line, as the prosecution asserted. They were Jewish nobility but only in the sense of having been born into great wealth. Etinger, who knew no Russian and had to speak in German through an interpreter, was a landowner and merchant. Landau composed operettas. A commentator in *Kiev Opinion* wrote that the two men would be at home "on Paris boulevards, at a table with cigars in their mouths, flowers in their buttonholes, sipping aperitifs on the veranda at four in the afternoon."

Indeed, "Etinger and Landau" were quintessential, even exaggerated specimens of Western European assimilated Jews. Out of their native habitat in Kiev, they were a strange species to be gawked at. In the Russia of Nicholas II, a Jew could be thoroughly "acculturated," like Oskar Gruzenberg, but never truly "assimilated." Jews were so excluded from major institutions—universities, the army, the government—and prohibited from physically even inhabiting vast parts of the empire, that they could never belong to the overall society. Etinger, on the other hand, had grown up in a country where the notion that a Jew could not live wherever he wished would seem bizarre and where Jews were highly integrated into the most prestigious state institutions. The Austro-Hungarian army had twenty-five thousand Jewish officers who would soon distinguish themselves in the Great War. (In its entire history, the Russian Imperial Army produced only nine Jewish officers and one general.) As for Landau, he had come to feel more at home in Berlin than in his native Kiev, where he was officially not even permitted to stay in his own mother's house, located in a fashionable neighborhood where Jews, with few exceptions, could not legally reside. (His mother, as the widow of a wealthy merchant, was classified as an exception, while he was not.) Upon their arrival in Kiev in December 1910, Etinger and Landau registered falsely with the police as residing in approved "Jewish" areas. Both men, in fact, stayed with their families in forbidden neighborhoods. Gruzenberg, perhaps letting his emotions get the better of him, declared to the court that these farcical indignities were "not a comedy, but a tragedy." Anti-Semitism was certainly a scourge in Western Europe, as it was in Russia, but such grotesque forms of state-sponsored discrimination were unthinkable in a civilized society, a point Gruzenberg left unspoken, but that was obvious enough to sophisticated spectators if not the jurors.

In the end, Etinger and Landau's testimony and an examination of their passports and other documents clearly showed that, while each man had indeed visited Kiev in December 1910, they had both left in January 1911, weeks before Andrei's murder. The prosecution was undone: the two men could never have crossed paths at the incriminating time with Beilis's controversial cow.

Foundering, the prosecution cast about for other Etingers and Landaus. These men, perhaps, were not quite the right ones, but they had relatives. What of them? The defense objected: many Etingers and certainly endless Landaus could be produced at will. When the prosecution pointed to an Israel Landau mentioned in the court record, Gruzenberg asked that Samuel Landau be recalled to the stand.

"Are you the son of Israel Landau?" Gruzenberg asked.

"Yes."

"Is your father dead?"

"Yes."

"When did he die?"

"1903."

"Where is he buried?"

"In Kiev, in the Jewish cemetery."

The prosecution had been flummoxed yet again.

The trial's twelfth day—October 6, 1913—was extraordinarily dull. Many a ticketholder, even quite a few reporters, deserted their prized seats for hours. But the testimony was remarkable in that it actually bore directly on Mendel Beilis's guilt or innocence. One after the other, shaggy-haired workers from the Zaitsev factory testified that operations had been in full swing on the day of Andrei Yushchinsky's disappearance. The factory grounds had been filled with men hauling bricks, shouting, cursing, and presenting their receipts to be signed by Beilis. If Andrei had been abducted there that day, it would not just have occurred in broad daylight, but before a large audience. And the dozens of signed receipts showed that the defendant had been quite busy with his work.

The same day that the jurors in Kiev were nodding off at the hours of mind-numbing testimony about brick deliveries, five thousand miles away, in the Chicago Loop, a tumultuous scene was unfolding. An uninformed bystander might have thought it the scene of an incipient riot. At around one p.m., thousands of people thronged the streets of the city's commercial, cultural, and governmental center, massing on the intersection of Clark and Randolph Streets and blocking traffic. Reserve police officers had to be called in to keep the crowd under control and prevent people from being trampled. At first the crowd streamed toward a rally at the Garrick Theater. The first fifteen hundred people or so at the head of the crowd were admitted, with thousands remaining outside. The throng was unusually diverse—"Jew and Gentile, Catholic and Protestant, white men and negroes"—as a *Chicago Tribune* reporter described it. But they were united in protest against the despicable mockery of justice in Russia.

America had lagged greatly behind Europe in coming to Beilis's defense. The first open letters of protest, signed by scores of eminent persons, had been published in France and Germany a year and a half earlier, in the spring of 1912. Paris had been the scene of the first large protest after the trial began, in a gathering addressed by the great socialist leader Jean Jaures. In Germany, Zionist groups organized protests all over their country. Even Germany's moderately conservative National Liberal Party, not regarded as terribly philo-Semitic, sent a representative to a pro-Beilis meeting to sign a petition.

America had taken its time, but now demonstrations held across the country dwarfed those in the Old World. Mass meetings were held in Cincinnati and in Canton, Ohio; in Fort Smith, Arkansas; in Kenosha, Wisconsin; in Pittsburgh, Pennsylvania. Six thousand people took part in a protest organized by the Socialist Party in Detroit. But the most impressive mass protest, in the United States or the world, would occur this day in Chicago.

The Garrick Theater was supposed to have been the only venue that day, but the overflow stretched a block and a half to George M. Cohan's

Grand Opera House, which was quickly opened up to accommodate another fourteen hundred protesters. Hundreds more still thronged the streets. Impromptu speakers shuttled between the theaters to brief the crowd.

In the Grand Opera House, Judge Edward O. Brown of the Illinois Appellate Court presided, with a hundred dignitaries seated behind him onstage. He introduced the world-renowned settlement house pioneer and social reformer Jane Addams, founder of Chicago's Hull House, who declared that outbreaks of racial and religious bigotry and superstition were a pestilence to be stamped out. "It seems to me," Addams told a cheering audience, "that this question of persecution must be governed by the same social control that exterminated the black plague and cholera epidemic . . . Something of the same sort must be done in the moral world. Nations must come together and say that things once believed must no longer be tolerated."

America's most prominent black leader, Booker T. Washington, told of how inspiring he found it "to see hundreds of men and women struggling to get into a meeting for the purpose of seeing that justice is brought a great people." He was joined by a local black pastor, the Reverend Archibald J. Cary, who said he was taking part in the protest as a member of a people who knew something about oppression; he went on to thank Julius Rosenwald, president of Sears, Roebuck, and Co., and one of the country's great philanthropists, for looking beyond his own creed as a Jew in funding a Young Men's Christian Association for the black community. (Rosenwald, a trustee and benefactor of Booker T. Washington's Tuskegee Institute, later gave millions in matching grants for the education of black children throughout the South in so-called Rosenwald Schools.)

Illinois's governor, Edward F. Dunne, wired a message to the gathering, branding anyone who advanced the blood accusation "as a malignant person or gullible fool." Father P. J. O'Callaghan of the Paulist Fathers proclaimed, "The greatest glory of the Catholic Church is that it is Jewish and the greatest honor any man may have is that he may say in some sense that he is of the House of Israel. The greatest work we can do is stamp out the hatred of the Jews by men who call themselves Christians."

The speakers' attacks on the tsarist regime and the defense of the Jews implied no self-righteousness where America was concerned.

Rabbi Emil Hirsch, Chicago's most prominent Reform Jewish leader, closed the Grand Opera House event with "an appeal for justice for the American Negro" as well as a reprimand to Chicago clubs that excluded Jews and thereby fomented prejudice. For Rabbi Hirsch, as for Jane Addams and men like Julius Rosenwald, the Beilis case was part of a much larger cause. "The railroading of Beilis to the gallows is a grave attack on elemental justice," Hirsch wrote soon afterward in the Reform Jewish journal the *Advocate,* "but so is every lynching of Negroes. The Pale of Russia is an insufferable hell. What about the attempt of certain states to create new ghettos for Negro families? The Talmudic admonition must not go unheeded . . . 'One who would reprove others should have a care to perfect himself first.' "

The first act of protest by a Washington politician had occurred two days earlier, with the introduction of a resolution by a Jewish member of the House of Representatives, Adolph J. Sabath of Illinois. Numerous other members of Congress soon proposed their own resolutions or otherwise spoke out. Speaker of the House Champ Clark of Missouri declared on the House floor, "The ritual murder prosecution . . . is the most preposterous performance of the age and finds no parallel since [trials for] witchcraft." The pro-Beilis movement in Congress not only condemned the trial in Kiev but demanded action by the American government. Denouncing the "outrageous and unfounded charge" against the Jews, the Sabath resolution called on "the Secretary of State . . . to convey through our Ambassador at St. Petersburg the sentiments of the American people" about the trial. However, neither Secretary of State William Jennings Bryan nor the American ambassador to Russia, Charles S. Wilson, were inclined to do anything of the kind.

Their hesitancy had nothing to do with domestic politics. Unlike France or Great Britain, America had no significant pro-Russian interest group. The entire American press, both respectable and yellow, was solidly on the side of the defendant. The *New York Times* headlined its first editorial on the case, "The Czar on Trial." William Randolph Hearst's newspapers adopted Beilis as a cause. Hearst's *New York American* headlined one article, "And Yet It Moves," a reference to Galileo's trial for heresy. But the American government would never criticize the prosecution of Beilis in public. Nor, it is nearly certain, did it ever do so in private. There were two reasons for the government's reluctance. The first was straightforward: the administration was focused at the time on reinvigorating commercial ties with Russia (even though during his 1912 presidential campaign Woodrow Wilson had, for reasons of political expediency, spoken out in favor of abrogating the Russo-American commercial treaty). The second reason was less obvious: the State Department fretted that the national uproar over the Jewish defendant could ricochet in ways that would complicate the situation in, of all places, Mexico.

In a series of diplomatic cables between Washington and St. Petersburg, Secretary of State Bryan and Ambassador Wilson hashed out how to react to the trial in Kiev. Wilson cabled his first report on the case six days into the trial. It was remarkably ill-informed. "I have been much surprised to find that every Russian with whom I have talked, of every class of society, firmly believes Beilis guilty of the crime with which he is charged," Wilson wrote. Moreover, he added, "the [Russian] Government feels itself backed up by the almost universal public opinion in taking any measures against the Jews in Russia." The ambassador was apparently ignorant of widespread opposition to the tsarist regime, to anti-Jewish measures in particular, and, specifically, to the prosecution of Beilis.

Around this time, the Russian ambassador to the United States, Boris Bakhmetev, met with Secretary Bryan to discuss the case. Bryan struck him, he reported, as possessing "no knowledge of the issue." He briefed Bryan on Russia's position, reassuring him that the Jews as a people were most certainly not on trial. In his report to the foreign minister after the meeting, the ambassador complained that "American Yids have not passed up the convenient opportunity to quickly use the Kiev case to attempt to stir up new attacks on Russia" and singled out for scorn the irksome "Representative Sabath, himself a Yid."

Bakhmetev need not have worried about pernicious Jewish influence on the American government. Two weeks later, Ambassador Wilson sent a telegram to Washington relaying his conversation with Russian foreign minister Sergei Sazonov—which had to do with the chaotic situation in Mexico. In February 1913, eight months before the Beilis trial began, General Victoriano Huerta had overthrown the Mexican revolutionary government in power since 1910, had the president and vice president killed, and established himself as dictator. President Woodrow Wilson wanted Huerta deposed but had few allies on this other than Russia. Sazonov informed Ambassador Wilson that Russia was "more than ready" to support the United States in regard to the Mexican situation. However Sazonov, insisting the trial "was entirely an internal matter," warned that congressional action in the Beilis case "could result in the preclusion of Russian support." Ambassador Wilson recommended to Bryan that the United States make no public protest regarding the Beilis case, given "the unfortunate effect such criticism may have . . . on important questions pending between [Russia and the United States]."

Secretary Bryan took the ambassador's advice. He would not place the moral argument for lodging a protest against the trial, no matter its verdict, over what he saw as the interests of the United States.

Day Thirteen. Oskar Gruzenberg believed he was being proven right in a prediction he had made two years earlier, but he could derive no satisfaction from this. Until this point, the trial could not have gone better for the defense. The prosecution had suffered an unbroken run of fiascoes. But now the defense itself was to be put on trial. Gruzenberg had foreseen this turn of events in late 1911, when he had warned his colleague, Arnold Margolin, Beilis's first attorney, not to pursue his covert investigation of Vera Cheberyak. No good could come of it, he had believed. Margolin, together with the bumbling journalist Stepan Brazul-Brushkovsky, had been duped by this villain, who had gone to the authorities with her wild story about being offered a forty-thousand-ruble bribe to confess to Andrei's murder. Margolin soon found himself under investigation for tampering with a witness. Now, instead of defending Beilis in court, he sat as a soon-to-be disbarred attorney about to be called as a witness himself. Gruzenberg was still highly optimistic about the outcome of the trial, but Margolin's testimony would give the prosecution the chance to counterattack.

To the end of their days, Gruzenberg and Margolin would disagree over the impact on the trial of what the newspapers called the "private investigation." Margolin understood he had been taking a risk, but he believed his scheme had unmasked Vera Cheberyak as a likely accomplice to the crime, allowing her to become the focus of the trial, much to the defense's benefit. In his view, thanks to himself, there would now be a six-day run of witnesses related to the question of Cheberyak's role in

Andrei's disappearance, concluding with the two gang members who Gruzenberg himself agreed were the likely killers.

Gruzenberg disputed this view. In his memoir of the case, he exhibits such embarrassment over the episode that he refrains from ever mentioning Margolin in connection with it, calling him only a "talented lawyer, deeply devoted" to the case, who had made a serious mistake. Gruzenberg agreed that the chance to question and confront the two purported killers, Boris Rudzinsky and Vera Cheberyak's half-brother Peter Singaevsky, was a tremendous opportunity for the defense. He would have had to concede that these disreputable figures would almost certainly not be taking the stand had it not been for Margolin's efforts, which attracted massive public attention, making the two criminals infamous, with their pictures reproduced in newspapers across the empire. But the private investigation gave too many gifts to the prosecution. For who were the upcoming defense witnesses? They were, arguably: a fool of a journalist (Brazul), a disgraced attorney (Margolin), a disgraced detective (Krasovsky), a young woman who appeared to be mentally unbalanced (Ekaterina Diakonova), and a revolutionary fop (Makhalin). While these witnesses would certainly divert attention from the defendant, they might also give the prosecution the chance to make the defense look foolish and dishonest. Gruzenberg, from his point of view, had to make the best of it—limit the damage, exploit the opportunities.

The testimony of Brazul took up most of the day. He thoroughly agitated Vera Cheberyak, who repeatedly scurried to a windowsill to pour herself a glass of water. But observers agreed the journalist was an ineffective witness for the defense; civil prosecutor Shmakov caught him in a slew of inconsistencies. Vladimir D. Nabokov, who covered the trial for *Speech,* found that while Brazul was "undoubtedly sincere," he came off as "unthoughtful, gullible," someone easily bamboozled. The correspondent for the *Jewish Chronicle* was harsher, saying that Brazul came across as "an honest, thick-skinned busybody with an exaggerated opinion of his detective talents."

Margolin took the stand next. As a professional advocate of the first rank, he conducted himself with immense skill. As the prosecution probed his dealings with Vera Cheberyak, along with Brazul and two or three other of Brazul's colleagues in the city of Kharkov in December 1911, he was never trapped in contradictions. In fact, he himself came armed to point out errors in Vera Cheberyak's account (what shirt he had been wearing, the layout of his hotel room, and so forth) that ate up time and neutralized the prosecution's attacks. As Shmakov questioned him aggressively, Margolin responded in kind. When asked if he had offered Vera Cheberyak forty thousand rubles to admit to the crime, he answered, "I think that only a demented person could do such a thing."

"I want a yes or no answer," Shmakov retorted.

"I just answered no," Margolin replied. "After all, no one has yet subjected my mental faculties to any doubt."

The prosecution did make Margolin look less than candid around his efforts to keep the Kharkov meeting a secret. Margolin unconvincingly contended that he had done nothing to "hide" the meeting but had merely been "silent" about it. However, it was obvious that he had gone to some lengths to keep the meeting from being publicly known.

Margolin, though, made sure he would fire the final salvo at the most auspicious moment. When the judge summoned Vera Cheberyak to the stand for an eye-to-eye confrontation with the witness, she told the court she recognized Margolin, though "he was a lot fatter then." She reaffirmed her tale about the forty-thousand-ruble bribe, and Margolin denied it.

Then, with Vera Cheberyak standing beside him, Margolin explained why her behavior made sense only if she had been an accomplice in Andrei's murder. Why had this known criminal made such efforts to implicate others, while seeking no reward at all for herself? "Only someone who was defending herself against a threatening danger," he argued, "who was trying to deflect suspicion from herself toward other persons, who wanted to lead astray the investigative authorities" would behave in such a way. When he finished, Vera Cheberyak remained silent.

On the morning of the fourteenth day, an unusually large crowd swarmed the court tearoom to fortify themselves before the session began. No one wanted to miss a single word of the day's proceedings. The courtroom was going to be as packed as it had been six days earlier for Vera Cheberyak's main testimony. Nikolai Krasovsky— former acting chief detective of the Kiev police force, former provincial police official, former lead investigator into the murder of Andrei Yushchinsky—was about to take the stand. His various "formers" had not been joined by any current position, the Beilis affair having provided him only with vilification in the far-right press, respect if not adulation in the liberal press, and worldwide fame. In Europe and the United States the reportage portrayed him as the Russian Sherlock Holmes who had cracked the case. But at home Krasovsky was unemployed and unemployable.

The detective had enjoyed a twenty-year career of successes followed by drastic disappointments. An intelligent man who had for some reason failed to finish his gymnasium education, he had entered the police force, risen by dint of his competence to the post of acting chief detective, only to be sent to the provinces when his rival, Evgeny Mishchuk, beat him out for the Kiev post. Then he had been specially recalled to Kiev to handle the politically sensitive murder case, with consequences that now made him hero, villain, and star witness.

The day had brought some welcome news for Beilis's supporters. Prince A. D. Obolensky, former ober-procurator (or lay administrator) of the Russian Orthodox Holy Synod, the governing body of the Church, condemned as "blasphemy" the prosecution's references to the Holy Bible. (He had earlier denounced the ritual-murder charge, in general, noting that "the use of blood is contrary to all the teachings of the Jewish religion.") The day before, King Constantine of Greece had denounced the myth in an audience with the rabbis of Salonika and invited the chief rabbi to his yacht to tell him personally: "You may assure the entire Jewish population that the calumny will never be repeated in my kingdom." (King Constantine seems to have been the only head of state to denounce the blood accusation in connection with the Beilis trial.) A number of Russian Orthodox clergymen had also publicly denounced the blood accusation in recent days. But in the courtroom the entire focus was on the former detective.

Krasovsky began by testifying for almost four and half hours, nearly uninterrupted, with only occasional questions by the judge, as he recounted his investigation of the Yushchinsky murder. He spoke calmly, precisely, and in an unhurried manner. The jurors, whose attention had understandably wandered at times, listened with unbroken attentiveness. As Krasovsky testified, Vera Cheberyak looked so nervous, it seemed to a reporter she might get up at any moment and scream. As it was, she merely began dashing to the window to gulp down repeated glasses of water.

Krasovsky told of his initial queasiness at the prospect of a case that would promise him nothing but "intrigues and trouble"; his initial suspicions that led him to arrest the dead boy's stepfather and other family members; his realization that he had made a mistake, that the family was innocent, and that Vera Cheberyak was likely involved in the crime. Following this breakthrough came his struggles with the intrigues against him, as Kiev's chief prosecutor, Grigory Chaplinsky, in league with the Black Hundreds, blocked his honest investigation. He told of his grateful return home to his provincial post, only to be cashiered from the police force on false charges. He then returned to Kiev with "the goal of restoring my reputation and seeing this case to its end," that is, solving the crime.

From Krasovsky the jury first heard an account of two seemingly sensational pieces of evidence—or, from the prosecution's point of view, unfounded speculations—that implicated Vera Cheberyak and her gang. These were the "story of the switches" and the "Christian letters." Along with the "the body in the carpet," and Zhenya Cheberyak's deathbed scene, these completed the quartet of haunting tales that formed the core of the case's legend.

Of the four different incidents, only Zhenya's deathbed scene was undoubtedly true. It had been testified to by the most credible eye witnesses. But the veracity of the "story of the switches" and the "Christian letters," as well as the "body in the carpet," was more open to question.

Krasovsky had heard from a number of witnesses that Andrei, Zhenya, and another boy had gone out one day to cut switches from some shrubs. They had quarreled over who would keep the best one. (Zhenya: "If you don't give me yours, I'll tell your aunt that you didn't go to school, and you came here to play." Andrusha: "And if you tell on me, I'll write to the police that at your mother's thieves are constantly hiding and bringing stolen things.") The argument had supposedly led to suspicions that Andrei had betrayed Cheberyak's gang. The prosecution forced Krasovsky to admit that story was at best thirdhand—he had heard it from a watchman with whom he'd struck up a conversation near a water main outlet, who had heard it from someone else, who said she had heard it from a boy known only as Sasha F., who had supposedly witnessed Zhenya and Andrei's argument. Neither Krasovsky nor any other investigator could find that boy. This did not mean the story was not true, just that it was not proven. But perhaps the efficient Lukianovka rumor mill had simply fabricated a scene that would explain the killing, just has it had when Andrei's mother and stepfather had been under suspicion and within days the story spread of their being seen loading into a cab, carrying a sack with Andrei's body.

The "Christian letters" were the two missives anonymously sent to Andrei's mother and to the city coroner days after the body was discovered. Their author recounted how he had supposedly seen the boy in the company of an "old Jew" around the time of his murder and pointed to the Jews as the culprits. The judge did not allow the letters into evidence but permitted Krasovsky to describe them. Krasovsky claimed that the letters' author described the wounds with great accuracy, even though the missives were posted before the coroner's autopsy had been completed. He and Brazul also contended that the letter had been written by one of Vera Cheberyak's gang members, Nikolai "Nicky the Sailor" Mandzelevsky, "at her dictation."

Unfortunately, only one of the letters, the one addressed to Andrei's mother, survives in the archives. It does not mention the specific number of his wounds. The handwriting does not match that of Nicky the Sailor or that of several other Cheberyak gang members for whom there are handwriting samples. Perhaps the letter to the coroner did describe the wounds. But even if the description were accurate, the prosecution pointed out, an early newspaper account gave a fairly accurate sense of the number of wounds on the body, which had, in any event, been on public view for hours after being removed from the cave. The letters' contents were spooky ("What if . . . the Jews need blood for the Passover holiday and a thin boy will be their victim"), but it could not be proved that either one had any connection to the killers.

The bulk of the prosecution's brutal cross-examination focused on Krasovsky's decision to arrest Andrei's family. Why had he arrested the boy's stepfather, Luka Prikhodko, even though the man had a credible alibi? Why did Krasovsky arrest not only him but also his elderly father and even the brother of Andrei's biological father? The prosecutor sarcastically asked Krasovsky if he had ever considered arresting Andrei's elderly grandmother, too. (Krasovsky, in one of his less adept answers, responded, "There was no need.") Why had the detective ordered that Luka Prikhodko's hair be cut and dyed, so as to maximize his resemblance to a man that a witness had seen near the scene of the crime? How could he justify such chicanery? Krasovsky looked evasive and unconvincing and at times stumbled under the prosecution's furious assault.

Vladimir D. Nabokov, always the most morally subtle and clear-eyed of observers, did not so much defend Krasovsky as explain him. This old police hand, he admitted, was an imperfect hero. But it was not fair to judge him outside the context of his time and place. "Of course his methods were reprehensible," Nabokov wrote in *Speech,* but, as a man who had served his whole career in the Russian police force, "where could he have been expected to glean the principles of respect for human dignity?" Krasovsky, overall, came across as a man who had, whatever his flaws, tried to correct his mistakes after he recognized them and who always pursued the truth as he saw it.

For two years Oskar Gruzenberg had feared the consequences of what he viewed as Arnold Margolin's reckless investigation of the case. So far the defense had weathered the prosecution's assault. However, with the appearance of the young seamstress Ekaterina Diakonova, the defense would find its case veering into the hallucinatory.

Diakonova was Vera Cheberyak's onetime friend who Krasovsky had wooed by taking her out dozens of times to restaurants on the hunch that she knew more than she was telling about the crime. Eventually, she had appeared to provide useful information. She claimed to have dropped by Cheberyak's on the day Andrei had disappeared and seen the three suspected gang members scurrying around suspiciously and hurriedly covering something with a coat in the corner as she entered the apartment. She and her sister Ksenia identified pieces of perforated paper found near Andrei's body as being very similar to ones used at Cheberyak's for a game called Post Office. It also appeared that she could identify a piece of embroidered pillowcase found in Andrei's pocket as coming from the Cheberyaks' apartment.

Testimony over the paper and pillowcase went on at great length. If the items could have been established as coming from the Cheberyaks' apartment, they would have constituted the first physical evidence linking Cheberyak to the crime. The testimony, though, while suggestive of a connection, was frustratingly inconclusive. The defense objected that

Ekaterina Diakonova was unfairly forced to try to draw the pillowcase design from memory. Rare is the person, they said, who could draw from memory the pattern of a piece of clothing he or she was actually wearing, let alone a pattern unseen for years. Still, the defense could not come close to proving the origin of the items.

But Ekaterina Diakonova had much, much else to say. From the pretrial depositions, Gruzenberg knew what was coming, which is why he must have been worried.

Diakonova, a thin woman of twenty-four, with her hair done up in a massive chignon, told the court that on three occasions she had had long conversations about the case with a mysterious masked man. The exchanges had lasted hours and had supposedly taken place while she and the man stood in the street. At one of the meetings, the man had supposedly told her that they needed to kill Krasovsky, Lieutenant Colonel Ivanov of the Gendarmes, and Investigator Fenenko. Why the masked man would talk to her of all people, she could not explain. Karabchevsky gamely attempted to mitigate the story's incredibility. "Have you ever seen people who fly on airplanes, or ride on motorcycles?" he asked hopefully. Perhaps the man had on that kind of mask? No, she answered, it was a smooth black mask that clung closely to his face, held in place by a hat with earflaps fastened under his chin.

Diakonova went on to tell a tale of how, the day after Andrei's murder, a fearful Vera Cheberyak asked Ekaterina to stay overnight. They slept together in the same room and, in the middle of the night, Ekaterina poked her stockinged foot through the grate of the bed. She felt an object, wrapped up in cloth, standing in the corner. It felt to her like a body and it was deathly cold.

"When I was sleeping, it seemed to me that someone was standing there," she told the court. "I woke up. Cheberyak said to me, 'Why did you wake up? Sleep.' I don't know what was standing, but near the wardrobe, there was something, I don't know what, but when I pushed it with my foot, it seemed to me that something was standing there. She again told me: 'Don't pay it any attention, sleep.' I fell asleep. And then in the morning, she said, 'Let's drink tea.'" By that time, whatever had been standing in the corner had disappeared.

On the stand, Diakonova also asserted that Adele Ravich had told her, too, about seeing a body wrapped in a carpet. This story had not been in her original deposition and subjected her to the suspicion that she was merely mimicking the old man Vyshemirsky's account. But she added her own embroidery, asserting that before Adele Ravich had ever told her the story, she herself had seen the boy's body lying in a carpet *in a dream*. Moreover, she had told Cheberyak herself of her vision. "I tell her: 'You know, I had a dream that I saw Andrusha lying in a carpet in your big room.' She says: 'Please don't tell the detectives that' . . . and she started to threaten me, what would happen to me if I told about that."

Diakonova's stories were not believable. And yet—could they be believed? Observers repeatedly used the word "sincerity" to describe her demeanor, as she told her tales in a "crystalline" voice that projected to the back of the courtroom. She looked humanly nervous on the stand, but the prosecution could not rattle her. And if the prosecution had its Jews in strange black garments, and secret Semitic rites, why could the defense not have a mysterious masked man, objects appearing in the night, or reality first seen in a dream? As the young woman testified hour after hour, sober-minded journalists found themselves softening and suspending their disbelief. "The more you hear her testimony, the more convincing it seems," one wrote. It all might be "in the realm of psychosis or hallucination," one commentator wrote sympathetically, "but had definitely made a sincere impression." With her "sincerity and naive mixture of fantasy and reality," in one reporter's assessment, she had blunted the prosecution's attacks. This was the most the defense could have hoped for.

And if the young woman had a certain enchanting effect on sophisticated correspondents, what of her effect on the peasant jurors, the sort who might consider the stuff of supernatural folklore—*domovois* (goblins) and ghostly emanations—to constitute part of everyday reality? Perhaps they, too, would be swayed by her tales. And who, really, was to say that they were not true?

Day sixteen. Beilis sat in the dock, wholly expressionless, wholly motionless, with an occasional glance at the jurors the only movement a patient observer could detect. All around him, people tensed with anticipation at the testimony of the young revolutionary Sergei Makhalin. Makhalin had teamed up with the anarchist-communist Amzor Karaev to lure Vera Cheberyak's half brother, Peter Singaevsky, into confessing to Andrei's murder. Both Karaev and Makhalin claimed to have witnessed the confession, but only Makhalin would testify at the trial. The state had connived to prevent the court appearance of Karaev, then in Siberian exile. Karaev's deposition would be read aloud to the jury, but the credibility of the radicals' story would essentially rest on Makhalin alone.

Gruzenberg, the defense team's leader, had no idea of just how disastrously vulnerable a witness Makhalin was. Unknown to him, the revolutionary had been an informer, code-named "Deputy" and "Vasilevsky," in the pay of two branches of the secret police. If this fact was revealed, the prosecution could easily portray him as an unprincipled mercenary. As Makhalin prepared to take the stand, officials at the highest levels of the government were debating whether to unmask him, thereby improving the prosecution's chances.

The intentional public exposure of an agent was nearly unthinkable. But civil prosecutor and Duma member Georgy Zamyslovsky, having somehow learned of Makhalin's past employment, angrily insisted that the information so helpful to the prosecution had to be made public. Moreover, he threatened to embarrass the secret police if his demand was not met. He relayed a message to Stepan Beletsky, head of the national Department of Police, that if the prosecution lost, he would go to the floor of the Duma to hold the secret police responsible, accusing it of corruption. The minister of the interior, Nikolai Maklakov, the archconservative brother of Beilis's attorney Vasily Maklakov, acceded to a plan to reveal in court that Makhalin had been an informer who had been terminated the previous year for fraudulent use of expense money. (The fraud charge was likely false, concocted for the purposes of destroying Makhalin at the trial—no evidence in the archives supports it.) Lieutenant Colonel Pavel Ivanov of the Gendarmes, due to testify in three days, would unmask Makhalin as an informer before the jury.

Makhalin turned out to be an unnervingly fantastic witness. Although he had lately come into a modest inheritance, and was attired in a foppish costume, he testified, as Nabokov wrote, with "deadly simplicity, resourcefulness," and common sense. The prosecution failed to trip him up. Moreover, Makhalin made a powerful moral impression. He recounted how, as a fourteen-year-old boy, he had witnessed a pogrom in the town of Smela, south of Kiev, that had radicalized him. When the Yushchinsky case emerged, he understood the forces of hatred it could unleash. He resolved to discover the real killers, exonerate an innocent man, and prevent acts of mass murder.

As Makhalin spoke, Nabokov thought to himself that by now everyone had surely forgotten about Beilis except his family. "But suddenly, completely unexpectedly, into Makhalin's rapid, well-crafted stream of words, there intruded distracting sounds. I turned and saw the defendant had completely bent over, and was covering his face in his hands, as convulsive, uncontrollable sobbing shook his entire body. Beilis had reminded us he was there."

One commentator noted that, at this trial, one had to make an unusual distinction: Mendel Beilis was merely the "defendant," while Peter Singaevsky was "the accused." Singaevsky testified on the eighteenth day of the trial, the day after Makhalin had completed his testimony, along with his fellow suspect in Andrei's murder, Cheberyak gang member Boris Rudzinsky. Both men had been transported to Kiev from Siberia, where they had been serving sentences for armed robbery. Singaevsky was by far the more important witness, as he had supposedly confessed to the crime in Makhalin's presence.

He was led into the courtroom and up to the witness stand by four guards, two in front and two behind. Observers describe him as looking utterly dim-witted. Drawings depict a normal-looking fellow, although, had he been a fugitive, the police could have described him as having a right ear noticeably higher than his left.

Vera Cheberyak bent over and cried softly, whether out of true feeling for her half brother or out of fear for herself. People had noted a change in her dress and demeanor. Her self-confidence seemed to be deserting her. In court she cast her eyes downward. Gone were her jaunty velvet hats with brilliantly colored feathers. Her head was now covered with a plain black scarf. As she listened to her brother testify, she grew more agitated than ever, her trips to the windowsill for water increasing in frequency.

Beilis stared intently at Singaevsky. The witness, of course, denied having confessed to the crime. The prosecution argued that it was ridiculous to think that two young revolutionaries could gain the confidence of an experienced criminal. But except for the matter of his purported confession, Singaevsky's account almost perfectly matched Makhalin's, even in the most seemingly far-fetched details. Singaevsky, for example, confirmed that, at his request, Karaev attempted to send a message to Rudzinsky, then in jail, using sign language. If one thing was certain, it was that Makhalin and Karaev had won Singaevsky's confidence.

Singaevsky had no alibi for the time of Andrei's murder but had made comic attempts to concoct one. The previous year he and Rudzinsky had confessed to the robbery of an optical goods store in Kiev on the night of March 12, 1911, the day of Andrei's disappearance. They freely admitted they were confessing to the robbery to prove they could not have committed the murder. But Andrei had been killed in the morning, which would have left them plenty of time for another crime. Some early reports had erroneously placed the time of the murder in the evening, apparently misleading the pair into believing the robbery would exonerate them. (In any event, they were very likely lying about being involved in the robbery, as they were never charged.)

Zamyslovsky attempted to contort the story into something that would exculpate his witness. Surely, he asked Singaevsky, it would be impossible to commit two such complex crimes in the same day? Robbery was, after all, an all-consuming endeavor. You had to spend days planning the crime. And, of course, even if he had committed a murder in the morning, he would not have had time to hide a body in the evening if he were committing a robbery? "Exactly right," Singaevsky replied.

On cross-examination, Gruzenberg adopted a restrained, nonaccusatory manner. He asked with brutal simplicity, "Why do you think that, if on the night of the twelfth . . . you were committing a robbery, then at 10 or 11 in the morning you couldn't have committed a murder?" Without Zamyslovsky to prompt him, Singaevsky was helpless. At first, he could not answer. Then he responded that in the morning he had been at home with his confederate, Ivan "Red Vanya" Latyshev, who was, of course, dead, having jumped or fallen out of a window at a police station earlier in the year. Singaevsky clearly had no alibi. And why had Singaevsky, Latyshev, and Rudzinsky all left Kiev for Moscow the day after the murder? Singaevsky admitted they were penniless and had to borrow money for train tickets.

"So, you have no money," Gruzenberg asked, "the three of you have committed a burglary, and you put the [stolen] things in one suitcase. Why would all three of you go to Moscow?"

Singaevsky responded, "I wanted to see Moscow because I'd never been there."

When the defense was finished, Judge Boldyrev said, gesturing to the space beside Singaevsky, "Makhalin, come here." The courtroom fell silent for the eye-to-eye confrontation. The judge asked Singaevsky if he knew the man now standing beside him. After a very long pause, he said, "Yes."

It was not so much what Singaevsky said as how he looked while standing next to his accuser that made such an unforgettable impression on those present. Looking like a guilty man, of course, is not in itself evidence. Still, the visceral reaction of people who witnessed the confrontation, as reported in the press, was striking:

"When Makhalin went up to stand next to Singaevsky, the latter flinched. When Singaevsky's and Makhalin's eyes met, Singaevsky seemed close to giving himself away. He looked lost and on his face was an expression of horror."

"On Singaevsky's face . . . one could see pure mortal fear."

"When Singaevsky saw Makhalin . . . his face transformed to such a degree, and on his face was written so much horror that it was chilling."

When the spectators left the courtroom during the break, many were heard to say, "We have seen the killer."

11

"Gentlemen of the Jury!"

The morning of the Beilis trial's nineteenth day was marked by a notable change in mood as the power of rumor descended on the court for the first time. Certainly, the occasional rumor had been known to circulate—for example, that the jury was leaning eight to four to convict. But rumor as a force rippling through the crowd had, strangely, never arisen until now.

The trial was ripe for a wave of unconfirmed items of intelligence. The spectators, Vladimir Nabokov noted in his daily column, were awaiting "some kind of sensation." While the trial was generally sensational, this day promised a thrill: a spy story, with double agents, backstabbing, provocateurs, and a witness's finger pointed dramatically at a helpless figure in the courtroom. The eighteenth day had severely damaged the prosecution, but the whispering suggested all was not what it seemed and the defense would now be undone.

Lieutenant Colonel Pavel Ivanov, who had headed the Gendarmes' investigation into the Andrei Yushchinsky case, was due to testify in the morning session. Would he really expose the revolutionary Sergei Makhalin as a renegade police informer in open court? If he did, he would discredit this important defense witness who had claimed to have tricked one of Andrei's real killers into confessing.

Nabokov, a former Duma member, noted jurist, and founding member of the liberal Kadet Party, was not naive concerning government intrigues. He had once been imprisoned for three months for antigovernment activity. But the idea that one government faction was battling another to pull off some coup de théâtre seemed to him "fantastic" and "improbable." Nabokov was wrong. Civil prosecutor and Duma member Georgy Zamyslovsky had threatened to embarrass the secret police and the whole Interior Ministry if it did not agree to expose in court Makhalin's past as the informer code-named "Vasilevsky" and

"Deputy." The record suggests that state prosecutor Oskar Vipper approved of his colleague's stance.

Before Ivanov could take the stand and confirm the rumor or not, the court had to hear yet another witness testify about the defendant's cow. Ekaterina Maslash, a fruit seller, was grilled harshly by the prosecution, but she firmly avowed that Beilis had no cow in the spring of 1911. After another uninformative witness testified, Vera Cheberyak, her head humbly clad in a scarf instead of a hat, returned for an eye-to-eye confrontation with a journalist named Yablonovsky, who she was now contending had actually offered her the forty-thousand-ruble bribe. He said he was not even at that notorious Kharkov meeting; she did not exactly recognize him but was sure he was the right man "by the way he folded his hands."

Finally, the judge called Lieutenant Colonel Ivanov.

Three days earlier, under pressure from civil prosecutor Zamyslovsky, the highest authorities had given Ivanov permission to unmask his former operative, Sergei Makhalin. Both the national chief of police, Stepan Beletsky, and interior minister Nikolai Makakov had signed off on the decision. But the secret police, uneasy about exposing their sources and methods to public view, kept urging Zamyslovsky to withdraw his ultimatum. To betray an agent publicly would harm their ability to recruit others, they argued. They made a tempting counter-proposal: instead of exposing only one witness, Ivanov would testify that all of them—Makhalin, Karaev, Brazul, and Krasovsky—were in the pay of the Jews. Ivanov would assert he had proof that Jewish money funded the so-called private investigation implicating Vera Cheberyak and her gang. The day before Ivanov was to testify, Zamyslovsky dropped his demand to expose Makhalin as an informer. It was far better for Ivanov to declare him and all his comrades to be tools of the Jewish conspiracy.

Like Nabokov, the defense dismissed the rumors that Ivanov was in league with the prosecution and fully expected him to be a helpful witness. They knew that Ivanov believed Beilis to be innocent. One of the more intriguing figures in the entire affair, Ivanov was a man whose instincts had been to do what was right. He had recommended that the police arrest Vera Cheberyak and her gang for Andrei's murder. He had planted the informer Ivan Kozachenko in Beilis's cell but then drove the man to confess on his knees that he lied about Beilis's offer to pay him to poison witnesses. When the prosecution included Kozachenko's falsehood in the indictment, Ivanov confided the truth to the venerable conservative editor and publisher of the *Kievan,* Dimitry Pikhno, an opponent of the blood accusation. The defense knew about this conversation and now counted on Ivanov to tell the truth.

On the witness stand, however, Ivanov denied even meeting with Pikhno. The editor had since died and could not contradict the witness. In response to a series of simple questions about whom he had spoken to and what he had told them, Ivanov repeatedly pleaded amnesia. "I don't remember this," he said. "I cannot remember a conversation that happened two or three years ago." "I don't remember."

Ivanov's evasions likely went unnoted by the jurors while his accusation that Jewish money had funded the independent investigation was all too understandable.

"Is it known to you whether Brazul-Brushkovsky, Makhalin, and Karaev received sums of money from someone?" asked state prosecutor Vipper.

"In that regard, it is a reliable fact that in the files of the Gendarmes' office, there is reliable information, that all persons taking part in the private investigation received compensation," Ivanov replied.

Brazul, he told the court, had received at least three thousand rubles. The covert funding had even covered Brazul's therapeutic visit to a Crimean resort after the group had completed implicating Vera Cheberyak and her gang. As for Karaev and Makhalin, Ivanov said each man received daily payments of fifty rubles. Krasovsky had also received money, he testified, though he didn't know how much. Asked about the source of the money, Ivanov remained vague, though he did mention a lawyer named Vilensky, an associate of Beilis's first attorney, Arnold Margolin.

Gruzenberg and his team were shocked. The spectators were witnessing, if not a coup de théâtre, then a truly unusual sight: Russia's foremost defense attorneys, knocked off balance.

Defender Karabchevsky, stunned by Ivanov's testimony, pressed him to reveal the name of the person who supplied him with this information. "Are we supposed to just take you at your word and not have the opportunity to verify it?" he asked. Ivanov vouched for the "reliability" and even "infallibility" of his source but, "in view of my official obligations," said he could not reveal it.

Gruzenberg was irate. No witness had the right to conceal information from the court.

He addressed the judge. "Why don't you, Your Excellency, explain to him that his 'official duty' has no place here, and that here his only duty is to serve the truth?" But Judge Boldyrev rejected the argument, maintaining that the source of the information was irrelevant. Zamyslovsky then took the opportunity to provoke his opponent. "I would like to point out," he said, "that this witness [Ivanov] was called at the request of the defense."

"It does not matter by whom the witness was called," Gruzenberg retorted. "There are no witnesses for the defense or for the prosecution. There are only honest witnesses and dishonest witnesses." Now the attorney was showing his rash and reckless side. To imply that a government official was a liar constituted a gross, and punishable, breach of decorum. Judge Boldyrev called a recess, after which he warned Gruzenberg of "extreme measures" in the event of another such outburst.

The prosecution relentlessly probed the question of covert subsidies to Brazul, Krasovsky, and the rest. Their logic was not unreasonable. Did Margolin and, perhaps, other well-to-do members of the Jewish community indeed fund the investigators? Krasovsky and Karaev were, after all, unemployed. Makhalin, as a freelance tutor before he received his inheritance, had no money to spare. Brazul insisted he had bankrolled much of the venture on his newspaperman's salary but that, too, seemed questionable. Where did the money come from for the trip to Kharkov, and the wining and dining of Vera Cheberyak and the Diakonova sisters?

Nabokov seems to have been the first observer to confront this question unflinchingly. "I believe that Jewish people of means did not only have the right to spend their money on a private investigation but it was their moral responsibility to do so," he wrote in his commentary the day after Ivanov's testimony. If Jews used their money to rescue one of their brethren who stood falsely accused, that "does not deserve condemnation but the reverse." With a flourish, Nabokov added that he gladly offered the right wing this helpful "new material."

Lieutenant Colonel Ivanov was the last of the trial's witnesses addressing facts or circumstances relating to the case. Now came the expert witnesses—on forensic pathology, psychiatry, and religion. In his daily report on the trial, a Department of Police agent struck a perverse note of optimism. "In general the evidence against Beilis is very weak," he wrote, "but ... the dim jurors may convict on the basis of tribal enmity."

On the twentieth day, the courtroom was nearly empty as the judges read aloud the autopsy reports on the victim and lengthy, lulling descriptions of the material evidence. A funereal solemnity filled the air. Beilis, the jurors, the attorneys for both sides, and the row of experts sat through it all nearly stock-still. To Stepan Kondurushkin of *Speech,* the proceedings resembled the traditional Russian Orthodox reading of the psalter over the body of the deceased:

> The eyelids are covered with dried clay. The ears and nose are intact, the external ear canals, nostrils and lips are covered with dried clay, the mouth is closed, the teeth are intact ...
>
> The twine was wound twice around [the right wrist] and tied in a knot, then the left wrist was secured to the right, the twine crisscrossed, wound twice around the wrists, and then knotted ...
>
> Underdrawers. Children's. Of white cloth with blue stripes. Button at the waist missing ... The ends of the cord are frayed. The area of the frontal opening is soaked with a brownish-red substance, evidently blood.

The funeral analogy was more than apt; the words were intoned in the presence of the victim's remains. On a table in front of the judges' bench, sitting there like a coffin, was an open wooden box with jars containing his preserved organs. The pathologists explained the jars could be opened to display their contents—the boy's punctured lungs, his liver and right kidney, a part of his brain, and the target of the final wounds, his heart.

After two days of preliminaries, the first expert witness, the pathologist Dr. Dimitry Kosorotov, finally took the stand. Kosorotov, together with the psychiatrist Dr. Ivan Sikorsky and the Catholic priest, Father Justin Pranaitis, formed a trio that would supposedly demonstrate the ritual nature of Andrei Yushchinsky's murder. Dr. Kosorotov, however, could claim a unique distinction: of all the witnesses, he alone is known to have extracted a bribe for his testimony that was paid for, in principle, by the tsar himself.

After the death of its original witness on the autopsy, Dr. Nikolai Obolonsky, the prosecution had drafted Dr. Kosorotov, who had obliged them by affirming that the wounds on Andrei "were inflicted with the goal of collecting the greatest quantity of blood," a conclusion that no other pathologist had been willing to draw so explicitly. But as the trial approached, Dr. Kosorotov became difficult. The proceedings, he complained to the prosecution, would take up so much of his time. His university in St. Petersburg would dock his pay. The official state rate of compensation for a witness was not nearly sufficient.

The doctor clearly knew his importance to the state's case and meant to exploit it. Alarmed, the prosecution sent out a distress call to St. Petersburg that reached all the way to justice minister Ivan Shcheglovitov and interior minister Nikolai Maklakov, who quickly agreed to secure the doctor's cooperation.

Six days before the trial began, the national chief of police, Stepan Beletsky, paid Dr. Kosorotov a call. Beletsky had with him a sum of four thousand rubles in cash, money disbursed from the tsar's secret Ten Million Ruble Fund for expenses to be kept off the official budget books. Beletsky, fearing to insult the doctor by being too direct, began by flattering him about the significance of his testimony in such a historic case. Kosorotov had no need for the polite prelude. The two men agreed on a price, four thousand rubles, the exact amount Beletsky happened to have with him. But because Zamyslovsky, the civil prosecutor, had said to pay out only half the agreed-on sum, with the balance to be delivered if the testimony proved satisfactory, Beletsky politely fibbed that he unfortunately had only two thousand rubles with him. He assured the doctor he would receive the balance on his return home from the trial.

Kosorotov did not disappoint his benefactors. He proved to be the most coherent prosecution witness so far. "If they had wanted only to kill [the boy]," he explained to the jury, "they could have hit him with a stone and he would have been dead." With an awl, "the killers still could have immediately plunged it into the heart," causing death instantaneously. But the killers did not do that, which, he reasoned, meant the goal was not murder, but something else—"torture and wounding in such places as are rich in blood."

The doctor gestured to the jar holding Andrei's dissected heart. The organ contained only two small clots the size of a pea. "That's all the blood remaining in Yushchinsky's heart," he declared. From the amount of blood contained in the internal organs and from the autopsy reports, he concluded that Andrei had lost more than half his blood. The perpetrators, he believed, would have collected the blood from the wounds to the right side of the neck, which bled profusely.

The medical experts for the defense then took the stand. Dr. Evgeny Pavlov, who held the honorary title of court-surgeon, and Dr. Alexander Kadyan, both professors from St. Petersburg, were far more distinguished than Dr. Kosorotov. They had no doubt that from the first blow, the killers—they agreed there had been more than one—had intended to kill. That is why they first went for the head, with blows that punctured the skull and penetrated into the brain. The heart, they explained, is actually not an easy target, something Andrei's body attested to: of the eight stab wounds in the area of his heart, only three had hit their mark. Dr. Pavlov explained that the preserved organs were now in nothing like the state they were in at the time of death; most of the blood in them would have been squeezed out during the dissection and more would have leached out over time into the formalin preservative. The autopsy, in fact, indicated that while the blood loss was significant, the veins were filled with blood, there were rose-colored tissues, and not a single organ was bloodless.

The doctors made clear that the notion that the crime had been committed to harvest the boy's blood was absurd. Any layman could see that the best way to obtain blood was to open up a vessel near the skin. As Dr. Kadyan put it: "If you want to get blood from the arm you make a cut and lower the limb so blood will flow. It's the same with a leg. If you cut open a vein, the blood will flow." Moreover, the natural tool for the purpose would be a knife that could make a clean cut, not an awl that could only puncture. To open a vessel with a puncture wound requires a very experienced hand. A layman, even with fair aim, would likely push a vessel aside rather than pierce it. In any event, Dr. Kadyan pointed out, not a single one of the wounds corresponded to the location of a major blood vessel.

Moreover, to collect blood from the head, as Kosorotov insisted had been done, the killers would have had to turn the boy upside down. "The idea that you would wound the head . . . the very uppermost part of the body in order to obtain blood is"—Dr. Kadyan said, using the

English word—"nonsense." The bleeding from the wounds to the neck was, in any case, mostly internal. The numerousness of the wounds was surely not an aid to collecting blood but, if anything, the reverse. The wounds to the vital organs, neck, and skull were undoubtedly meant to kill. The two dozen remaining wounds had no clear purpose and tell a story of killers in a frenzy. All in all, the signs pointed to a murder committed on the spur of the moment "with whatever weapon was at hand."

The penultimate witness for the prosecution was Dr. Ivan Sikorsky, professor emeritus of psychiatry at St. Vladimir University in Kiev. If not for Sikorsky, the ritual-murder case against Mendel Beilis would almost certainly never have been brought. After Andrei's murder, the authorities had asked Sikorsky to review the evidence and try to draw conclusions about the killer or killers. (Later in the century Sikorsky might have been called a "profiler.") In May 1911, two and half months before Beilis's arrest, he rendered his expert assessment: the "psychological basis" of the crime was "the racial revenge and vendetta of the sons of Jacob." The terrible deed, he contended, was typical of child murders committed by Jews throughout the ages.

Dr. Sikorsky was, by far, the prosecution's most distinguished expert. He was a scientist of international reputation—or, at least, had been until he became involved in the Beilis case: he was under assault by his colleagues at home and in Western Europe, condemned and derided as a man who had sacrificed his professional honor to superstition and religious hatred.

Dr. Sikorsky's illness in the spring of the previous year occasioned the initial postponement of the trial, nearly driving Beilis out of his mind. Now, a year and a half later, on the trial's twenty-fourth day, Sikorsky remained a very ill old man. His personal physician was in attendance in the courtroom and he was allowed to sit in a chair to testify. Nabokov also noted "signs of mental deterioration," an assessment widely shared.

The doctor initially testified more or less coherently. "The murder of Andrei Yushchinsky," he began, "differs from ordinary murders, but is extraordinarily similar to those unusual murders which have been noted from time to time even into our day. I have in mind the mur-

Mikhail "Frog" Nakonechny,
shoemaker, man of conscience,
and star witness for the defense.

Stepan Brazul-Brushkovsky,
the ambitious Kiev journalist
whose sensational reportage
turned the case upside down.

Prime Minister Peter Stolypin.
A man with a tragic fate, he was probably
the only person who could have
stopped the trial.

Georgy Zamyslovsky, attorney for
Andrei's mother, who functioned
as a coprosecutor.

Alexei Shmakov, attorney for
Andrei's mother, who functioned
as a coprosecutor.

Oskar Vipper, the state prosecutor,
was high strung and easily unnerved.

Judge Fyodor Boldyrev,
the chief trial judge.

Religious texts being carted into court
for the expert testimony on religion.

The courthouse on St. Sophia Square in Kiev remains unchanged to this day.

The jury. They were largely peasants, identifiable
by their traditional bowl haircuts and caftans.

Court in session. Witnesses stood facing the judges.
Prosecutor Oskar Vipper is at the lectern at upper left.

Father Justin Pranaitis,
the prosecution's expert on
the Jewish religion.

Dr. Ivan Sikorsky, psychiatric expert
for the defense.

Dr. Dimitry Kosorotov,
forensic pathologist for the prosecution.

A Beilis case document bearing the characteristic mark that Tsar Nicholas placed on briefing materials he had read—a slash flanked by two dots—indicating that he was keeping track of developments in the case.

Tsar Nicholas II, the empress Alexandra, and their children. Nicholas declared that his "inner voice" counseled him to repress the Jews. *(Courtesy Library of Congress)*

Mendel Beilis and his family after the trial.

Beilis in the mid-1920s.

Andrei Yushchinsky's grave as it appears today in
Lukianovka Cemetery in Kiev. Renovated by reputed
far-right-wingers in the mid-2000s, the grave stands out as
being unusually well cared for.

ders of children by means of bloodletting while the victims are alive."
He noted a number of "secondary signs" that Andrei's murder shared
with others of its kind. There was the season in which the crime was
committed—spring; the age of the victim—around twelve or thirteen
years old; the lack of any clear motive for the crime; the leaving of the
body unburied and uncovered; and the number of wounds. He asserted
the wounds were often a multiple a seven—"that is, 14, 21, 49 etc."—
and added the further qualifier "approximately." Andrei's wounds were
officially reckoned at forty-seven—in other words, "approximately"
forty-nine. Contradicting every other expert, even the prosecution's
own Dr. Kosorotov, Dr. Sikorsky maintained that Andrei's killers had
conducted the butchery and bloodletting "skillfully," showing a knowledge of anatomy. Finally, it was characteristic of such crimes that "there
appears some kind of unseen hand"—a Jewish conspiracy—"which
tries to direct the investigator on a false path." In sum, he said the evidence clearly suggested that the murder of Andrei Yushchinsky had
been "committed by fanatics from among the Jews." Child murder by
this nation's "community of killers," he told the court, "is no invention,
no myth, no imaginary product of the Middle Ages, but a criminal reality of the twentieth century."

Now the professor began to ramble. "Their capital," meaning Jewish
money, "is thrown around so as to persecute those who would unmask
them. Those who want to fight this evil must be prepared to face enormous monetary force." The judge told Sikorsky to confine himself to
psychiatric expertise, but the witness persisted. "Talmudism, Jewish
capital, the Jewish press, all arm themselves, unify themselves, for the
struggle with the unmaskers." Stranger things started coming out of
the professor's mouth. "Russian society has reached a dead end, from
which it has to be brought out. Bankers, doctors, sexual psychopaths,
go around like a pack of dogs."

Dimitry Grigorovich-Barsky initiated a fusillade of defense objections by proclaiming, "This is definitely not expert testimony." Taking
note of the objection, the judge again cautioned the professor to confine
himself to psychiatry, to no effect.

"We protest against all of this," Karabchevsky told the judge a few
minutes later.

Zamyslovsky, taking the opportunity to provoke the defense, declared, "Servants of the Jews!"

"We are serving justice, not the Jews," Karabchevsky shot back.

After Zamyslovsky repeated his insult, Zarudny rose to object to the entirety of Sikorsky's testimony. "I am defending only the accused, I am not defending the Jews, but at this moment I am defending the Russian court," he told the judge.

"The Russian court has no need of your defense," Boldryev replied. He allowed Sikorsky to testify essentially unimpeded.

But in his cross-examination, Karabchevsky honed in on Sikorsky's fundamental weakness with a crafty question to which he must have known the answer.

"Could you tell us from where you obtained these words, so we can check them?" he asked, regarding one quotation the professor had adduced.

"That was published in a book entitled *The Damascus Ritual Murders,*" he responded, and then volunteered ingenuously, "which I believe was prepared by Mr. Shmakov." The supposed expert was relying on the work of one of the very prosecutors who had been questioning him.

"Ah, by Mr. Shmakov!" Karabchevsky declared. "I have no more questions!"

Yet the attacks by the defense apparently did not undermine Sikorsky to the jury. As they listened in on the jurors' conversations, police spies had picked up something encouraging. An agent reported to headquarters in St. Petersburg, "Sikorsky's expert testimony, according to the gendarmes, made a strong impression on the jurors, convincing them of the existence of ritual murder." At the same time, though, the agent reported a worrisome sign. The jury had noticed the odd hollowness at the center of the case. "How can we judge Beilis," jurors were heard to say, "when they do not even mention him?"

As the trial edged toward its conclusion, Mendel Beilis would go utterly unmentioned during three days of testimony critical for the state. With experts opining on the Jewish religion and its relation to ritual murder, the prosecution sought to convince the jury that killings like Andrei's were a reality deeply rooted in Jewish history and theology.

The final witness for the prosecution, and its only purported expert on Judaism, would be the priest from Tashkent, Justin Pranaitis. The prosecution moved to acquaint the jury with one of the texts on which he would rely, *The Book of the Monk Neophyte,* said to have been written in Romania in the early nineteenth century. Its author describes himself as a Jewish convert to Christianity who took monastic orders and assumed the name Neophyte. He asserts an intimate and intricate knowledge of his people's secret rites. Lengthy excerpts of *The Book of Neophyte* were read into the record as the jury listened:

> A curse was pronounced upon [the Jewish people] by the prophet Moses who said: the Lord will strike you with the boils of Egypt in the buttocks, and the horrible scab and itch from which you will not heal . . . We clearly see that the damnation has been fulfilled . . . since all European Jews have a scab on the buttocks, all Asian ones have mange on the head, all African ones have boils on the legs, and the Americans have a disease of the eyes, that is suffer from trachoma, as a result of which they are ugly and stupid. The wicked rabbis found a medicinal remedy that consists of curing the afflicted with Christian blood . . .

All Jews, Neophyte attested, are obligated to kill Christians for three reasons:

> a) the extraordinary hatred which they bear toward Christians, and the assumption that, in committing such a murder, they are making a sacrifice to God . . . b) the numerous magical actions which the Jews perform with the blood itself, c) and also the uncertainty of the rabbis as to whether Jesus was the son of Mary, the true Messiah, and whether, given this circumstance, they might be saved by sprinkling themselves with the aforementioned blood.

He also reveals that the Jews put Christian blood to a remarkable number of other uses.

> At the beginning of each season, from the air there appears on [the Jews'] food some sort of blood which they call "tekifa," and if a Jew eats this food he will immediately die . . .
> The wicked rabbis . . . smear a steel fork with the blood of a Christian martyr, putting it on the top of the food, so that the above-mentioned blood from the air does not fall upon this food . . .
> When Jews marry, they have a custom that the young people fast

the whole day . . . and in the evening after the ceremony, a rabbi comes . . . and gives them both, the bride and groom, a boiled egg, sprinkled instead of salt with the ash of a burned rag that has been dipped in the blood of a Christian martyr . . .

On their Passover, preparing matzo with many devilish Jews . . . they put a little of the powder with the blood of the Christian martyr on one piece of matzo. And on the day they begin their Passover . . . every Jew, even the smallest of them, is obliged to eat a part of it . . .

Beilis's attorney Vasily Maklakov, considered one of the Duma's greatest orators, knew beforehand about the reading of the *Book of Neophyte,* yet still seemed dumbfounded about how to respond to such obvious absurdity. He quoted derisively from the text and then declared sarcastically to the jury, "So this is the 'scholarly' work on which the prosecution is basing the indictment." If a juror did not find it *self*-refuting, then what, really, could the defense do?

Father Justin Pranaitis, a clean-shaven old man in a black cassock, with a full head of steel gray hair, spoke very softly, from time to time muttering an execration, such as: "The extermination of Christians is the main goal of the Jewish Talmudists' existence. Toward that end are directed all prayers, all deeds." Such epigrammatic moments were exceptional during his eleven hours of meandering testimony. Pranaitis embarked on a lecture clotted with references to Jewish texts—the Talmud, the Shulkhan Arukh, the Gemara, the Mishnah, the Tosefta, and the Zohar—personages such as the ancient Jewish historian Josephus Flavius and the Baal Shem Tov (the founder of Hasidism), and contemporary Christian defenders of the Jews. Judge Boldyrev, exasperated, repeatedly warned him to hew to his expertise. But nothing could restrain his digressions, including one on the origin of playing cards, in particular the Jack of Diamonds.

The prosecution was itself largely to blame for encouraging Pranaitis's maddening detours, by organizing the testimony around twenty-nine theological questions, some of them obscure in the extreme. (For example, Question 19: "What effort did the Frankists make to reveal human sacrifice among the Jews during the dispute in Lvov in 1759?") As for the murder of Andrei Yushchinsky, Pranaitis had only one directly relevant thing to say: he pointed to a group of thirteen wounds on Andrei's right temple, as representing the Hebrew word *"echad"* ("one," as in "God is One"), to which the Kabbalah gave a numerical value of thirteen.

Why not look at the *total* number of wounds, the defense argued. Moreover, the true number of wounds on Andrei's right temple was, in all likelihood, not thirteen, but fourteen. An autopsy photograph seemed to show thirteen punctures at first glance but, on closer inspection, the defense experts showed that one of the puncture marks was a double wound—the weapon had struck in nearly the same place twice. Even Kosorotov, the prosecution's own expert, agreed that the true count was very possibly fourteen.

The prosecution had a far greater problem than the attack on their witness's numerology. Once Father Pranaitis departed from his prepared opening statement, he seemed lost. This became evident under questioning by the prosecution itself. Shmakov would formulate a question, often citing a lengthy textual quotation, and Pranaitis would invariably respond with, "I don't know," "I don't remember," "I can't explain," or silence. To Nabokov, Pranaitis resembled a seminary student failing an exam: "Sweating, wiping his brow, looking with wide frightened eyes at his tormentors"—that is, the very prosecutors who had called him as a witness—"Pranaitis's whole figure expressed physical suffering." Shmakov grew openly angry at his foundering witness; Beilis's supporters began smiling and sometimes even burst into laughter.

The defense, oddly, did a better job of eliciting answers from the witness. Father Pranaitis had mentioned an eighteenth-century Jewish convert named Serafimovich who had attested to the ritual killings of Christians. "Would you please tell us," Gruzenberg asked, "does he not say that when they [the Jews] drew the blood of a [Christian] child, that it ran white as milk?"

"Yes," Pranaitis answered, "that is the case, though why it was white, I cannot say."

Karabchevsky took over, initiating an exchange about ritual-murder trials of the Middle Ages. "How were those trials conducted? With the use of torture?"

"Yes, there was severe torture," he responded, "but due to this torture one can say that the truth was revealed. Of course, this is not good, but if a person will not confess, you have to torture him."

A reporter at the trial, Benzion Katz, who was editor of Russia's only regularly published Hebrew-language newspaper, *Ha-Zeman* (The Time), approached Karabchevsky with additional ammunition to discredit Pranaitis. He had evidence that the priest was not just highly ignorant but a fraud. The man who had once attempted to pass off a worthless painting as an Old Master had passed off others' work as his own. He had plagiarized *The Talmud Unmasked* and *The Jewish Blood Secret* from other anti-Semitic pseudo-scholars, even copying their typographical errors. This was why he had such trouble answering simple questions.

Katz was confident that Pranaitis, contrary to his claims, was wholly ignorant of Semitic languages. He proposed a ploy to destroy Pranaitis's credibility beyond all doubt. The attorneys would ask the priest to translate the headings of a number of Talmudic tractates, or sections, that he himself had mentioned, as well as a trick question that would definitively expose his ignorance.

"Maybe he will answer correctly, and then your ploy will backfire," Karabchevsky objected. Gruzenberg agreed, but eventually Katz won the pair's agreement to the plan. The defense first presented its experts on Judaism, including two non-Jewish scholars: Professors P. K. Kokovtsov of the University of St. Petersburg, one of Russia's most distinguished Hebraists; and I. G. Troitsky, of the St. Petersburg Theological Seminary; as well as the chief rabbi of Moscow, Jacob Mazeh. Kokovtsov testified in detail about the ancient Jewish prohibition against ingesting blood, which required the most careful butchering to drain the fluid completely from slaughtered animals. Food that came into contact with blood was considered unclean and not fit to eat. The idea that any Jew would ingest blood in the name of his religion was utterly absurd. A less likely foundation for a Jewish sect could hardly be imagined. Kokovtsov cracked that, if he heard some Jews were caught with an exsanguinated corpse, he "would sooner believe they were preparing to eat it than consume its blood."

After a recess, Pranaitis was recalled to the stand.

"In your testimony," Karabchevsky asked him, "it seems you mentioned the tractate Hulin. Is there such a thing?"

"I don't remember," Pranaitis replied.

"But you know the tractate Hulin? How do you translate that title? What is it about?"

Pranaitis was silent.

"You can't say anything?"

There was no response.

"Let's go on. What about Makshirin? What does that mean?"

"That's liquid," Pranaitis responded. The response was vaguely on target—the tractate deals with the circumstances under which contact with liquid renders food unclean.

Shmakov jumped up to object. "The defense is giving the witness an examination. That is unacceptable."

Judge Boldyrev overruled the objection. He had little choice. He could not forbid the defense from asking the witness to clarify the meaning of terms he himself had used. "You cited the tractate Yevamot?"

"I will not answer."

"And Eruvin?"

Silence.

Karabchevsky's final question, devised by Benzion Katz, was, "Where did Baba Bathra live and what was she famous for?"

Baba Bathra ("The Lower Gate") is not a person but a Talmudic tractate dealing with the rights and responsibilities of property owners. "Baba" means "old woman" in Russian, so the defense counted on Pranaitis's falling into the trap. As the historian Maurice Samuel put it, the question was similar to asking, "Who lived at the Gettysburg address?"

Pranaitis responded, "I don't know."

Several Jewish spectators burst into laughter and Benzion Katz himself began laughing so uncontrollably that he was ejected from the courtroom, which did not trouble him at all. "Many congratulated me," he later recalled, "for having brought Pranaitis to his knees."

The two police agents reporting on the trial to St. Petersburg both agreed that Pranaitis's testimony had been a fiasco. The priest had demonstrated "ignorance of the texts," "insufficient familiarity with Hebrew writings," and, generally, no more than "dilettantish" knowledge. In sum, "he looked as if he could not answer the simplest questions." One additional aspect of Pranaitis's pitiful testimony is of note. Zamyslovsky asked the priest at one point, "You have not found papal bulls which would directly condemn the accusation that the Jews commit ritual murder, is that correct?"

"Yes," Pranaitis responded. "There are no such bulls." In his pretrial testimony the priest had further contended that any such purported bulls were forgeries. Both statements were false. In fact, several popes had condemned the blood accusation, beginning with Innocent IV in 1247. But the papal declarations could be introduced by the defense only if the Vatican authenticated them for the Russian court. To secure the authentication, the British journalist and Jewish activist Lucien Wolf drafted a letter in the name of Lord Lionel Rothschild to the Vatican secretary of state, Cardinal Merry del Val. For some reason, the letter was sent off only as the trial began. The cardinal replied eleven days later with a letter attesting to the accuracy of a report written in 1756 by Cardinal Lorenzo Ganganelli—the future Pope Clement XIV—which quoted papal pronouncements against the blood accusation, and generally cast extreme doubt on the charge. The secretary of state's response arrived promptly enough to be of use to the defense—if the defense had seen it. But the state made sure the defense would not be able to introduce evidence that would be too awkward for the Catholic Pranaitis to dismiss. Forwarding the letter to Kiev was the responsibility of the Russian ambassador to the Vatican, Dimitry Nelidov. He made sure it would not arrive in time. In a letter to foreign minister Sazonov shortly after the trial, the ambassador expressed his displeasure at the "readiness of the Curia [the papal court] . . . to please the Jews" and boasted that the cardinal's missive "could have no significance, since it would arrive in Kiev after the verdict."

Ambassador Nelidov's letter is one of the most remarkable in the archives for another reason. In the left margin of the first page, in blue pencil, is a vertical slash flanked by two dots. This was the personal mark Tsar Nicholas had a habit of inscribing on briefing materials he had read. Documentary evidence of the tsar's involvement in the Beilis case is scant. The record does indicate that he was briefed on it a number of times. This mark is the clearest indication of how closely the tsar must have been following the case and his awareness of the tactics of his minions.

By the time the summations began on the trial's twenty-ninth day, Mendel Beilis was in declining health. He had fainted repeatedly during the proceedings and a physician had found him to be suffering from "anemia of the brain" brought on by the strain. The endless days of testimony had also been hard on the jurors, two of whom had needed medical attention.

With eight attorneys participating—three for the prosecution and five for the defense—the summations would take up five days of the trial. Then the judge would read his charge to the jury and send the twelve men off to deliberate. A great deal was left to endure. Still, in less than a week, Mendel Beilis might finally know his fate.

State prosecutor Oskar Vipper was the first to address the jurors. Officially, he was the only prosecutor in the trial, with his two colleagues technically representing only the mother of the victim. When Vipper spoke, he spoke for the state.

Why, he asked, was the world so interested in this case? Surely, there was only one reason. "If a non-Jew, a Russian, were accused of this crime," he continued, "would there be such a commotion?" Surely not. The world had taken notice only because Mendel Beilis, a Jew, "sits in the dock and we have the audacity to accuse him . . . of committing this evil deed out of fanatical motives." Recently another trial had attracted such attention, he said. "One has only to recall the Dreyfus case—how a single person was accused of treason and the whole world was concerned about him only because he was a Jew."

Vipper denied indicting the Jewish people as a whole. "Once and for all, nothing of the sort is true," he proclaimed. "We are accusing only a single fanatic." But he did not shrink from accusing the Jews as a whole of attempting to cover up the truth. From the very beginning of the case "all means were used to confuse and obscure" the investigation. He had no doubt the Jews were behind these efforts. "Some kind of unseen hand, in all likelihood, raining down gold," was at work. If evidence was lacking—if the Lamplighters or the Wolf Woman did not say what was needed—the primary reason was a Jewish conspiracy to suppress it.

Vipper struck the note of helplessness that characterizes many anti-Semitic screeds against Jews. "I will say candidly—let people criticize me for this if they wish—that I personally feel that I am in the power of the Jews, in the power of Jewish opinion, in the power of the Jewish press." That the Jews lacked legal rights was of no consequence. "In fact they rule our world," he proclaimed. "We feel ourselves under their yoke."

In the seventh hour of an oration lasting some ten hours, when jurors and spectators must have been nodding off at his recapitulation of trial testimony, Vipper surprised the courtroom. He was adding a new name to his list of unindicted accomplices. The list—which included the hay and straw dealer Shneyerson, with his suspiciously "noble" Jewish surname, and included nearly every Jew at the Zaitsev factory—was already rather long. He now found room in it for Vera Cheberyak.

Could Vera Cheberyak have been involved in Andrei's murder? Vipper could not rule it out. She and Beilis, he maintained, were "apparently well-acquainted." Now Beilis's cow ambled into his argument. "When the question of the cow was raised here," he told the jury, "I attached to it, as indeed I still do, substantial significance." The animal, he hinted, served as the excuse for frequent contact between Cheberyak and the defendant. "She went to buy milk from him," he said, adding suggestively, *"as she herself did not deny."* Vera Cheberyak could well have been complicit in Andrei's death, Vipper declared. "Just like other witnesses," such as Shneyerson, "she could possibly take her place in the prisoner's dock." This gambit by the prosecutor was a bid to outflank the defense, which had put Cheberyak's guilt at the center of its strategy. Whether it would persuade or confuse the jurors remained to be seen.

By the end his summation, Vipper could barely be heard. An anxious man, he was now in a state of nervous exhaustion, which he oddly admitted to the jury before making his final plea. Beilis, despite his ill health, remained attentive throughout the daylong speech. When Vipper called on the jury to "look at this fanatic who committed this evil deed with his own hands" and "pronounce the verdict upon him that he deserves," he did not visibly react.

Civil prosecutor Georgy Zamyslovsky delivered his summation the next day. By all accounts his performance was far superior to that of Vipper. He projected confidence. His well-constructed and straightforward oration focused on convincing the jury, although he did spin out an extended metaphor about ultraviolet rays: just as there was an invisible spectrum, so, too, there were "ultraviolet clues" that could not be seen but were nonetheless present. In the main, though, he attempted to rely on the factual record. He presented the jurors with a stark choice: either Cheberyak or Beilis. Nabokov gave Zamyslovsky high marks. He feared the speech might be quite effective "should the jurors, in the end, give in to subtle, competent hypnosis, which counted on their ignorance and racial prejudice."

Civil prosecutor Alexei Shmakov spoke for five and a half hours, in a feverishly incoherent speech that leapfrogged from overly detailed recapitulations of the evidence to obscure digressions and back again. He treated the jurors to a defense of the ancient Greek sophist Apion before moving on to Vera Cheberyak, dismissing as a "legend" that she was involved in the murder. Soon, however, he insisted, like Vipper, that Beilis and Cheberyak might have been accomplices. "Why not Beilis and Vera?" he asked. "That is perfectly possible." Then he told the whole story of the Jewish holiday of Purim despite Judge Boldyrev's repeated warnings that it was irrelevant. The jury, if it was paying attention, learned much about the Persian grand vizier, Haman; the Jewish heroine, Esther; and the tasty Purim treat known as Hamentaschen, which Shmakov insisted the Jews sometimes made with human blood. He, too, spoke a great deal of the "unseen hand" and the worldwide Jewish conspiracy, with its "horrific, overwhelming weapon—the press."

On the afternoon of the thirty-first day—October 23, 1913—Vasily Maklakov gave the first summation for the defense. Of the five members of the defense team, he possessed the most powerful intellect. He had an unusual talent for arguing questions from both sides and getting into the minds of those he might be inclined to despise. Perhaps most important, as a speaker, he was direct and plainspoken.

Maklakov began by imploring the jury to focus solely on the defendant. He would not seek to disprove the blood accusation against the Jews. He only wanted them to disregard it as wholly irrelevant to their one and only responsibility: deciding the defendant's guilt or innocence. He even went so far as to concede that fanatics might arise anywhere, and "perhaps . . . there could have been some among the Jews." But it was not for the jurors to settle a dispute that had been going on for centuries. They would need all their wisdom simply to decide the case before them.

"The prosecution says it is convinced Beilis is guilty," he continued. At this point, Beilis broke down. He was given a glass of water and Maklakov proceeded.

Maklakov liked to assume a jury's common sense and rely on logic and the law. He conceded that the jurors had the right to question the credibility of some defense witnesses, so he would clear the stage of anyone about whom they might have doubts. "I will rely only on what is totally reliable, on what the prosecutors themselves acknowledge to be true," he told them. Gone were Ekaterina Diakanova and her masked man; Zinaida Malitskaya and her claim that she had heard Andrei and his killers scuffling overhead; and even, for now, Detective Krasovsky. But what remained was a strikingly convincing case against Vera Cheberyak.

"After Andrei disappeared, when people were looking for him everywhere, when there were notices in the newspapers, she uttered not a word about seeing him on that fateful day, March 12," he told the jury, "She alone held the key to helping find Andrei, but she did not show anyone that key." He posed a series of questions. "Why did she so diligently hide all this? . . . What so worried her that she forbade Zhenya to speak? . . . Why, if she was innocent, did it occur to her that people would suspect her of the child's murder?"

He then moved on to the centerpiece of his oration. "And now," he told the jury, "we come to the most frightening and mysterious episode in this case—the death of her son."

The courtroom was about to be transfixed by his dramatic recounting of Zhenya Cheberyak's deathbed scene. Maklakov began with one of his characteristic lawyerly concessions to gain the jurors' confidence. Some, such as Detective Krasovsky, had accused Vera Cheberyak of wanting her children dead. That was not true, he said.

> But together with that natural love of a mother for her children there was another feeling in her, a feeling of horror and fear for herself . . . The unfortunate Cheberyak had to think at that moment not of saving her son, nor of giving him peace. She did not dare to cry at the detectives, "Get out of here, this is death, this is God's business." She could not do that. She was afraid. She wanted to use her dying son. She asked him: "Zhenya, say that I had nothing to do with it." And what did Zhenya answer? "Mama, leave me alone, it hurts." The dying boy did not fulfill her request. He did not say what would have been so easy for him to say. If only it had been true, he could have told the detectives, "Leave my mother alone, I myself saw Beilis drag Andrusha to the brick kiln." Why did he not say that? And when he wanted to speak, this unfortunate mother, as witnesses have testified, kissed him to prevent him from speaking. Before he died, she gave him the Judas kiss so that he would not speak.

At those words, the spectators drew in their breath and shifted in their seats. At least one juror was seen to wipe away a tear. Maklakov went on to a give an elegant accounting of the prosecution's flaws, posing a series of questions that answered themselves. Would anyone, even a group of fanatics, grab a child in broad daylight in front of several witnesses? Even if one accepted that scenario, why did none of the children who were supposedly with Andrei immediately tell their parents? Why did not all of Lukianovka immediately know what had happened? The answer was obvious: "No one knew about it, simply because it never happened. The whole story was the invention of Cheberyak."

In a keen psychological move, Maklakov appealed to the jurors' national pride. Imagine, he asked,

> all of Lukianovka, knowing that their child, a Christian child, had been dragged off to the brick kiln by a Jew and then found dead in a cave . . . If what the prosecutor described had really happened . . . then all of Lukianovka would have arisen. These simple Russian people would have risen up, fearing no one, and we would not have had to sit in judgment of Beilis. There would be nothing left of the Zaitsev factory. There would be nothing left of Beilis. There would be no trial.

Unspoken was the message that the jurors themselves were the kind of men who surely would have joined in avenging the poor Christian boy's murder. Maklakov then moved nimbly to appeal to the jurors' basic sense of fairness. "You have been told in various ways," he said, "that the Jews are our enemies, that they do not consider us [non-Jews] to be human beings, and they [the prosecutors] are inviting you to have the same feelings toward them. Do not give in to that invitation." The jurors were free to convict Beilis if they believed the evidence warranted it. But he implored them to consider only the evidence, and nothing else, and refuse to be accomplices in "the suicide of the Russian justice system" by succumbing to an attempt to stir up their hatred.

Oskar Gruzenberg, the only Jew on the defense team, spoke next. He felt, with some reason, that he had to explain himself as a Jew before he did anything else. "Ritual murder," he began, "the use of human blood . . . a frightful accusation, frightful words, which had been buried long ago. But they are powerful and enduring, as you have heard, and now rise from the grave." He then turned to his personal beliefs. "If I for one minute thought that Jewish teachings allowed the use of human blood—I say this clearly, knowing that these words will become known to Jews throughout the world—that not for one minute would I consider it possible to remain a Jew. I am deeply convinced, I have no doubt, that there are no such crimes among us and there cannot be." Returning to his funereal metaphor, he declared "these accusations, rising from the graveyard, drag us back to it, where they have been exhumed from thousand-year-old tombs long ago crumbled to dust."

Though not as elegantly as Maklakov, Gruzenberg went on to do an excellent job of detailing the numerous flaws, lapses, inconsistencies, and omissions in the prosecution's case. How could the prosecutors defend Vera Cheberyak as innocent of murder and then just a short time later label her as a possible accomplice? If she was a suspect, why did the authorities not take the most elementary steps to investigate her? If the prosecution was so sure that Shneyerson was involved, why was he not sitting in the dock with Beilis? The prosecution maintained that Andrei's blood was needed for the dedication of a prayer house being built by the Zaitsevs. If so, why did the Zaitsevs not stand accused as well? Gruzenberg's relentlessly logical dissection of the prosecution's case took up most of his six-hour oration. In closing, however, Gruzenberg returned to a declamatory mode.

> I firmly hope that Beilis will not be allowed to perish . . . But if I am wrong, what of it? Hardly two hundred years have passed since our forefathers were burned at the stake for similar charges. Without complaint, with a prayer on their lips, they went to their unjust punishment. How are you, Beilis, better than they? So, too, ought you to go. In your days of suffering at hard labor, when you are seized by despair and grief, take heart, Beilis. Repeat often the words of the prayer uttered by the dying. "Hear, O Israel: the Lord is our God, the Lord is One." Terrible is your destruction. But more terrible still is the very possibility of such accusations here [in this court], made under the cover of reason, conscience and the law.

Was this melodramatic conclusion—however moving to the Jews in the courtroom and those who read it in newspapers around the world—helpful to Mendel Beilis? Maklakov argued that any attempt by the attorneys to defend the Jews as a group, or argue generally against the existence of ritual murder, was misguided and even risked the life of their client. "Gruzenberg held the opinion that world Jewry sat in the dock and it was necessary to defend not only Beilis but the Jews as a whole," he recalled decades later, while "I was always on the side of defending only Beilis, and not the Jews." He may have been exaggerating their differences. In his memoirs, Gruzenberg agreed with Maklakov that "in court there should be only one goal"—to prove the defendant's innocence, but in his summation, to a degree, he departed from that principle. Perhaps Maurice Samuel's judgment—that "the more eloquent he became, the more futile it sounded"—is too harsh. Gruzenberg argued in his memoirs that he considered it his "duty" to say certain things of broader importance in his address to the jury and "took the liberty" of saying them. But the wisdom of taking that liberty could be questioned.

On the thirty-second day of the trial Alexander Zarudny and Nikolai Karabchevsky delivered the final summations for the defense. Zarudny's was unfortunate. Instead of letting their experts' words speak for themselves and dismissing the blood accusation as nonsense, he decided to play Shmakov's opponent regarding the minutiae of things Jewish. The Temple in Jerusalem, for example, was not illuminated by thirteen candles, as Shmakov held (there were not even candles in biblical times) but with a seven-branched oil-lit candelabrum, and the prosecutor was thoroughly wrongheaded about the Jewish ritual of circumcision. Zarudny's broader sentiments were irreproachable and sometimes eloquently expressed. "The court is a kind of temple," he told the jury. "As in a temple, one prays for one's enemies, one must judge even them with complete impartiality, without any prejudice." But the fine sentiments were lost in the thicket of allusions to the "the 248 positive commandments," "the Seven Noahide Laws," and "Exodus 37, verses 17 through 23."

The final summation belonged to Nikolai Karabchevsky. It would be easy to judge his oration as harshly as Zarudny's. He failed to tailor his grandiloquent style to the mostly uneducated jury. He spoke of the prosecution's attempt to prove its case "by means of the negative system of formal proofs." He used words like "axiom," "idyll," "extraterritorially," and "casus." Yet he did reinforce many of the points made by Gruzenberg and Maklakov—for example, the matter of Andrei's missing coat. The prosecution itself conceded that all the evidence suggested that it had been left at the Cheberyaks' house. Why had Vera

Cheberyak not told anyone about it? "You cannot get away from the coat," Karabchevsky emphasized. "Against Beilis there is, strictly speaking, no evidence," he went on to say. And not to be underestimated is the tremendous presence Karabchevsky projected, which everyone, including Beilis, found so striking. Some said that a performance by Karabchevsky had to be experienced firsthand; perhaps his summation in the Beilis case made a greater impression on the jury than the words on the page suggest.

On the thirty-third day of the trial, after rebuttals that added nothing of importance, the judge gave Mendel Beilis the final word.

"Defendant Beilis," he asked, "do you have anything to tell the gentlemen of the jury?"

Beilis stood up quickly. "Gentlemen of the jury," he said, speaking rapidly in his Yiddish-inflected Russian and looking directly at them, "I could say much in my defense. I am tired. I have no strength to say what I could. You can see that I am innocent. I ask you to acquit me so that I can see my poor children who have been waiting for me for two and a half years."

Then Beilis was taken back to prison. He lay down on his cot knowing this might be his last night of captivity or the prelude to a life of hard labor.

The trial was nearly over, but far away, in America, Jewish leaders were still arguing over how, and how vocally, to help Mendel Beilis. Three days earlier the noted Reform rabbi Max Heller had taken the American Jewish leadership to task for its inaction. "Has the Jewish people ever afforded the world a more doleful and piteous spectacle of disunion and disorder than what it is presenting just now?" he asked in an article entitled "Statesmanship," published in the *American Israelite*. He may have had in mind the nation's leading Jewish lobbying organization, the American Jewish Committee, whose executive body first met about the case only on the thirty-second day of the trial— that is, the day before the end of summations. The only significant action the committee had taken to help Beilis was to organize the open letter to Tsar Nicholas from a group of prominent Christian clergymen. As they met, the committee's leaders felt reason to be optimistic; their State Department sources were saying the Russian government believed Beilis would be acquitted. Still, they agreed it was prudent to have a plan of action should he be convicted. After discussing how they might pressure the Wilson administration into appealing to the Russian government, they came to no consensus.

Jewish organized labor and the thriving socialist movement had also been slow to organize in Beilis's defense. Midway through the trial, Abraham Cahan, the editor of the leading Yiddish newspaper, *Forverts* (Forward), had berated a New York gathering of twelve hundred socialists for being so preoccupied with local issues that they "ignore the evil-doing in Russia." Only on the thirty-third day did a group of predominantly Jewish, or Jewish-led, unions—including the furriers, laundry, and millinery workers, as well as socialist movement chapters—decide to organize a protest. But the hour for protests had passed.

October 28, 1913. At eight a.m., Mendel Beilis was taken to the prison office and handed over to his security detail. As usual before departing, this crew strip-searched him. Beilis endured the degrading routine without complaint. But then, just as his convoy was about to depart, the deputy warden demanded that the prison guards search Beilis as well. Beilis removed everything but his undershirt, which he had always been allowed to retain when searched. But now the deputy warden demanded he remove every piece of clothing. The needless humiliation sent Beilis into a rage. He tore off the undershirt, ripped it to pieces, and threw it in the guard's face. The deputy warden pulled out his pistol and aimed it at him with such a wild look in his eyes that it seemed to Beilis he might really pull the trigger. Had this been any other insolent prisoner, shooting him would have been nothing out of the ordinary. Luckily, a courthouse security officer grabbed the pistol from the deputy warden's hand. After the head warden came in and chastised Beilis for "starting trouble," the convoy finally headed off.

Beilis found St. Sophia Square filled with mounted police and surrounded by Cossacks on foot. The authorities would allow no crowd that could cause trouble to gather in the square. The thousand people or so who came to await the verdict had to squeeze onto the sidewalks, pressing themselves against the buildings around the square's perimeter. Judging by press reports, the throng was entirely pro-Beilis or else held their tongues. Supporters of the prosecution gathered at the other end of the square, in St. Sophia Cathedral, where Vladimir Golubev's right-wing youth group, Double Headed Eagle, held a requiem for Andrei.

Once court was in session, the prosecution formally moved to put into effect its insurance policy. The jury's first charge would be to decide, irrespective of Beilis's guilt, the manner in which the crime had been committed and its location. "Has it been proven," the charge read,

> that on the twelfth of March, 1911, in one of the buildings of the [Zaitsev] brick factory belonging to the Jewish surgical hospital, thirteen-year-old Andrei Yushchinsky . . . had wounds inflicted on him with a pointed instrument on the crown, and sides, and back of his head, and also on his neck, causing injuries to the veins in the brain, arteries of the left temple, and veins in the neck, resulting in copious blood loss, and that after Yushchinsky had lost up to five glasses of blood, there were inflicted on him, with the same weapon, wounds to the torso, causing injuries to the lungs, liver, right kidney, and heart, to the latter of which were directed the final wounds; and that these wounds, totaling forty-seven, caused Yushchinsky's torturous suffering, resulting in the almost complete loss of blood and in his death?

The question did not mention the word "ritual" or "religious." The jury could avoid ruling on the killers' motivation, but the wording served the purposes of the supporters of the blood accusation well enough. "Complete loss of blood" suggested that the intention had been to drain it from the body. Measuring the blood in "glasses" was suggestive of collecting and consuming it. The description of the crime accorded with the prosecution's contention that the killers had waited for some time so as to let the blood flow out, and only then finished the boy off. And, of course, placing the location of the crime at the Jewish-owned Zaitsev factory implied Jewish culpability.

The second question concerned the guilt or innocence of the defendant. The wording was almost exactly the same as the first question except that it began, "Is the defendant Menahem Mendel Tevyev Beilis guilty of having conspired with others unknown . . . in a plan motivated by religious fanaticism, to deprive thirteen-year-old Andrei Yushchinsky of his life . . ." Here the jury *was* asked to rule on motivation. Still, the prosecution avoided the word "ritual." It did not need to push the jury on this point. The phrase "religious fanaticism" was sufficient. If Beilis was found guilty, no one would doubt that he had been convicted of ritual murder.

The defense argued that there was no basis in law for the first question and that the way both were formulated was prejudicial. Judge Boldyrev overruled the objections and prepared to give his charge to the jury. This was his moment. Boldyrev's superiors had promised him a promotion should he perform his duties at the trial to their satisfaction. Now he would prove himself worthy.

Boldyrev's two-hour address was as biased toward the prosecution as he could manage without shedding all pretense to juridical propriety. "Essentially," Nabokov wrote in his daily analysis, "it was a summation for the prosecution, deliberate and well thought out." In summarizing the thirty-three days of testimony for both sides, Judge Boldyrev gave a more compelling account of the prosecution's point of view, though he was always careful to add that the jury could reject it. He stated, "You know that the body was drained of blood," even though the experts for the defense disputed that contention. "Why did the killers allow blood to flow?" he asked. "What was the point of looking at their victim, as blood flowed out of him?" He saved his major nod to respectability for the end. "A great deal was said here about the Jews," he told the jurors. "Forget all of that. You are deciding the fate only of Beilis."

The judge handed the list of charges to the foreman and sent the jurors off to deliberate. Expressionless, the twelve men filed out of the courtroom, led by the foreman, whose fawning demeanor toward the judge and prosecutor had so aroused Gruzenberg's distrust. Gruzenberg made a final motion, asking the judge to call the jury back and amend his charge with material from the defense. Boldyrev denied the motion, and the waiting began.

Most of those who had only read about the trial—including, confidentially, senior Russian officials—believed the jury would vote to acquit. But they were thinking in terms of logic and of evidence. Most of the observers who had actually sat through the trial, Nabokov among them, believed that Beilis would be found guilty.

The defendant's lead attorney was ready for the worst. Gruzenberg confessed to a reporter that, as he waited, he could think only of reasons the jury would convict. The jurors were "exceptionally ignorant." He had seen their faces, growing more "confused, helpless, embittered, sullen" with each passing day. The relentless talk of "Jewish domination," "all-powerful Jewish gold," and blood sacrifice, beaten into their heads for thirty-three days, must have succeeded in arousing in these simple Russians an instinctive ethnic animosity. His last hope had been Judge Boldyrev's charge to the jury. But when the judge sent the jurors off, Gruzenberg could only think to himself, "Beilis is finished."

Russian jurors usually came back with a verdict quickly. After an hour passed, some pro-Beilis spectators argued that hesitance to convict was a good sign, but several attorneys in the crowd outside the courtroom said that long deliberations usually went against the defendant. Quite a few spectators, certain of the guilty verdict and overcome with anxiety, were heard to say, "I can't take this," and left the courthouse.

After one hour and twenty minutes of deliberations a bell sounded inside the building. The jury had reached a verdict. The spectators stopped arguing and dashed into the courtroom to take their seats. Mendel Beilis was led in, leaning heavily on his guards, who sat him down in the prisoner's dock for the last time.

Court procedure could not be rushed. The bailiff cried out, "Court is in session! Please rise!" Everyone rose. The four judges entered and took their places at the bench, and then everyone sat down again. At 5:40 p.m. the bailiff announced, "The jury is entering! Please rise!" Everyone rose. The foreman handed Judge Boldyrev the sheet of paper with the verdicts. The judge read it and handed it back to him. Then all took their seats, except for the foreman, wearing his pince nez, who still stood before the bench, the piece of paper in his hand. The judge told him to proceed. The foreman began to read the first question, about whether the crime had been committed on the premises of the Zaitsev brick factory and in what manner.

The question was long, but he was obliged to recite it in its entirety. The words—"blood loss," "five glasses," "forty-seven"—escaped his lips in a soft, quavering voice until he finally reached "and in his death." The foreman then uttered two more words: "Yes, proven." Regardless of the defendant's guilt, the crime had been committed in the manner the prosecution had contended.

The foreman then moved on to the second question. After he finished reading it, he pronounced three more words. Beilis began to sob violently, though people noticed there were no tears. He fell forward onto the railing of the dock. He rose up a number of times and then fell back again. He was reacting physically to the verdict, but it seemed to people that he gave no sign of understanding what it meant. In fact, he understood, but at first could not believe the three words: *"Net, ne vinoven."* "No, not guilty."

The chief guard tried to give Beilis a glass of water, but Zarudny grabbed it from him, saying curtly, "Beilis is not yours anymore, he belongs to us," and handed it to Beilis himself. Judge Boldyrev then told Beilis, "You are a free man. You may take your place among the public." His guards stood aside, but Beilis did not move. The judges withdrew for a few minutes and returned to declare the case resolved. Beilis, still crying, managed to half stand and bow.

He was held in the courthouse for nearly two hours until the crowd had dispersed. At seven thirty p.m. a police wagon took him back one last time to the prison, where he signed for the return of his belongings. Then he was conveyed to the Zaitsev brick factory, heavily guarded by police and night watchmen. At nine thirty p.m. he finally walked through the door of his home into his family's arms.

The next morning Beilis awoke as the man everyone in Kiev wanted to meet. "Old people and children, fashionably turned-out ladies and simple peasant women, workers and students, and little schoolchildren," a *Kiev Opinion* reporter wrote, "they all make their way to the Zaitsev factory." So many people were asking directions that at Alexandovskaya Square the tram conductor took to crying out, "Take Number 16 to Beilis's!" Someone set up a sign outside the home saying "Beilis Station." The arriving visitors stood in line to spend a moment with the world-famous defendant. Over the course of two days Beilis shook thousands of hands.

Telegrams arrived by the hundreds. One, from Chicago, was in English. When someone was found to read it, it turned out to be an offer from an impresario to perform in his theater for a twenty-week run for twenty thousand rubles. Beilis laughed.

The onetime brick factory clerk was utterly exhausted. He would have loved to leave the city, go somewhere to rest. But for now he would remain in Kiev, he told a reporter, "so that the Unionists"—that is, the Black Hundreds—"won't say that I ran away."

Beilis's supporters were overwhelmed by joy at the acquittal. But in the trial's aftermath, the double verdict allowed both sides to claim victory. Civil prosecutor Zamyslovsky admitted that he was, of course, disappointed at the not-guilty verdict but insisted that the main goal— demonstrating the nature of the crime—had been accomplished. "The peculiarities of that act, given in detail," he contended, "leave no doubt about the ritual character of the murder." Beilis's attorneys argued that the positive verdict on the first question in no way confirmed that the crime was a ritual murder. The question posed to the jury contained no reference to religion. To find that the crime took place somewhere on the Zaitsev factory's thirty-three acres of grounds in itself meant noth- ing. Moreover, the prosecution had argued that if Jews had committed the murder, then Beilis must be involved. So, in exonerating Beilis, the jury must have exonerated the Jews. To paint the trial's results as vic- tory for the prosecution, Gruzenberg declared, was "a comic effort that deserves pity."

How had the jurors reached their decision? According to the popular right-wing newspaper *New Times,* the vote on Beilis's guilt had been a six-six tie. This rumor grew into fact, but there was no proof of it. The verdict led some to speculate it had been rigged by the state. The Anglo-Jewish journalist and activist Lucien Wolf had little doubt that the outcome "was engineered by the authorities with the idea of throw- ing dust in the eyes of foreigners, while at the same time preserving the blood accusation." Herman Bernstein, secretary of the American Jew- ish Committee, concluded that the verdicts were clearly "prearranged" to satisfy both public opinion in the West and the Black Hundreds in Russia. Such suspicion was reasonable, but the archival record, which includes numerous secret communications, contains absolutely nothing to support it. It is nearly certain that the jurors came to the decision on their own. As Gruzenberg told a reporter, "The muzhichki"—the little peasants—"they stood up for themselves." Gruzenberg further recounts in his memoirs that the jury's initial vote was seven to five to convict "but when the foreman began taking the final vote one peasant rose to his feet, prayed to an icon, and said resolutely, 'I don't want to have this sin on my conscience—he's not guilty.'" (This beautiful and oft-repeated story unfortunately remains unconfirmed.)

Agent Pavel Liubimov, in his final, secret report to the chief of the national police, called the Beilis trial a "political Tsushima"—referring to the sinking of the Russian fleet by the Japanese in 1905—"which will never be forgiven." Many in the government undoubtedly did view it as a disaster on a par with a military defeat. Yet whatever the verdict, the case could only have ended as a fiasco for the regime. The whole affair, Vasily Maklakov wrote soon after the trial, was a sign "of a dangerous internal illness afflicting the state itself." A regime that could prosecute such a bizarre case suffered from the kind of rot that only reform—or revolution—could root out. A jury's decision one way or the other could not alter that profound reality.

For the government officials directly involved in it, the case was an undoubted success. In St. Petersburg, ten days after the verdict, a victory banquet was held "in honor of the heroes of the Kiev trial." The minister of justice, Shcheglovitov himself, and prosecutor Oskar Vipper were the guests of honor. Also present was Alexander Dubrovin, founder of the Union of Russian People, the group synonymous with the term "Black Hundreds." Congratulatory telegrams were sent to the absent heroes—including Chaplinsky, Dr. Kosorotov (who had been paid the balance of his four-thousand ruble bribe for a job well done), Dr. Sikorsky, and others—praising them for their "noble patriotic courage" and "great moral dignity."

These men had correctly calculated that the case would advance their careers. They were showered with praise, promotions, and material rewards. Kiev's chief prosecutor, Grigory Chaplinsky, was appointed to Russia's highest court, the Senate. Judge Boldyrev received his promised appointment as chief judge of the Kiev Judicial Chamber, as well as an illegal pay increase. Civil prosecutor Zamyslovsky was paid twenty-five thousand rubles from the tsar's secret fund to write a book about the case.

What of Tsar Nicholas? What was the sovereign's view of the trial's outcome? The day of the verdict found him at the Livadia Palace near Yalta, on the Black Sea, where he had gone to relax with the empress Alexandra and their family. When a member of his entourage informed him of the news from Kiev, Nicholas delivered his opinion: "It is certain that there was a ritual murder. But I am happy that Beilis was acquitted, for he is innocent."

This jury of common folk, in its wisdom, had found its way to the result most pleasing to their tsar. To Nicholas, who believed his rule to be divinely ordained, it must have seemed in the natural order of things. Yet in his ingrained and deepening fatalism, Nicholas took limited comfort even from welcome events. The tsar was given to speaking humbly of the impotence of the human will and of his own powerlessness to influence the course of history. As he had told Prime Minister Stolypin just a few years earlier, he knew he was destined for "terrible trials." He often invoked a verse from the righteous sufferer Job on whose feast day he had been born:

For what I feared has overtaken me;
What I dreaded has come upon me.

12

"The Smell of Burning, Blood, and Iron"

Who Killed Andrei Yushchinsky?

On November 27, 1913, in the town of Fastov, about fifty miles south-west of Kiev, the body of a boy, aged eleven or twelve, was found in a timber yard, lying across neatly stacked boards, stabbed to death. Beneath him was a pool of blood. On his neck, tracing a line from ear to ear, were thirteen puncture wounds.

The immediate, feverish response by the Black Hundreds and in the right-wing press was predictable. Here, without a doubt, they raged, was another Jewish ritual murder. The number of stab wounds was a kabbalistic one, they said, and proof that Jews were the killers. They made this claim in the face of a most inconvenient fact: the victim, Yossel Pashkov, was a Jew. Moreover, his apparent killer was a Christian. The authorities quickly apprehended a career criminal named Ivan Goncharuk, who had a lengthy record (the exact nature of his crimes is not clear) that included ten convictions. The local prosecutor's office soon presented what it considered conclusive proof of Goncharuk's guilt. But the Black Hundreds insisted that the supposed Jewishness of the victim was a fiendish deception. (That the victim was circumcised was seen as part of the plot.) They were convinced the body was that of a Christian child.

However implausibly, the case followed the Beilis template with remarkable faithfulness. Justice minister Ivan Shcheglovitov took an interest in the investigation. Grigory Chaplinsky had just stepped down as chief prosecutor in the Kiev region but had not yet left to take up his new post as a senator. Chaplinsky consulted with the justice minister on the Fastov case and the course it took undoubtedly reflected the two men's wishes.

In December 1913, the acting chief prosecutor, a former Chaplinsky underling named Vodokovich, launched a new investigation, its mission to answer the question: Was the apparent victim in the Fastov case really Yossel Pashkov, or had his father, a tailor named Froim Pashkov, in fact killed a Christian child, contriving to pass off the body as that of his son? Proving the theory would require two elements: a missing Christian child and a hidden Jewish child, Yossel, who was still alive. That the authorities would entertain such an insane theory is a mark of their determination, or desperation, to instigate another ritual murder case and rescue their reputations in the wake of their defeat in the Beilis affair.

As in the Beilis case, police investigators resisted supporting the blood accusation. A detective in Fastov obstinately found no evidence of ritual murder. The prosecutor judged him to be "biased in favor of the Jews" and he was soon replaced. The right-wing press spun a story about how the Jewish boy Yossel had fled to America, or perhaps to some other country, "together with Beilis." But for some time the state had trouble coming up with a suitable missing Christian child. By January 1914, however, it had made progress. The parents of a missing boy named Boris Taranenko were brought in to the morgue to view the badly decayed corpse of the Fastov victim. They swore it was their son. Yossel's father and his clerk were charged in Boris's murder and put in prison. (Boris had disappeared in Zhitomir, more than a hundred miles to the west; the authorities never attempted to explain how he ended up in Fastov.) Professor Ivan Sikorsky, reprising his role as expert on the Jews' psychiatric profile, offered his opinion to the popular right-wing paper *New Times* that, although "committed in a crude fashion" (the boy's blood had pooled wastefully below his body), this was clearly a ritual murder.

In mid-February, Nikolai Chebyshev, Chaplinsky's designated replacement as the Kiev region's chief prosecutor, finally assumed the post. Known for prosecuting the instigators of pogroms, Chebyshev had a reputation for courageous and unimpeachable integrity. He quickly corrected course in the Fastov case. An autopsy specialist positively identified the body as that of Yossel, the boy's father and the clerk were freed, and Ivan Goncharuk was convicted of the boy's murder. In June, the authorities found the missing Boris Taranenko—he had run away from home but was quite alive—and returned him to his parents.

Could Ivan Goncharuk have been Andrei Yushchinsky's killer?

Apparently no one asked that question for nearly a century. The authorities never investigated the possibility, or any other alternative hypothesis, for that matter. The first person to propose the idea, in 2005, was the noted Russian historian Sergei Stepanov. He correctly pointed out that, despite much suspicious behavior on the part of Vera Cheberyak and her gang, no direct evidence ever connected them to the murder. As for the revolutionaries/informers Karaev and Makhalin, it was entirely possible that they were lying when they claimed that Vera Cheberyak's half brother, Peter Singaevsky, had confessed to them. Nothing but their testimony implicated Singaevsky.

There is only one obstacle to the lone-killer theory: experts for both the defense and prosecution agreed that Andrei's murder was not the act of a single maniac but of several people. However, one prominent defense witness disagreed with this view, though he did not say so at the trial. Vladimir Bekhterev, a world-renowned neurologist and leading authority on the physiology of the brain, had testified as a psychiatric expert, after examining all the autopsy reports, photographs, and physical exhibits. In a lengthy article published not long after the trial, he wrote:

> Although the other experts have argued that Yushchinsky's murder was committed by at least two persons, because of the complexity of the murder, involving infliction of many wounds and suffocation, we think that it may be assumed that the murderer could well be a single individual, and that there is no need to postulate possible accomplices. After all, does it really require many people to knock out a boy in a surprise attack and, having inflicted a number of serious blows with an awl to the head and right side of the neck, finish him off by suffocating him and delivering more blows? Clearly not.

Bekhterev's argument seems persuasive. But as the historian Stepanov acerbically points out, "no one had any use for a sadistic murderer." Both sides in the case were interested only in the multiple-killer theory. The defense had postulated that Andrei had been killed by Cheberyak's gang; the prosecution averred the murder had been committed by a band of fanatical Jews. It can never be proven whether Goncharuk or some other maniac was responsible for Andrei's killing, but the possibility cannot be eliminated.

But what of Vera Cheberyak's conduct after Andrei's murder, which seemed so suspicious to people as to constitute virtual proof of her guilt? Why would she give false testimony against an innocent man, enlist her own daughter and husband in her perjury, as well as—infamously—beseech her dying son to exonerate her?

Cheberyak was, after all, a suspect in a murder. If she had nothing to do with the crime, she needed to find a way to convince the authorities of her innocence. She was a woman who, in any situation, knew no other way out than to lie, deceive, and manipulate. A deeper psychological explanation also suggests itself. Cheberyak, after spending her life consorting with the detritus of society, had finally found a stage that presented her talents to those she considered worthy of appreciating them. She discovered an opportunity to bend to her will prominent men—prosecutors, Duma members, government ministers. And whether she was guilty or innocent, she made sure to make the most of her role.

For all this speculation, the theory that Andrei was killed by Vera Cheberyak's gang remains the most plausible one. After the trial, Nikolai Krasovsky immediately set about proving it beyond a doubt. In February 1914, Krasovsky boarded an ocean liner bound for New York. His mission was to locate Adele Ravich, the woman who had supposedly seen Andrei's body in Vera Cheberyak's apartment and fled to America. When Krasovsky arrived in New York he was treated as a celebrity, "entertained at the Café Boheme in Second Avenue," the *New York Times* reported, "by a number of [the city's] Russian residents."

Living up to his reputation as "Russia's Sherlock Holmes," he soon found Adele Ravich and her husband, Amerik, possibly in Hoboken, New Jersey, where the 1930 U.S. census records them as living. Krasovsky claimed that he secured affidavits from the couple that would force the reopening of the case. "I am confident," he told the *Times,* "that the outcome of the new trial will be the final destruction of popular faith in the old ritual-murder myth." But when Krasovsky returned to Kiev, Arnold Margolin disagreed. Margolin writes in his memoirs that while the Raviches' testimony was "highly interesting, tending to confirm that Vera Cheberyak had taken part in the murder," it was not sufficient to reopen the case under Russian law. Margolin is frustratingly vague about the content of the affidavits, but it seems certain that the couple did not confirm seeing Andrei's body in Vera Cheberyak's apartment.

Krasovsky still hoped to prove his case. But within four months a new Time of Troubles threw Russia into chaos and brought an end to all hopes and efforts to bring the killers of Andrei Yushchinsky to justice.

1917

One day in early March 1917, Oskar Gruzenberg answered a telephone call in his apartment in St. Petersburg, where he had been watching a revolution unfold outside his window. The call was from a colleague who had been assigned by the new Provisional Government to secure the files of the Department of Police. "Would you like to look through the secret materials on the Beilis case?" he asked. Gruzenberg, needless to say, immediately agreed. The files would be brought over forthwith.

This moment had only been made possible by an unprecedented catastrophe for Russia. On August 1, 1914, just nine months after Mendel Beilis had left the Kiev courtroom a free man, Russia had been plunged into war. The "smell of burning, blood, and iron" that the poet Alexander Blok had sensed in the spring of 1911 had been a portent of the greatest carnage the world had yet seen, with Russia suffering more than nine million dead and wounded in its conflict with the Central Powers, Germany and Austria. Fate did not grant the empire the twenty-year breathing space that Prime Minister Peter Stolypin had known it must have if it was to reform and survive.

The outbreak of World War I had at first been accompanied by a patriotic upsurge, national unity, and hopes that Russia might prevail. The tsar's army even attained a few victories, but by the fall of 1915, Nicholas II had become, in Vasily Maklakov's famous allegory of the time, the "mad chauffeur," driving Russia to "inescapable destruction." As if to speed the disastrous course, Nicholas, over the extreme protests of his ministers, took personal command of the armed forces. The tsar's decision, as one minister noted, was "fully in tune with his . . . mystical understanding of his imperial calling." For Nicholas, Russia's salvation lay in the dictates of his "inner voice" and the miraculous bond of Tsar and People. But Nicholas's departure for the front left the empress Alexandra, advised by Rasputin, holding power in Petrograd (as the Germanic-sounding Petersburg had been patriotically renamed). The result was utter bureaucratic chaos as one minister after another was promoted in reward for his obsequiousness, or cast out for supposed disloyalty, in the farcical game known as "ministerial leapfrog." Over its final seventeen months, the government ran through four prime ministers, five ministers of the interior, three foreign ministers, three ministers of war, three ministers of transport, and four ministers of agriculture.

The system could not endure the strain of the war and its misman-agement. The end, when it came, came suddenly, triggered by random events. The death agony commenced in Petrograd on February 23, 1917, International Women's Day, the occasion for a large demonstra-tion of women in the center of the city demanding equal rights and pro-testing against bread shortages. Strikes by some two hundred thousand Petrograd workers followed. The weather was unseasonably warm, encouraging large crowds of all sorts of people to take to the streets either as demonstrators or as sympathetic bystanders. Cossack troops showed hesitance in controlling the crowds. Nicholas then issued an order for the Petrograd garrison to put down the disorder. On Febru-ary 26, troops fired on demonstrators in the city center, killing dozens of them, but widespread mutinies in the armed forces followed. In the end, the troops would not fire upon the people. Nicholas had become a nonentity, his orders ignored by his senior generals, who unanimously agreed that he should abdicate. Within four days the tsarist regime had collapsed. On February 27, the Duma began forming a provisional government.

The revolution was perceived as utterly inevitable and yet, some-how, a surprise. "The most striking thing," Blok wrote in his diary three months later, "was the utter unexpectedness of it, like a train crashing in the night, like a bridge crumbling beneath your feet, like a house falling down."

Russia's new leadership quickly moved to hold the enemies of the people, including Mendel Beilis's prime persecutors, accountable for their crimes. The former justice minister, Ivan Shcheglovitov, was the first high official to be arrested, seized in his kitchen on the evening of February 27 by a student who had, on his own initiative, flagged down a few soldiers. The former minister was hustled into custody, wearing no topcoat in the freezing cold. Moments after the arrest, Nikolai Karabchevsky's assistant in the Beilis trial, Boris Utevsky, happened to catch sight of the prisoner, who struck him as "pallid, unshaven, flabby, frightened, but angry and full of hate." Shcheglovitov was marched to the Tauride Palace where the Duma convened. There he was confronted by the well-known attorney and Duma member Alexander Kerensky, who would soon become Russia's justice minister (and later, briefly, the government's leader). Shcheglovitov stood there, head bowed, his face still red from the cold, as Kerensky proclaimed, "Citizen Shcheglovitov, in the name of the people I declare you under arrest!"

He was held in the palace for some time until soldiers led him off to a large motorcar that inched along as crowds swarmed around it, the driver periodically calling out, "Automobile of the Provisional Government!," to which the crowd responded with cries of "Hurrah!" and parted to make way. The scene was repeated again and again until the vehicle arrived at its destination, the gates of the Peter and Paul Fortress where the prisoner was locked in a cell.

Former interior minister Nikolai Maklakov, who was arrested the next day with two other officials, suffered rougher treatment. Maklakov related the experience to a fellow inmate who later set down his words:

> Around us an enraged crowd snarled, cursing us, and sometimes hitting and pushing us to the complete indifference of our guards. Some huge fellow jumped on my back and squeezed me with his legs . . . Finally we came to the Peter and Paul Fortress. At the gates someone hit me on the head. I fell and, unconscious, was taken by the guards to my cell.

The former head of the Department of Police, Stepan Beletsky, was also arrested and locked up in the fortress. With his ministers imprisoned and his government in ruins, still to be dealt with was the sovereign emperor—stranded in his imperial train two hundred miles southwest of Petrograd, powerless, but still Tsar of all the Russias. The task of securing his abdication fell to Vasily Shulgin, the righteous anti-Semite and Duma member who had so famously opposed Beilis's prosecution, and former Duma chairman Alexander Guchkov. By the time the two men sat down in the luxuriously appointed imperial railway car sitting room, outside the town of Pskov, the tsar had already reached the most difficult decision of his life. A few weeks earlier, Prime Minister Kokovtsov had thought Nicholas "on the verge of a mental breakdown." But now the tsar was calm. His infamous fatalism, such a maddening quality to his advisers, a wellspring of obstinacy, now eased his path toward acceptance of the inevitable. He had always believed he was destined to rule Russia but also to endure "terrible trials" and go to his death unrewarded. Now his own prophecy was fulfilled. According to one witness, he expressed "his strong conviction that he had been born for misfortune, that he brought Russia great misfortune." His advisers had persuaded him that he could not continue to rule. "If it is necessary for Russia's welfare that I step aside," he said, "I am prepared to do so." He would abdicate for the good of the nation—in favor of his brother, the Grand Duke Michael, rather than his incurably ill son Alexis, explaining to Shulgin and Guchkov, "I hope you will understand the feelings of a father."

Upon returning to Petrograd with the tsar's signed abdication decree, Shulgin immediately proceeded to the house where the Grand Duke Michael was secretly residing. Vladimir D. Nabokov and another jurist were summoned there to draft Michael's renunciation of the throne. Nicholas's brother had no desire to be tsar. For some reason the business was conducted in a child's study. The document that Nabokov wrote out at a small school desk, surrounded by toys, was one of the most consequential in Russia's history. Signing it, the grand duke brought to a close three centuries of rule by the Romanov dynasty.

A few days later, Gruzenberg, after receiving the surprise telephone call from his colleague, was poring over the secret Beilis files. "By evening I had been furnished with five volumes," he recalled in his memoirs. "I seized the materials greedily and spent the entire night reading them." He learned of the illegal surveillance of the jurors, of the correspondence among high officials who believed Beilis to be innocent. He read letters that had been intercepted by the government, containing important information for the defense that had never been delivered. Also included were copies of letters Gruzenberg himself had written late at night to his son and daughter back in the capital after exhausting days at court. The files contained correspondence about placing under surveillance people who had written sympathetically to the defense.

The whole disgusting business was laid bare. "When I finished reading the secret materials," Gruzenberg recalled, "dawn was already breaking. I went to the window and looked at the empty street, then across from my apartment at a [regimental barracks], bedecked with red flags and I said to myself, 'We can thank fate that a people in revolt has swept away the dishonorable tsarist regime like a cobweb.'"

Gruzenberg had some reason for optimism about the future of his country. The state apparatus was now in the hands of men like himself. In fact, members of Mendel Beilis's defense team, as well as their prominent supporters, were playing a significant role in the just-established Provisional Government. The new justice minister, Kerensky, called Karabchevsky for advice on organizing the department. He appointed as his deputy Alexander Zarudny who, in four months, would become justice minister himself. Gruzenberg was made a senator, as Russia's Supreme Court justices were called. Vasily Maklakov held a series of temporary posts in the government. Nabokov was appointed head of the chancellery, essentially the chief of staff. The government convened what it called an Extraordinary Commission to investigate the crimes of Tsar Nicholas's regime, which included high officials' perversion of justice and grossly corrupt actions in the Beilis affair. Shcheglovitov, Nikolai Maklakov, and Beletsky were subjected to harsh questioning about their actions in the case. The two former ministers defended their conduct, though Shcheglovitov admitted that some of the state's actions had been illegal. But Beletsky repeatedly expressed deep shame over his involvement in the conspiracy to frame an innocent man. "My conscience is forcing me to speak," he told the commission. "I want to confess and be of use." Perhaps he was just trying to save himself, yet his condemnation of the blood accusation sounded sincere. "This legend lived, lives, and maybe will live," he declared, "until it is expelled from people's minds."

Unfortunately, the red flags that gladdened Gruzenberg's heart did not bode well for Russia's future. At first, red was simply the color of joy at the tsarist regime's fall. The entire city was festooned with red flags. But, beginning in April, Nabokov noted something ominous about the flags. Once pure red, they were now written over with slogans denouncing ministers and calling for the new government's removal. On April 3, Vladimir Lenin, leader of the Russian Social Democratic Workers Party (b)—better known as the Bolsheviks—had returned to

Russia from his decade-long exile in Switzerland. Within three weeks, the Provisional Government was facing Bolshevik-inspired demonstrations and riots. The Bolsheviks did not take power in April, but they would soon enough. "Strictly speaking," Nabokov later wrote, the next six months "were one continual process of dying." "Glorious February" would become an historical dead end. The victory of humane men like Nabokov, who wanted to turn Russia into a democratic state based on the rule of law, had been a chimera. Lenin's October Revolution would sweep nearly all of them away.

Fates

Some prominent figures in the Mendel Beilis trial died amid the battles and privations of World War I. But Lenin's revolution would decide the destinies of most of the players in the case, some of whom would die at the hands of Russia's new leaders, while others would escape into exile.

Vladimir Golubev, who had first named Mendel Beilis as a suspect in Andrei Yushchinsky's murder, was killed in 1915 while fighting in the First World War.

Alexei Shmakov, the attorney for Andrei's mother, who was effectively Vipper's co-prosecutor, died in 1916.

After the trial, Father Justin Pranaitis returned to Tashkent, where he was soon embroiled in a scandal, caught embezzling some fifteen hundred rubles in donations from a Catholic charity that he headed. He died just before the revolution, in January 1917.

Dr. Ivan Sikorsky died in 1917, as well, in time to escape any retribution for his role in the Beilis trial.

Shmakov's cocounsel, Georgy Zamyslovsky, fled to the Caucasus region during the civil war that followed the Bolshevik Revolution. He died of typhus in the city of Vladikavkaz in 1920.

Ivan Shcheglovitov, Nikolai Maklakov, and Stepan Beletsky were all executed by the Bolsheviks in 1918.

Prosecutor Oskar Vipper fled to the city of Kaluga, about a hundred miles south of Moscow, keeping a low profile as a minor official in the Provincial Food Committee. He was eventually discovered, and in September 1919 he was tried for his role in the Beilis case by the Moscow Revolutionary Tribunal. The prosecutor asked for the death penalty.

The tribunal, deciding mercy was in order, sentenced him "to be confined in a concentration camp until the complete establishment in the Republic of the communist system." Vipper did not survive the year.

Sergei Makhalin at first prospered after the revolution, serving in some sort of official post (exactly what is not known). But, according to a contemporary newspaper report, he soon found himself accused of having had connections to the tsarist secret police—which was true—and "to the well-known anti-Semite A. S. Shmakov," which almost certainly was not. After the accusations were made, his execution quickly followed.

In January 1914, thanks in part to testimony from her blinded ex-lover Pavel Mifle, Vera Cheberyak was convicted of selling stolen property to the Gusin watch store. She was sentenced to two months in prison. No reliable information exists on her life over the next four years. What is certain is that she was executed by the Bolsheviks in Kiev in 1918. According to an agent of the Bolshevik secret police, the Cheka, who was captured and interrogated by the "White" forces that were battling the "Reds," Cheberyak was shot along with a number of others as punishment for their connection to the Union of Russian People—the Black Hundreds—which had played such a prominent role in propagandizing for the blood accusation against the Jews. The most credible account of how she died was published in the early 1960s in the New York Yiddish newspaper *Tog-Morgn Zhurnal* (Day-Morning Journal). A long-time journalist for the paper, Chaim Shoshkess, reported that he was locked up in a Bolshevik prison in the city of Kharkov in 1920 when a prison overseer named Antizersky boasted to his Jewish prisoners that he had interrogated the infamous Vera Cheberyak in the Kiev Cheka headquarters and that he had ended the life of the "wonderful lady," as he mockingly called her, with his own hand. "She was on her knees beating her head against the ground, begging everyone for her life," he told the prisoners. "But after three days of 'speaking' with her I gave her a bullet in the neck." Her half brother, Peter Singaevsky, was also said to have been shot by the Bolsheviks.

Vladimir D. Nabokov was shot to death in Berlin in 1922 while trying to defend his friend, the former Kadet Party leader Paul Miliukov, from an assassination attempt by right-wing Russian émigrés. His son, Vladimir Vladimirovich, went on to write such classic novels as *Lolita* and *The Gift*.

After his abdication, Nicholas Romanov, his wife, Alexandra, and their five children became captives, first of the Provisional Government, then of the Bolsheviks. Nicholas and his family were executed—shot and bayoneted to death—by their Bolshevik guards in July 1918 in the Russian city of Ekaterinburg, twelve hundred miles east of Moscow, in the basement of the mansion where they were being held. In August 2000 Nicholas and his family were canonized by the Russian Orthodox Church.

All of Beilis's attorneys but one immigrated to Western Europe.

Just before the October 1917 revolution, Vasily Maklakov was appointed the Provisional Government's ambassador to France and remained there for most of his life. He died in Switzerland in 1957.

Nikolai Karabchevsky also immigrated to France, dying in Paris in 1925.

Oskar Gruzenberg died in Nice, France, in December 1940. When he was dying, a Christian colleague volunteered to give his blood for a transfusion. After the procedure, Gruzenberg found the strength to joke, "Well, how can anyone say now that Jews do not use Christian blood." He died that night. In 1950, in accordance with his last wishes, his remains were reinterred in Israel.

Alexander Zarudny, who was a member of a small socialist party, made his peace with the Bolsheviks and remained in the Soviet Union until his death in 1934.

Stepan Brazul-Brushkovsky also remained in the Soviet Union, but had the misfortune of living until the bloodiest year of Stalin's Great Terror. He was arrested and shot in 1937.

After the Bolshevik Revolution, Nikolai Krasovsky moved to the Polish city of Rovno. (The city, called Rivne, is now part of Ukraine.) He was last heard from in 1927 when he wrote a letter to a French Zionist activist, attempting to secure payment for his memoirs, the publication of which, he maintained, would eliminate all doubt about who had killed Andrei Yushchinsky. "Having emigrated and therefore having endured all possible material privations," he wrote, "these material benefits would finally extricate me from this difficult situation which, in any case, I did not deserve." Krasovsky, as far as is known, received no help. His memoirs, it can be hoped, survive in some archive, waiting to be found.

Arnold Margolin was unusual, though not unique among elite Jews, in his strong identification with the Ukrainian culture and nation and in his belief that both the Ukrainians and the Jews should have their own homeland. He served as a supreme court justice and vice minister of foreign affairs in the short-lived independent Ukrainian People's Republic in 1918–1919, before the country was reconquered by the Bolsheviks. In 1922, Margolin immigrated to the United States. Within a few years he had passed the state bar exams in Massachusetts and New York and was a practicing attorney again, specializing in Russian law. During and after World War II he advocated for settlement of Jewish refugees in Palestine and in other countries. Margolin, who died in Washington in 1956, lived to see the creation of the state of Israel. His vision of an independent Ukraine only came to pass with the fall of the Soviet Union in 1991. In 2000, the U.S. Department of State established the annual Fulbright-Margolin Prize for Ukrainian writers, named for Senator J. William Fulbright and Arnold D. Margolin, "the outstanding Ukrainian lawyer and diplomat."

The strangest fate belonged to Vasily Shulgin. He fled Russia after the revolution, ending up in Yugoslavia. In 1944, during World War II, he was captured by Soviet forces, taken back to Russia, and sentenced to a long prison term for his anti-Soviet activity. Upon being freed in 1956 he, at least outwardly, became a Soviet patriot, penning an ardently pro-communist piece of propaganda, *Letters to Russian Emigres.* In 1965, he appeared in a fascinating documentary, *Before the Court of History,* in which he recounted the story of the abdication of Tsar Nicholas in the very railway car where the historic event occurred. Shulgin died in 1976 in the city of Vladimir at the age of ninety-eight.

As for the trial's exonerated defendant, within weeks of the verdict Mendel Beilis came to realize that his notoriety would make life in Russia impossible. No one could guarantee his safety or that of his family. In the spring of 1914, the Beilises immigrated to Palestine, where, to Mendel's delight, he immediately felt at home. "The land of Israel had an invigorating effect on me," he wrote in his memoirs. "It gave me new life and new hope." He loved the hills and the fields and just breathing the air. And he felt something new: a sense of freedom. "I saw for the first time a race of proud, uncringing Jews," he wrote, "who lived life openly and unafraid." His first few months in Palestine may have been the happiest of his life.

But the outbreak of World War I disrupted this idyll, as Great Britain and the Ottoman Empire fought for control of the Holy Land. The Beilis family was forced to move from the town of Petah Tikva when Ottoman forces drove them out and destroyed their home. To his parents' great distress, their son Pinchas, barely seventeen, joined the Ottoman army because it was fighting the Russians. He soon deserted, putting himself at risk of execution. Beilis, meanwhile, grew short of money as he failed to find a way to make a decent living in wartime Palestine, and promises of help from the Jewish community always seemed to fall through. The Beilises were struck by personal tragedy when Pinchas, having survived the war, committed suicide. In 1922, hoping to improve his fortunes, Beilis reluctantly decided to move to America. The family settled in the Bronx. People in America still remembered him. He was feted in Chicago by social reformer Jane Addams and in Cincinnati by a "Mr. Manischewitz"—one of the five Manischewitz brothers, the most famous matzo makers in the world. But in America, too, he could not thrive. He was willing to do any kind of work, but people were reluctant to give the famous Beilis too menial a job. He found himself all but unemployable. He tried his hand in a printing business and at selling life insurance but failed. His memoirs, *The Story of My Sufferings,* self-published in 1925 with the help of Arnold Margolin and others in the American Jewish community, sold reasonably well, bringing in some money. Beilis could have made a fortune had he moved to America in 1913 and taken up offers to capitalize on his renown (for example, a $40,000 offer from Hearst's *New York American* for a twenty-week speaking tour). He had no regrets, though, telling the *Jewish Daily Bulletin* in 1933 that he could never do anything that "involved my exploiting myself as a Jew and as a Jewish victim of an unjust and cruel persecution. So I refused. And I would still refuse today." Yet twenty years of struggle did wear him down. By the early 1930s his main means of support was peddling his book door to door, which exhausted him. "I am not yet sixty," he told an interviewer the year before his death, "but it's as though I've lived through a thousand years." When he died in 1934, four thousand people attended his funeral, a final manifestation of the fame that he had tried to avoid and had found such an awful burden.

Echoes

In Russia, for a few years after the verdict, "Beilis" became a derogatory epithet for "Jew." Somewhat more strangely, during World War I some Russians nicknamed German zeppelins "Beilises," because Jews were supposedly pro-German traitors. (Jews were also sometimes called "Vilyush," a mocking diminutive of Kaiser Wilhelm.)

Within a decade or so, however, Mendel Beilis, once one of the most famous people on earth, had largely faded from memory in Russia and in the world. But the blood accusation did not disappear. It lived on— predominantly outside of Russia.

Its survival in the West should not have been surprising. In the Western condemnation of the Beilis trial there had arguably been no small element of hypocrisy. During the trial, prosecutor Oskar Vipper had complained to the jury:

> Some foreign newspapers refer to our Russia as a barbarous country where such indictments, where such cruel blood accusations are permitted . . . But it turns out that abroad such indictments are brought as well . . . Consequently attacks on Russia, from this point of view, are incorrect and unfounded.

Vipper's complaint was defensible. The Beilis affair could be seen as the climax of a wave of ritual murder cases in Eastern and Central Europe, the majority of which, as noted earlier, arose in Germany and Austria-Hungary. Between the early 1880s and 1913 there were at least as many recorded cases—approximately a hundred—as there had been in the previous seven hundred years ("cases" being defined here as accusations that were investigated or at least received considerable popular attention).

The last actual ritual-murder trial outside of Eastern Europe occurred in the Prussian town of Konitz, in 1900. The victim was an eighteen-year-old student, Ernst Winter, who had been neatly dismembered, his body parts scattered throughout the town, wrapped in packing paper. The case sparked anti-Semitic riots—the town's synagogue was set on fire and Jewish homes vandalized—though thankfully no one was killed. A Jewish butcher and his son, Adolph and Moritz Lewy, were charged in the murder. They turned out to have solid alibis and the charge was dismissed. A third Jew was tried and acquitted. (Moritz Lewy, however, was convicted of perjury for denying that he knew the victim, based on extremely flimsy evidence. The kaiser, in his mercy, cut the four-year sentence in half.)

Historians have reached no consensus on the precise reasons for the revival of the blood accusation with a half-dozen full-fledged trials in Europe in the latter part of the nineteenth century. But the wave was undoubtedly linked to the rise of modern anti-Semitism that culminated in some of the worst horrors of the twentieth century. Jew-hatred was now the province of "experts" who could testify in court. As the historian David Biale writes, "a folkloric belief that had remained relatively underground in central Europe after the Reformation was now given a certain bogus dignity as 'scientific.' " The blood accusation's revival, then, was arguably a warning sign. In reaction to the Beilis affair, Russia's European critics might have done well to look inward, for the trial could be seen as a symptom, to borrow Vasily Maklakov's words, of a "dangerous internal illness" afflicting the heart of Europe itself. During the trial, in fact, Vipper was quite explicit in confessing that he had been inspired by certain recent European trials.

In the decades after his trial, Mendel Beilis never entirely lost his place in history. He was reliably mentioned in any tract on Jewish ritual murder or its refutation. In 1926, the official newspaper of Germany's rising Nazi Party, *Volkischer Beobachter*, devoted a six-part series to the Beilis affair, calling it a "test of strength between the Russian state and people and the Jews." In the 1930s, Julius Streicher, editor of the infamous Nazi weekly *Der Sturmer*, energetically propagandized for the ritual-murder charge, devoting special issues to the subject that listed Beilis in the pantheon of Jewish child-killers. "Look at the path which the Jewish people has traversed for millennia," Streicher declared at a Nazi rally. "Everywhere murder, everywhere mass murder!" The Nazi regime itself, it is true, never adopted the blood accusation as a major part of its official propaganda. There were no Nazi versions of the Beilis trial. Still, as Biale has argued, the blood accusation was more important to the Nazi cause than it might initially appear. Thanks to the efforts of Streicher and others, the charge "lurked in the background, providing additional mythic ammunition" that aided in "the demonization of the Jews . . . [making] it easier for the Nazis to isolate their victims and then deport them to their deaths." As the most notorious example of its kind, the Beilis case surely helped the ritual-murder myth maintain its vitality. Of note is that in May 1943, the head of the SS, Heinrich Himmler, sent several hundred copies of a book on Jewish ritual murder, which included an entire chapter on the Beilis trial, for distribution to the *Einsatzgruppen,* the mobile death squads that killed more than a million Jews in Eastern Europe. The tomes, Himmler explained to a top lieutenant, were important reading "above all to the men who are busy with the Jewish question."

In Poland, during and after World War II, there were signs that the Kiev case had survived in the collective memory. Residents of German-occupied Poland called the product rumored to be made from human fat in the Auschwitz concentration camp "Beilis Soap." (Poles therefore took care to avoid the soap cakes distributed by the German authorities.)

After the war, as the historian Jan T. Gross has documented in horrifying detail, Poles perpetrated pogroms that killed hundreds of the Jews who had managed to survive German extermination. In many cases, the violence was sparked by rumors of ritual murder. The first postwar pogrom was in the city of Rzeszow on June 12, 1945. No one was killed but a large number of Jews were beaten, Jewish property was vandalized, and two hundred Jews fled the city. According to a local newspaper account, the public was enraged by "the wildest rumors" of a ritual murder committed "by Jews who needed blood [transfusions, to fortify themselves] after returning from the camps."

The most notorious postwar pogrom in Poland took place on July 4, 1946, in the town of Kielce, where a mob killed forty-two Jews and left some eighty wounded. A Jewish delegation attempted to secure a statement condemning anti-Semitism from the bishop of Lublin, Stefan Wyszinski, later named a cardinal and primate of Poland. According to a report on the meeting, Wyszinski declined to issue a special condemnation of anti-Semitism and "during the discussion of how the crowd was agitated by the myth that Christian blood is necessary to make matzo, the bishop clarified that during the Beilis trial a lot of old and new Jewish books were assembled and the matter of blood was not definitively settled." (It should be noted that another bishop, Teodor Kubina of Czestochowa, together with local officials, issued an uncompromising proclamation that began: "All statements about ritual murders are lies. Nobody . . . has ever been harmed by Jews for ritual purposes.")

In Russia, Jewish ritual murder reared up once more as a highly public issue—almost exactly eight decades after Mendel Beilis's arrest in the middle of the night. The occasion was the discovery in a forest outside Sverdlovsk (as Ekaterinburg had been renamed) of several sets of buried skeletal remains, believed to be those of Tsar Nicholas II and his family. The excavation that commenced in mid-July 1991 was reminiscent of the botched handling of the Yuschinsky crime scene. Over the protests of a forensic archaeologist, ready with her brushes and tools, untrained investigators hurriedly grabbed at the hundreds of bones, many of which splintered or disintegrated entirely as they were stuffed into bags.

After the Soviet Union collapsed a few months later, the new Russian government created a commission to establish the identities of the victims and plan an appropriate interment. DNA samples were taken from the remains and compared to samples from several living relatives of the imperial couple. In September 1995, the commission's lead investigator announced his conclusion: the remains were, beyond all doubt, those of Nicholas and Alexandra, and three of their daughters, as well four others in their retinue who had been murdered along with them. (One of the two younger daughters—either Maria or Anastasia—and the boy Alexis were unaccounted for, fueling speculation they had escaped, though the evidence strongly suggested that the perpetrators had burned these bodies.)

After the bodies were identified, the Holy Synod of the Russian Orthodox Church shocked authorities and the public by declaring that it could not accept the accuracy of the commission's report. The Church asked for clarification on ten questions, two of which attracted widespread attention. The synod wanted to know: Had the tsar been decapitated after his death? And could the commission "confirm or refute the ritual character of the murder"?

The notion that the massacre of the imperial family was a Jewish ritual crime had persisted since the early 1920s when it was propagated by anticommunist Russian propagandists and popularized in the West by the *Times* of London's Russia correspondent, Robert Wilton, who wrote a lurid book on the subject. In this scenario, Jews were solely responsible for killing the tsar, his wife, and their children. They had cut off the head of the tsar and sent it to the Kremlin, and they had left behind, in Wilton's words, "mysterious inscriptions in the death chamber." When the White forces briefly captured the Ipatiev House in Ekaterinburg where the Romanovs had been killed, they found scrawled on the basement walls some runic-looking marks and two garbled lines of poetry in German by the German Jewish poet Heinrich Heine. The quotation was from a poem about the death of King Balthazar, the biblical figure who sees "the writing on the wall." Belsazar—the correct rendering of Balthazar in German—was misspelled "Belsa*tzar.*" Some might see the work, at worst, of a punning executioner and some idle doodling. But in the eyes of the Far Right, all the scribblings were "kabbalistic signs" pointing to the murders' ritual character.

The Holy Synod's ghoulish inquiries in 1995 testified to the abiding obsession of extreme Russian nationalists with what one historian has called the "gothic version" of the murders. Critics argued that for the commission to address the ritual scenario was to dignify it. But the commission's chairman, the noted democratic reformer Boris Nemtsov, opted to deal with it matter-of-factly. In January 1998, the commission's chief investigator, V. N. Solovev, informed the synod of his unequivocal conclusion, which he later summed up in a newspaper interview: "The motives [for the murders] were of a political character and were in no way connected with secret religious cults." Unsurprisingly, latter-day Black Hundreds, a rising force in postcommunist Russia, would not accept this conclusion; they insisted that the investigation was "fraudulent" and designed "to conceal the ritual character of the crime." As for the Russian Orthodox Church, it merely refused to accept the identification of the remains, calling the results inconclusive. The Church's position did not change even after additional tests reckoned that the odds of a coincidental match with Romanov DNA were more than a billion to one.

When the imperial family's remains were interred in the Peter and Paul Cathedral in St. Petersburg in July 1998, Patriarch Aleksy and other high Church officials refused to attend. The priests presiding over the service did not utter the victims' names; the ceremony was treated as a ritual that would be performed for unknowns. The refusal of the Church to acknowledge the identity of the remains could, of course, only encourage speculation about the nature of the murders, which continues in the far-right-wing media to this day. In the post-Soviet era, the sensational accounts of Wilton and the White Russians from the 1920s have been republished and embellished in new versions. One especially popular one, marketed as scholarly nonfiction, features a mysterious rabbi who supervises the ritual.

Then there is the strange case of Alexander Solzhenitsyn, the anticommunist hero and winner of the Nobel Prize in Literature who died in 2008. Though a deeply conservative Russian nationalist, he in no way advocated for the truthfulness of the blood accusation. Yet, in one of his final works, *Two Hundred Years Together,* about the Russians' relationship with the Jews, he struggles with the Beilis case. He begins with the right question: "How was it possible in the twentieth century, without a factually based indictment, to instigate such a trial that threatened an entire people?" But, as the Russian journalist and historian Semyon Reznik writes, while Solzhenitsyn makes it clear he "does not approve of those who conducted the Beilis case, he tries in every way he can to shield them, to obscure the clarity of the picture."

Solzhenitsyn writes that "Beilis was indicted, on the basis of dubious evidence, because he was a Jew." The evidence, of course, was not "dubious" but better said to have been nonexistent or fabricated by the state. Solzhenitsyn's account contains numerous other inaccuracies that invariably cast Beilis's defenders in a bad light and make his prosecution seem, if not defensible, then a less evil act than it was. On major points he accepts the prosecution's view of the evidence. Andrei Yushchinsky, he writes, "was killed in an unusual manner: forty-seven wounds were inflicted on him, with apparent knowledge of anatomy," with wounds whose "apparent goal was to drain his blood while alive." All those allegations, of course, were contradicted by the defense experts—and in the matter of the perpetrators' supposed anatomical knowledge, by an expert for the prosecution. It is surely indicative of the modern-day persistence of the blood accusation that one of the greatest Russian literary, political, and moral figures of the last century could not honestly come to terms with the case of Mendel Beilis.

A Well-Tended Grave

For decades, the grave in Section 34, Row 11, Plot No. 4 of the Lukianovka Cemetery in Kiev had been abandoned, lacking even a proper grave marker. The first sign of renewed interest in the site came in 2003 when a group of about fifteen men dressed in facsimiles of tsarist officers' uniforms came from St. Petersburg, along with two Russian Orthodox priests, to pay their respects at the final resting place of Andrei Yushchinsky.

Soon after that visit—without official permission, according to the cemetery's director—neat new shrubbery appeared on the plot, as well as a new cross with two metal plates bearing inscriptions. In the decrepit cemetery, where many graves had turned into weed-filled sinkholes, Andrei's plot now stood out as unusually well tended.

The inscription on the first plate read:

Here lie the remains of the saintly boy-martyr Andrei (Yushchinsky).
Crowned with the martyr's wreath in his thirteenth year, on 12
    March 1911.
Sainted, martyred, Andrei, pray to God for us.

In calling Andrei a "martyr," the inscription was inappropriate, since the poor boy's murder, horrible though it was, had nothing to do with his faith. Beneath the first plate someone had affixed another one, bearing a much more plainspoken and provocative inscription:

Andrei Yushchinsky, martyred by the Yids in 1911.

In February 2004, after reports of this anti-Semitic act incited an uproar, the cemetery sought a court order to remove the plate—a legal necessity, according to the director—but within days someone had made off with the offensive plaque, rendering legal action unnecessary.

Andrei's grave site continued to attract the attention of the Russian and Ukrainian Far Right. In February 2006, the grave was renovated again, thanks to the efforts of a group from a large private Ukrainian university, the Inter-Regional Academy of Personnel Management, known by its Ukrainian acronym MAUP, which has been cited by the U.S. State Department and the Anti-Defamation League as a disseminator of anti-Semitic propaganda. The major addition was a rectangular marble tablet placed over the grave, inscribed with the text of the first question to the jury—about the forty-seven wounds and five glasses of blood—which, given the affirmative verdict, supposedly confirmed the existence of ritual murder. Local Jewish groups were outraged by the inscription, but because it was a quote from a court proceeding that was not overtly inflammatory, no legal basis could be found to have it removed. It remains there today.

It would be mistaken to exaggerate the extent of anti-Semitism in

Ukraine. Ukraine does not sponsor official anti-Semitism. When anti-Semitic incidents have occurred, the government has condemned them. Nonetheless, Andrei Yushchinsky's grave site has become a place of pilgrimage for far-right true believers. Every year, on the anniversary of the murder, a sizeable and organized group comes to pay its respects to the Boy Martyr, a thirteen-year-old child whose memory is both celebrated and abused. Smaller groups of mourners make their way there as well. In springtime a visitor will find Andrei's grave covered with fresh flowers.

Acknowledgments

I have many people to thank.

My amazing agent, Renee Zuckerbrot, plucked me off the Internet to suggest I write "a book," when I had no idea what that book would be, and then saw the potential in this story. Altie Karper acquired the book for Schocken and gave me consistent encouragement during the long process of researching and writing.

Leonid Finberg, head of the Judaica Institute in Kiev, the go-to person for anyone doing research on Ukrainian Jewish history, was indispensable in helping me secure access to archival documents. He also provided me with my indefatigable research assistant, Olga Savchuk.

Thanks also go to my other research assistants: Nicole Warren, who scouted out every possible mention of the case in blurry microfilms of Russian newspapers, and also read through the manuscript, making many useful comments; and Nataliya Rovenskaya, Kateryna Demchuk, Jane Gorjevsky, and Lydia Hamilton.

Katia Shraga transcribed handwritten documents that even native Russians found impossible to read and imparted to me some of her skill.

Professors Natan Meir and Yohanan Petrovsky-Shtern provided very helpful research advice along the way. Professor Robert Weinberg was generous with his time, reading and commenting on drafts of several chapters.

David Groff gave me the benefit of his immense editorial acumen throughout the writing of this book. Alexander Zaslavsky and Caroline Howard contributed many incisive and constructive comments on the manuscript.

Jay Beilis, Mendel's grandson, and his cousin Hilda Edelist were generous with their memories and information about their family and put me onto material I otherwise would not have found.

Mark Stein, coeditor of a new edition of Mendel Beilis's memoir, shared much interesting material.

Carrie Friedman-Cohen located and translated Beilis's lost memoir in the Yiddish newspaper *Haynt* and translated most of the Yiddish material in this book; Jessica Kirzane also contributed Yiddish translation work.

Alex Ratnovsky, of the Yeshiva University library, provided indispensable assistance.

My wife, Lilia, fulfilled multiple roles: graphic artist, Russian-language consultant, critical and sensitive reader. I owe her more than I can express.

Source Notes

The major source for information about the Mendel Beilis case is the three-volume trial transcript, which was printed daily in the newspaper *Kievskaia Mysl'* and published in three volumes as *Delo Beilisa: Stenographicheskii Otchet*. These will be cited as: STEN I, II, and III. The transcript is a unique and extraordinary document, the product of a private effort, as Russian trial proceedings were not routinely transcribed in full.

The transcript, however, was recognized at the time by both sides as being not entirely accurate. I have supplemented or used alternative versions of witness testimony as recorded by reporters for the newspapers *Rech'*, *Kievskaia Mysl'*, and *Kievlianin* and, occasionally, other sources.

In 2005, the State Archive of the Kiev Region, Gosudarstvennyi Arkhiv Kievskoi Oblasti (GAKO), put out seven reels of microfilm with some five thousand pages of documents about the case. *Dokumenty po delu Beilisa (The Beilis Case Papers)* was published by the U.S. firm Eastview Information Services. This material is cited as "GAKO-DpdB" by reel number and in standard archival notation.

I also obtained hundreds of pages of additional documents from the Kiev State Archive. This material is cited as "GAKO" in standard archival notion.

After the February 1917 revolution, the Provisional Government convened an Extraordinary Commission to investigate the crimes of the tsarist regime, including the prosecution of Beilis. The testimony was published in *Padenie Tsarskogo Rezhima (The Fall of the Tsarist Regime)*, cited as "*Padenie*."

Another indispensable source: a collection of depositions given to the Extraordinary Commission by key figures in the Beilis case, published in book form in 1999 as *Delo Mendelia Beilisa: Materialy Chrezvychainoi sledstvennoi komissii Vremennogo pravitel'stva o sudebnom protsesse 1913 g. po obvineniiu v ritual'nom ubiistve (The Case of Mendel Beilis: Materials of the Extraordinary Investigative Commission of the Provisional Government about the Trial of 1913 on the Accusation of Ritual Murder.)* This work is cited as *Materialy Chrezvychainoi*.

Special mention must be made of the Russian jurist and historian Alexander Tager, author of *Tsarskaia Rossiia i delo Beilisa* (published in English as *The Decay of Czarism: The Beiliss Trial*), and two indispensable articles in the journal *Krasnyi Arkhiv*, collecting important documents about the case.

His effort was heroic and his fate tragic, as he perished in the Stalinist purges of the 1930s. His works are still the only source for much of what we know about the case.

The sources for the personal experiences of Mendel Beilis are his autobiography, *The Story of My Sufferings,* and the multipart interview with him published in the Yiddish newspaper *Haynt* in November–December 1913, "Mayn Lebn in Turme un in Gerikht" (My Life in Prison and the Court). Where the accounts overlap, I have generally preferred the *Haynt* version, given its proximity to the events. Beilis also gave an interview to the Hearst papers, which published a multipart series in the spring of 1914. The material unfortunately contains so many obvious errors and exaggerations that I have used it very sparingly.

Abbreviations

GAKO (*Gosudarstvennyi Arkhiv Kievskoi Oblasti*)
GAKO-DpdB (GAKO-*Dokumenty po delu Beilisa*)
STEN (*Delo Beilisa: Stenographicheskii Otchet*)

Archival Notation

f. *fond* (collection)
d. *delo* (file)
op. *opis'* (inventory)
l. *list* (folio)
ob. *oborot* (verso)

Preface

xi   "The Yids have tortured": Samuel, *Blood Accusation*, p. 17.
xii   *Protocols*: *The Protocols of the Elders of Zion* originated in Russia and were originally spread in the West after the Russian revolution by Russian émigrés. Their fabrication has generally been ascribed to the Russian secret police, but recent scholarship has raised serious doubts about that theory. See Michael Hagemeister, "The *Protocols of the Elders of Zion:* Between History and Fiction," *New German Critique* 103, vol. 35, no. 1 (Spring 2008): 83–95; Ruud and Stepanov, in *Fontanka 16,* "conclusively rule out police involvement," p. 215.
xiii   A hundred years: Weinberg, "The Blood Libel in Eastern Europe," pp. 284–85.
xiv   Beilis case has been strangely neglected: Samuel's *Blood Accusation* has been considered the standard account; Robert Weinberg's *Blood Libel in Late Imperial Russia: The Ritual Murder Trial of Mendel Beilis* is an

excellent collection of documents with narrative introductions to each chapter; until the present work, Tager, *Tsarskaia Rossiia i delo Beilisa* (*Tsarist Russia and the Beilis Case*), first published in 1933, was the only full-length, nonfiction account of the case based on primary sources; Katsis, *Krovavyi navet,* comprises an exhaustive analysis of the trial testimony on religion; Pidzharenko's *Ne ritual'noe ubiistvo* is an odd mixture of fictional recreations with original documents, some of them available nowhere else.

xv   "master libel": Julius, *Trials of the Diaspora,* p. 69.

xv   Middle East: The Syrian defense minister, Mustafa Tlas, wrote a book called *The Matzah of Zion* in 1986, which was being reprinted and cited into the 2000s. From an October 2001 article in the Egyptian newspaper *Al-Ahram*: "The bestial drive to knead Passover matzahs with the blood of non-Jews is [confirmed] in the records of the Palestinian police where there are many recorded cases of the bodies of Arab children who had disappeared being found, torn to pieces without a single drop of blood. The most reasonable explanation is that the blood was taken to be kneaded into the dough of extremist Jews to be used in matzahs to be devoured during Passover." Such references can be found ad nauseam. Judith Apter Klinghoffer, "Blood Libel," *History News Network,* December 19, 2006, http://hnn.us/articles/664.html; Julius, *Trials of the Diaspora,* pp. 96–101; Frankel, *The Damascus Affair,* p. 419. (The cover of Tlas's book is reproduced on p. 421. Frankel transliterates the name as Talas.) Less than three years before he became president of Egypt, Mohammed Morsi described Zionists as "these bloodsuckers who attack the Palestinians, these warmongers, the descendants of apes and pigs." David D. Kirkpatrick, "Morsi's Slurs Against Jews Stir Concern," *New York Times,* January 14, 2013, http://www.nytimes.com/2013/01/15/world/middleeast/egypts-leader-morsi-made-anti-jewish-slurs.html?_r=0.

1. "Why Should I Be Afraid?"

3   buried treasure: Stepanov, *Chernaia Sotnia* (1992), p. 266.

3   caves had been uncovered: *Evropeiskaia Rossiia: Illiustrirovannyi geograficheskii, sbornik* (Moscow: I.I. Kushnerov i ko., 1909), p. 419; Vladimir Antonovich, "Kiev v dokhristianskoe vremia," in *Moia spovid': Vibrani istorichni ta publistichni tvori* (Kiev: Lybid', 1995), p. 578, http://litopys.org.ua/anton/ant22.htm.

3   pulverize the stone to powder: Antonovich, "Kiev," p. 578.

3   two thousand human skeletons: "Kiev," *Encylopaedia Britannica,* vol. 15, p. 788.

3   "Lukianovka children's games": STEN I, p. 605, reproducing: *Kievskaia Mysl',* "Zagadochnaia Ubiistvo na Luk'ianovke" ("A Mysterious Murder in Lukianovka"), March 22, 1911.

4   crest of the slope: description draws on Vladimir Korolenko, "1. Na
     Luk'ianovke (vo vremia dela Beilisa)," subheading VI, published in
     October 1913. Korolenko's articles about the case were published in a
     number of Russian newspapers, including *Rech'* and *Russkie Viedmosti*.
     http://ldn-knigi.lib.ru/JUDAICA/Korol_Stat.htm.

4   The entrance to the cave: Description of the discovery of the body draws
     on the indictment, depositions, and witness testimony in STEN I. Indict-
     ment, pp. 17–21; Elandsky, pp. 115–17; Sinitsky, pp. 118–21.

6   "It's Goblin": STEN I, p. 304.

7   avoided saying his last name: Statement of Georgy Konovalov, GAKO-
     DpdB (reel 3) f. 183, op. 5, d. 4, l. 387.

7   insisting: Statement of Konovalov, GAKO-DpdB (reel 3) f. 183, op. 5,
     d. 4, l. 387; statement of Vladimir Kostiuchenko, GAKO-DpdB (reel 3)
     f. 184, op. 5, d. 4, l. 399; also statement of Polishchuk, GAKO-DpdB
     (reel 2) f. 2, op. 229, d. 264, l. 63.

8   "Why should I be afraid": STEN I, p. 362.

8   borscht: STEN I, p. 86.

9   "very receptive": STEN I, p. 54.

9   Pavel Pushka, saw Andrei: STEN I, p. 69.

10   bought for thirty kopeks: STEN I, p. 46.

10   lamplighter named Kazimir Shakhovsky: based on Shakhovsky's testi-
     mony and depositions in STEN I, pp. 172–79.

11   The neighbor delivered: Beilis, *My Sufferings,* pp. 26–27.

12   done the priest: Beilis, *My Sufferings,* p. 25.

12   "beaten our millionaires": Meir, *Kiev,* p. 126.

12   Jonah Zaitsev, a sugar magnate: Meir, *Kiev,* p. 226.

13   "The Yids have tortured": The translation is based on Samuel, *Blood
     Accusation,* p. 17, and Weinberg, *Blood Libel in Late Imperial Russia,*
     chapter 1, document 8.

13   Nikolai Pavlovich: Stepanov, *Chernaia Sotnia* (2005), p. 361.

14   "consumed by a sense of doom": Lincoln, *In War's Dark Shadow,* p. x.

14   "smell of burning": Lincoln, *In War's Dark Shadow,* p. 386.

14   living "on a volcano": Pipes, *Russian Revolution,* p. 194; Rogger, "Russia
     in 1914," p. 95.

14   "a mad chauffeur": David Christian, *Imperial Power and Soviet Russia*
     (New York: St. Martin's Press, 1997), p. 170; Figes, *A People's Tragedy,*
     p. 276.

14   strong fatalism: Steinberg, "Nicholas and Alexandra: An Intellectual
     Portrait," pp. 13–14.

14   "salient characteristic": Massie, *Nicholas and Alexandra,* p. 114;
     Fuhrmann, *Rasputin,* p. 16.

15   official badges: Lincoln, *In War's Dark Shadow,* p. 331.

15   modern political terrorism: Geifman, *Thou Shalt Kill,* p. 21.

15   "sign of good manners": Geifman, *Thou Shalt Kill,* p. 42.

16   Contrary to suspicions: This is the consensus of the last generation of scholarship despite reasonable suspicions to the contrary. See Klier and Lambroza, *Pogroms*.

16   "how the pogroms happened": "Conclusion and Overview," in Klier and Lambroza, *Pogroms,* p. 344.

16   "Mad Monk" Iliodor: For a fascinating account of his rise and fall and Tsar Nicholas's attitude toward him, see Dixon, "The 'Mad Monk' Iliodor."

17   "Jews as a race of superhuman": Langer, "Corruption and Counterrevolution," p. 137.

17   "delicate, beautiful": Dixon, "Mad Monk," p. 377.

17   "filthy" songs: Dixon, "Mad Monk," p. 396.

18   losing all sense of reality: Contemporary observers viewed Iliodor as a warning sign of the regime's decay. The monk, in the opinion of Count A. A. Uvarov, revealed "the astonishing lack of resistance to evil exhibited by the clergy, and especially the civil power." As Dixon argues, it says much about the regime that such a figure was allowed to become "a disruptive political instrument." Dixon, "Mad Monk," p. 413.

18   self-destruct: Just a few years later Iliodor scandalized the right by recanting his reactionary, anti-Semitic views and writing a sensational, confessional autobiography. He moved to America, starred as himself in a silent film, *The Fall of the Romanoffs,* got into a lawsuit over the rights to his story, then moved back to Russia, then returned to America in 1923, and became a Baptist preacher. He died in New York in 1952. See Dixon, "Mad Monk," pp. 409–13.

19   "walked the halls alone": STEN I, p. 58.

19   "There were times when Andrusha's mother": STEN I, p. 301.

19   "I know that Alexandra": STEN I, p. 400.

19   "Since I had no children": STEN I, p. 87.

20   "I would scream": STEN I, p. 88.

21   "They broke everything": STEN I, p. 84.

21   "because of a nosebleed": Stepanov, *Chernaia Sotnia* (1992), p. 269.

21   "didn't know whether to live or die": STEN I, p. 111.

21   had long known: Beilis's wife, Esther, recalled having an altercation in a store with Cheberyak who she said called her a "*zhidovka,*" the feminine of "Yid." Esther had heard from her neighbors that "in the house she's the man and her husband is the woman." *Rech',* September 25, 1913.

2. "The Vendetta of the Sons of Jacob"

22   "cold and cloudy weather": *Kievlianin,* April 10, 1911.

22   "Why should we worry about cholera": Hamm, *Kiev,* p. 48.

23   "blood of the unfortunate Yushchinskys": *Moskovskie Vedomosti,* April 23, 1911.

23   Fenenko had been assigned: GAKO DpdB (reel 3) f. 183, op. 5, d. 4, l. 4.

23   indication that Fenenko was chosen: *Materialy Chrezvychainoi*, p. 92; *Rech'*, September 22, 1913.

24   Fenenko regarded his integrity: Shulgin, *The Years*, 116; Margolin, *Jews of Eastern Europe*, pp. 161, 164.

24   autopsy report: V. M. Bekhterev, "The Iushchinskii Murder," pp. 24–33.

24   the first wounds: V. M. Bekhterev, "The Iushchinskii Murder," pp. 10–14.

26   minister of justice was being copied: Pidzharenko, *Ne ritual'noe*, p. 13.

27   public requiem for Andrei: Pidzharenko, *Ne ritual'noe*, pp. 22, 31.

27   The authorities did not want a pogrom: Klier and Lambroza, *Pogroms*, pp. 231, 348; E. Semenoff, *The Russian Government and the Massacres*, pp. 193–94.

27   owe his position to the empress Alexandra: Gerasimov, *Na lezvii*, p. 171; Fuller, *The Foe Within*, p. 89; Stepanov, *Zagadki*, p. 162.

27   "pogrom must be avoided": Ruud and Stepanov, *Fontanka 16*, p. 249 (Russian edition, p. 304).

28   "inflames people's passions": *Novyi Voskhod* (1911) no. 17; Lowe, *The Tsars and the Jews*, p. 287.

28   "Black Hundred idealist": Stepanov, *Chernaia* (2005), 367.

29   William of Norwich: This section draws heavily on Langmuir, *Toward a Definition*, pp. 209–36. There are two accounts in antiquity of ritual murder by Jews, but Langmuir argues that they played no role in the creation of the medieval myth. The first dates to the second century B.C. during the reign of the Seleucid king Antiochus IV Epiphanes who, on sacking the Temple in Jerusalem, supposedly learned that Jews had the custom of fattening up and eating a Greek (obviously not Christian) captive. The story was repeated and embellished by the first-century Greek sophist Apion and refuted by the Roman Jewish historian Flavius Josephus in his *Against Apion*. The second account, and first known accusation of the ritual murder of a Christian, dates to around A.D. 415 in Inmestar in Syria. During Purim celebrations there, Jews were said to have so abused a Christian boy, tied to a cross to represent the biblical villain Haman, that he died. Neither tale gained wide currency. See Langmuir, *Toward a Definition*, pp. 212–16.

29   "did not alter the course": Langmuir, *Toward a Definition*, pp. 234–35.

30   "a certain poor maid-servant": Quotes about William of Norwich are from Langmuir, *Toward a Definition*, p. 222, and Thomas of Monmouth, *Life and Miracles*, pp. 28, 93–94.

30   Chaucer's story: In the words of Alan Dundes, there is "little doubt that the most famous literary articulation of Jewish ritual murder is Chaucer's 'The Prioress's Tale'" (*The Blood Libel Legend*, p. 91). Strictly speaking, it is not an example of the blood libel, since there is no mention in it of the draining or ingesting of blood. Chaucer, though, may well have been aware of that charge against the Jews, given that it had already been in existence for a century and a half.

31 Fulda: Langmuir, *Toward a Definition,* pp. 264–65, 275, 278; Strack, *The Jew and Human Sacrifice,* pp. 179, 240–41.

31 papal bull from Innocent IV: Langmuir, *Toward a Definition,* p. 265; Smith, *The Butcher's Tale,* p. 94.

32 most reliable count: Smith, *The Butcher's Tale,* p. 123. For the best overview of the history and sources of the blood accusation, see Smith, chapter 3, pp. 91–133.

33 "Golubev has quieted down": Tager, *Tsarskaia,* p. 66.

33 On April 18: Tager, *Tsarskaia,* p. 67.

33 Black Hundred thugs: *Haynt,* April 28, 1911, p. 2.

34 Jews and Gentiles could mix easily: Meir, *Kiev,* p. 203.

34 "Bronze Horseman": Stepanov, *Chernaia* (1995), p. 123.

34 views were extreme: Lowe, *The Tsars,* p. 286.

34 "pursue the whole malignant sect": Tager, *Tsarskaia,* pp. 84–85.

35 boisterous floor fight: Samuel, *Blood Accusation,* p. 27.

35 "most fearful two days": *Haynt,* May 8, 1911.

35 Liadov—vice director: Tager, *Tsarskaia,* pp. 86–87. In *Materialy Chrezvychainoi*—depositions of Liadov, pp. 68–71; Fenenko, pp. 56–58; Chaplinsky, p. 208.

38 ritual-murder theory: *Haynt,* May 13, 1911.

38 "patiently refrain": *Haynt,* May 8, 1911, p. 2.

39 record was disturbingly mixed : Klier, *The Blood Libel,* p. 14. Klier's article is available in English only in an unpublished manuscript. It was published in Russian as: "Krovavyi navet v Russkoi pravoslavnoi traditsii," in M. Dimitriev, ed., *Evrei i khristiane v pravoslavnykh obshchestvakh vostochnoi evropy,* pp. 181–205 (Moscow: Indrik, 2011).

39 David Blondes: "Blondes, David Abramovich," *Evreiskaia entsiklopediia Brokgauza i Efrona,* http://brockhaus-efron-jewish-encyclopedia .ru/beje/02-7/014.htm.

40 the "Christian Letters": GAKO-DpdB (reel 3) f. 183, op. 5, d. 4, 1. 413–418.

40 "At the market they're saying": Tager, *Tsarskaia,* pp. 89–90.

41 "Now it seems to me": Tager, *Tsarskaia,* p. 88.

42 "if the Jews were beaten up": *Materialy Chrezvychainoi,* p. 56.

42 danger of a pogrom: GAKO-DpdB (reel 3) f. 183, op. 5, d. 4, 1. 32.

42 Brandorf recommended: GAKO-DpdB (reel 3) f. 183, op. 5, d. 4, 1. 22, 22 ob.

43 spiritual awakening: On the imperial couple's mental world, see Mark Steinberg's superb "Nicholas and Alexandra: An Intellectual Portrait." On spiritual life and God-seeking: Steinberg, "Russia's Fin de Siècle," pp. 80–81; on lower classes, Steinberg, *Proletarian Imagination,* pp. 228–29, and Steinberg and Coleman, "Introduction" in *Sacred Stories.*

43 Nizier-Vachod: Steinberg, "Nicholas and Alexandra: An Intellectual Portrait," p. 12.

43   Sikorsky's worldview: Menzhulin, *Drugoi Sikorskii,* pp. 243, 311, 320–22.
44   races could be divided into two types: Menzhulin, *Drugoi,* p. 317.
44   "hereditary degeneration": Menzhulin, *Drugoi,* p. 155.
44   "but gone rotten": Menzhulin, *Drugoi,* pp. 25–26.
44   fanatical anti-Semitism: Menzhulin, *Drugoi,* pp. 371–73.
45   Their autopsy report differed: STEN II, pp. 245–46.
45   Ambrosius: STEN II, pp. 144–45; GAKO-DpdB (reel 3) f. 183, op. 5, d. 4, l. 170 ob.
47   "racial revenge and vendetta": STEN I, p. 30.
48   "a certain Yid": Tager, *Tsarskaia,* 90; Stepanov, *Chernaia* (2005), p. 367.

3. *"A Certain Jew Mendel"*

49   "By order of": STEN II, p. 536.
49   "King of Thieves": "Korol' vorov," *Rannee Utro,* November 12, 1908, http://starosti.ru/article.php?id=16887; Stepanov, *Zagadki,* p. 213.
49   "It seemed as if a dark cloud": Shulgin, *The Years,* p. 62.
49   Krasovsky displayed: Pidzharenko, *Kriminal'nyi sysk Kieva,* pp. 204–38.
50   Tallish and kindly: Stepan Kondurushkin, "Vpechatleniia," *Rech',* October 14, 1913.
50   defendants appealed for help: *U Tolstogo, 1904–1910: Iasnopolianskie zapiski D.P. Makovitskogo,* vol. 3. (Moscow: Izdatel'stvo nauka, 1979), p. 241.
50   Tolstoy told: *New York Times,* August 9, 1908, p. SM6.
51   "intrigues and trouble": STEN I, p. 536.
52   "regarding the factual side": Tager, *Tsarskaia,* 94.
52   "Worldwide Yid": *Russkoe Znamia,* May 14, 1911.
53   "was not distinguished by": *Materialy Chrezvychainoi,* p. 91.
54   detailed survey: STEN I, pp. 542–44.
55   "one of his own": STEN I, p. 161.
55   having an affair: STEN I, p. 398.
55   "promissory note": STEN I, p. 97; GAKO-DpdB (reel 3) f. 183, op. 5, d. 4, l. 69.
56   Chirkov: STEN I, pp. 21, 41, 87.
56   "not especially reputable": STEN I, p. 66.
56   Alexandra would often boast: STEN I, p. 99.
56   lived on the interest: GAKO f. 864, op. 10, d. 5, l. 10.
56   Alexandra had behaved quite suspiciously: STEN I, p. 131.
57   the police arrested Fyodor: STEN I, p. 561. Suspicion about him, STEN, p. 161; GAKO-DpdB (reel 3) f. 183, op. 5, d. 4, l. 68 ob.–69 ob.
57   Yashchenko: STEN I, pp. 140, 539; *Rech',* September 30, 1913.
57   "He ended his investigation": Stepanov, *Chernaia* (1992), p. 274.
58   "Nezhinsky's story": GAKO-DpdB (reel 3) f. 183, op. 5, d. 4, l. 72–73.
58   Father Glagolev: Kal'nitskii, "Ekspertiza professora Glagoleva," p. 164.

58 sat himself down: Mikhailov memoir, pp. 6–9. This memoir, by a tsarist officer named Vasily Alexandrovich Mikhailov, is based on notes of a conversation with Mishchuk in 1918 when both were fleeing the Bolsheviks. The memoir, composed many years later, contains factual errors about the Beilis case but has the palpable feel of truth when relating Mishchuk's personal experiences.

59 "Cheberiachka": Tager, *Tsarskaia,* p. 88.

60 "lowest of the low": STEN I, pp. 161, 467, 400.

60 Cheberyak was volatile: STEN I, p. 308.

60 Cheberyak freely admitted: STEN I, p. 468.

60 tried for the crime: Margolin, *The Jews,* 169.

61 her gang included: STEN I, p. 468.

62 he usually made himself scarce: STEN I, p. 284.

62 into a stupor: STEN II, pp. 20, 23.

62 semen on the wallpaper: STEN II, p. 167.

62 police informer: Mikhailov memoir, p. 13. This is the only source for Vera Cheberyak being an informer, but the accusation seems plausible.

62 "Vera . . . would visit me": f. 864, op. 10, d. 11, l. 104.

62 A neighbor noticed: STEN II, p. 27.

62 stretch one day's dinner: STEN I, p. 663.

62 Gusin watch store: GAKO f. 864, op. 10, d. 11, l. 3–4; STEN I, p. 548; STEN II, p. 42.

63 Nadia Gaevskaya: GAKO-DpdB (reel 4) f. 183, op. 5, d. 5, l. 263; STEN I, pp. 467–69.

63 The next day: STEN I, pp. 503, 549, 571; STEN II, pp. 43, 53.

63 stashed stolen goods: STEN II, p. 47.

63 "She looked somehow upset": STEN II, pp. 24–25.

64 denied he'd seen: GAKO-DpdB (reel 3) f. 183, op. 5, d. 4, l. 36 ob.

64 A theory of the case: *Materialy Chrezvychainoi,* p. 306; Tager, *Tsarskaia,* p. 98; the notion that the Andrei's murder was part of a plot to foment a pogrom was oft-repeated but unsupported by any evidence. Margolin did not take it seriously; see, *Jews of Eastern Europe,* p. 189.

64 "Relations between Krasovsky and Mishchuk": Pidzharenko, *Ne ritual'noe,* pp. 64–65.

65 clippings: GAKO-DpdB (reel 3) f. 183, op. 5, d. 4, l. 72–73.

65 Krasovsky supervised: STEN I, p. 169.

65 In Luka's presence: STEN I, p. 111.

66 officers searched the Cheberyaks' home: GAKO-DpdB (reel 2) f. 2, op. 229, d. 264, l. 18.

66 Kirichenko, recalled: STEN II, p. 41.

67 Cheberyak detained: *Materialy Chrezvychainoi,* pp. 94–95; Tager, *Tsarskaia,* p. 96.

68 "I'll be free of her": STEN II, p. 21.

68 beaten the rap: STEN II, p. 597.

68   "I was afraid": STEN I, p. 301.
69   "very drunk" Fyodor: GAKO-DpdB (reel 3) f. 183, op. 5, d. 4, l. 68 ob.–69.
69   A pattern had emerged: This point is made by Stepanov in *Chernaia* (1992), p. 279.
69   Cheberyak was held: Tager, *Tsarskaia*, p. 101; *Materialy Chrezvychainoi*, p. 94; GAKO-DpdB (reel 3) f. 183, op. 5, d. 4, l. 66–68 ob.
70   liberal press rejoiced: Stepanov, *Chernaia* (2005), pp. 362–63.
70   slip of paper: Stepanov, *Chernaia* (2005), p. 363; STEN I, pp. 114, 560; GAKO f. 864, op. 10, d. 5, l. 11–12.
70   "heaping testimony": Hans Gross, *Criminal Investigation,* p. 55, http://archive.org/stream/criminalinvestig00grosuoft/criminalinvestig00grosuoft_djvu.txt.
71   "Unfortunately, one cannot": Tager, *Tsarskaia,* pp. 103, 106.
71   "wasted shells": Korolenko, *Delo Beilisa,* "1. Na Luk'ianovke," subheading III.
72   deposition: STEN I, pp. 177–80.
72   "consorting with criminals": GAKO-DpdB (reel 3) f. 183, op. 5, d. 4, l. 92.
72   cooperating with Golubev: Tager, *Tsarskaia,* p. 126.
72   "The place where Cheberyak": STEN I, p. 179.
73   "Shakhovskaya told me": Stepanov, *Chernaia* (1992), p. 278.
73   On July 20: Tager, *Tsarskaia,* p. 104.
73   "I forgot to mention": STEN I, p. 179.
74   clay grinders: description in Korolenko, "1. Na Luk'ianovke," subheading III.
74   "The day before yesterday": STEN I, p. 192.
75   Korolenko the writer would point out: Korolenko, "Na Luk'ianovke," subheading III.
75   "an agitated Golubev": *Materialy Chrezvychainoi,* p. 209.
76   "What filth": STEN I, p. 546.
76   "conspiratorial expression": *Materialy Chrezvychainoi,* p. 209. Ruud and Stepanov hypothesize that Beilis and his son were initially detained out of fear for their safety and to preserve public order and that, at this point, the prosecution of Beilis was not inevitable. I do not believe a full reading of the record supports this theory. See Rudd and Stepanov, *Fontanka 16,* pp. 256–61.
76   "[Chaplinsky] explained to me": *Materialy Chrezvychainoi,* p. 227.
77   "exceptional interest": Tager, *Tsarskaia,* pp. 118–19.
77   At three o'clock in the morning: Tager, *Tsarskaia,* 106; Beilis, *My Sufferings,* pp. 36–38; Beilis, "Mayn Lebn in Turme," *Haynt,* November 18, 1913.

4. "Andrusha, Don't Scream"

79   At five o'clock: Beilis, "Mayn Lebn in Turme," *Haynt,* November 19, 1913, p. 3; Beilis, *My Sufferings,* p. 39.

79   Okhrana chief was well-known: Zuckerman, *The Tsarist Secret Police,*
      p. 77; Ruud and Stepanov, *Fontanka 16,* pp. 181–82.
80   "What do I need": Beilis, "Mayn Lebn in Turme," *Haynt,* November 19,
      1913, p. 3.
80   Kuliabko left Beilis: Beilis, *My Sufferings,* p. 40.
81   "You can understand": Beilis, "Mayn Lebn in Turme," *Haynt,* Novem-
      ber 19, 1913, p. 3; Beilis, *My Sufferings,* pp. 41–42.
82   The door opened: Beilis, "Mayn Lebn in Turme," *Haynt,* November 20,
      1913, p. 3; Beilis, *My Sufferings,* p. 41.
82   children's voices: Beilis, *My Sufferings,* pp. 41–42; Beilis, "Mayn Lebn in
      Turme," *Haynt,* November 20, 1913, p. 3.
83   "no insurance": Beilis, *My Sufferings,* p. 39.
83   "rogues": Baron, *The Russian Jew,* p. 9.
83   half-million: Gitelman, *A Century,* p. xiii.
83   Dubnow: Hamm, *Kiev,* p. 133.
84   "ghetto": Meir, *Kiev,* p. 34.
84   poor Jews: Khiterer, "Social and Economic," p. 308; Meir, *Kiev,* p. 34.
84   "migraine": Khiterer, "Social and Economic," p. 124.
84   "cheese pies": Khiterer, "Social and Economic," p. 181.
84   A new life: Meir, *Kiev,* p. 104; Khiterer, "Social and Economic," p. 163.
84   For perhaps every ten or so: This is a rough guess. There appears to be
      no estimate of the number of Jews illegally living in Kiev before World
      War I. But in 1910, according to Natan Meir, more than one thousand
      Jewish families were expelled from the city. Meir, *Kiev,* p. 130.
85   "For what purpose": "Daily Raids in Kiev," *Haynt,* March 30, 1911, p. 2.
85   "Where can": Khiterer, "Social and Economic," p. 181. A somewhat
      different translation can be found in Sholem Aleichem, *From the Fair,*
      trans. Curt Leviant (New York: Penguin Books, 1986), p. 238.
85   in the small village of Neshcherov: "Mendel Beilis's Own Story of His
      Life and Persecution," *New York American,* February 15, 1914. Beilis's
      purported multipart memoir in this Hearst paper is extremely unreliable,
      but this fact is probably accurate. Beilis did talk to a Hearst reporter
      and it's known from a reliable source that Beilis worked in Neshcherov.
      Beilis, "Mayn Lebn in Turme," *Haynt,* November 25, 1913, p. 4.
86   pogroms traumatized: Baron, *Russian Jew,* p. 45.
86   "Temporary Rules": Baron, *Russian Jew,* p. 48.
86   "Why do they": Baron, *Russian Jew,* pp. 45–46.
86   twenty rubles: Petrovsky-Shtern, personal communication.
86   not the catastrophe: Petrovsky-Shtern, *Jews in the Russian Army,* pp.
      150, 191–92.
87   "The Jewish soldier": Petrovsky-Shtern, *Jews in the Russian Army,* p. 196.
87   opportunity came: Beilis, *My Sufferings,* pp. 23–24.
87   brandy distillery: Beilis, "Mayn Lebn in Turme," *Haynt,* November 21,
      1913, p. 4.

88   rich man's home: Samuel, *Blood Accusation,* p. 56.
88   Kiev's population: Meir, *Kiev,* p. 108.
88   "peaceful future": Beilis, *My Sufferings,* p. 25.
88   news soon leaked out: Tager, *Tsarskaia,* p. 109.
88   His conversion: Stepanov, *Chernaia* (2005), p. 362.
88   telegram: GAKO-DpdB (reel 3) f. 183, op. 5, d. 4, l. 78.
89   "I never told": STEN I, p. 180.
90   "deal with him": Tager, *Tsarskaia,* p. 110.
90   Ulyana Shakhovskaya was formally questioned: STEN I, pp. 192–93.
90   three in the morning: STEN I, p. 292.
91   "Because of a shit": STEN I, p. 292.
92   "indictment": *Materialy Chrezvychainoi,* p. 95.
93   "I can present no information": STEN I, p. 596.
93   Though utterly convinced: Margolin, *Jews of Eastern Europe,* pp. 163–64.
93   Chaplinsky's order: Tager, *Tsarskaia,* p. 109; Pidzharenko, *Ne ritual'noe,*
      pp. 74–77.
95   "I have nothing to consider": Beilis, "Mayn Lebn in Turme," *Haynt,*
      November 21, 1913, p. 4.
96   "My husband": GAKO f. 864, op. 10, d. 15, l. 95.
98   "confuse and entangle": Beilis, *My Sufferings,* p. 46.
98   "I must send you": Beilis, "Mayn Lebn in Turme," *Haynt,* November 25,
      1913, p. 3.
98   Darofeyeva: GAKO-DpdB (reel 3) f. 183, op. 5, d. 4, l. 395–395 ob.,
      l. 401.
99   "ruin you": STEN I, p. 332.
100   pear trees: STEN II, p. 21.
100   Vasily at first: STEN I, p. 330.
100   silent film: Morozov and Derevianko, *Evreiskie Kinematografisty v
      Ukraine,* pp. 57–61.
100   "In his delirium": Stepanov, *Chernaia* (1992), p. 281; STEN I, p. 286.
101   covered his mouth: STEN I, pp. 283–84.
101   Sinkevich: STEN I, pp. 332–34.
101   communicate something to the boy wordlessly: STEN I, p. 333.
102   Polishchuk told Fenenko: Tager, *Tsarskaia,* p. 121.
102   *Contemporary Word:* Stepanov, Chernaia (2005), p. 370; Tager, *Tsar-
      skaia,* pp. 123–24.
103   "[Zhenya's] death": Tager, *Tsarskaia,* p. 124.

      5. "You Are a Second Dreyfus"

104   culture of professionalism: Zuckerman, *The Tsarist Secret Police,*
      pp. 58–80.
104   The officer escorting: Beilis, "Mayn Lebn in Turme," *Haynt,* Novem-
      ber 26, 1913, p. 4; Beilis, *My Sufferings,* pp. 49–50.

105 In the waiting area: Beilis, *My Sufferings*, p. 50.
106 Moments after he entered: Beilis, *My Sufferings*, p. 51; Beilis, "Mayn Lebn in Turme," *Haynt*, November 26, 1913, p. 4.
106 piece of a mouse: Beilis, *My Sufferings*, p. 52.
107 impromptu courthouse: Beilis, "Mayn Lebn in Turme," *Haynt*, November 28, 1913, p. 4.
107 *Kiev Opinion*: In Russian, *Kievskaia Mysl'*, literally *Kiev Thought*.
108 Fenenko was astonished: Fenenko's account of this episode in GAKO-DpdB (reel 2) f. 2, op. 229, d. 264, l. 196–98.
110 Krasovsky arrived: GAKO-DpdB (reel 2) f. 2, op. 229, d. 264, l. 200 ob.–201 ob.
110 two or three days: GAKO-DpdB (reel 2) f. 2, op. 229, d. 264, l. 198 ob.
110 Chaplinsky threatened: *Materialy Chrezvychainoi*, pp. 53, 81–82.
110 Mishchuk and his codefendants: "Delo Mishchuka v senate," *Rech'*, February 8, 1913; Tager, *Tsarskaia*, p. 195.
111 "If you don't give me": STEN I, p. 547.
112 "rubbed out": STEN I, p. 564.
112 Evgeny Mifle: GAKO-DpdB (reel 4) f. 183, op. 5, d. 5, l. 263 ob.
112 took with great seriousness: Verner, *The Crisis*, p. 68; Figes, *A People's Tragedy*, p. 22.
113 Peter Badmaev: "Protokol doprosa G.N. Badmaeva" (Deposition of G. N. Badmaev) from the official report on Stolypin's assassination, http://www.doc20vek.ru/node/1731; Fuhrmann, *Rasputin*, p. 177; Radzinsky, *Rasputin*, p. 146.
113 "semi-literate": Radzinsky, *Rasputin*, p. 132; Fuhrmann, *Rasputin*, p. 62.
114 "When in trouble": Wortman, *Scenarios*, vol. 2, p. 410.
114 Nicholas had entrusted: Radzinsky, *Rasputin*, p. 143.
114 "two infusions": Radzinsky, *Rasputin*, p. 147.
114 lack of previous experience: Stepanov, *Zagadki*, p. 5.
115 security preparations: Ascher, *Stolypin*, p. 369.
115 "most humble": Tager, *Tsarskaia*, p. 122.
116 bomb: Ascher, *Stolypin*, p. 369; *Rech'*, August 30, 1911; *Moskovskie Vedomosti*, August 30, 1911.
116 crossed himself: Ioffe, "Delo Beilisa," p. 333, and personal communication; Beilis conveys Grigorovich-Barsky's account in *My Sufferings*, p. 69.
116 "We must not forget": Lincoln, *In War's Dark Shadow*, p. 30; Massie, *Nicholas and Alexandra*, p. 15.
117 "I'm a Unionist": Stepanov, *Chernaia* (2005), p. 203.
117 Rogger: Rogger, *Jewish Policies*, pp. 109–10.
118 "The Jews throw bombs": Ascher, *Stolypin*, p. 170.
118 "fighting on two fronts": Figes, *A People's Tragedy*, p. 224.
118 contentious meetings: Ascher, *Stolypin*, p. 168.
119 "an inner voice": Rogger, *Jewish Policies*, p. 93; Steinberg, "An Intellectual Portrait," p. 16.

119 "Tsar's mystical attitude": Ascher, *Stolypin,* p. 169.

119 "stamped out": Steinberg, "An Intellectual Portrait," pp. 16–17.

119 political agenda: Figes, *A People's Tragedy,* p. 245; Rogger, *Jewish Policies,* pp. 41–44.

120 Shcheglovitov: Zviagintsev, *Rokovaia femida,* pp. 201–11; Gruzenberg, *Yesterday,* pp. 78–82.

121 "taking over Siberia": Tager, *Tsarskaia,* p. 130.

122 security: Ascher, *Stolypin,* p. 369; Stepanov, *Zagadki,* p. 5.

123 "Death is following": Stepanov, *Zagadki,* p. 157. The story has been told many times, as in Massie, *Nicholas and Alexandra,* p. 238. The story originated with a reliable source, the Duma member and conservative journalist Vasily Shulgin, who heard it directly from the official given the task of being Rasputin's minder while in Kiev.

123 "I want to be buried": About the will, with a slightly different translation, see Figes, *A People's Tragedy,* p. 223. The Russian text ("Ia khochu byt' pogrebennym . . .") appears in many sources.

124 One bullet: Ascher, *Stolypin,* p. 372.

124 "At first": Stepanov, *Zagadki,* p. 10; Ascher, *Stolypin,* p. 369.

124 "crossed himself": Ascher, *Stolypin,* p. 373.

124 "Kill him!": Stepanov, *Zagadki,* pp. 10–11.

124 fragments of the Order: Stepanov, *Zagadki,* p. 13.

125 Bogrov: Ascher, *Stolypin,* pp. 376–78.

125 thugs: Ascher, *Stolypin,* p. 375.

125 Bogrov's motives: Stepanov, *Zagadki,* pp. 61–133; Ascher, *Stolypin,* pp. 384–86; for an argument that Bogrov's motives stemmed primarily from his Jewishness, see Khiterer, "Social and Economic," pp. 404–8.

125 morbidly curious readers: Morrissey, *Suicide and the Body Politic,* p. 314.

125 "Let my drop": Morrissey, *Suicide and the Body Politic,* p. 325.

126 "depressed, bored": Stepanov, *Zagadki,* p. 195.

126 "most decisive measures": Ascher, *Stolypin,* p. 375.

127 Jewish conspiracy: Stepanov, *Chernaia* (2005), pp. 285–86.

6. *"Cheberyak Knows Everything"*

128 good-fitting boots: Petrovsky-Shtern, *Jews in the Russian Army,* p. 147.

129 an "analysis": Beilis, "Mayn Lebn in Turme," *Haynt,* November 28, 1913, p. 4; Beilis, *My Sufferings,* pp. 56–57.

130 Aaron: Details of Aaron Beilis's life and personality from personal communication with his granddaughter, Hilda Edelist.

130 Margolin: Khiterer, "Arnold Davidovich Margolin," pp. 146–50.

131 "who had always worked": "A Conversation with Mendl Beilis's Brother" (in Yiddish), *Haynt,* February 9, 1912, p. 3.

131 Margolin did his best: Margolin, *Jews of Eastern Europe,* pp. 164–66.

132 "indecisive and timid": Margolin, *Jews of Eastern Europe,* p. 173.

133 "something foolish": Gruzenberg, *Yesterday,* p. 105.

133 "The first word": Gruzenberg, *Yesterday,* p. 12.

133 spiritually stranded: Donald Rawson, introduction to Gruzenberg, *Yesterday,* p. xv.

133 The poor woman was led off: Gruzenberg, *Yesterday,* p. 18.

133 funeral: Gruzenberg, *Yesterday,* pp. 19–20.

134 struggled with his religious and national identity: Khiterer, "Arnold Davidovich Margolin," pp. 147–48.

134 "iron whip": Gruzenberg, *Yesterday,* p. 3.

135 "an offensive": Stepanov, *Chernaia* (2005), p. 373.

135 "bad friend": STEN I, p. 646.

136 "dubious person": Tager, *Tsarskaia,* p. 134.

136 "I clearly heard": GAKO f. 864, op. 10, d. 5, l. 37–38; STEN II, p. 27.

137 Fenenko knew: *Materialy Chrezvychainoi,* pp. 58–59.

137 Ivan Kozachenko: Beilis, *My Sufferings,* pp. 58–61; GAKO f. 864, op. 10, d. 5, l. 7–8, 16; GAKO f. 864, op. 10, d. 5—*Protokoly* (statements), separately numbered section, pp. 39–52.

138 Lieutenant Colonel Pavel Ivanov: *Materialy Chrezvychainoi,* p. 272.

139 "Do not worry": GAKO f. 864, op. 10, d. 5—*Protokoly,* p. 51.

139 "My dear wife": GAKO f. 864, op. 10, d. 5—*Protokoly,* pp. 39–40.

140 legal bill: GAKO f. 864, op. 10, d. 5—*Protokoly,* p. 48.

140 "stir up a riot": STEN I, p. 370.

141 Kozachenko's story: His statement is in GAKO f. 864, op. 10, d. 5—*Protokoly,* pp. 40–43; mentioned in indictment, STEN I, p. 35.

141 "I screamed at Kozachenko": *Materialy Chrezvychainoi,* p. 195.

142 Chaplinsky had no intention: Tager, *Tsarskaia,* pp. 136, 141–42.

142 "A cold shiver": Beilis, "Mayn Lebn in Turme," *Haynt,* December 2, 1913, p. 4.

143 Brazul knew Krasovsky: STEN I, p. 475.

144 at Zhenya's funeral: GAKO-DpdB (reel 3) f. 183, op. 5, d. 4, l. 402.

144 midwife and "healer": Pidzharenko, *Ne ritual'noe,* p. 116.

144 "I'm a woman": STEN I, pp. 478–79.

144 "talking in her sleep": STEN II, p. 100.

145 "got it good": STEN I, p. 479.

145 "divining": STEN I, p. 500.

145 "quixotic": STEN I, p. 521.

145 "'Cheberyak knows everything'": Margolin, *The Jews of Eastern Europe,* p. 168.

146 "small, thin restless": Margolin, *The Jews of Eastern Europe,* p. 169.

146 Kharkov: STEN I, pp. 479–80.

146 Margolin's father: GAKO f. 864, o. 10, d. 5—*Protokoly,* p. 92.

147 Grand Hotel: GAKO-DpdB (reel 2) f. 2, op. 229, d. 264, l. 181.

147 The meeting: Margolin tells the story in his statement to investigators,

GAKO-DpdB (reel 2) f. 2, op. 229, d. 264, l. 28 ob.–31, and in Margolin, *The Jews of Eastern Europe,* pp. 174–77.

147 "noble avenger": GAKO-DpdB (reel 2) f. 2, op. 229, d. 264, l. 31.

148 "being hunted": STEN I, p. 527.

148 "untarnished case": Gruzenberg, *Yesterday,* p. 111.

148 "Thank God": STEN II, p. 119.

149 poorly paid: GAKO f. 864, op. 10, d. 9. l. 118 ob.

149 "state of affairs": GAKO f. 864, op. 10, d. 5—*Protokoly,* p. 100.

150 "Zhenya came running": GAKO f. 864, op. 10, d. 5—*Protokoly,* pp. 100–101.

150 "most profuse bleeding": GAKO f. 864, op. 10, d. 5—*Protokoly,* pp. 110, 113.

151 suddenly and summarily dismissed: STEN I, p. 547.

7. *"Who Is a Hero?"*

152 holes in the soles: Beilis, *My Sufferings,* p. 62.

152 "completely unreligious": GAKO f. 864, op. 10, d. 5—*Protokoly,* pp. 130–31.

152 "frozen feet": Beilis, "Mayn Lebn in Turme," *Haynt,* December 2, 1913, p. 4.

153 the infirmary: Beilis, *My Sufferings,* pp. 64–65.

153 important person: Beilis, "Mayn Lebn in Turme," *Haynt,* December 2, 1913, p. 4.

153 Margolin, received word: Margolin, *The Jews of Eastern Europe,* p. 243.

154 Margolin encouraged Brazul: Margolin, *The Jews of Eastern Europe,* pp. 178–79.

154 "gang of thieves": Stepanov, *Chernaia* (1992), p. 288; Tager, *Tsarskaia,* pp. 150–51.

154 escorting him: GAKO f. 864, op. 10, d. 11, l. 3b., l. 103–104b.

155 indictment: GAKO-DpdB (reel 3) f. 183, op. 5, d. 4, l. 168. The entire text of the first indictment can be found in l. 165–69.

155 visitors' chamber: Beilis, "Mayn Lebn in Turme," *Haynt,* December 2, 1913, p. 4; "Beilis's Own Story," *Literary Digest,* December 6, 1913, pp. 1136–37.

156 typhoid fever: Beilis, *My Sufferings,* p. 79.

156 "slow blood loss": GAKO-DpdB (reel 3) f. 183, op. 5, d. 4, l. 166–67.

157 "read between the lines": Margolin, *The Jews of Eastern Europe,* p. 182.

157 requiem: *Rech',* March 12, 1912.

157 stalked into the ball: *Rech',* March 14, 1912; *Rech',* March 15, 1912.

158 "firm basis": Tager, *Tsarskaia,* p. 151; Tager, "Tsarskoe pravitel'stvo," p. 165.

158 "Personal. Top Secret": Tager, *Tsarskaia,* p. 117; Tager, "Tsarskoe pravitel'stvo," p. 167.

158 "inadequacy of the evidence": Tager, *Tsarskaia,* p. 160; Tager, "Tsarskoe pravitel'stvo," p. 167.

159 Opanasenko: Tager, *Tsarskaia,* pp. 171–72; GAKO-DpdB (reel 3) f. 183, op. 5, d. 4, l. 386.

160 "felt like a bullet": Beilis, "Mayn Lebn in Turme," *Haynt,* December 4, 1913, p. 3.

161 first mention: *Jewish Chronicle,* May 5, 1911; *New York Times,* May 15, 1911.

162 most hospitable soil: Szajkowski, "The Impact of the Beilis Case," pp. 198, 203.

162 "No one has ever accused": Samuel, *Blood Accusation,* p. 238.

162 "vendetta of the Jews": Samuel, *Blood Accusation,* p. 239.

163 "ministers of foreign affairs": Szajkowski, "Paul Nathan," p. 179.

163 solicited no Jews: Szajkowski, "The Impact of the Beilis Case," pp. 199–200.

163 open letters: Szajkowski, "The Impact of the Beilis Case," p. 209; Samuel, *Blood Accusation,* p. 232; *Rech',* March 12, 1912.

163 fine-tuned: *Rech',* March 17, 1912.

163 *Times* letter: *Times* of London, May 4, 1912.

164 Baron Heyking: *Times* of London, May 10, 1912.

164 "end in the exoneration": Tager, *Tsarskaia,* p. 161; Tager, "Tsarskoe pravitel'stvo," p. 170.

165 Shcheglovitov immediately: Tager, *Tsarskaia,* pp. 162–63.

166 character straight out of Dostoyevsky: Samuel, *Blood Accusation,* p. 148.

166 "spark of truth": STEN I, p. 677.

166 "seamy side": Geifman, *Thou Shalt,* p. 154.

167 pistol-packing: Montefiore, *Young Stalin,* p. 10.

167 bandit gangs: Geifman, *Thou Shalt,* pp. 126, 135, 25.

167 Karaev: STEN II, p. 666.

168 lenient sentences: Geifman, *Thou Shalt,* pp. 223–26.

168 Karaev agreed: STEN I, p. 681.

168 Makhalin dropped by: STEN I, p. 669.

169 Ferdydudel: GAKO-DpdB (reel 2) f. 2, op. 229, d. 264, l. 345.

169 restaurant Versailles: GAKO-DpdB (reel 2) f. 2, op. 229, d. 264, l. 347.

171 thrown up: STEN I, p. 214.

171 "ministerial brain": STEN II, p. 7.

171 outdoor latrine: STEN II, p. 7.

172 "Brazul's Declaration": GAKO-DpdB (reel 3) f. 183, op. 5, d. 4, l. 410–12, 409–409 ob.

172 "outcry in the Yid press": Tager, *Tsarskaia,* p. 187.

172 "unfavorably disposed": Tager, *Tsarskaia,* p. 186.

172 "completely sufficient material": Tager, *Tsarskaia,* p. 159.

172 "chase my well-wishers": Tager, "Tsarskoe Pravitel'stvo," p. 173.

173 under the code name: *Padenie,* vol. 3, p. 370.
174 one hundred rubles: Stepanov, *Chernaia* (1992), p. 300.
174 "agent provocateur": Stepanov, *Chernaia* (2005), p. 381.
175 She told Karbovsky: GAKO-DpdB (reel 3) f. 183, op. 5, d. 4, l. 402.
175 Tager, who reviewed: Tager, *Tsarskaia,* p. 190.
175 "a Jew, very plump": GAKO-DpdB (reel 2) f. 2, op. 229, d. 264, l. 264.
175 Margolin: His version of Kharkov meeting is in GAKO-DpdB (reel 2) f. 2, op. 229, l. 26–33 ob. and in STEN I, pp. 522–29.
176 filed libel suits: *Rech',* July 8, 1912.
176 neutralizing Nikolai Krasovsky: Kovbasa, 16 kopeks—*Rech',* August 8, 1912; Lottery ticket—*Rech',* May 24, 1912, and June 4, 1913. More on charges in *Rech':* September 1, 1912; September 2, 1912; October 10, 1912; November 14, 1912; December 21, 1912.
176 Sherlock Holmes: Melamed, "Krasovskii," p. 167; Samuel, *Blood Accusation,* p. 46.
177 Makhalin had the good sense : Tager, *Tsarskaia,* pp. 248, 238.
177 "Yushchinsky's murderer!": *Rech',* July 13, 1912.
178 "caught Zhenya and Andrusha": Ludmila Cheberyak's deposition of August 13, 1912, in GAKO-DpdB (reel 2) f. 2, op. 229, l. 13–16 ob.

8. *"The Worst and Most Fearful Thing"*

179 "It would be curious": Beilis, *My Sufferings,* pp. 77–79.
180 "healthy shoots": Verner, *The Crisis,* p. 43.
180 seventeenth-century costume: Hughes, *The Romanovs,* p. 221.
180 Han-Gaffari: *Rech',* January 3, 1912.
180 run away: Wortman, *Scenarios,* vol. 2, p. 318.
180 "Above all": Verner, *The Crisis,* p. 15.
181 saw himself as the heir: Wortman, *Scenarios,* vol. 2, p. 491.
181 wear a full beard: Wortman, *Scenarios,* vol. 2, p. 190.
182 "has the kike come": Wortman, *Scenarios,* vol. 2, p. 483.
182 "invisible threads": Wortman, *Scenarios,* vol. 2, pp. 481, 489.
182 enjoyed favor of the tsar: Wortman, *Scenarios,* vol. 2, pp. 460–61.
183 belief in the existence: Wortman, *Scenarios,* vol. 2, p. 505.
183 "no purely rational": Rogger, *Jewish Policies,* p. 51.
183 "missing faith": Rogger, *Jewish Policies,* pp. 53, 51.
184 "jail is hell": Beilis, *My Sufferings,* pp. 81, 83.
184 "You liked to stab": Beilis, *My Sufferings,* p. 80.
184 court acquitted him: *Rech',* February 6, 1913; Margolin, *The Jews of Eastern Europe,* p. 203.
185 convicted of forgery: GAKO f. 866, op. 10, l. 36.
185 "1 ruble": GAKO f. 866, op. 10, l. 31.
185 "Illegitimate": GAKO f. 866, op. 10, l. 35.
186 "greatest quantity of blood": Tager, *Tsarskaia,* pp. 80–81.

187 "poison me": Beilis, "Mayn Lebn in Turme," *Haynt,* December 5, 1913, p. 3.

187 "you can starve": Beilis, *My Sufferings,* pp. 98–100.

188 request a copy: GAKO-DpdB (reel 3) f. 183, op. 5, d. 4, l. 128–128 ob.; Beilis, *My Sufferings,* pp. 120–22.

189 brothers Gorenstein: Pidzharenko, *Ne ritual'noe,* p. 158.

189 dashed for a window: GAKO-DpdB (reel 4) f. 183, op. 5, d. 5, l. 231 ob.; Tager, *Tsarskaia,* p. 153; Pidzharenko, *Ne ritual'noe,* p. 158; Margolin, *The Jews of Eastern Europe,* p. 208, speculates on Latyshev's feelings of guilt.

189 forty-two pages: *Rech',* September 29, 1913.

190 "No one can know": Beilis, "Mayn Lebn in Turme," *Haynt,* December 5, 1913, p. 3.

190 "blind man's buff": Margolin, *The Jews of Eastern Europe,* p. 181.

190 "resolute, steadfast": Tager, *Tsarskaia,* p. 256.

191 Catholic "import": Klier, *The Blood Libel,* pp. 23, 9.

191 Church, as such, had never advocated: Klier, *The Blood Libel,* p. 10; Klier, *Imperial Russia's,* p. 427. In the historian Laura Engelstein's assessment: "Most voices within the Russian Orthodox community endorsed the blood ritual myth and its relevance to the [Beilis] trial, but some dissociated themselves from anti-Semitism in general and this belief in particular." She also notes that "the [church] hierarchy did not issue an opinion on the matter, thus implicitly supporting the accusation." Engelstein, *The Keys to Happiness,* pp. 326 and 326n123.

191 Liutostansky: Klier, *Imperial Russia's,* pp. 423–24.

192 sure he would be murdered: Tager, *Tsarskaia,* p. 255.

192 "disagreeable" information: Tager, *Tsarskaia,* pp. 261–63.

193 all Jews would stand in the dock: Klier, *Imperial Russia's,* p. 426.

193 minority opinion: Tager, *Tsarskaia,* pp. 112–14. Tager and Margolin indicate Kamentsev and Ryzhov resigned over the case, but this is not clear from the record.

194 rode alone: Massie, *Nicholas and Alexandra,* p. 239.

194 "absence of": Wortman, *Scenarios,* vol. 2, pp. 468, 464.

194 "Now you can see": Massie, *Nicholas and Alexandra,* p. 239.

195 "blindly devoted": Wortman, *Scenarios,* vol. 2, pp. 468, 467–68.

195 resolved to reestablish: Wortman, *Scenarios,* vol. 2, p. 502.

195 "The belief or non-belief": Wortman, *Scenarios,* vol. 2, p. 505.

196 publication in Germany: Quotations are from the Russian translation, *Mneniia inostrostrannykh.* Ziemke, p. 31; Forel, p. 76; Wagner-Jauregg and Obersteiner, p. 91. Also quoted in Tager, *Tsarskaia,* p. 175. The British report is translated in *Mneniia,* pp. 49–58. The original is quoted in: "A Foul Libel Repelled," *Colonist* (New Zealand), July 15, 1913, p. 2, http://paperspast.natlib.govt.nz/cgi-bin/paperspast?a=d&d=TC 19130715.2.8. Wagner-Jauregg, ironically, was an anti-Semite who later

joined the Nazi Party, though he was married to a Jewish woman and had Jewish assistants. Sengoopta Chandak, review of *Julius Wagner-Jauregg* by Magda Whitrow, *Bulletin of the History of Medicine* 70, no. 1 (Spring 1996): 147–48.

197 real purpose was to punish: Cohen, "The Abrogation," p. 7.

197 "lack real leadership": Lifschutz, "Hedei Alilat-Hadam Al Beilis Be-Amerikah" (hereafter, "Repercussions"), p. 209.

197 wary of acting: "Politics," *Encyclopaedia Judaica,* 2nd ed., vol. 16 (Detroit: Macmillan Reference USA, 2007), p. 350.

198 "Jews, Jews, Jews": Oney, *And the Dead,* p. 347.

198 "American Beilis": Lifschutz, "Repercussions," p. 207.

198 Anti-Semitism was only one factor: Oney, *And the Dead,* p. 347.

198 "filthy, perverted": "Leo Frank," *Encyclopaedia Judaica,* 2nd ed., vol. 7, p. 193.

199 As committee members pondered: The American Jewish Committee, Minutes of the Meeting of the Executive Committee held on November 8, 1913, pp. 12–15. American Jewish Committee Archives. Available at: http://www.ajcarchives.org/ajcarchive/DigitalArchive.asp; Lifschutz, "Repercussions," p. 212.

199 Kramer's Comedy Theater: Lifschutz, "Repercussions," p. 210.

199 "Mendel Beilis epidemic": Berkowitz, "Mendel Beilis Epidemic," p. 201.

200 performing a duet: *Moment* (Yiddish), "How Beilis Is Being Performed in America," *Moment,* December 29, 1913, p. 3.

200 romantic subplot: Berkowitz, "Mendel Beilis Epidemic," p. 210. Berkowitz notes Beilis's daughter's age as eight, but she was five.

200 "voice of the people": *Moment,* "How Beilis Is Being Performed."

200 "few dollars": Berkowitz, "Mendel Beilis Epidemic," p. 201.

200 "It is this not knowing why": Beilis, "Mayn Lebn in Turme," *Haynt,* December 2, 1913, p. 4.

201 "failure to observe formalities": *Rech',* October 11, 1913.

201 Brazul was charged with lèse-majesté: Margolin, *The Jews of Eastern Europe,* p. 207; *Materialy Chrezvychainoi,* pp. 298–99.

201 fortress: Pares, *Russia and Reform,* pp. 363–64.

201 Karaev wrote a letter: Tager, *Tsarskaia,* pp. 238–39.

202 dandyish getups: Samuel, *Blood Accusation,* p. 147.

202 "accompanying a groom": Beilis, *My Sufferings,* pp. 123–24.

202 "go in good health": Beilis, "Mayn Lebn in Turme," *Haynt,* December 7, 1913, p. 3.

202 looked out the window: "Beilis's Own Story," *Literary Digest,* December 6, 1913, pp. 1134–37, 1143–44; Beilis, *My Sufferings,* p. 125.

203 "I will pay you": Beilis, *My Sufferings,* p. 126.

203 Karabchevsky: Beilis, *My Sufferings,* pp. 127–30.

203 led him into the courtroom: Beilis, "Mayn Lebn in Turme," *Haynt,* December 12, 1913, p. 3.

9. *"Yes, a Jew!"*

204 "A place can scarcely": Vladimir Nabokov, "Na protsesse," *Rech'*, September 25, 1913.
204 news organizations: *Rech'*, August 29, 1913; *Rech'*, August 26, 1913.
205 simple peasants: Beilis, "Mayn Lebn in Turme," *Haynt*, December 12, 1913, p. 3; Korolenko, "Na Luk'ianovke," subheading III, http://ldn-knigi.lib.ru/JUDAICA/Korol_Stat.htm.
205 "strangers to the high aims": Aleksandr Tager speculated that Chaplinsky's right-hand man, A. A. Karbovsky, rigged the jury. Tager, *Tsarskaia,* p. 231.
205 three times as great: Korolenko, "2. Gospoda prisiazhnye zasedateli."
206 "state of mind": Tager, *Tsarskaia,* pp. 231–34.
206 "my bellicose": Gruzenberg, *Yesterday,* p. 38; Samuel, *Blood Accusation,* p. 177.
206 "legal ladies": Utevskii, *Vospominaniia,* p. 24.
207 man obsessed: Utevskii, *Vospominaniia,* 149; Karabchevskii, "Rech' v zashchitu Ol'gi Palem," *Sudebnye rechi,* http://az.lib.ru/k/karabchewskij_n_p/text_0050.shtml266. Trial of Egor Sazonov: Karabchevskii, "Rech' v zashchitu Sazonova," *Sudebnye rechi,* http://az.lib.ru/k/karabchewskij_n_p/text_0050.shtml (Search term: "gremuchei rtut'iu"); Utevskii, *Vospominaniia,* p. 152; Kucherov, *Courts,* pp. 229–30.
207 Zarudny: Troitskii, *Sud'by rossiiskikh advokatov,* pp. 82–92, http://www.sgu.ru/files/nodes/9851/rus_ad.pdf; Karabchevskii, *Chto moi glaza videli* (Chapter Six), http://az.lib.ru/k/karabchewskij_n_p/text_0030.shtml.
208 Maklakov: Dedkov, *Konservativnyi liberalism,* pp. 221–31; Zviagintsev, *Rokovaia femida,* pp. 227–34.
208 Grigorovich-Barsky: *Rech'*, September 25, 1913.
209 "In the world": Ruud and Stepanov, *Fontanka 16* (Russian edition), p. 323.
209 "fair and honest": Margolin, *The Jews of Eastern Europe,* p. 217.
209 "not by nature": Gruzenberg, *Yesterday,* p. 113. For Margolin's similar assessment of Zamyslovsky, see Margolin, *The Jews of Eastern Europe,* p. 218.
209 "Fedya": Utevskii, *Vospominaniia,* pp. 26–31.
210 "course of hydrotherapy": Tager, "Protsess Beilisa," p. 92.
210 He stayed motionless: *Jewish Chronicle,* October 10, 1913; S. Ansky, "Vpechatleniia," *Rech'*, September 26, 1913.
211 "Yes, a Jew!": STEN I, p. 3; Beilis, *My Sufferings,* p. 136.
211 "dark-complexioned": Nabokov, "Na protsesse," *Rech'*, October 12, 1913.
211 "beautiful, restlessly": *Rech'*, September 26, 1913.
212 "near to fainting": Beilis, *My Sufferings,* p. 136.

212 "old friends": Beilis, *My Sufferings,* p. 137.

212 sat nervously: *Rech',* September 27, 1913.

212 strong, clear voice: *Kievskaia Mysl',* September 27, 1913.

212 "Do you admit": STEN I, p. 37.

213 deeply resonant sobs: Vladimir Bonch-Bruevich, *Kievskaia Mysl',* September 27, 1913; S. Ansky, "Vpechatleniia," *Rech',* September 26, 1913.

213 "Did you love him": STEN I, p. 41.

214 "maybe the Jews": STEN I, p. 84.

214 "We must inform": Bonch-Bruevich, *Kievskaia Mysl',* September 29, 1913.

214 hours on end: Stepan Kondurushkin, "Vpechatleniia," *Rech',* September 29, 1913.

214 "strange impression": Tager, "Protsess," p. 96.

214 police were on trial: *Rech',* September 28, 1913; noted in secret police reports—Tager, "Protsess," p. 97.

214 "disappeared": STEN I, p. 82; *Rech',* September 28, 1913.

214 Tartakovsky: STEN I, p. 291.

215 jumpy, unnerved: Tager, "Protsess," p. 96.

215 "scribbled over": STEN I, p. 164.

215 The price quickly: *Rech',* September 28, 1913; Tager, "Protsess," p. 97. The *Kievan* had no set newsstand price but would ordinarily have cost a few kopeks.

215 "The Beilis indictment": Shulgin, *The Years,* pp. 114–15. The closest parallel to Shulgin as a defector from the Left was the philosopher Vasily Rozanov, a decadent sensualist known as "Russia's Nietzsche," who was (and still is) regarded as a brilliant literary stylist. In a series of articles published in the leading right-wing newspaper, *New Times* (*Novoe Vremia*), he scandalized Russia's cultural and intellectual world by proclaiming Beilis's guilt. In one passage, Rozanov argued that Andrei's wounds formed a mystical, coded message that said the boy was a sacrificial victim to God. One critic professed mock admiration that Rozanov could tease out a whole sentence from the wounds, while poor Father Pranaitis could only manage a single Hebrew word, "*echad.*" In reaction to his support of the prosecution, Rozanov was himself put on trial by his intellectual peers and nearly expelled from the avant-garde Religious-Philosophical Society. In the end, the members voted only to severely rebuke, not expel him, but he left the group. He collected his articles in a book, *The Olfactory and Tactile Relation of Jews to Blood* (*Oboniatel'noe i osiazatel'noe otnoshenie evreev k krovi*). See Harriet Murav, "The Beilis Ritual Murder Trial," pp. 247–58; Engelstein, *The Keys to Happiness,* pp. 324–27; Matich, *Erotic Utopia,* pp. 243-45 and p. 299n73.

216 harass the press: Tager, *Tsarskaia,* p. 208.

216 fining Nabokov: Vladimir Nabokov, *Speak Memory,* p. 176.

216 striking workers: *Rech'*, September 26, 1913.
216 although they considered: *Rech'*, September 28, 1913.
218 "So you are": STEN I, p. 144.
218 Daria Chekhovskaya: STEN I, p. 157.
219 " 'day of the black beards' ": Kondurushkin, "Vpechatleniia," *Rech'*, September 30, 1913.
219 "Did the detectives": STEN I, pp. 175–76, 181, 183.
220 "full deck": *Kievlianin*, September 30, 1913.
220 "Yes": STEN I, pp. 191, 195.
220 fined him ten rubles: *Rech'*, July 11, 1912.
220 confiscated: *Rech'*, June 25, 1912.
220 night of September 5: *Rech'* September 9, 1912.
221 "No, I can talk": STEN I, p. 200.
221 A refreshed Golubev: STEN I, pp. 201, 206.
222 erupted in laughter: STEN I, p. 204; *Rech'*, October 1, 1913.
222 piled into twenty-five carriages: Bonch-Bruevich, *Znamenie*, pp. 68–76; STEN I, pp. 215–19; Kondurushkin, "Vpechatleniia," *Rech'*, September 30, 1913.
222 "dancing couple": STEN II, p. 27.
223 "Of course, we knew him!": Korolenko, "Na Luk'ianovke," subheading VI, http://ldn-knigi.lib.ru/JUDAICA/Korol_Stat.htm.
223 Vipper the prosecutor fretted: Kondurushkin, "Vpechatleniia," *Rech'*, September 30, 1913.
223 shambled: Bonch-Bruevich, *Znamenie*, p. 61.
223 air of hopeful confidence: Samuel, *Blood Accusation*, p. 70.
223 "What do you know": STEN I, p. 222; *Rech'*, October 2, 1913.
224 crossing herself: *Jewish Chronicle*, October 24, 1913, p. 20.
224 "nauseous case": *Times* of London, October 15, 1913.
225 Simon of Trent: Po-Chia Hsia's gripping *Trent 1475* is the definitive account.
225 Tiszaeszlar: Yehouda Marton, "Tiszaeszlar," *Encyclopaedia Judaica*, 2nd ed., vol. 19, p. 735; *Gale Virtual Reference Library*. The dead girl, whose name was Eszter Solymosi, was later established to have committed suicide by throwing herself into a river. The Tiszaeszlar case was of considerable political significance. Anti-Semitic parliament deputies vocally supported the case, which was accompanied in 1883 by violent attacks on Jews in Budapest and elsewhere. In some areas, the authorities declared a state of emergency to protect Jewish lives and property. In the trial's aftermath, an anti-Semitic party was founded that won seventeen seats in the Hungarian parliament.
225 Talberg: *Materialy Chrezvychainoi*, p. 81.
226 He complained: *Materialy Chrezvychainoi*, p. 147.
226 Koshko: Koshko, "O dele Beilisa," pp. 165–66, 173–77. Koshko later became the head of criminal investigations for the entire empire, so

his opposition to the Beilis case did not obstruct his advancement. The value of Koshko's memoir, written years after the trial, is mainly in the account of the conversation with Shcheglovitov. Regarding details of the case, it contains significant factual errors and needs to be used with caution.

227   "Let him [Beilis] be acquitted": Stepanov, *Chernaia* (1995), p. 392.

227   "severely unnerves": Tager, "Protsess," p. 98.

228   "the judge skillfully": Tager, "Protsess," p. 101.

228   Boldyrev was aware: *Materialy Chrezvychainoi,* pp. 171, 186.

228   "sheds rivers": Berkowitz, "Epidemic," pp. 204–205; see also, "Ritual Murder Play: Actor Acting in His Stage Version of Beiliss Case to Crowds," *New York Times,* November 21, 1913.

228   "three-dimensional newsreels": Stefan Kanfer, Stardust Lost: The Triumph, Tragedy and Mishugas of the Yiddish Theater in America" (New York: Vintage Books, 2007), p. 114.

228   "deep Jewishness": Berkowitz, "Mendel Beilis Epidemic," p. 205.

229   assimilationists to be "furious": *Jewish Chronicle,* October 17, 1913, pp. 23–24.

229   "discreet diplomacy": Szajkowski, "The Impact of the Beilis Case," p. 205.

229   state legislatures: 1914 *American Jewish Yearbook,* p. 135; Lifschutz, "Repercussions," note 39.

229   "elegant women": Bonch-Bruevich, *Znamenie,* pp. 95–96.

230   gold buttons: *Kievlianin,* October 3, 1913.

230   ravenous: *Kievlianin,* October 3, 1913.

230   "illiterate Jews": STEN I, p. 276.

230   "gesticulation": *Jewish Chronicle,* October 24, 1913, p. 20.

230   elegantly dressed: *Rech',* October 3, 1913; Bonch-Bruevich, *Znamenie,* p. 90.

230   Polishchuk, startlingly: STEN I, pp. 282–84.

231   chestnut hair: Bonch-Bruevich, *Znamenie,* pp. 93–94; *Rech',* October 3, 1913.

231   the girl told the court: STEN I, pp. 295–97.

232   eye-to-eye: STEN I, p. 298.

232   feather pom-pom: Bonch-Bruevich, *Znamenie,* p. 96.

232   Beilis could stare: Viktor Sosedov, "Otryvki," *Kievlianin,* October 4, 1913.

232   skeptical reporter: *Kievlianin,* October 3, 1913.

232   "Would you be so kind as to read aloud": STEN I, p. 303.

233   "metallic": *Kievlianin,* October 3, 1913. Vialtseva's voice can be heard on YouTube by searching her name in Russian letters (Vial'tseva).

233   "running away": *Rech',* October 3, 1913.

233   eyewitnesses and liars: *Kievlianin,* October 3, 1913.

233   sent Zhenya: STEN I, p. 309.

234 "Were you questioned": STEN I, p. 310, pp. 310–13.

236 "boy suddenly shrank": *Kievlianin,* October 5, 1913.

236 "slightly increased": Tager, *Tsarskaia,* p. 125; Tager, "Protsess," p. 98.

236 "lying bitch": Tager, *Tsarskaia,* p. 199.

   10. "We Have Seen the Killer"

237 feed had become too expensive: STEN I, pp. 359, 273, 393.

238 "annoying formality": *Kievlianin,* October 11, 1913.

238 "What do you think happened": *Rech',* October 6, 1913.

238 Vyshemirsky: Beilis, *My Sufferings,* pp. 140–45; STEN I, pp. 403–9. The
   core of Beilis's account is accurate, but Beilis presents Vyshemirsky as
   far more well-spoken than he actually was.

239 "In any normal trial": "Iz zaly suda," *Kievskaia Mysl',* October 6, 1913.

240 "on Paris boulevards": "Vpechatleniia," *Kievskaia Mysl',* October 7,
   1913.

240 one general: Petrovsky-Shtern, *Jews in the Russian Army,* pp. 134–35.

240 more at home in Berlin: GAKO f. 864, op. 10, d. 5, l. 35.

241 "not a comedy": *Rech',* October 6, 1913.

241 "in the Jewish cemetery": *Rech',* October 7, 1913.

241 workers from the Zaitsev factory testified: STEN I, pp. 433–60.

242 in the Chicago Loop: All details about the rally are from "Overflow
   Crowd and a Speaker at Beilis Trial Protest Mass Meeting," *Chicago
   Tribune,* October 20, 1913, p. 1; on its organization, "'Ritual Murder
   Protest Today,'" *Chicago Tribune,* October 19, 1913, and "Set Beilis Pro-
   test Meeting," *Chicago Tribune,* October 16, 1913.

242 Mass meetings were held in Cincinnati: *American Jewish Yearbook,*
   p. 136; Lifschutz, "Repercussions," note 39. Oddly, in New York, the
   America city with the biggest Jewish population, a protest of five hundred City College students appears to have been the largest one. Lifschutz, "Repercussions," note 39.

244 Hirsch wrote: "Editorial Notes," *The Advocate: America's Jewish Journal* 46 (1913): 338.

244 Champ Clark: Lifschutz, "Repercussions," note 41.

244 Sabath resolution: "Congress Takes Up Defense of Beiliss; Representative Sabath Offers a Joint Resolution of Protest," *New York Times,* October 18, 1913, p. 4.

244 "Czar on Trial": *New York Times,* October 9, 1913.

244 "And Yet": Lifschutz, "Repercussions," note 35.

245 "much surprised": Lifschutz, "Repercussions," note 52.

245 "no knowledge": Tager, *Tsarskaia,* p. 218.

246 "more than ready": Lifschutz, "Repercussions," p. 218.

246 "unfortunate effect": Lifschutz, "Repercussions," p. 218. Wilson argued,
   with some foundation, that Beilis would, in any event, be acquitted.

The Russian foreign minister himself, who was sharing the consensus of elite opinion—the trial was, after all, clearly going badly for the prosecution—had told Wilson he was "certain" of such an outcome. See Lifschutz, "Repercussions," note 50.

247 "talented lawyer": Gruzenberg, *Yesterday,* p. 111.

247 glass of water: *Rech',* October 8, 1913.

247 "unthoughtful": Nabokov, "Na protsesse," *Rech',* October 8, 1913.

247 "honest, thick-skinned": *Jewish Chronicle,* October 24, 1913, p. 23.

248 "mental faculties": STEN I, p. 528.

248 eye-to-eye: STEN I, p. 535.

248 swarmed the court: *Kievskaia Mysl',* October 9, 1913.

249 Prince A. D. Obolensky: *Kievskaia Mysl',* October 9, 1913. *American Jewish Yearbook,* p. 17.

249 King Constantine: *Rech',* October 7, 1913; *Jewish Chronicle,* October 11, 1913.

250 "story of the switches": see note to p. 111.

251 "Christian letters": GAKO-DpdB (reel 3) f. 183, op. 5, d. 4, l. 413-18.

251 early newspaper account: STEN I, p. 606.

252 "methods were reprehensible": Nabokov, "Na protsesse," *Rech',* October 9, 1913.

253 needed to kill: STEN I, p. 601.

253 "airplanes, or ride on motorcycles": STEN I, p. 623.

253 felt to her like a body: STEN I, p. 618.

253 "When I was sleeping": STEN I, p. 607.

254 " 'I had a dream' ": STEN I, p. 623.

254 "sincerity": *Rech',* October 10, 1913; *Kievlianin,* October 10, 1913.

254 "psychosis": *Kievianin,* October 10, 1913.

254 wholly expressionless: Nabokov, "Na protsesse," *Rech',* October 11, 1913.

255 acceded to a plan: *Materialy Chrezvychainoi,* pp. 172–73.

255 "deadly simplicity": Nabokov, "Na Protsesse," *Rech',* October 11, 1913.

256 "Beilis had reminded us": Nabokov, "Na Protsesse," *Rech',* October 11, 1913.

256 "defendant": Nabokov, "Na protesse," *Rech',* October 11, 1913; Kondurushkin, "Vpechatleniia," *Rech',* October 11, 1913.

257 Zamyslovsky attempted: STEN II, pp. 66–68.

257 On cross-examination: STEN II, pp. 71–73.

258 eye-to-eye: STEN II, pp. 73–74.

258 visceral reaction: Tager, *Tsarskaia,* p. 250.

11. *"Gentlemen of the Jury!"*

259 rumor: Tager, "Protsess," p. 101.

259 "some kind of sensation": Nabokov, "Na protsesse," *Rech',* October 14, 1913.

259 once been imprisoned: Vladimir Nabokov, the son, writes in his autobi-ography, *Speak Memory* (p. 29): "My father spent a restful, if somewhat lonesome three months in solitary confinement, with his books, his col-lapsible bathtub and his copy of J. P. Muller's manual of home gym-nastics." V. D. Nabokov served the sentence in 1908 as punishment for taking part in the "Vyborg Manifesto," a protest against the disbanding of the First Duma by Tsar Nicholas.

259 "fantastic": Nabokov, "Na protsesse," *Rech'*, October 12, 1913.

260 Maslash: STEN II, p. 96.

260 "folded his hands": STEN II, p. 101.

260 Three days earlier: Tager, *Tsarskaia*, p. 251; *Materialy Chrezvychainoi*, p. 173; Testimony of Beletsky, *Padenie*, vol. 3, pp. 370–71, 375.

261 Ivanov confided: *Materialy Chrezvychainoi*, p. 131; Tager, *Tsarskaia*, pp. 141–44.

261 Jewish money: STEN II, pp. 107–8.

262 "only honest": STEN II, p. 115.

262 "I believe": Nabokov, "Na protsesse," *Rech'*, October 14, 1913.

263 "tribal enmity": Tager, "Protsess," p. 106.

263 reading of the psalter: Kondurushkin, "Vpechatlaniia," *Rech'*, October 15, 1913.

263 "The eyelids": STEN II, pp. 151, 165.

263 box with jars: STEN II, p. 160.

263 Kosorotov: Tager, *Tsarskaia*, pp. 80–83; *Materialy Chrezvychainoi*, pp. 64, 112, 187–88; Testimony of Beletsky, *Padenie*, vol. 3, pp. 381–82; Beletsky explains how the Ten Million Ruble Fund worked in *Padenie*, vol. 3, pp. 379–80.

264 "If they had wanted": STEN II, p. 178.

265 dissected heart: STEN II, p. 173.

265 "That's all the blood": STEN II, p. 176.

265 collected the blood: STEN II, p. 177.

265 nothing like the state: STEN II, p. 187.

265 filled with blood: STEN II, p. 192.

266 "nonsense": STEN II, p. 209.

266 "with whatever weapon": STEN II, p. 212.

266 "mental deterioration": Nabokov, "Na protsesse," *Rech'*, October 23, 1913.

266 "The murder": STEN II, p. 253.

267 "of unseen hand": STEN II, p. 254.

267 "Their capital": STEN II, p. 256.

267 "Bankers, doctors, sexual psychopaths": S. El'patevskii, "Vpechatle-niia," *Kievskaia Mysl'*, October 19, 1913.

267 defense objections: STEN II, p. 258.

268 "Could you tell us": STEN II, p. 263.

268 "How can we judge Beilis": Tager, "Protsess," p. 111.

269 *Book of Neophyte*: STEN II, pp. 303–307.

269   "boils": This passage derives from Deuteronomy 28:27 where Moses tells his people that if they do not obey God's commandments and laws, "The Lord will smite thee with the botch of Egypt, and with the emerods, and with the scab, and with the itch, whereof thou canst not be healed."

270   Maklakov: STEN II, pp. 307–308.

270   "The extermination": STEN II, p. 318.

270   Jack of Diamonds: *Rech',* October 21, 1913.

270   "Frankists": STEN II, p. 362. Frankism was an eighteenth-century heretical religious movement centered around the charismatic leader Jacob Frank. According to the *YIVO Encyclopedia of Jews in Eastern Europe,* "The Frankists initially thought of themselves as a branch of Judaism opposed to the authority of the rabbis and rejecting some elements of rabbinic tradition. Subsequently, Frankists redefined themselves as a separate religious group, practically independent from hitherto existing forms of both Judaism and Christianity." In 1759, Frank converted to Catholicism; http://www.yivoencyclopedia.org/article.aspx/Frankism.

271   Even Kosorotov: STEN II, p. 223.

271   "Sweating, wiping": Nabokov, "Na protesse," *Rech',* October 21, 1913.

271   Shmakov grew openly angry: "Iz zaly suda," *Kievskaia Mysl',* October 21, 1913.

271   burst into laughter: El'patevskii, "Vpechatleniia," *Kievskaia Mysl',* October 22, 1913.

271   "why it was white": STEN II, p. 339.

272   plagiarized: Shnayer Leiman, "Benzion Katz: Mrs. Baba Bathra," p. 52n3.

272   "ploy will backfire": Leiman, "Benzion Katz: Mrs. Baba Bathra," p. 55.

272   "would sooner believe": Nabokov, "Na Protesse," *Rech',* October 23, 1913.

272   Pranaitis was recalled: Based on STEN II, pp. 434–35, and Leiman, "Benzion Katz: Mrs. Baba Bathra," pp. 55–56. The Baba Bathra episode, vividly recounted by Katz, does not appear in the transcript, which was widely recognized to be imperfect.

273   "Many congratulated": Leiman, "Benzion Katz: Mrs. Baba Bathra," p. 56.

273   "ignorance": Tager, "Protsess," pp. 111–13.

273   "papal bulls": STEN II, p. 336.

274   made sure it would not arrive: Tager, "Tsarskoe pravitel'stvo," p. 345; on the effort to obtain the Vatican's authentication, see Szajkowski, "The Impact of the Beilis Case," pp. 356–59. The historian David I. Kertzer mischaracterizes this episode in *The Popes Against the Jews,* pp. 227–28, 230–36, entirely omitting the role of Ambassador Nelidov in ensuring the letter would not arrive in time for the trial, and blaming the Vatican for the failure of the letter to be introduced at the trial. Lawlor, in *Were the Popes Against Jews?,* pp. 125–46, corrects some of Kertzer's

errors but unfortunately confuses the chronology by failing to take into account the thirteen-day difference between the Julian calendar used in Russia and the Gregorian one used in the West. Kertzer is on firmer ground in his harsh assessment of the Vatican's failure to condemn the blood libel at the time of the Beilis trial, or afterward. Kertzer points out that Catholic publications regarded as close to the Vatican published articles advocating for the ritual murder charge. The semiofficial Vatican periodical *Civilta Cattolica* published two articles on the Beilis trial in the spring of 1914 by a Jesuit, Father Paolo Silva, entirely supporting the prosecution's point of view. In the articles, titled "Jewish Trickery and Papal Documents—Apropos of a Recent Trial," Father Silva wrote that "the murder [in Kiev] was committed by people who wanted to extract the blood" and that the Jews regard blood as "a drink like milk" (Kertzer, p. 236). The Catholic newspapers *L'Unita Cattolica* in Florence and *L'Univers* in France also supported the ritual-murder charge. See also Charlotte Klein, "From Damascus to Kiev: *Civilta Cattolica* on Ritual Murder," in *The Blood Libel Legend,* pp. 194–96, and passim on *Civilta*'s advocacy of the blood libel from 1881 to 1914, pp. 180–96. Lawlor (see above) defends the Vatican's conduct.

274 vertical slash: The document's significance was first noted by Alexander Tager. Tager, *Tsarskaia,* photostat following p. 160; Tager, *Decay of Czarism,* photostat no. 9. Reproduced in the photo section of this book.
274 "anemia of the brain": STEN III, p. 192.
274 medical attention: Samuel, *Blood Accusation,* p. 219.
275 "If a non-Jew": STEN III, p. 4.
275 "unseen hand": STEN III, p. 5.
275 "under their yoke": STEN III, p. 18.
276 "question of the cow": STEN III, p. 38.
276 "prisoner's dock": STEN III, p. 41.
276 "pronounce the verdict": STEN III, p. 57.
276 "ultraviolet clues": "Iz zaly suda," *Kievskaia Mysl',* October 25, 1913.
276 feared the speech: Nabokov, "Na protsesse," *Rech',* October 25, 1913.
277 dismissing as a "legend": STEN III, p. 95.
277 "Why not Beilis and Vera?": STEN III, p. 96.
277 Hamentaschen: STEN III, p. 108; "Iz zaly suda," *Kievskaia Mysl',* October 25, 1913.
277 "unseen hand": STEN III, p. 98.
277 "overwhelming weapon": STEN III, p. 98.
277 "perhaps": STEN III, p. 124. In his memoirs, written two decades later, Maklakov wrote that he himself was, in principle, willing to acknowledge the possibility that somewhere Jewish fanatics had committed ritual murders. "In such an admission," he insisted, "there is nothing insulting," arguing that a religion is not responsible for fanatical sects that commit awful acts in its name. In 1956, he carried on correspon-

dence on this topic with his contemporary, the Jewish attorney Mark Vishniak, who reproached him for taking such a position. Indeed, the argument that unspecified Jewish ritual murders may have occurred at some time or some place is clearly fallacious. Of the scores of known cases *in the record,* not a single one proved to be well-founded. There-fore, it has been pointed out, the notion that there are unknown cases with unknown evidence in which unknown Jews were actually guilty is illogical. See Maklakov, *Iz vospominanii,* pp. 256–57; O. Budnitskii, "V.A. Maklakov i evreiskii vopros," pp. 53–54.

277 "The prosecution": STEN III, p. 124.

277 "I will rely only": STEN III, p. 136.

278 "She alone": STEN III, p. 136.

278 "most frightening": STEN III, p. 137.

278 "But together": STEN III, p. 138.

278 At those words: El'patevskii, "Vpechatleniia," *Kievskaia Mysl',* Octo-ber 26, 1913.

279 "invention of Cheberyak": *Ubiistvo Iushchinskogo,* "Rech' V.A. Mak-lakova," p. 64; STEN III, p. 145. The text in Maklakov's published version differs slightly from that in the transcript. Maklakov's text has been generally preferred here, given the attorneys' own complaints about inaccuracies in the transcript. See Margolin, *The Jews of Eastern Europe,* p. 156.

279 "all of Lukianovka": *Ubiistvo Iushchinskogo,* "Rech' V.A. Maklakova," p. 64; STEN III, p. 145.

279 "You have been told": *Ubiistvo Iushchinskogo,* "Rech' V.A. Maklakova," p. 87; STEN III, p. 155.

279 "suicide": *Ubiistvo Iushchinskogo,* "Rech' V.A. Maklakova," p. 84; STEN III, p. 154. In the published version of the speech (p. 87), Makla-kov warns more declaratively that, in the event of an unjust verdict, "it will be forever remembered that a court of Russian jurors, out of hatred for the Jewish people, turned away from the truth." It is not clear if he actually said those words in court.

279 "frightful accusation": STEN III, p. 155.

280 "I firmly hope": STEN III, p. 193.

281 "I was always on the side": Budnitskii, "V.A. Maklakov i evreiskii vopros," pp. 53–54.

281 "the more eloquent": Samuel, *Blood Accusation,* p. 225.

281 "took the liberty": Gruzenberg, *Yesterday,* pp. 107–8.

281 candelabrum: STEN III, p. 203.

281 "court is a kind of temple": STEN III, p. 195.

281 allusions: STEN III, p. 203.

281 "negative system": STEN III, p. 214.

281 "axiom": STEN III, pp. 214, 217.

282 "the coat": STEN III, p. 213.

282 "Defendant Beilis": STEN III, p. 272; Bonch-Bruevich, *Znamenie,* p. 184.

282 Jewish leaders: Lifschutz, "Repercussions," pp. 213–14.

283 Jewish organized labor: Lifschutz, "Repercussions," pp. 210–11.

283 At eight a.m.: Beilis, *My Sufferings,* pp. 182–83.

283 St. Sophia Square filled: Viktor Sosedov, "Otryvki," *Kievskaia Mysl',* October 29, 1913; *Rech',* October 29, 1913.

284 The jury's first charge: The text of both questions appears in STEN III, p. 299.

285 prejudicial: On the prejudicial formulation of the two questions, see Nabokov, "Delo Beilisa," *Pravo,* no. 44 (November 3, 1913): 2522–24.

285 Nabokov wrote: Nabokov, "Na Protsesse," *Rech',* October 29, 1913. Nabokov analyzes Boldyrev's prejudiced charged to the jury in "Delo Beilisa," *Pravo,* no. 45 (November 10, 1913): 2577–80.

285 "You know that the body": STEN III, p. 289.

285 Most of those: Tager, *Tsarskaia,* p. 229; Bonch-Bruevich, *Znamenie,* p. 186.

286 Gruzenberg could only think: "Beseda s pris. pov. O.O. Gruzenbergom," *Rech',* October 30, 1913. Gruzenberg's candid admission of pessimism, made to a reporter soon after the verdict, is at odds with his account of his state of mind in his memoirs. "I had not the slightest doubt about the outcome of the trial," he wrote. "I believed, indeed I knew, that the conscience of a Russian would never condone the destruction of an innocent person." Gruzenberg, *Yesterday,* p. 105.

286 After an hour passed: Bonch-Bruevich, *Znamenie,* p. 186; Bonch-Bruevich, "Reziume predesedatelia," *Kievskaia Mysl',* October 29, 1913.

286 quavering voice: Bonch-Bruevich, "Prigovor," *Kievskaia Mysl',* October 29, 1913; Bonch-Bruevich, *Znamenie,* pp. 188–89.

287 could not believe: "Osvobozhdenie Beilisa," *Kievskaia Mysl',* October 29, 1913.

287 "Beilis is not yours": Samuel, *Blood Accusation,* p. 249; Beilis, *My Sufferings,* p. 188.

287 "free man": STEN III, p. 299.

287 "Old people and children": "U Beilisa," *Kievskaia Mysl',* October 30, 1913.

287 "Beilis Station": Beilis, *My Sufferings,* p. 203.

287 Telegrams: "U Beilisa," *Kievskaia Mysl',* October 30, 1913.

287 "won't say that I ran away": "U Beilisa," *Kievskaia Mysl',* October 30, 1913.

288 "peculiarities of that act": "G.G. Zamyslovskii o prigovore," *Kievskaia Mysl',* October 30, 1913; on prosecution claiming victory, see also Samuel, *Blood Accusation,* p. 253.

288 "comic effort": "Beseda s pris. pov. O.O. Gruzenbergom," *Rech',* October 30, 1913.

288 *New Times:* Samuel, *Blood Accusation,* p. 250.
288 "engineered": Szajkowski, "The Impact of the Beilis Case," pp. 215, 216.
288 "The muzhichki": "Beseda s pris. pov. O.O. Gruzenbergom," *Rech',* October 30, 1913.
288 "but when the foreman": Gruzenberg, *Yesterday,* p. 186.
288 "political Tsushima": Tager, "Protsess," p. 123.
289 "dangerous internal illness": V. A. Maklakov, "Spasitel'noe predoster-ezhenoe," p. 137.
289 victory banquet: Tager, *Tsarskaia,* pp. 281–82.
289 promotions, and material rewards: *Padenie,* vol. 3, p. 378; *Padenie,* vol. 4, pp. 207, 426–27; Tager, *Tsarskaia,* pp. 281-82.
289 "It is certain": Hans Rogger, *Jewish Policies,* p. 48, citing, A. I. Spirido-vich, *Les dernières années de la cour de Tzarskoïé-Sélo* (Paris: Payot, 1928), vol. 2, p. 447.
290 He often invoked: The verse is Job 3:25. The straightforward translation used here is similar in tone to the standard Russian Orthodox translation that Nicholas would have quoted. The memoirs of the French ambassador to Russia, Maurice Paleologue, are an oft-cited source for Nicholas's penchant for citing Job. Paleologue used an ornate French translation of the passage that was awkwardly retranslated into English and sometimes quoted as Nicholas's words. Paleologue's account is reproduced in Fuhrmann, *Rasputin,* p. 16.

12. *"The Smell of Burning, Blood, and Iron"*

291 neatly stacked: Stepanov, *Chernaia* (2005), p. 394.
291 Fastov case: The story of the case is told in Tager, *Tsarskaia,* pp. 287–95.
292 Chebyshev: According to Chebyshev, the decision to appoint him to succeed Chaplinsky was made by the entire council of ministers, not just by Shcheglovitov, because the government wanted to change course. "Protsess Beilisa: Razoblachenie Bol'shevikov," *Vozrozhdenie,* August 24, 1933, p. 3.
292 Goncharuk was convicted: Stepanov, *Chernaia* (2005), p. 394.
293 Bekhterev: Bekhterev, "The Iushchinskii Murder," p. 68n2.
293 "no one had any use": Stepanov, *Chernaia,* p. 395.
294 most of her role: Samuel, *Blood Accusation,* p. 35, hints at a similar point, writing, "All in all, we seem to have in Vera Cheberyak a woman born out of her time and setting. In the Italy of Cesare Borgia and Caterina Sforza she might have found an adequate field for her talents . . . [but] she was fated to operate in mean circumstances with mean accomplices."
294 "Café Boheme": "Will Exonerate Beilis: Ex-Russian Police Official Says He Will Clear Up Ritual Murder Myth," *New York Times,* April 23, 1914.
294 Margolin disagreed: Margolin, *The Jews of Eastern Europe,* p. 236.

295 Gruzenberg answered: Gruzenberg, *Yesterday,* p. 121.

295 "fully in tune": Figes, *A People's Tragedy,* p. 270.

296 "ministerial leapfrog": Figes, *A People's Tragedy,* p. 277.

296 "The most striking": Figes, *A People's Tragedy,* p. 351.

297 "pallid, unshaven": Utevskii, *Vospominaniia,* p. 33.

297 Shcheglovitov stood: Zviagintsev, *Rokovaia femida,* pp. 211–12; N. N. Sukhanov, *The Russian Revolution, 1917: Eyewitness Account,* vol. 1, ed. and tr. Joel Carmichael (New York: Harper, 1962), p. 52.

297 soldiers led him off: Zenzinov, "Fevral'skie Dni," p. 238.

297 "enraged crowd": Andrei A. Ivanov and Anatolii D. Stepanov, eds., *Chernaia sotnia: istoricheskaia entsiklopediia* (Moscow: Institut Russkoi Tvivilizatsii, 2008), p. 308.

298 "mental breakdown": Figes, *A People's Tragedy,* p. 339.

298 "born for misfortune": Pipes, *The Russian Revolution,* p. 312.

298 tsar's signed abdication: Figes, *A People's Tragedy,* pp. 339–44; Pipes, *The Russian Revolution,* pp. 310–17.

298 school desk, surrounded by toys: Figes, *A People's Tragedy,* p. 345; Nabokov, *V. D. Nabokov and the Russian Provisional Government,* p. 53; Vasily Shulgin, *Dni,* p. 277.

298 "I seized the materials": Gruzenberg, *Yesterday,* pp. 121–24.

299 "My conscience": *Padenie,* vol. 3, pp. 347, 358.

299 Once pure red: Nabokov, *V. D. Nabokov and the Russian Provisional Government,* p. 34.

300 "one continual process": Nabokov, *V. D. Nabokov and the Russian Provisional Government,* p. 35.

300 Pranaitis: Tager, *Tsarskaia,* pp. 272–73.

300 Vipper: Krylenko, *Sudebnye,* p. 58; Tager, *Decay of Czarism,* p. 249.

301 Makhalin: Reznik, *Skvoz' chad,* p. 177.

301 Cheberyak was convicted: GAKO, f. 864, op. 10, d. 11.

301 According to an agent: Reznik, *Skvoz' chad,* p. 177.

301 Cheberyak was shot: Tager, *Decay of Czarism,* p. 249.

301 Shoshkess: Chaim Shoshkess, "My Meeting with Mendel Beilis," *Der Tog–Morgn Zshurnal,* December 1, 1963, p. 6.

301 Nabokov was shot: Nabokov, *Speak Memory,* p. 193; Boyd, *Vladimir Nabokov: The Russian Years,* pp. 190–93.

302 "Well, how can anyone": Kucherov, *Courts,* p. 268; Gruzenberg, *Ocherki,* p. 56.

302 Brazul-Brushkovsky: Reznik, *Skvoz' chad,* p. 176; Samuel, *Blood Accusation,* p. 255. The Jewish Telegraph agency published an obituary for Brazul in January 1924, but apparently in error.

302 Rovno: Melamed, "Krasovskii," p. 164.

302 "did not deserve": Melamed, "Krasovskii," p. 165.

302 Margolin: On his life after the revolution, see Khiterer, "Arnold Davidovich Margolin," pp. 145–67.

303 Fulbright-Margolin Prize: Khiterer, "Arnold Davidovich Margolin," p. 163.

303 strangest fate: Shulgin, *The Years,* p. xiv.

303 documentary: The documentary is on Youtube: https://www.youtube .com/watch?v=sKPUoLAc2G4.

303 "invigorating effect": Beilis, *My Sufferings,* p. 221.

303 "uncringing Jews": Beilis, *My Sufferings,* p. 225.

303 destroyed their home: Beilis, *My Sufferings,* p. 234.

304 committed suicide: Beilis, *Blood Libel,* p. 218. Beilis tells of Pinchas's suicide in the last chapter of his memoirs, which was not included in the original English edition but is translated for the first time in the valuable new edition coedited by Beilis's grandson.

304 Addams: Beilis, *Blood Libel,* p. 220.

304 "exploiting myself": Beilis, *Blood Libel,* p. 227.

304 "not yet sixty": Chaim Shoshkess, "My Meeting with Mendel Beilis," *Der Tog–Morgn Zshurnal,* December 1, 1963, p. 6.

304 derogatory epithet: S. Ansky, *The Enemy at His Pleasure,* pp. 28–29, 4.

305 Vipper had complained: STEN III, p. 52.

305 Between the early 1880s: Biale, *Blood and Belief,* p. 126.

305 Konitz: The definitive work on the Konitz case is Michael Walser Smith's *The Butcher's Tale.*

306 "folkloric belief": Biale, *Blood and Belief,* p. 130.

306 *Volkischer Beobachter:* Rogger, *Jewish Policies,* pp. 55 and 243n44.

306 "Everywhere murder": Raul Hilberg, *The Destruction of the European Jews,* 3rd ed., vol. 3 (New Haven, CT: Yale University Press, 2003), p. 1095.

306 "lurked in the background": Biale, *Blood and Belief,* p. 137.

307 Himmler explained: Hilberg, *The Destruction of the European Jews,* vol. 3, pp. 1095–96.

307 "Beilis Soap": Weinreich, *Hitler's Professors,* p. 200.

307 Rzeszow: Gross, *Fear: Anti-Semitism in Poland After Auschwitz,* p. 74.

307 Wyszinski declined: Gross, *Fear,* pp. 149–50.

308 The excavation: Slater, *The Many Deaths of Tsar Nicholas II,* p. 26.

308 created a commission: Slater, *The Many Deaths,* p. 28.

308 The Church asked: Slater, *The Many Deaths,* pp. 30–32.

308 Jewish ritual: Slater, *The Many Deaths,* pp. 71–80.

309 "The motives": Reznik, *Rastlenie nenavist'iu,* p. 114, citing *Moskovskie Novosti,* March 1–8, 1998, p. 2; Solovev rendered his official opinion on the ritual question in January 1998. Slater, *The Many Deaths,* p. 31.

309 Church officials refused: Slater, *The Many Deaths,* p. 155.

309 In the post-Soviet era: Slater, *The Many Deaths,* p. 74.

310 "How was it possible": Aleksandr Solzhenitsyn, *Dvesti let vmeste,* p. 446.

310 "tries in every way": Semyon Reznik, "Vmeste ili Vroz': Zametki o knige A.I. Solzhenitsyna, 'Dvesti let vmeste," *Zhurnal Vestnik Online,* May 15, 2002, http://www.vestnik.com/issues/2002/0515/win/reznik.htm.

310 group of about fifteen men: "Antisemitizm na Kievskom Kladbishche," *Segodnia,* February 21, 2004. http://www.segodnya.ua/oldarchive/c225 6713004f33f5c2256e40004f79d9.html.

311 "in his thirteenth year": This is incorrect. Andrei was thirteen years old when he died. "In his thirteenth year" would mean he was twelve.

311 someone had made off: Eduard Doks, "Kto Khochet Vozrodit' Krovavyi Navet," *Evreiskii obozrevatel',* March 2004, http://www.jewukr.org/observer/eo2003/page_show_ru.php?id=531.

311 grave was renovated: "Pam'iati nevinno ubiennogo," *Personal Plus,* no. 8 (159) February 22–28, 2006, http://www.personal-plus.net/159/471.html

311 State Department: *Contemporary Global Anti-Semitism: A Report Provided the United States Congress* (2008), pp. 5, 32, http://www.state.gov/documents/organization/102301.pdf.

311 Anti-Defamation League: "Ukraine University of Hate: A Backgrounder on MAUP (Interregional Academy of Personnel Management)," ADL, November 3, 2006, http://www.adl.org/main_anti_semitism_international/maup_ukraine.htm.

311 no legal basis: Anshel Pfeffer, "A Grave with a Particularly Sad Story," *Haaretz,* February 8, 2008. http://www.haaretz.com/print-edition/news/a-grave-with-a-particularly-sad-story-1.238892.

311 anti-Semitism in Ukraine: In the Ukrainian parliamentary elections in October 2012, the ultranationalist Svoboda (Freedom) Party, widely regarded as xenophobic and anti-Semitic, shocked observers by winning 12 percent of the vote and representation in parliament. In the 2007 elections, it had won less than 1 percent of the vote. The party's leader, Oleg Tyagnibok, denies charges that he hates foreigners and Jews, though he had previously been expelled from parliament for using ethnic slurs, has referred to the "Jewish-Russian mafia" that supposedly runs the country, and has called for an end to "the criminal activities of organized Jewry" in his country. David M. Herszenhorn, "Ukraine's Ultranationalists Show Surprising Strength at Polls," *New York Times,* November 8, 2012.

312 fresh flowers: Pfeffer, "A Grave," *Haaretz,* February 8, 2008; Paul Berger, "Was Kiev Beating Anti-Semitic Act?: Some See Return of Old Hatreds, But Others Have Doubts," *Jewish Daily Forward,* June 8, 2012; Weinberg, "The Blood Libel in Eastern Europe," p. 283; author's visit to grave, spring 2011.

Bibliography

Sources in Russian

Bonch-Bruevich, Vladimir. *Znamenie vremeni: ubiistvo Andreia Iushchinskogo i delo Beilisa*. Moscow: Gosudarstvennoe Izdatel'stvo, 1921.

Budnitskii, Oleg. "V.A. Maklakov i evreiskii vopros." *Vestnik Evreiskogo Universiteta* 19 (1999): 42–94.

Dedkov, Nikita. *Konservativnyi liberalizm Vasiliia Maklakova*. Moscow: AIRO-XX, 2005.

Delo Beilisa: Stenographicheskii Otchet. 3 Vols. Kiev: 1913.

Delo Mendelia Belisa: Materialy chrezvychainoi sledstvennoi kommissii vremennogo pravitel'stvo o sudebnom protsesse 1913 g. po obvineniu v ritual'nom ubiistve. Edited by R. Sh. Ganelin, V. E. Kel'ner, and I. V. Lukoianov. St. Petersburg: Dimitrii Bulanin, 1999.

Gerasimov, A.V. *Na lezvii s terroristami*. Paris: YMCA Press, 1985.

Gruzenberg, O.O. *Ocherki i rechi*. New York: 1944.

Ioffe, G. Z. "Delo Beilisa." In *Tsarskaia Rossiia i delo Beilisa: issledovaniia i materialy*, pp. 327–50. Moscow and Jerusalem: Gesharim, 1995.

Kal'nitskii, Mikhail. "Ekspertiza professora Glagoleva." *Egupets* 19 (2010): 151–64.

Karabchevskii, Nikolai. *Chto moi glaza videli*. Berlin: Izd. Ol'goi Diakovoi, 1921. http://az.lib.ru/k/karabchewskij_n_p/text_0050.shtml.

———. *Rechi: 1882–1914*. Petrograd: M.O. Vol'f, 1916.

Katsis, Leonid. *Krovavyi navet i russkaia mysl': istoriko-teleologicheskoe issledovanie dela Beilisa*. Moscow and Jerusalem: Gesharim, 2006.

Klier, Dzhon (John). "Krovavyi navet v Russkoi pravoslavnoi traditsii." In M. Dimitriev, ed., *Evrei i khristiane v pravoslavnykh obshchestvakh vostochnoi evropy*, pp. 181–205. Moscow: Indrik, 2011.

Korolenko, Vladimir. Articles on the Beilis case published in fall 1913 *Rech'* and *Russkie Viedmosti*. Collected at http://ldn-knigi.lib.ru/JUDAICA/Korol_Stat.htm.

Koshko, A. F. "O dele Beilisa." *Novyi Zhurnal* 91 (1968): 162–83.

Krylenko, N.V. *Sudebnye rechi*. Moscow: Iuridicheskaia literature, 1964.

Maklakov, Vasilii. *Iz vospominanii*. New York: Chekhov Publishing House, 1954.

————. "Spasitel'noe predosterezhenoe: smysl dela Beilisa." *Russkaia Mysl'* 11 (1913): 135–43.

Melamed, Efim. "Krasovskii, 'Izvestnyi po delu Beilisa . . .'" *Egupets* (Kiev) 20 (2011): 164–75.

Menzhulin, Vadim. *Drugoi Sikorskii: neudobnye starnitsy istorii psikhiatrii.* Kiev: Sfera, 2004.

Mikhailov, V. A. "Delo Beilisa." Unpublished manuscript. Bakhmeteff Archive, Columbia University.

Morozov, Iurii, and Tat'iana Derevianko. *Evreiskie kinematografisty v Ukraine 1910–1945.* Kiev: Dukh i Litera, 2004.

Nabokov, V. D. "Delo Beilisa (Nachalo)." *Pravo*, No. 44 (November 3, 1913): 2519–2524.

————. "Delo Beilisa (Okonchanie)." *Pravo*, No. 45 (November 10, 1913): 2569–2580.

————. "Dva obvinitel'nykh akta. (Delo Beilisa)." *Pravo*, No. 47 (November 24, 1913): 2593–2702.

Radzinsky, Edvard. *"Gospodi . . . spasi i ismiri Rossiiu"—Nikolai II: Zhizn i Smert'.* Moscow: Vagrius, 1993.

————. *Rasputin: zhizn' i smert'.* Moscow: ACT, 2007.

Reznik, Semyon. *Rastlenie nenavist'iu: krovavyi navet v Rossii: istoriko-dokumta'nye ocherki o proshlom i nastoiashchem.* Moscow and Jerusalem: DAAT/Znanie, 2001.

————. *Skvoz' chad i fimiam.* Moscow: Academia, 2010.

————. "Vmeste ili Vroz': Zametki o knige A.I. Solzhenitsyna, 'Dvesti let vmeste." *Zhurnal Vestnik Online,* May 15, 2002. http://www.vestnik.com/issues/2002/0515/win/reznik.htm.

Ruud, Charlz, and Sergei Stepanov. *Fontanka 16: politicheskii sysk pri tsariakh.* Moscow: Mysl', 1993.

Pidzharenko, Aleksandr. *Kriminal'nyi sysk Kieva vo II pol. XIX–nach. XX vv.* Kiev: KVITS, 2006.

————. *Ne ritual'noe ubiistvo na Luk'ianovke: kriminalnyi sysk Kieva v nach. XX v.* Kiev: KVITS, 2006.

Shulgin, Vasily. *Dni; 1920.* Moscow: Sovremennik, 1989.

Solzhenitsyn, Aleksandr. *Dvesti let vmeste.* Moscow: Vagrius, 2006.

Stepanov, Sergei A. *Chernaia Sotnia.* Moscow: Eksmo-Iauza, 2005.

————. *Chernaia Sotnia v Rossii, 1905–1914.* Moscow: VZPI, 1992.

————. *Zagadki ubiistva Stolypina.* Moscow: Progress-Akademiia, 1995.

Tager, Alexander S. "Protsess Beilisa v otsenke deparmenta politsii." *Krasnyi Arkhiv* 44 (1931): 85–125.

————. *Tsarskaia Rossiia i delo Beilisa.* 2nd ed. Moscow: Sovietskoe Zakonodatel'stvo, 1934.

————. "Tsarskoe pravitel'stvo i delo Beilisa." *Krasnyi Arkhiv* 54–55 (1932): 162–204.

Troitskii, Nikolai. *Sud'by rossiiskikh advokatov.* Saratov: Saratovskii Gos.

Universitet, 2003. http://www.sgu.ru/faculties/historical/sc.publication/
history_rus/rus_ad.

Ubiistvo Iushchinskogo: Mneniia inostrannykh uchenykh. St. Petersburg:
L. Ia. Ganzburg, 1913.

Utevskii, B. S. *Vospominaniia iurista.* Moscow: Iuridicheskaia Literatura,
1989.

Varfolomeev, Yu. *V. A. S. Zarudnyi: Iurist i obshchestvennyi deiatel'.* Saratov: Nauchnai kniga, 2002.

Zenzinov, V. "Fevral'skie dni," *Novyi Zhurnal* vol. 35 (1953), pp. 208-240.

Zviagintsev, Aleksandr. *Rokovaia femida: dramaticheskie sud'by znameni-
tykh rosiiskikh iuristov.* Moscow: Astrel', 2010.

Sources in Hebrew and Yiddish

Beilis, Mendel. "Mayn Lebn in Turme un in Gerikht: Dertseylt fun Mendl
Beylis" (My Life in Prison and the Court: Recounted by Mendl Beilis).
Haynt (Warsaw): November 18, 1913, p. 3; November 19, 1913, p. 3; No-
vember 20, 1913, p. 3; November 21, 1913, p. 4; November 25, 1913, p. 4;
November 26, 1913, p. 4; November 28, 1913, p. 4; December 2, 1913, p.
4; December 4, 1913, p. 3; December 5, 1913, p. 3; December 7, 1913, p. 3;
December 12, 1913, p. 3.

Lifschutz, E. "Hedei Alilat-Hadam Al Beilis Be-Amerikah" (Repercussions
of the Beilis Blood Libel in America). *Zion* 28, nos. 3–4 (1963): 206–22.

Sources in English

The American Jewish Yearbook 5674, vol. 16. Philadelphia, 1914.

Ansky, S. *The Enemy at His Pleasure: A Journey Through the Pale of Settlement During World War I.* New York: Metropolitan Books, 2002.

Ascher, Abraham. *P. A. Stolypin: The Search for Stability in Late Imperial
Russia.* Stanford, CA: Stanford University Press, 2001.

Baron, Salo W. *The Russian Jew Under Tsars and Soviets.* New York:
Schocken Books, 1987.

Beilis, Jay, Jeremy Simcha Garber, and Mark S. Stein. "Pulitzer Plagiarism."
Cardozo Law Review de Novo (2010): 225–41. http://www.cardozolaw
review.com/Joomla1.5/content/denovo/BEILIS_2010_225.pdf.

Beilis, Mendel. *Blood Libel: The Life and Memory of Mendel Beilis.* Edited
by Jay Beilis, Jeremy Simcha Garber, and Mark S. Stein. Chicago: Beilis
Publishing, 2011.

———. *The Story of My Sufferings.* New York: Mendel Beilis Publishing
Co., 1926.

Bekhterev, V. M. "The Iushchinskii Murder and the Expert Psychiatric-
Psychological Opinion." Translated by Lydia Razran Stone. *Journal of*

Russian and East European Psychology 41, no. 2 (March–April 2003): 7–70.

Berkowitz, Joel. "The 'Mendel Beilis Epidemic' on the Yiddish Stage." *Jewish Social Studies* New Series 8, no. 1 (Autumn 2001): 199–225.

Biale, David. *Blood and Belief: The Circulation of a Symbol Between Jews and Christians*. Berkeley: University of California Press, 2008.

The Blood Libel Legend: A Casebook of Anti-Semitic Folklore. Edited by Alan Dundes. Madison: University of Wisconsin Press, 1991.

Boyd, Brian. *Vladimir Nabokov: The Russian Years*. Princeton: Princeton University Press, 1990.

Charques, Richard. *The Twilight of Imperial Russia*. New York: Oxford University Press, 1974.

Cherniavsky, Michael. *Tsar and People: Studies in Russian Myths*. New York: Random House, 1962.

Cohen, Naomi W. "The Abrogation of the Russo-American Treaty of 1832." *Jewish Social Studies* 25, no. 1 (January 1963): 3–41.

Dixon, Simon. "The 'Mad Monk' Iliodor in Tsaritsyn." *Slavonic and East European Review* (January–April 2010): 377–415.

Edvard, Radzinsky. *The Last Tsar: The Life and Death of Nicholas II*. Translated by Marian Schwartz. New York: Anchor Books, 1992.

———. *The Rasputin File*. Translated by Judson Rosengrant. New York: Anchor Books, 2001.

Egan, Clifford L. "Pressure Groups, the Department of State, and the Abrogation of the Russian-American Treaty of 1832." *Proceedings of the American Philosophical Society* 115, no. 4 (August 1971): 328–34.

Engelstein, Laura. *The Keys to Happiness: Sex and the Search for Modernity in Fin-de-Siècle Russia*. Ithaca and London: Cornell University Press, 1992.

———. *Slavophile Empire: Imperial Russia's Illiberal Path*. Ithaca, NY, and London: Cornell University Press, 2009.

Figes, Orlando. *A People's Tragedy: The Russian Revolution, 1891–1924*. New York: Viking Penguin, 1996.

Frankel, Jonathan. *The Damascus Affair: Ritual Murder, Politics, and the Jews in 1840*. Cambridge: Cambridge University Press, 1997.

Fuhrmann, Joseph T. *Rasputin: A Life*. New York: Praeger, 1990.

Fuller, William C. *The Foe Within: Fantasies of Treason and the End of Imperial Russia*. Ithaca, NY: Cornell University Press, 2006.

Geifman, Anna. *Thou Shalt Kill: Revolutionary Terrorism in Russia, 1894–1917*. Princeton, NJ: Princeton University Press, 1993.

Gitelman, Zvi. *A Century of Ambivalence: The Jews of Russia and the Soviet Union: 1881 to the Present*. Bloomington: Indiana University Press, 2001.

Gross, Hans. *Criminal Investigation: A Practical Handbook for Magistrates, Police Officers, and Lawyers*. London: The Specialist Press, Ltd., 1907.

Gross, Jan T. *Fear: Anti-Semitism in Poland After Auschwitz*. New York: Random House, 2006.

Gruzenberg, O. O. (Oskar). *Yesterday: Memoirs of a Russian-Jewish Lawyer.* Edited and translated by Don C. Rawson. Berkeley: University of California Press, 1981.

Hamm, Michael F. *Kiev: A Portrait, 1800–1917.* Princeton, NJ: Princeton University Press, 1993.

Harcave, Sidney. *The Russian Revolution of 1905.* New York: Collier, 1970.

Hughes, Lindsay. *The Romanovs: Ruling Russia, 1613–1917.* London and New York: Continuum, 2008.

Ivanits, Linda J. *Russian Folk Belief.* Armonk, NY: M. E. Sharpe, 1989.

Julius, Anthony. *Trials of the Diaspora: A History of Anti-Semitism in England.* Oxford and New York: Oxford University Press, 2010.

Kertzer, David. *The Popes Against the Jews.* New York: Vintage Books, 2002.

Khiterer, Victoria. "Arnold Davidovich Margolin: Ukrainian-Jewish Jurist, Statesman and Diplomat." *Revolutionary Russia* 18, no. 2 (2005): 145–67.

———. "The Social and Economic History of Jews in Kiev Before February 1917." Ph.D. diss., Brandeis University, 2008.

Kieval, Hillel J. "Death and the Nation: Ritual Murder as Political Discourse in the Czech Lands." In *Languages of Community: The Jewish Experience in the Czech Lands*, pp. 181–97. Berkeley: University of California Press, 2000.

———. "Representations and Knowledge in Mediaeval and Modern Accounts of Jewish Ritual Murder." *Jewish Social Studies: History, Culture, and Society* 1, no. 1 (September 1994): 52 72.

———. "The Rules of the Game: Forensic Medicine and the Language of Science in the Structuring of Modern Ritual Murder Trials." *Jewish History* 26 (2012): 287–307.

Klier, John D. "The Blood Libel in the Russian Orthodox Tradition." Unpublished manuscript.

———. *Imperial Russia's Jewish Question, 1855–1881.* Cambridge: Cambridge University Press, 1995.

Klier, John D., and Shlomo Lambroza, eds. *Pogroms: Anti-Jewish Violence in Modern Russian History.* Cambridge: Cambridge University Press, 1992.

Kucherov, Samuel. *Courts, Lawyers, and Trials Under the Last Three Tsars.* New York: Frederick A. Praeger, 1953.

Langer, Jacob. "Corruption and Counterrevolution: The Rise and Fall of the Black Hundred." Ph.D. diss., Duke University, 2007.

Lawlor, Justus George. *Were the Popes Against the Jews?* Grand Rapids, MI: Wm. B. Eerdmans, 2012.

Langmuir, Gavin I. *Toward a Definition of Anti-Semitism.* Berkeley: University of California Press, 1990.

Laqueur, Walter. *Black Hundred: The Rise of the Extreme Right in Russia.* HarperCollins, 1993.

———. *Russia and Germany: A Century of Conflict.* New Brunswick, NJ, and London: Transaction Publishers, 1990.

Leikin, Ezekiel. *The Beilis Transcripts: The Anti-Semitic Trial That Shook the World.* Northvale, NJ, and London: Jason Aronson, Inc., 1993.

Leiman, Shnayer Z. "Benzion Katz: Mrs. Baba Bathra." *Tradition* 42, no. 4 (2010): 51–57.

Lieven, Dominic. *Nicholas II: Twilight of the Empire*. New York: St. Martin's Press, 1993.

Lincoln, W. Bruce. *In War's Dark Shadow: The Russians Before the Great War*. New York: Dial Press, 1983.

Lindemann, Albert S. *The Jew Accused: Three Anti-Semitic Affairs: 1894–1915*. Cambridge: Cambridge University Press, 1991.

Lowe, Heinz-Dietrich. *The Tsars and the Jews: Reform, Reaction and Anti-Semitism in Imperial Russia, 1772–1917*. Chur, Switzerland: Harwood Academic, 1993.

Margolin, Arnold. *The Jews of Eastern Europe*. New York: Thomas Selzer, 1926.

Massie, Robert K. *Nicholas and Alexandra*. New York: Atheneum, 1967.

Matich, Olga. *Erotic Utopia: The Decadent Imagination in Russia's Fin De Siècle*. Madison: University of Wisconsin Press, 2005.

Meir, Natan. *Kiev: Jewish Metropolis*. Bloomington: Indiana University Press, 2010.

Montefiore, Simon Sebag. *Young Stalin*. New York: Random House, 2007.

Morrissey, Susan K. *Suicide and the Body Politic in Imperial Russia*. Cambridge: Cambridge University Press, 2012.

Murav, Harriet. "The Beilis Ritual Murder Trial and the Culture of Apocalypse." *Cardozo Studies in Law and Literature* 12, no. 2 (Autumn–Winter 2000): 243–63.

Nabokov, V. D. *V. D. Nabokov and the Russian Provisional Government*. Edited by Virgil D. Medlin and Steven L. Parsons. New Haven, CT: Yale University Press, 1976.

Nabokov, Vladimir. *Speak Memory: An Autobiography Revisited*. New York: G. P. Putnam's Sons, 1966.

Nathans, Benjamin J. *Beyond the Pale: The Jewish Encounter with Late Imperial Russia*. Berkeley: University of California Press, 2002.

The Occult in Russian and Soviet Culture. Edited by Bernice G. Rosenthal. Ithaca, NY, and London: Cornell University Press, 1997.

Oney, Steve. *And the Dead Shall Rise: The Murder of Mary Phagan and the Lynching of Leo Frank*. New York: Vintage Books, 2004.

Pares, Bernard. *Russia and Reform*. London: Archibald Constable & Co., 1907.

Petrovsky-Shtern, Yohanan. *Jews in the Russian Army: 1827–1917*. Cambridge: Cambridge University Press, 2009.

Pipes, Richard. *The Russian Revolution*. New York: Alfred A. Knopf, 1990.

Po-Chia Hsia, R. *The Myth of Ritual Murder: Jews and Magic in Reformation Germany*. New Haven, CT, and London: Yale University Press, 1988.

———. *Trent 1475: Stories of a Ritual Murder Trial*. New Haven, CT: Yale University Press, 1992.

Pogroms: Anti-Jewish Violence in Modern Russian History. Edited by John D. Klier and Shlomo Lambroza. Cambridge: Cambridge University Press, 1992.

Rogger, Hans. *Jewish Policies and Right-Wing Politics in Imperial Russia*. Berkeley: University of California Press, 1986.

——. *Russia in the Age of Modernization and Revolution: 1881–1917*. London and New York: Longman, 1983.

——. "Russia in 1914." *Journal of Contemporary History*, vol. 8, no. 4 (October 1966): 95–119.

Ruud, Charles A., and Sergei A. Stepanov. *Fontanka 16: The Tsar's Secret Police*. Montreal: McGill-Queen's University Press, 1999.

Sacred Stories: Religion and Spirituality in Modern Russia. Edited by Mark D. Steinberg and Heather J. Coleman. Bloomington: Indiana University Press, 2007.

Samuel, Maurice. *Blood Accusation: The Strange Story of the Beiliss Case*. New York: Alfred A. Knopf, 1967.

Semenoff, E. *The Russian Government and the Massacres: A Page of the Russian Counter-Revolution*. London: John Murray, 1907.

Shulgin, V. V. (Vasily). *The Years: Memoirs of a Member of the Russian Duma: 1906–1917*. Translated by Tanya Davis. New York: Hippocrene Books, 1984.

Slater, Wendy. *The Many Deaths of Tsar Nicholas II: Relics, Remains and the Romanovs*. London: Routledge, 2007.

Smith, Michael Walser. *The Butcher's Tale: Murder and Anti-Semitism in a German Town*. New York: Norton, 2002.

Steinberg, Mark D. "Nicholas and Alexandra: An Intellectual Portrait." In Mark D. Steinberg and Vladimir M. Khrustalev, eds., *The Fall of the Romanovs: Political Dreams and Personal Struggles in a Time of Revolution*, pp. 1–37. New Haven, CT: Yale University Press, 1995.

——. *Proletarian Imagination: Self, Modernity and the Sacred in Russia: 1910–1925*. Ithaca, NY: Cornell University Press, 2002.

——. "Russia's Fin De Siècle." In Ronald Grigor, ed., *The Cambridge History of Russia*, vol. 3, pp. 67–94. Cambridge: Cambridge University Press, 2006.

Steinberg, Mark D., and Heather J. Coleman. "Introduction: Rethinking Religion in Modern Russian Culture." In Mark D. Steinberg and Heather J. Coleman, eds., *Sacred Stories: Religion and Spirituality in Modern Russia*, pp. 1–22. Bloomington: Indiana University Press, 2007.

Strack, Herman L. *The Jew and Human Sacrifice: An Historical and Sociological Inquiry*. London: Cope and Fenwick, 1909.

Strickland, Lloyd, and Eugenia Lockwood. "Editors' Introduction." *Journal of Russian and East European Psychology* 41, no. 2 (March–April 2003): 3–6.

Szajkowski, Zosa. "The Impact of the Beilis Case on Central and Western

Europe." *Proceedings of the American Academy for Jewish Research* 31 (1963): 197–218.

———. "Paul Nathan, Lucien Wolf and the Versailles Treaty." *Proceedings of the American Academy for Jewish Research* 38–39 (1970–1971): 179–201.

Tager, Alexander. *The Decay of Czarism: The Beiliss Trial.* Philadelphia: Jewish Publication Society, 1934.

Thomas of Monmouth. *The Life and Miracles of Saint William of Norwich.* Translated and edited by Augustus Jessop and Montague Rhodes James. Cambridge: Cambridge University Press, 1896.

Trachtenberg, Joshua. *The Devil and the Jews: The Medieval Conception of the Jew and Its Relation to Anti-Semitism.* Philadelphia: Jewish Publication Society, 1983.

Tuchman, Barbara. *The Proud Tower: A Portrait of the World Before the War, 1890–1914.* New York: Macmillan, 1966.

Verner, Andrew M. *The Crisis of Russian Autocracy: Nicholas II and the Russian Revolution.* Princeton, NJ: Princeton University Press, 1990.

Weinberg, Robert. "The Blood Libel in Eastern Europe." *Jewish History* 26 (2012): 275–85.

———. *Blood Libel in Late Imperial Russia: The Ritual Murder of Mendel Beilis.* Bloomington: Indiana University Press, 2013.

———. "The Trial of Mendel Beilis: The Sources of the 'Blood Libel' in Late Imperial Russia." In Michael S. Melancon and Donald J. Raleigh, eds., *Russia's Century of Revolutions: Parties, People, Places: Studies in Honor of Alexander Rabinowitch,* pp. 17–36. Bloomington, IN: Slavica, 2012.

Weinreich, Max. *Hitler's Professors: The Part of Scholarship in Hitler's Crimes Against the Jewish People.* New Haven, CT: Yale University Press, 1999.

Wistrich, Robert S. *Anti-Semitism: The Longest Hatred.* New York: Schocken Books, 1991.

Wortman, Richard S. *Scenarios of Power: Myth and Ceremony in Russian Monarchy.* Vol. 1: *From Peter the Great to the Death of Nicholas I.* Princeton, NJ: Princeton University Press, 1995.

———. *Scenarios of Power: Myth and Ceremony in Russian Monarchy.* Vol. 2: *From Alexander II to the Abdication of Nicholas II.* Princeton, NJ: Princeton University Press, 2000.

Zuckerman, Fredric. *The Tsarist Secret Police in Russian Society, 1880–1917.* New York: New York University Press, 1996.

Index